Advance Praise for *Musaliar King*

This book is a must-read to better understand the ravages of colonialism, especially the resistance to colonial forces in Malabar and the sentiment that has permeated the colonial narrative in other regions that have experienced colonialism such as Mauritius.

Ameenah Gurib-Fakim
Sixth President of the Republic of Mauritius (2015–2018)

Scholarly studies of popular resistance to European colonial regimes have sometimes allowed the colonizer's literary and archival evidence to dominate the historical narrative to the neglect of indigenous perspectives. In his meticulous study of the anti-colonial resistance movement that erupted in rural Malabar in 1921, Dr Panakkal examines not only British colonial literature but also local diaries, letters, religious documents, poetic works and oral traditions. Armed with this corpus of evidence, the author reveals the movement's deep social complexities, notably the firm alliances between Muslim and Hindu freedom fighters, contrary to the standard British assertion that popular opposition to oppressive colonial rule could usually be attributed to sectarian hatred.

Ross Edmunds Dunn
Professor Emeritus of History, San Diego State University, United States of America

Musaliar King is a transformative exploration of the decolonial historiography of Malabar. This book challenges established historical paradigms, unveiling marginalized narratives with precision. In my experience, acknowledging diverse histories is crucial for lasting peace, and Panakkal's work aligns with this imperative. His dedication to decolonization resonates globally, offering valuable insights for those who are interested in a more inclusive understanding of the past. As an African who was born during the French colonial rule in Senegal, I recognize parallels between our histories, which emphasizes the book's universal relevance. *Musaliar King* is a commendable contribution, urging us to reconsider historical narratives and fostering a broader dialogue on decolonization.

Adama Dieng
Former United Nations Under-Secretary-General and Special Adviser on the Prevention of Genocide

Abbas Panakkal is an intrepid scholar from Kerala—the historic region of Malabar in South India—who is dedicated to fostering harmonious relations between the different faiths in his native land and worldwide. His book, *Musaliar King*, concerns the resistance against the British by the population of his region in 1921–1922 under the leadership of Ali Musaliar, who had the support of both Muslims and Hindus. The book meticulously investigates the documents concerning the events of this period, in particular the collection of notes and documents regarding Ali Musaliar in the possession of his grandson Muhammed Ali. As well as being a thorough study of the events of the two noted years, it demonstrates that the Hindu and Muslim communities could not only live in peace and harmony together but also, in opposition to an external force, assist each other in shared goals. This is a pivotal point, central to Abbas Panakkal's personal dedication to interfaith harmony.

Mehrdad Shokoohy
Emeritus Professor of Architecture and Urban Studies,
University of Greenwich, United Kingdom

With this case study of an early-20th-century episode of resistance to British imperialism, Abbas Panakkal makes an important contribution to the historiography of the decolonization of British India and the generic field of subaltern studies. The book is situated in a regional setting with which the author maintains a personal connection. Through detailed archival research and the collection of orally transmitted sources, Panakkal also highlights the role of local women and the relation between Hindu and Muslim residents, while his critical examination of photographic material enables an important correction of earlier mistaken identifications of those involved in the 1921 resistance.

Carool Kersten
Professor of Islamic Studies, Catholic University Leuven, Belgium

This captivating monograph delves into the intricate tapestry of Malabar's history, offering a scholarly exploration of the nuanced interplay between communal coexistence and anti-colonial resistance. Through a decolonial lens, it meticulously dissects the dynamics of Hindu–Muslim unity and the concerted struggles against Portuguese and British dominion. It challenges the colonial historiographical paradigm by presenting a nuanced account of the Malabar resistance that transcends the simplified binaries of sectarian narratives. By integrating primary sources and critical analysis, this study instead illuminates the multifaceted nature of resistance, highlighting the complexities of historical resistance and the power of collective solidarity.

Sebastian R. Prange
Author of *Monsoon Islam*,
Department of Asian Studies, University of British Columbia, Canada

While contextualizing the cultural and social setting of Malabar before and under colonial rule, *Musaliar King* emphasizes the absence of exclusive religious roles and the clear demarcation between those who supported the British regime and those who opposed it. Countering colonial narratives of religious fanaticism, Abbas Panakkal portrays Malabar as a land of pluralism, interfaith engagements, intercultural understanding, peculiar feminism and social cohesion 'long before any of these abstract phrases were fashionable'. This is a profound and timely contribution to both a better knowledge of history and the struggle for a peaceful and prosperous future in the region.

Marco Ventura
Professor of Law and Religion, the University of Siena, Italy

From a deeply grounded local perspective, Panakkal's work opens up new lines of discussion that challenge established narratives of Malabar's distinctive historical patterns of Muslim–Hindu communal interactions and culturally contextualized gender dynamics with a critical eye toward how both of these distinctive traditions were dramatically transformed in the early 20th century. In doing so, he highlights important points of contrast between the experience of Muslims in southern India and those of the north that can contribute new perspectives on both colonial historiography and broader contemporary conversations.

R. Michael Feener
Professor of Cross-Regional Studies, Kyoto University, Japan

This richly documented study, by an author who clearly knows what he is talking about, offers a rigorous postcolonial reassessment of the much-studied 1921–1922 incidents. Panakkal critiques the existing Eurocentric coverage with its distorted record of how Malabar's diverse people resisted colonial suppression. Reflecting the effectiveness of 'doing' new history, this decolonial analysis scrutinizes local sources, including prison diaries that have remained hidden, and other sources that were misinterpreted to justify colonial perspectives. Of most contemporary relevance for India is the finding that local Muslims and Hindus worked together to oppose colonial rule.

Werner Menski
Emeritus Professor of South Asian Laws,
SOAS, University of London, United Kingdom

Musaliar King is a literary gem for aficionados of history, offering a profound understanding of the events that have shaped the history of Malabar in India. Panakkal's meticulous research debunks controversial colonial narratives and resolves misidentifications, unveiling the spirit within Malabar's own stories about solidarity and sacrifice. One of the book's most captivating aspects is its exploration of a contentious photograph, masterfully challenging its authenticity. This captivating journey transcends the mere exploration of historical facts; instead it results in a symphony of identity, sacrifice and community resilience. Panakkal's work serves as a much-needed correction for historians and the general public alike, shifting the spotlight onto the valiant deeds often overshadowed by colonial narratives. Readers are invited on a transformative journey where historical understanding is reshaped, where the inherent valor embedded in Malabar's history takes center stage.

Afifi al-Akiti
Faculty of Theology and Religion,
University of Oxford, United Kingdom

Panakkal has provided a detailed picture of resistance against colonial rule in the first quarter of 20th-century colonial India. He provides fascinating details of micro-details of village life and the events that engulfed his ancestral village. This is a must-read to understand history from below.

Ebrahim Moosa
Professor, The Keough School of Global Affairs,
The University of Notre Dame, United Sates of America

In this abundantly detailed and highly readable account, Abbas Panakkal unpacks the struggles of Malabaris towards the freedom of their homeland. This story of the politics and poetics of resistance is relatively unacknowledged in most textbooks on India's past. Sufis, scholars, peasants, men, women and youth from a variety of backgrounds came together to challenge and overcome waves of European colonization. A pioneering decolonial work that would reshape the contours of Asian historiography, *Musaliar King* is a must-read, an empowering and moving book.

Khairudin Aljunied
The Faculty of Arts and Social Sciences,
National University of Singapore

This is an important book on the resistance against the British in 1921. It advances our understanding in particular by not relying on the colonial record but by making considerable use of indigenous sources. We are shown a society in which there is much intercommunal unity.

Francis Robinson
Professor Emeritus of History, Royal Holloway,
University of London, United Kingdom

MUSALIAR KING

MUSALIAR KING

Decolonial Historiography of Malabar's Resistance

Abbas Panakkal

B L O O M S B U R Y
NEW DELHI • LONDON • OXFORD • NEW YORK • SYDNEY

BLOOMSBURY INDIA
Bloomsbury Publishing India Pvt. Ltd
Second Floor, LSC Building No. 4, DDA Complex, Pocket C – 6 & 7,
Vasant Kunj, New Delhi, 110070

BLOOMSBURY, BLOOMSBURY ACADEMIC INDIA and the Diana logo are trademarks of Bloomsbury Publishing Plc

First published in India 2024
This edition published 2024

Bloomsbury Academic India
An imprint of Bloomsbury Publishing Plc

ISBN: HB: 978-93-56409-12-5; eBook: 978-93-56407-99-2
2 4 6 8 10 9 7 5 3 1

Typeset by Manipal Technologies Limited
Printed and bound in India by Replika Press Pvt. Ltd.

CONTENTS

LIST OF FIGURES

INTRODUCTION

The Decolonial Historiography of Resistance in Malabar

The historiography of my village unfolds across three distinctive epochs: the period before 1921, the tumultuous years of 1921 itself and the subsequent era. The socio-geographical landscape of our community underwent profound transformations in the wake of the cataclysmic events of 1921–1922. This epoch witnessed a staggering loss of lives, the forced displacement of families, the diaspora of young aspirants in search of livelihoods in distant locales and the protracted suffering endured by the elderly. Those who actively participated in the movement found themselves incarcerated for lengthy durations. Virtually no household was immune to the tragic narratives of post-movement tribulations. Curiously, instead of condemning the incident, our community articulates these narratives with pride, venerating the resilience and mettle exhibited by their forebears. This period is thus characterized also by the narratives of widows and orphans who, against all odds, discovered fortitude amidst the turbulence.

As it traversed the corridor of time into adulthood, the society encountered analogous accounts in neighboring hamlets, each replete with its nomenclature and episodes yet unified by a shared undercurrent of profound anguish and affliction. Seasoned matriarchs, the repositories of oral history, had meticulously committed to memory stirring ballads that exalted the valiant exploits linked to various episodes. Collectively, the denizens of the region embraced an abiding reverence for their community and its sagacious leadership. The old mosque of Tirurangadi emerged as a veritable repository of memories and narratives, a historical bastion of ideological resistance against the British colonial apparatus. During the auspicious commemoration of the seventy-fifth anniversary of the seminal events of 1921, I embarked on a pilgrimage to this venerable mosque. My odyssey also encompassed a retracing of the path leading back to Tirurangadi Kacheri,[1] thus allowing for a nuanced appreciation of the pivotal events that once transpired on these hallowed grounds.

These investigations evoked the metaphorical image of a kaleidoscope, each visit revealing diverse facets of the events that transpired in August 1921. The vivid image of individuals leaping from the mosque's pinnacle into the river was conjured up by the narratives I had heard, with the Mamburam[2] mosque perpetually looming in the background as I sought glimpses of the riverside from Kizhakkepalli.[3] The sturdy wooden door that served as the portal to the mosque from the burial ground situated along the Western periphery of the compound wall, a testament to traditional artisanship, bore the scars of numerous bullet impacts. Unquestionably, the mosque itself constituted a monument commemorating the resistance against the dominion of British colonial rule.

The mosque's architectural facade has since undergone a transformation, transitioning from its erstwhile traditional aesthetic to an Arab-centric petrodollar-influenced 'Islamic' architectural paradigm. Regrettably, this metamorphosis has entailed the erasure of the nostalgic architectural vestiges that once adorned the old mosque. Among these relics that vanished are the wooden doors that bore such indelible imprints of history. During my academic exploration, I also encountered a minority of contrarian voices stemming from pro-British lineages and landowning elites who historically maintained close affiliations with the colonial establishment.

In the narratives that form the cornerstone of our primary historical accounts, one discerns recurrent motifs that reverberate across the annals of human experience. These motifs encompass acts of resistance against prevailing circumstances, familial migrations spanning geographical expanses, the founding of orphanages as bastions of solace and the transplantation of institutions, all woven into the fabric of historical occurrences. Importantly, these collective struggles have begotten diasporic communities that span the globe. The phenomenon of human mobility, inherent in these narratives, transcends temporal and spatial boundaries. My personal experiences have afforded me the privilege of engaging with individuals who embody these narratives, their lived experiences echoing through the corridors of time. In particular, my lasting connection with Muhammed Ali Musaliar stands out. He is the grandson of Ali Musaliar, a prominent luminary of the 1921 struggle, and has also taken on the role of a local historian and collector and guardian of rare manuscripts and textual documents from various parts of Malabar.[4] Muhammed Ali Musaliar meticulously transcribed the oral traditions and narratives originating from his maternal lineage. An integral aspect of this lineage preservation is the naming convention, which passes from grandfather to grandson, an observance initiated by Muhammed Ali Musaliar's mother. This practice underscores the profound reverence assigned to the concept of generational heritage in this cultural context.

In this academic context, an interview was conducted during the seventy-fifth anniversary commemoration with Ali Musaliar's daughter, Amina, which shed light on her father's religious and familial practices. Specifically, she recalled memories of his return from the mosque, often carrying a wooden writing board and a few texts, and the lingering sweetness of jaggery on her tongue from the candy he brought for her. These memories evoke nostalgia and affection. The river flowing near his house also links the Tirurangadi mosque, and Ali Musaliar crossed the Kadalundi River to commute between the mosque and his residence. The tradition of her father, who she affectionately referred to as *Vappa*, consistently bringing home traditional candy further reinforces the emotional and generational bonds within the family unit. This personal anecdote provides valuable insight into the cultural tradition and familial relationships.

Shifting Horizons: The Evolution of Malabar's Boundaries over Time

The boundaries of Malabar were subject to periodic changes driven by political considerations and the strategies of reigning rulers. The precise political boundaries of Malabar, as described in 'Qissat Shakruti Farmad' and *Tuhfat al Mujahidin*, exhibit variations. In the 'Qissat', Malabar initially encompassed a broader region, reflecting the accounts of earlier travelers.[5] Over time, the territorial delineations in the 'Qissat' and the *Tuhfat* underwent transformations due to the fluctuating political borders of Malabar. By the 16th century, the territorial extent appears to have diminished from Barkur to Kanjarakut/Kasaragod. According to the 'Qissat', the king of Malabar meticulously documented the boundaries and allocated lands to provincial rulers in a note. This division covered a span of 140 *parasangs* (*farsakh*), equivalent to 805 kilometers in Malabar. Originally, the allocated lands likely constituted a more extensive area, including crucial port towns from Barkur to the southern tip of Thengapattanam (Taqipatan in the 'Qissat').[6] The *Tuhfat*, reflecting the 16th-century perspective, adjusted Malabar's boundaries, shortening them to extend from Kasaragod in the north to Kanyakumari (Kumhuri) in the south, aligning with the political realities.[7]

Positioned as a central hub in the Indian Ocean, Malabar served as a natural crossroads for long-range monsoon navigation. The term *Malabar* has its origins in the contributions of Arab and Persian traders who frequented the coast even before the rise of Islam in Arabia.

Notable travelers of the time highlighted Malabar in their early writings. The inhabitants, along with their rulers, displayed openness to diverse religions and cultures introduced by traders, fostering a harmonious assimilation in the region. The name 'Malabar' is derived from the local vernacular, with *Mala* signifying hill and the affix *bar* potentially originating from either the Arabic word *barr* or the Persian word *bar*.[8] This etymology is widely accepted in the region and has been elucidated by both ancient and modern writers.[9]

The Malabar region had a longstanding tradition of anti-colonial resistance dating back to the 16th century. Muslims and Hindus collaboratively persevered in their resistance against colonial forces. This exploration delves into the 16th-century historical backdrop, employing a thorough categorization of primary source materials. At the heart of this study is Shaykh Zayn al-Din I's (c. 1467–1522 CE) manuscript 'Tahrid ahlul Iman', which was a call for resistance in the face of Portuguese incursions, reflecting the period's strife and the localized adaptation of Jihad.[10] Additionally, the contributions of Shaykh Zayn al-Din II (1530–1583 CE), particularly through his seminal book *Tuhfat al-Mujahidin*, highlight the era's significant cultural consolidation in Malabar.[11] These scholars, along with Qazi Muhammed, played pivotal roles in the colonial resistance, maintaining communal harmony with the Hindu king and his Nair soldiers. This collective effort not only underscores the importance of unity in the face of external threats but also showcases the balance of religious and cultural identities in the region's sociopolitical landscape.

Decoding Discourse: A Comprehensive Exploration of Texts and Contexts

The colonial era was a crucible for numerous insurgencies, which has engendered extensive inquiry. The prevailing discourse surrounding these historical upheavals often gravitates toward the vantage point of colonial historiography, heavily reliant on primary sources culled from the annals of British archives. Nevertheless, the academic pursuits in this book have ventured down a distinctive avenue, one that invokes the collective memory and oral narratives of those who witnessed the formidable struggles against the prevailing administration. In addition to these invaluable oral testimonies, my research has unveiled a repository of compelling documentary evidence, including the poignant correspondence emanating from the confines of colonial prisons, which reveals the tribulations of those detained for their unwavering commitment to resistance. Noteworthy among these archival discoveries is the diary of a remarkable woman, Chakeri Thithachumma, the daughter of the eminent Malayalam poet Chakeri Moideen Kutty.[12] In this text, she pens a vivid account of her pivotal role in the Malappuram *Nercha*,[13] an annual festival celebrated with fervor and zeal. The diary serves as a poignant testament to the tumultuous events of her compelled departure from her domestic haven, precipitated by the looming specter of imminent danger.

This meticulously inscribed document is a significant historical artefact that challenges prevailing interpretations of colonial-era struggles. It transcends the narrow confines of a one-dimensional Eurocentric historiography, which typically focuses on the oppression of Hindu landlords while neglecting the actions taken against landlords regardless of their religious affiliations as long as they supported the colonial regime. The chronicled accounts of Muslim landlords forced to forsake their abodes under the specter of life-threatening peril clarify the multifarious challenges that confronted diverse segments of society during this transformative epoch.[14]

In the aftermath of the violent interventions in the Malabar region by the British colonial forces, a concerted effort was undertaken to systematically undermine the heritage and historical legacy of the community. This endeavor was characterized by a calculated strategy of linguistic warfare, with the explicit intent of portraying them as fanatical, illiterate and lacking in erudition. This linguistic subterfuge aimed to justify the brutalities perpetrated by the British and, concurrently, cast doubt upon the character, ethos and motivation of those who actively resisted such sociocultural incursions. To realize this objective, the British authorities resorted to the deployment of pejorative terminology in official reports and newspapers, such as 'Mappila War Knife', 'Khilafat King', 'Outrage', 'Revolt', 'Rebellion' and 'Marauding Mappilas', which were widely disseminated as labels affixed to those individuals and groups that opposed British colonial presence. These sticky tags were artfully employed to construct a distorted narrative of events and, more perniciously, malign the victims of the British military's relentless brutality, especially women and children.[15]

The campaign of denigration extended to the realm of documentation, where colonial officials published contrived monographs, manipulative official records and news stories strategically placed in international newspapers. These publications were instrumental in conferring a veneer of legitimacy upon British actions, both within the colonial sphere and beyond its borders. Notably, R.H. Hitchcock, a negative figure associated with the suppression of the resistance, contributed to this nefarious effort. Hitchcock characterized the Moplahs of Malabar as fanatic and ignorant individuals.[16] In this narrative, the Malabaris were unfairly stigmatized as a community with perceived intellectual limitations. The British went on to exploit categories like ethnicity, religion and literacy as pretextual justifications for forcibly displacing this community from their ancestral homelands. R.H. Hitchcock, in crafting his colonial version of events, aimed to validate both his and Collector Thomas's perspectives, supporting their decision to wage war on the people. Additionally, he sought to rationalize all the massacres and brutal slaughtering carried out under martial law by providing a supportive narrative. The deliberate manipulation of language and the dissemination of deceptive stories played a central role within the broader framework of British colonialism. These tactics not only served to legitimize the colonial endeavor but also significantly contributed to the creation of a distorted historiographical record.

C. Gopalan Nair, through his written works, manifested a continued allegiance to colonial interests, even after his retirement from an official position in the imperial apparatus. He adopted a linguistic style reminiscent of the colonial administration, characterized by its use of harsh and inflammatory language in the service of colonial objectives. This linguistic phenomenon permeates the narratives penned by this 'native writer' as he unabashedly deployed his literary prowess in favor of the British cause. Nair, a retired government officer under the aegis of the Madras government, collated source materials from various outlets, such as newspaper reports, government press releases, legislative council debates and other primary and secondary sources. In a tribute to Captain McEnroy, Nair unequivocally expresses his disdain for the indigenous population. This homage was constructed around an event that transpired on 26 August 1921 in Pukkottur during McEnroy's march to 'relieve Malappuram'. Nevertheless, it is imperative to contextualize this event from the perspective of the native inhabitants of the region, who perceived the British actions as an outright invasion of their land and a challenge to their property rights. In his portrayal of Captain McEnroy, Nair deliberately crafts a heroic persona, emphasizing McEnroy's achievements with a relatively modest contingent of no more than 125 men, including the Leinsters and the Special Police. Concurrently, Nair depicts the indigenous forces as fanatical adversaries, referring to them as a 'rebel horde of about 4,000 Moplah fanatics' and claiming that the British defeated them, resulting in approximately 400 casualties. A noteworthy aspect of Nair's rhetoric is the recurring use of the pronoun 'them', which effectively marginalized and othered the native population who had valiantly sacrificed themselves in defense of the land. Furthermore, Nair asserts in his tribute that McEnroy had saved the 'Eranad Hindus' from mass conversion to the Muslim faith. Gopalan Nair claims: 'His success saved difficult situation during the first week of the Moplah rebellion when Government forces were not available in sufficient numbers to check the rebellion and also saved the Emad Hindus from wholesale conversion to Moslem faith.' While this narrative might appear as a benevolent act on the surface, it warrants critical scrutiny within the broader context of colonial objectives and its ramifications for the indigenous populace. The utilization of linguistic manipulation and biased narratives by individuals like C. Gopalan Nair underscores the imperative for a comprehensive reevaluation of colonial-era texts and their impact on historical understanding.[17]

C. Gopalan Nair's propagandistic stance, particularly the vitriolic allegations levied against proponents of the Non-Cooperation Movements, appears calculated to sow discord and disunity between Hindus and Muslims in the region. In his narratives, Nair unequivocally espouses settler viewpoints, framing the resistance of the Moplahs as a confrontation against the British government. He primarily portrays the resistance as an outgrowth of the Khilafat Movement, largely neglecting to provide a counter-narrative that could have defended Mahatma Gandhi and the Non-Cooperation Movement. Instead, Nair aligns himself with the British narrative, asserting that the suppression of 'evil passions' through Gandhi's teachings gave way to a surge in violent acts, including widespread murder, looting and rapine.[18] Moreover, Nair perpetuates the colonial stereotype of the Ernad Moplah as an ignorant, illiterate and fanatical figure, thus reinforcing a negative image of the local populace. Overall, Nair's writings serve to undermine the unity and cohesion of the local populace while echoing the prevailing British narratives of the time.[19]

K. Madhavan Nair (1882–1933), a notable lawyer and a prominent leader in the Indian National Congress, was the inaugural secretary of the Pradesh Congress Committee in the early months of 1921. His stature within the Congress party during this pivotal juncture in India's struggle for independence was substantial. Notably, Madhavan Nair authored a book titled *Malabar Kalapam*, which is of scholarly interest due to its posthumous publication and allegations of internal fabrication in the biography.[20] Madhavan Nair's active engagement in the Non-Cooperation Movement, a pivotal campaign with Congress support, led to his imprisonment for six months, spanning from mid-February to mid-August 1921. This incarceration resulted from his principled refusal to adhere to the district collector's directives, which barred him from addressing a public gathering in Calicut (Kozhikode). Following his release from jail, a period marked by British-inflicted atrocities in the region, Nair endeavored to dissuade individuals from resorting to violent means. However, the momentum of the resistance proved insurmountable, thereby presenting a considerable challenge to him and his fellow activists in the national movement. What lends particular gravitas to Madhavan Nair's book on these epochal events is his direct involvement and comprehensive knowledge of the geographical locations and individuals central to the unfolding incidents. Notably, the book remained unpublished until 1971, five decades after 1921 and two decades after the author's death, a circumstance attributed to the agency of Madhavan Nair's spouse. This delay was a frequent point of discussion during my interviews with people from Pukkottur, Tirurangadi, Kolathur, Melattur and so on. It is believed that if the book had been published during Madhavan Nair's lifetime, it would have been more favorable to the Non-Cooperation Movement and could have avoided using British terminologies. The extended interval between the manuscript's completion and publication invites scrutiny into the circumstances surrounding this delay. The delay in publishing the book allowed potentially influencing the narrative. In the book, the preface posits that it was an appropriate course of action to compose a series of articles based on his firsthand involvement and knowledge of the events of 1921.[21] This decision was prompted, in part, by the absence of any inquiry into the incidents, even more than a year and a half following their occurrence. Mrs Madhavan Nair underscores that the author was unable to finalize the work according to his original intentions.[22] In a statement published in the book, K. Kelappan raises questions about how Gandhi's Khilafat message became either favorable or unfavorable to Muslim sentiments. He emphasizes the need for further study on this issue and highlights the impact of people who supported the British by presenting false arguments and misleading messages against the resistance movement.[23] The literary contribution of K. Madhavan Nair, an eminent leader in the Non-Cooperation Movement and a fervent advocate for independence, offers a distinctive vantage point on the historical events of his era. The circumstances surrounding the book's publication, as well as the allegations of internal fabrication, add layers of intrigue and scholarly significance to its exploration within the broader context of the struggle against colonial hegemony.

Khilafat Smaranakal, authored by Mozhikunnath Brahmadattan Namboodiripad (1897–1964), is noteworthy in the annals of historical literature. It represents a work penned by a contemporary actively involved in the struggles against colonial rule, affording it considerable academic significance. The book employs a nuanced narrative structure, delineating two distinct temporal segments. The initial chapters are primarily centered on the resistance itself, drawing from extant records and incorporating direct experiential insights. Conversely, the subsequent chapters were composed in the early years of the resistance, furnishing firsthand accounts of personal experiences during that epoch.

The author's note specifically mentions that his experience, which is included at the end of the book, had been published in a newspaper decades earlier. Additionally, the inclusion of an 'end note', featuring narrations by individuals recounting their experiences, augments the multifaceted paradigm.[24] Namboodiripad's approach affords readers intimate glimpses into various events while concurrently illuminating the motivations propelling the native fighters. Notably, the author's overarching perspective, encapsulated in his statements, underscores the pivotal significance of the resistance. During that era, British forces resorted to coercive measures against activists, thereby compelling the latter to adopt a defensive stance, including the use of force. These actions were impelled by a dual motivation: the desire to escape unbearable oppression and the enduring aspiration to establish a government more amenable to their interests. *Khilafat Smaranakal* performs a dual function as a chronicle of events and a lens through which to scrutinize the intricate motivations underpinning the indigenous resistance against the colonial powers. Its dual temporal structure, adeptly interweaving contemporary recollection with retrospective narration, enriches the academic understanding of the era and its broader significance within the context of colonial history.[25]

Malabar Congress leader K.P. Keshava Menon (1886–1978), in his book *Kazhinja Kaalam*, unwaveringly reveals the true causes of the issues that had been concealed by the colonial administration through various embedded writings. Keshava Menon staunchly rejects colonial propaganda, which attempted to portray religious fanaticism as the primary source of the disturbances, and instead emphasizes the extent to which government officials engaged in actions that provoked such a response. There is no doubt regarding the genesis of the issue of 1921, he wrote; it was born out of police repression. Its chief cause was the excessive violence used by the authorities to suppress the movements and not any *jenmi* (landlord) conflict or disputes concerning mosques. He also points out that when the unbearable police atrocities pushed them to their limits, the people decided to abandon their commitment to non-violence and meet violence with violence. Keshava Menon's work provides an accurate account of the events and the factors that led to the 1921 resistance.[26]

In the realm of academic research, a comprehensive examination of the Malabar issues began approximately half a century after the event, coinciding with the release of official records. D.N. Dhanagere's (1936–2017) work *Agrarian Conflict, Religion, and Politics: The Moplah Rebellion in Malabar in the Nineteenth and Twentieth Centuries* was published in 1977. This undertaking scrutinizes the peasant issues that were prevalent in Malabar and underscores them as the foundational impetus behind the resistance. Dhanagere's analysis posits that these concerns were further compounded by religious and ethnic identity factors, coupled with political alienation, notably during the period spanning from 1885 to 1920.[27]

Simultaneously, in 1977, Robert L. Hardgrave Jr. (1939–2023) contributed to the discourse with his study 'The Mappila Rebellion, 1921: Peasant Revolt in Malabar'. Hardgrave's examination adopts a colonial perspective concerning the prevailing issues of the time. It extensively employs colonial lexicon, languages and descriptors, potentially sidelining the vernacular accounts of the event. In line with this viewpoint, Hardgrave's analysis corroborates the pivotal role of agrarian discontent, accentuating the perceived threat to Islam, the influence of the Congress-Khilafat agitation, the impact of incendiary reports and the provocation orchestrated by government officials and law enforcement. Furthermore, Hardgrave alludes to the presence of additional, though as yet unidentified, underlying issues that contributed to the complex fabric. Employing colonial terminologies, this scholar expresses his opinions on the reports spread through a newspaper called the *Mail*. This print medium presented the anti-Muslim reaction in a series titled 'The Moplah Rebellion', in which they refer to certain 'innate characteristics of the Moplahs', such as 'mad fanatical fury', 'murderous spirit' and 'reckless disregard for life'. Hardgrave specifies that the report from the special correspondent exacerbated the sentiments of victimized Hindus in Malabar. The report implies that it was the fervent desire of these Hindus, after their terrible experiences, to see the Moplahs as a race exterminated from their country. Such inflammatory narratives in the reports played a significant role in fomenting Hindu fears and fostering hostility toward Muslims.[28]

M. Gangadhara Menon's (1933–2022) study examines the nationalist movement in the Malabar region, tracing its inception from Calicut. It charts the trajectory of this movement in parallel with the tenants' agitation, which sought legislative measures to counteract the oppressive exercise of *jenmi* power. The study further elucidates the spread of the 'Khilafat agitation', offering insight into the heightened excitement, emerging expectations and the underlying tensions characterizing the early months of 1921. However, despite its vernacular merits, Menon's study is ensconced within the colonial narrative, which is particularly evident in its initial recounting of the disturbance in Pukkottur. The choice of terminologies and titles such as 'Malabar Rebellion' in books illustrates a lingering influence of post-colonial perspectives, evident in the continued use of colonial language and frameworks to narrate vernacular history.[29]

In parallel, in his 1921 book *India in Transition*, M.N. Roy (1887–1954) characterizes the events in Malabar as 'the latest phase of agrarian trouble' in India. Roy emphasizes the economic dimensions, contending that the native populace in Malabar was economically disadvantaged, with agriculture serving as their primary source of livelihood. His narrative underscores the enduring dominance of moneylenders over the local population. It is essential to recognize that, at the time, Roy possessed limited information about the specific events in Malabar. His perspective primarily reflects a broader understanding of rural poverty in India as a whole, along with the prevailing perception that the colonial administration favored the interests of landholders over those of the impoverished rural populace.[30]

The Bengali intellectual Soumyendranath Tagore (1901–1974) authored *Peasant Revolt in Malabar*, in which he characterizes the events of 1921 as an organic and spontaneous 'uprising' of the Malabar peasantry against British imperial rule.[31] Notably, Tagore had already faced criticism for reportedly not having personally visited Malabar before penning his treatise, with detractors contending that his perspective was colored by his Marxist ideological stance.[32] However, even Elamkulam Manakkal Sankaran Namboodiripad (1909–1998), a prominent Communist ideologue hailing from Malabar who wrote on the subject in the early 1940s, did not discount the role played by agrarian discontent in these events. Leaders associated with the Congress-Khilafat movement raised their voices against both the British colonial administration and the *jenmi*. The oppression and exploitation meted out by colonial officials and landlords were no less severe in their effects upon Hindu peasants as they were on their Muslim counterparts.[33] Tagore advances the argument that the anti-Hindu sentiment expressed during this period was intricately tied to resistance against those Hindus who were overtly supportive of the British colonial regime. Therefore, the manifestation of 'anti-Hindu' actions, while unfortunate, could be better understood as directed not at the broader Hindu population but rather at those complicit in bolstering British interests. In this complex web of sociopolitical dynamics, Muslims also faced repercussions due to their association with the colonial power. Importantly, the significance lies not only in these instances but in their relatively modest number and proportional representation within the broader context.[34]

In another work, E.M.S. Namboodiripad explored further into the broader context of the Malabar issues, elucidating the foundational elements of the predicament in the Malabar region. These issues were intrinsically intertwined with the loss of indigenous hegemony that transpired upon the establishment of British dominion in the region. The resistance against the perceived beliefs and atrocities of the colonial power formed a paramount catalyst for the local population. E.M.S. expounds upon this notion as a key impetus behind the substantial involvement of the Muslim community in the anti-colonial struggle against the British. This commitment extended beyond mere agrarian or peasant-related grievances. In the eyes of the local population, their spiritual leaders assumed a focal role in this struggle, and thus, the act of resistance encompassed broader socio-religious dimensions. Furthermore, E.M.S. Namboodiripad articulates that the British colonial government was perceived as fundamentally antagonistic to the interests of the native population. The imperative of a 'jihad' against the colonial invaders became a rallying cry, as individuals were resolute in their willingness to sacrifice their lives in pursuit of this overarching objective, characterized by a profound sense of collective determination and aspiration for a more just and equitable order.[35]

A contemporaneous account of the Malabar resistance, *Malabar Lahala*[36] by Koyatti Moulavi, a native of Tirurangadi, claims that his book was informed not only by his own experiences but also by contemporary press reports and the proceedings of special courts. The book provides details of the political developments in Malabar, spanning from the inception of the Khilafat Movement to the eventual quelling of the resistance. In broad strokes, Moulavi's perspective positions the movement as primarily a struggle against British colonial rule, with the ultimate aim of securing independence. Pertinently, Moulavi's work is set within the context of imperial linguistic influences, as evident in the choice of the title, *Malabar Lahala*, mirroring the nomenclature employed by colonial narratives. Moulavi was not reticent in expressing his criticism of the leaders of the rebellion, who laid down their lives for the cause of their land. He laments the lack of effective leadership and argues that this leadership vacuum had catastrophic consequences, resulting in the loss of over 12,000 lives. It is essential to challenge this perspective, as leaders like Musaliar were resolute in seeking justice for those who were treacherously killed in Tirurangadi, making their own lives secondary to the cause of righteousness. Moulavi further argues that the issue at hand was not confined solely to the peasantry who endured the oppressive *jenmi* system in the region. He points out that in Tirurangadi, a significant proportion of the population, around 95 per cent, comprised Muslims who were not subject to the oppressive *jenmi* system. Yet, they too faced brutality when rallying peacefully at the British magistrate's office in Tirurangadi, underscoring the multifaceted nature of the grievances and motivations that fueled the mass resistance.[37]

Conrad Wood's assessment, informed by sources in the British administrative echelons, upheld a prevailing colonial paradigm that denigrated the inhabitants of the region as a 'largely illiterate population'.[38] In actuality, the populace exhibited a commendable level of literacy, proficiently engaging in reading and writing in their vernacular languages, which they held in obligate esteem. Ali Musaliar stands as a testament to this erudition. His traditional teaching centers became focal points in the landscape of the 1921 resistance. Therefore, the accusation of illiteracy, one must emphasize, emanated primarily from the British standpoint, where illiteracy meant the inability to engage with the English language or the idiom of the ruling oligarchy. Viewed from the prism of the Malabar populace, a significant proportion of British personnel were, conversely, characterized as 'illiterate', owing to their incapacity to decipher the vernacular languages and decode the indigenous scripts. Conrad Wood's assertion about the paucity of 'written records' left by the Muslim community, available for historiographical purposes, is entirely unfounded.[39] All extant documents, alongside textual and referential sources employed by Ali Musaliar and Variamkunnath Kunhamed Haji, were destroyed in the conflagration and annihilation orchestrated by the colonial forces. They did not permit even a vestige of the archival legacy of fallen freedom fighters like Variamkunnath Kunhamed Haji to endure.[40] Remarkably, even after the passage of three-quarters of a century after the event, I personally unearthed letters and diaries ensconced within the collections of landlords who were aligned with British interests. These relics proffer an alternative perspective on the events that unfolded. It is patently evident that Conrad Wood evinced minimal diligence in the exploration of the indigenous perspective—one fervently striving to extricate itself from the vestiges of colonial dominion. Conrad Wood's exposition tends toward exaggeration and bias. In the intervening decades, a trove of primary source materials have come to light, shedding illumination on hitherto obscured facets of the narrative. It is conspicuous that Conrad Wood uncritically aligned himself with British propaganda, particularly as it pertains to the alleged 'Hindu genocide', a stance that significantly impugns the scholarly objectivity intrinsic to his inquiry.[41]

Stephen Frederic Dale's book *Islamic Society on the South Asian Frontier* is a discourse within the colonial framework that tends to homogenize native populations as militant and illiterate. He also endeavors to instrumentalize Hindu–Muslim tensions as a component of British propaganda. Within this context, he portrays Ali Musaliar as a religious zealot and opportunist who sought to harness the Khilafat Movement for his own ambitions. Dale contends that Ali Musaliar's teachings veered toward militancy, rather than advocating legal recourse. In a milieu marked by colonial military excesses, wherein atrocities against the local populace were rampant, particularly toward women and children, the expectation that a leader would urge his followers to seek justice through colonial-administered courts appears implausible. Dale seeks to implicate Ali Musaliar's ideology, but it is important to contextualize Ali Musaliar's involvement against the broader backdrop of Gandhi's visit to Calicut, the establishment of the Congress and the emergence of the Khilafat Movement.[42]

Ali Musaliar's influence extended throughout the region, and his disciples from various educational centers where he had disseminated his teachings over the years actively supported him through this crisis. Collaboratively, British officials and local colonial supporters sought to lay siege to the mosque where Ali Musaliar instructed and led prayers.[43] Dale echoes narratives promulgated by the colonial administration, which marginalized non-Muslim associates of Ali Musaliar engaged in the same mission. Dale propagates a colonial logic insinuating that Musaliar advocated for the establishment of a distinct Islamic state within the Indian subcontinent. Furthermore, Dale sought to draw connections between Malabar and wider Indian contexts, positing that Indian Muslims' apprehensions about their own predicaments had significantly ignited the movement.[44] Notably, the regional population seldom aspired to religious nationhood but rather sought to safeguard their property, offspring and the dignity of women. As part of the British propaganda, the colonial administration magnified the figure of the 'Musaliar King', amplifying his influence, thereby posing a formidable setback to British operations in the region.

In K.N. Panikkar's book, the movement transformed from a religio-centric one driven by colonial animosity to an amicable 'peasant revolt'. This transformation is underscored by Panikkar's emphasis on contextualizing the movement within the socioeconomic fabric of its participants. In this metamorphosis, the movement became intrinsically linked with the livelihoods and social standing of its regional constituents. Within the annals of early anti-colonial resistance during the 16th century, participants are notably seen to be from two distinct strata of society: the coastal traders and their dependents and the agrarian communities of the hinterlands. Their motivations for engagement extended beyond mere vocational considerations. Rather, it was their deep-seated allegiance and symbiotic relationships with the leadership figures of various epochs that galvanized their participation. Although these leaders were part of the movements, they were not peasants themselves. This emphasizes a specific aspect of the broader Non-Cooperation Movement, which included people from different backgrounds and professions. Panikkar, however, emphasized the peasants. Panikkar posits that a seminal moment in the politicization of the peasantry was the visit of Mahatma Gandhi and Maulana Shaukat Ali to Malabar in August 1920.[45] This visit was part of their nationwide tour to solicit support for the Non-cooperation and Khilafat Movements. It signified a profound turning point, revitalizing the sociopolitical consciousness of the peasantry. Yet, crucially, the historical significance of Tirurangadi predates this visit, being previously recognized as a pivotal site in the anti-colonial resistance of the 16th century. Subsequent confrontations with colonial administrative forces continued to thrust Tirurangadi into the spotlight, culminating in the loss of Collector Conolly's life.[46]

Notably, Tirurangadi remained the epicenter of these issues, a theme that will be elaborated upon in the forthcoming chapters of this academic work. The incontrovertible enthusiasm witnessed during the visit of Gandhi and Shaukat Ali is underscored by the image of throngs of supporters who assembled at the railway station, bearing flowers and garlands. However, it is imperative to scrutinize claims made by the police force asserting that any fusion of religion with politics would have precipitated dire consequences in the zone.[47] The excerpt elucidates the multifaceted dynamics of resistance exhibited against landlords and colonial authorities within the context of colonial India. This resistance manifested itself through a spectrum of strategies, encompassing sporadic acts of defiance by small, localized groups, organized nonviolent strikes and protracted armed endeavors aimed at land seizure and the establishment of autonomous peasant self-governance.

Kathleen Gough's (1925–1990) contributions to this discourse are acknowledged, with particular attention drawn to her tendency to infuse a colonial narrative into her accounts. This colonial tint is exemplified by Gough's emphasis on the religious dimension of the resistance, especially against the backdrop of the struggles in the Malabar district spanning from 1836 to 1898. These narratives frequently portrayed the Muslim tenants as insurgents who engaged in acts of violence, including the killing of Hindu landlords, British officials and soldiers, before 1920. Gough's accounts overlook the contributions of non-Muslim leaders to the Khilafat and Non-Cooperation Movements, thereby potentially skewing the narrative by disproportionately foregrounding the religious facet of the resistance at the expense of other essential dimensions. This calls attention to the necessity for a more nuanced historiographical approach, one that considers the broader sociopolitical and economic factors that contributed to these historical events, transcending simplistic religious categorizations. Such an approach is pivotal in rendering a more comprehensive understanding of resistance in colonial India.[48]

British Primary Source Materials and Neighboring Narratives

During this study, a meticulous examination of British primary source materials has been diligently undertaken. This comprehensive review encompasses a spectrum of archival materials, including manuals, correspondences, treaties, agreements, official reports, literary works, articles, gazettes and contemporaneous newspapers. Such an extensive exploration was executed through the vantage point of a native resident hailing from a village situated in the locus of myriad anti-colonial struggles that transpired over a significant period, spanning from the 16th century to the dawn of the 20th century. Oral traditions, intricately interwoven with our social fabric, also chronicle instances of inter-community solidarity, notably, the protection of Hindus by their Muslim neighbors during the turbulent times, specifically against the depredations of the 'Lahalakkar' (proponent of *lahala*) and other exigent circumstances, as my field study in Vengara revealed. Certain infiltrators sought to exploit the situation for their personal gain. While this reality must be acknowledged, it should not be wielded to disparage entire resistance movements that were conceived and executed with genuine intent and whose participants made the ultimate sacrifice in defense of the honor and sovereignty of their land and people. There were instances of British agents infiltrating civilian protests with the purpose of furthering colonial propaganda, tactics rooted in the principles of divide and rule.[49] The colonial administration, in their efforts to expedite this agenda, released reports that besmirched entire factions engaged in the pursuit of a noble cause.

In the discourse surrounding the centenary observations of 1921–1922, a photograph purportedly depicting Variamkunnath Kunhamed Haji (1875–1922) surfaced and gained circulation, reportedly sourced from an article by Captain Harry in the magazine *Sciences et Voyages*, published on 10 August 1922. I obtained an issue of the same publication containing the alleged image was found, revealing a footnote referencing Muhammed Ali (Musaliar) but notably omitting any mention of Variamkunnath Kunhamed Haji in relation to the photograph. Consequently, the current evidence fails to conclusively establish the image attached to Captain Harry's article as that of Variamkunnath Kunhamed Haji. The accompanying caption to the prominently featured image of three men in association with this article asserts, 'Muhammed Ali, the mastermind of the Malabar Rebellion. When he was captured and executed, his followers became disillusioned and surrendered. The two Moplahs on both sides gave the signal to revolt by killing two British officers against the English sides.'[50] However, in the book titled *Sultan Variam Kunnan*, a contention arises that Ali Musaliar does not bear the name Muhammed Ali, thereby suggesting that the reference to 'Muhammed' in the caption likely pertains to Kunhamed Haji of Variamkunnath.[51] At the time of its public presentation, I posited that if the first half of 'Muhammed Ali' was attributed to Kunhamed Haji, a query arises about the name assigned to the other person on the opposite side.[52] Muhammed Ali Musaliar, the grandson of Ali Musaliar, personally communicated to me that his name Muhammed Ali was an homage to his grandfather, who had indeed possessed the full name Muhammed Ali.[53]

Captain Harry's article unveils the intricacies of British colonial propaganda directed against the anti-British movement in Malabar. The identification of the individuals featured in the published image, distinct from the presumed Variamkunnan, shows their pivotal roles in the Tirurangadi struggles. This revelation, earmarked for Chapter 3 of this monograph is crucial in the evolving landscape, highlighting the multifaceted attempts to assert proprietary rights over and aggrandize the struggle. Furthermore, this hasty assessment of the authenticity and authority of Variamkunnan's photo exposes a layered narrative where extremist factions, both religious and political, endeavor to manipulate the narrative. In doing so, they often neglect the nuanced interplay of inter-religious engagements that were integral to these historical movements.

In the post-colonial epoch, extensive scholarly investigations have scrutinized historical intricacies in the region. Nonetheless, a persistent issue reflected in studies conducted by indigenous historians is the perpetuation of colonial terminologies.[54] Designations such as 'rebellion', 'revolt' or '*lahala*', conventionally denoting armed resistance against an established governance or leadership, inadequately encapsulate the essence of the events in Malabar. The occurrences were not directed at the legitimate governance but rather constituted resistance against oppressive rule and intrusive forces. The prevalent usage of terms such as *Malabar Revolt* and *Moplah Rebellion* to delineate these struggles is emblematic of this issue. *Revolt* itself is a term crafted by the colonial administration, characterizing violent actions against a recognized government or ruler. Despite the passage of time and the advent of post-colonial scholarship, indigenous historians have introduced terminologies like *Malabar Lahala* and *Kalapam* (mutiny/revolt). This persistence of the colonial lexicon post-Independence underscores the enduring impact of colonialism on narrative constructs.

This study endeavors to disentangle itself from these entrenched colonial narratives. It aims to adopt terminology that more accurately reflects the nature of the historical events, seeking nomenclature that aligns with the nuanced aspects of resistance against oppressive governance and acknowledges the complexities inherent in the struggles of the Malabar region. Phrases like 'the prelude to the rebellion', 'religious animosity', 'Musaliar king', 'Khilafat king', 'waging war', 'Moplah Amazon' and 'feminists' were employed to justify the atrocities committed against the people, often demonizing them. For example, numerous individuals were massacred in the train carriage, and these incidents are narrated as a 'tragedy'.[55] However, if we consider these incidents as tragedies, then Conolly's death should also fall under the same category. Deliberate killings were described as tragedies in the colonial narrative. Women and children were brutally targeted, and these actions were justified through narratives that accused women of being feminists in that era. This study aims to address these issues and provide a decolonial narrative that accurately represents the struggles of Malabar.

Furthermore, to augment and triangulate these narratives, a substantial corpus of primary source documents has been meticulously scrutinized. This collation encompasses diaries, personal notes, official documents referred to as 'Malabar Resources', epistolary exchanges, religious edicts, articles, poetic compositions and published works of historical significance. These sources collectively offer a vivid and unfiltered window into the inhumane practices and cruelties meted out under the yoke of colonial administration. They are a poignant testament to the profound suffering and hardships endured by individuals who fell under the purview of colonial law enforcement agencies and military forces, who subsequently found themselves confined within the narrow spaces of carceral institutions. In undertaking this study, a concerted effort has been made to holistically comprehend the historical milieu by means of a multidisciplinary approach, rigorously subjecting these diverse primary source materials to analytical scrutiny. The aim is to contribute to a scrupulous understanding of the sociopolitical and cultural landscape of this historical epoch.

Mahatma Gandhi to Musaliar King: 1920–1922

The book is organized into two distinct parts. The initial segment, titled 'From Mahatma Gandhi to Musaliar King: 1920–1922', meticulously documents Gandhi's pivotal visit to Calicut and the consequential establishment of Non-Cooperation and Khilafat committees in the region. The opening chapter, 'Musaliar King: The Coinage to Conceal Colonial Carnage', critically analyzes the Tirurangadi event. It provides an extensive rebuttal to the conventional linkages between Malabar issues and Pukkottur, illustrating the depiction of Ali Musaliar as the regional monarch by colonial forces. This portrayal led to the titular concept of 'Musaliar king', which was derived from colonial coinage aiming to discredit influential local leaders. Chapter 2 engages with a contrived narrative propagated by the colonial press, depicting the Malabar region as 'Moplah Amazons'. These publications emerged during the period of Pukkottur issues, categorizing Muslim women as proponents of feminism. This perspective is examined in the context of its contentious role as a catalyst for feminist discourse. The subsequent chapter, Chapter 3, aims to unravel the identities of figures previously misidentified as Variamkunnath Kunhamed Haji. Utilizing documents from propaganda photographs published in *Sciences et Voyage*, this chapter diligently explores and elucidates the identities of individuals—namely Kunhi Kadir and Lava Kutty—depicted alongside Ali Musaliar in the aforementioned photograph. Chapter 4 delves into the historical narrative of the Khilafat Movement and its profound influence in the subcontinent. This section offers a nuanced analysis of Gandhi and Maulana's impact on the populace of Malabar, culminating in a thorough examination of the events of 1921 and 1922. This approach relies predominantly on primary sources as a foundational support for constructing arguments and cultivating a historiographical framework rooted in decolonial perspectives. Furthermore, it involves a critical analysis of colonial propaganda disseminated through historical news sources.

Portuguese to British Forces in Malabar, 1498–1900

The second section, 'Portuguese and British: 1498–1900', delineates the persistent resistance displayed by the local populace against historical colonial powers. It highlights the unwavering resilience of the Malabar people in staunchly opposing Portuguese and subsequent colonizers seeking dominion over the land. Chapter 5 explores the struggles that took place before the First War of Independence in colonial India, emphasizing the nuanced and inclusive nature of South India, particularly the Malabar region. Chapter 6 meticulously narrates the resistance sagas of two eminent figures—Sayyid Alawi and Sayyid Fazal—hailing from Mamburam. This section portrays their roles as proponents of resistance and harmony, countering prevalent colonial narratives portraying them as religious zealots. Chapter 7 comprehensively explores Conolly's death, which marked the continuation of Sayyid Fazal's expulsion from Malabar. This volume endeavors to present a decolonial historiography of the tumultuous struggles within Malabar, which were historically characterized by communal harmony and interfaith coexistence. It critically examines colonial narratives and propagandistic journalism that fueled discord by selectively emphasizing religious identities while omitting crucial details. The book seeks to unveil the actual perpetrators behind the atrocities of 1921, shedding light on the indoctrination aiming to impose martial law in the region. It underscores the inhumane aspects of colonial approaches, particularly highlighting the ethnic cleansing tactics deployed in the region, meticulously orchestrated by colonial forces under the guise of conflict and atrocities.

The village of Vengara has always been an integral part of the broader Tirurangadi region, and it is noteworthy that the historical *Mahal* affiliations of our village were initially connected with the Tirurangadi congregational mosque.[56] Eventually, this connection led to the establishment of our indigenous congregational mosque in Irukulam. Over the passing decades, I have had the privilege of embarking on numerous journeys to these historical centers. This contextual backdrop, enriched with its unique sociocultural tapestry, serves as the cradle for narratives and oral traditions passed down through generations. These narratives encapsulate the collective memory of families, recounting the tribulations endured during these pivotal historical junctures. Some families chose to relocate due to the profound loss incurred by the untimely demise of their parents during these tumultuous events. Indeed, like Ali Musaliar visited the tomb of Cherur Shaheeds (martyrs), an action that the British authorities considered to be the most significant provocation for inciting conflict in the region, the villages continue to draw strength and inspiration from these Shaheeds and Sufis. Among these sanctified sites, Mamburam Maqam consistently holds a prominent influential place.

PART I

MAHATMA GANDHI TO MUSALIAR KING
1920–1922

CHAPTER 1

MUSALIAR KING

The Coinage to Conceal Colonial Carnage

Around three decades ago, during the commemoration of the seventy-fifth anniversary of the 1921 Malabar resistance, I embarked on a meticulous journey to trace the vernacular historical paths of significant locales, including Mamburam, Tirurangadi, Tanur, Pukkottur, Nellikkuth and other regions of consequence. These areas were significant in the resistance against British colonial rule and were closely associated with Ali Musaliar, a prominent leader and scholar who operated traditional teaching centers, known as *Dar*s, at the heart of the resistance. His journey began as a teacher in Podiyat, near Pukkottur, where he served for four years. In 1907, he relocated to Tirurangadi and continued his religious teaching, while also establishing several traditional schools. Ali Musaliar was widely respected, and a significant number of his disciples went on to serve in various parts of Ernad and Valluvanad Taluks. Strong support for him from the local community led the British authorities to regard him as a prominent figure in the region. Interestingly, certain areas became centers of resistance because they were closely connected with Ali Musaliar. Once again, I immersed myself in the memory of the very grounds where the British perpetrated a treacherous massacre against peaceful demonstrators and the stories of individuals who met their demises during unforeseen waves of colonial brutality. This exploration revealed instances of unwavering support extended to Ali Musaliar, emphasizing the extraordinary selflessness displayed in the face of such adversity. Notably, the Tirurangadi Kacheri building emerged as a pivotal historical artifact, serving as the final resting place for British officers Johnstone and Rowley, who lost their lives during the actions executed by the colonial collector.

This chapter is devoted to a comprehensive examination of the primary factors underpinning the Malabar resistances of 1921, with particular attention to the loss of life among the native populace and the prominent British officers responsible. The death of two British

Figure 1.1
Map of British Malabar, 1807, Published by Francis Buchanan (1762–1829)

Source: Francis Buchanan, *A Journey from Madras through the Countries of Mysore, Canara and Malabar from London* (London: Cadell and Davies, 1807).

officers consistently occupied a central role in the narrative constructed by British authorities to rationalize their actions in the Malabar region (Fig. 1). While colonial reports and subsequent historiography traditionally emphasize the alleged theft of a gun by Vadakke Vitil Mammad and the police case against him as the initial catalyst for the ensuing catastrophes,[1] this research reveals an alternative perspective. It becomes apparent that the colonial collector and police superintendent harbored malevolent intentions to incite unrest in the region, resulting in the killings of innocent individuals in Tirurangadi, which also led to the death of British officials Johnstone and Rowley. The collector, E.F. Thomas sought retaliation for an incident in February 1921 when leaders of the Malabar Congress such as K. Madhavan Nair, U. Gopala Menon and Moideen Koya endeavored to bring Yakob Hassan to Malabar. Despite the district collector's prohibition on gatherings, they proceeded with their plans, leading to their arrest and subsequent six-month imprisonment. This incident incited unrest in Calicut, culminating in protesters assembling on Beach Road. They engaged in a confrontation with the district magistrate and the police, a tense standoff lasting for two hours. Hitchcock, in his book *A History of the Malabar Rebellion*, underscores this event as a significant protest, the first of its scale in seventy years since the exile of Sayyid Fazal Thangal of Mamburam.[2] The British authorities alleged that many of the protesters hailed from Tirurangadi.

Hitchcock notes that the attendees of Yakob Hassan's meeting numbered 12,000 people, primarily from Tirurangadi, and he drew a parallel with the substantial gathering of 8,000 to 12,000 during the exile of Sayyid Fazal (which will be addressed in Chapter 6). Upon the release of these leaders from prison after six months, further processions against British colonial rule ensued, a topic to be elaborated on later in this chapter. By associating the event predominantly with Muslims and Tirurangadi, Hitchcock tries to justify the carnage in Tirurangadi.[3]

Furthermore, it appears that Thomas, a pivotal figure in the colonial administration, was motivated by a desire to substantiate his initial assessment that the region would experience outbreaks of unrest and violence. This perspective was intended to urge the governor to implement all his proposed actions, thereby gaining consideration from higher authorities.

8 June 1921: Ali Musaliar's Ritualistic Visit to the Cherur Martyrs

Ali Musaliar's emergence as a prominent leader can be attributed to his profound influence in the Ernad and Valluvanad regions. While the British authorities acknowledged his leadership and occasionally referred to him as a king, he was primarily perceived and regarded as a spiritual and community leader.[4] The local populace seldom referred to him as a king; instead, they affectionately and respectfully addressed him as 'Musaliar *Uppapa*'.[5] This dialectical term reflects the deep reverence and intimate affection held for him personally, signifying his role as a scholarly figure who was like a beloved grandfather in their hearts.

On 8 June, the Tirurangadi mosque witnessed an increased turnout. Ali Musaliar, the head of the Tirurangadi mosque, led a tradition where he guided people to burial sites for special prayers for the deceased, commencing at the Kizhakkepalli (Fig. 1.2). They also offered prayers at the burial site of the Cherur battle that took place in 1843.[6] This traditional custom in Malabar is a part of religious rituals to commemorate departed individuals during significant events. In the case of martyrs, communities come together to perform special prayers, including the *nercha*, and engage in ritualistic processions to

Figure 1.2
Tirurangadi Kizhakkepalli Where Ali Musaliar Led the Congregational Prayers

Photograph by Lenseman Siraj

mark their death anniversaries. The British colonial administration accused Ali Musaliar of a serious offense, alleging that he was leading a procession of 300 to 400 Khilafat volunteers. Some of them were seen wearing uniforms, carrying cross-belts and knives and walking from the Kizhakkepalli to the burial site. This was a customary ritualistic practice during special occasions rather than any sinister plot. British officials attempted to portray these prayers as only being conducted before crucial events. Due to the historical significance of this site in anti-colonial struggles, British officers had previously prohibited gatherings and prayers at these graves.[7]

The British accused Ali Musaliar of praying for the success of the Khilafat Movement.[8] This was a misinterpretation, as such prayers were a common practice in Muslim culture, encompassing all aspects of life and well-being. The colonial administration in the district used this peaceful action as an excuse to agitate against the locals. The Cherur incidents were already a point of concern for the British, as they suffered significant losses in clashes with a relatively small number of determined individuals. The district superintendent of police judged this event as the first definite sign of a potential 'uprising'.[9] It is evident that the district administration had planned aggressive actions against the local population from July. The *Madras Mail*, a source of colonial propaganda, began a series on 'Moplahs of Malabar', recounting past 'atrocities' such as the 'murder of Hindus and defilement of temples'.[10] The colonial administration aimed to divide people based on their religion, using divisive narratives to pit Hindus and Muslims against each other. The *Madras Mail* emphasized 'violent excesses' and fabricated narratives about the 'fanatical and turbulent spirit' prevalent among the Moplahs. They also highlighted the perceived danger of sudden outbreaks of 'fanaticism', especially among the 'ignorant' and 'backward' Moplah inhabitants of Ernad and Valluvanad.[11]

While the colonial authorities viewed Muslims as a threat to maintaining peace and tranquility in the district, other reports highlighted peaceful coexistence between Muslims and Hindus, who lived and worked together like brothers in the region. During the field study for collecting local history in Vengara, I received direct narratives of Hindu–Muslim unity in the region. Hindu families were shielded by their Muslim neighbors, and a Hindu worker bravely sacrificed himself to protect his Muslim landlord from a group that attacked the landlord's house due to his support for the British.[12] Instances of this unity can also be seen in the leadership of the Non-Cooperation and Khilafat Movements. After the Tirurangadi incident, K.P. Keshava Menon described his journey from Calicut to Tirurangadi. It is interesting to observe the Hindu–Muslim unity within the group, including K.V. Gopala Menon, U. Gopala Menon, Kodungallur Shekhara Menon, Ponmadathu Moideen Koya, Manikkoth Gopala Menon, Abdurahiman, Kunhammad, K. Madhava Menon and T.V. Chathukutty Nair.[13]

Hitchcock encapsulated the yearlong events showcasing Hindu–Muslim solidarity and friendship, evident on reading between the lines. He noted that in April 1920, Hindus initiated agitation for non-cooperation, aiming to garner support from the Mappila community, highlighting the efficacy of communal unity and friendships. This narrative sheds light on how the colonial administration interpreted and depicted such interactions.[14]

Conrad Wood acknowledges that 'there is sufficient evidence to suggest that the agitation of 1920–1921 did, to some extent, succeed in mobilizing at least some Ernad Moplahs on a secular basis against Jenmi power'.[15] Notably, his study aligns with the notion that this mobilization did occur, albeit with some negative connotations about the limited scope of this harmony, as it was particularly confined to some issue.

Numerous non-Muslims also came to Mamburam to seek the blessings of Sayyid ʿAlawi Mawla al-Dawilah al-Ḥusayni Thangal. The police took note of the growth of the volunteer movement during the summer and reported fabricated cases of knife and sword manufacturing.[16]

29 July 1921: Ali Musaliar's Regular Friday Congregation Gained Attention

Ali Musaliar also championed the values of interreligious and intercultural engagement, making him a leader capable of uniting people from diverse backgrounds in the spirit of non-cooperation. On 29 July 1921, Ali Musaliar's regular Friday congregation prayer attracted attention as an act of resistance against the colonial government. British reports noted that a large group, half of which consisted of volunteers, attended the congregational prayers in Tirurangadi with a procession. Ali Musaliar's advocacy for the boycott of British actions became a significant issue in these reports. Muslim scholars discouraged people from joining the army and called for the resignation of those already enlisted.[17] Ali Musaliar's commitment to peaceful coexistence was evident in his approach during a meeting facilitated by the colonial administration. The meeting, which included Khan Bahadur Chekkuti, Karadan Moideen and Ali Musaliar, aimed to address the potentially 'dangerous' direction of the Non-Cooperation and Khilafat Movements.[18] During this meeting, Ali Musaliar concurred with the recommendations, which included refraining from displaying Khilafat emblems and wearing uniforms. This decision was reached with the participation of influential regional figures from the Chakeri family, as well as in alignment with the British authorities' assertion that such measures were necessary to preserve peace in the region. In addition to these measures, Ali Musaliar also made a plea that no punitive actions be taken against individuals who chose to attend the Friday congregation prayers in Khilafat uniform. This incident serves as a poignant testament to Ali Musaliar's remarkable unwavering commitment to the cause of peace.[19] To discredit this esteemed leader and provide a semblance of justification for the orchestrated massacre led by Collector Thomas, Hitchcock resorted to propagandistic claims in his published work. He alleges that a significant portion of the volunteers failed to uphold their commitments, seeking to cast a shadow of doubt on their integrity. Furthermore, Hitchcock erroneously contends that Ali Musaliar was seen attending the mosque in the company of a substantial number of bands,[20] an assertion aimed at tarnishing his reputation. These misrepresentations in Hitchcock's work illustrate a deliberate attempt to undermine Ali Musaliar's character and justify the tragic events surrounding Collector Thomas.[21]

30 July 1921: Propaganda Prelude to the Malabar Massacre

Incidents at Pukkottur *Kovilagam*[22] were highlighted as the prelude to violent colonial massacres in the Malabar region. It is indeed a matter of intellectual fascination to unearth the existence of counter-narratives that serve to challenge the prevailing colonial propaganda. Particularly, these descriptions seek to debunk the notion that the Hindu landlord of Pukkottur was attacked by Muslims under the guidance of a prominent employee, Vadakke Vittil Mammad. Notably, Tirumalpad,[23] the said landlord, borrowed funds from Muslim neighbors to meet his financial obligations to the employee, which becomes a salient element in this episode: 'Mammad insisted on getting the money then and there, but for want of ready cash three Mapillas of the locality who are tenants of the palace stood surety for the amount and gave a jewel to Mammad with promise to redeem it the next day'.[24] The dispute centered around the accusation of a stolen gun from the *kovilagam* and the accompanying financial predicament, as accentuated by the British, are pivotal elements within the broader context of the 'revolt' in Malabar. This emphasis on financial matters introduces a layer of intricacy and subtlety to the historical landscape, effectively subverting the conventional portrayal of these events. The presence of such nuanced counter-narratives serves as a valuable contribution to our comprehension of the historical milieu, as it illuminates the multifaceted dynamics at play, revealing mechanical details that often remain obscured within the overarching colonial narrative.[25]

In the colonial historiography of the Malabar region, particularly within the orbit of important events marked by substantial British involvement, a conspicuous inclination toward distortion becomes evident. British colonial authorities consistently exhibited a proclivity for constructing counter-narratives to obfuscate the substantive issues at hand. Notably, the genesis of the eventful incidents of 1921 has conventionally been ascribed singularly to the actions of Kalathingal Vadakke Vitil Mammad. However, a deeper motive can be discerned in the echelons of the colonial administration. This underlying motive appears to have revolved around the deliberate designation of the region as a crucible of insurgency, a strategic maneuver designed to secure augmented fiscal allocations and additional privileges from higher stratums of authority. Notwithstanding the discernible rhetoric that sought to portray the region as a bastion of fanaticism and militancy, such depictions crumbled under scrutiny during the visits of high-ranking colonial officials. Consequently, District Magistrate Thomas and Police Superintendent Hitchcock, steadfast in their determination to validate their claims, found themselves constrained to engineer instances of insurgency within the region. Events unfolding in locales such as Pukkottur and Tirurangadi were choreographed with meticulous precision by these officers. This calculated manipulation of events was a perilous gambit, imperiling not only the lives of the indigenous populace but also the harmonious coexistence that had hitherto characterized the region.[26]

The British historiographic interpretation of the 1921 resistance in the Malabar region is entwined with the historical account of Kalathingal Vadakke Vittil Mammad, a prominent figure who assumed a central role in catalyzing both the Khilafat and tenancy protests in Pukkottur. Notably, on 30 July 1921, M. Narayana Menon, the acting police inspector, along with his contingent of constables, forcefully entered and searched Vadakke Vittil Mammad's residence. This action stemmed from allegations implicating Mammad in the theft of a firearm from Nilambur *kovilagam*, the domicile of the local chieftains, where Mammad was the estate manager. Significantly, before this event, Mammad had been terminated from his position, precipitated by his association with the Khilafat-Non-Cooperation Movement—a stance that placed him in direct opposition to the pro-British landlords of Nilambur. When the police tried to arrest Mammad, around 2,000 individuals congregated in front of his house, resolutely determined to shield him from apprehension. Faced with this formidable gathering, Inspector M. Narayana Menon and his retinue tactically withdrew from the scene, presumably under the sway of a discernible sense of trepidation.[27]

The British records prominently characterize the Pukkottur incident as the 'prelude to the rebellion'.[28] However, this episode was orchestrated against a participant in the Non-Cooperation Movement to protect a local landlord who aligned with colonial interests. The correspondence by M. Narayana Menon, the inspector in the D. Division of Malappuram, addressed to the superintendent of police in Malabar, Calicut, on 2 August 1921, provides a comprehensive account of this occurrence. Regrettably, this incident was later depicted as a precursor to a spectrum of issues, with subsequent scholars also adhering to this colonial narrative,[29] which, in part, sought to obscure the malfeasance of the head of the Malabar District.

> I beg to report that on 28th July 1921 night the pathayapura attached to the Nilambur Kovilagam at Pukkottur was broken into by thieves by opening the lock with a false key and a single barrel breech loading gun, a sum of about Rs 130 in cash and some documents were stolen. Some of the documents were next day found torn and thrown in the tank close by. Probationary Sub-Inspector Govinda Menon of Manjeri who went to Pukkottur on other business on 29th knew of the occurrence and started inquiry into the case. On 30th forenoon he conducted a search in the house of one Vadakke Vittil Mammad of Pukkottur, a peon and a tenant of the Kovilagam. This Mammad

> was a gun licensee, but his license had been cancelled a few weeks ago, he is being an active non-cooperator and a member of Khilafat. Nothing was recovered during search.[30]

This report provides valuable insight into how colonial historiography employed a selective and biased narrative to shape events in Malabar to align with their perspective. In this context, Manager Mammad was relegated to a peon, a characterization seemingly incongruous with the fact that he had previously held a government-issued gun license. Mammad was accused of misappropriating ₹130 from a traditional safe locker belonging to a landlord. Contrary to the colonial claim, Tirumalpad owed Mammad an amount about three times bigger than what he was accused of stealing. This aspect is apparent in British primary documents, yet there was a lack of decolonial analysis, failing to illuminate the perspectives omitted in the colonial narratives.[31] This raises questions regarding the accuracy of the colonial account and underscores the need for a more nuanced examination of historical events. It also shows the existence of pre-existing tensions between Mammad and the landlord, the sixth Tirumalpad. Perapurath Ahamad Kutti, who held the position of *adhikari*,[32] was involved in the inquiry conducted by the sub-inspector at Pukkottur.[33] Official records, however, downplay his active involvement, stating that he 'did not actively participate in the search'.[34] A longstanding enmity had existed between Perapurath Ahamad Kutti and Vadakke Vittil Mammad, which further fueled the events. Vadakke Vittil Mammad firmly believed that the *adhikari*, Ahamad Kutti, and one of the *kariastans*,[35] Velayudhan Nayar, played a pivotal role in orchestrating the search, leading to his public humiliation. Additionally, there were suspicions regarding the sub-inspector's presence, with Mammad suspecting that he was acting at the behest of the village *munsif*[36] to suppress his activities.[37]

1 August 1921: Tirumalpad's Financial Settlement with Muslim Support

On the morning of August 1921, Pulakal Karunakara Menon, a relative of the Tirumalpad, reported to the acting inspector that on the night of 31 June, Mammad and his brother Kunhammad went to the *kovilagam* and demanded ₹355, contending that it was owed to them as arrears of pay and charges for work performed, along with two bags of rice. However, the Tirumalpad had only ₹5 to provide, and a chit was issued for the rice. Mammad, nonetheless, insisted on the immediate payment of the full amount due. Due to a shortage of liquid funds, three Muslims from the vicinity, who were tenants of the landlord, offered themselves as sureties for the outstanding amount. They also provided jewelry to Mammad, with a commitment to redeem it the next day. This episode reveals the presence of a personal dispute between the landlord and the non-cooperation volunteer, Mammad, as well as the personal animosity between Mammad and the village *adhikari*, Ahamad Kutti.[38] This historical account unequivocally establishes that the unfolding events lacked any sectarian underpinnings. The report underscores the proactive role played by members of the Muslim community in promptly assisting the Hindu landlord to address the situation involving Mammad and the Tirumalpad. This collective response serves as compelling empirical evidence that communal dynamics were not the driving force behind the sequence of events. Furthermore, Ahamad Kutti's collaborative partnership with both colonial authorities and the Hindu landlord highlights the absence of purely religious-based communal tensions. Ahmad Kutti, a Muslim, was closely involved with both a Hindu landlord and the British administration without any accusations of religious fanaticism or religious animosity, as often depicted in colonial documents.

K.N. Panikkar conspicuously delineates the appellation 'Kalathingal Muhammad' in his published chapter in the book edited by R. Desai, a nomenclature distinct from that attributed by Tottenham.[39] Noteworthy is the steadfast employment of this particular name throughout K.N. Panikkar's comprehensive work entitled *Against Lord and State: Religion and Peasant Uprisings in Malabar*.[40] This situation engenders a certain degree of ambiguity concerning the precise nomenclature of the individual who the British authorities highlighted as the instigator of the issues at hand. An examination of the complete family name reveals that he was known as 'Kalathingal Vadakke Vittil Mammad', with 'Mammad' serving as the colloquial abbreviation of 'Muhammed'.[41] Importantly, he was the secretary of the local Khilafat committee. Pukkottur played host to one of the most significant non-cooperation gatherings during this period. By mid-1921, the local people showed a clear interest in expressing their political dissent effectively, which was a significant moment in history.

When Hitchcock described this incident a few years later, it created even more venomous arguments and controversy:

> On 31st July 1921 a Mapilla of Pukkottur, who had a grievance against 6th Tirumalpad of Nilambur living in a kovilagam at Pukkottur raised the whole country side. Gangs of Mappillas 30 to 50 strong were collected for mile round at tea shops and praying sheds. The main body, led by the man with the grievance, over 600 strong was

> armed with spears and swords, several wearing Khilafat badges. The Inspector handled this admirably won over the man with the grievance and left for the kovilagam to reassure the inmates. But the crowd was beyond the control of the man who had raised them and by their cries showed they had come not to redress a grievance real or imaginary but determined to convert the kovilagam to a mosque, destroy the Tiramalpad and murder Deputy Superintendent Amu, the Parappur Adhikari and the Inspector because they were opposed to Khilafat.[42]

This case illustrates the evolving colonial narratives and their ramifications on intergroup dynamics, particularly with regard to religious tensions. The colonial authorities not only endeavored to obfuscate the religious affiliations of the *adhikari* but also promulgated a spurious hypothesis suggesting an attempt to convert the *kovilagam* into a mosque. Between 1922, when Tottenham first published the report, and 1925, when Hitchcock published it, there was a noticeable change in the colonial administration's tone, which became more contentious. Consequently, it becomes increasingly exigent to consider the colonial propaganda delineated in this account. In this narrative, Hitchcock chose to omit the account where Muslims played a pivotal role in assisting Tirumulpad to amicably resolve the dispute with Vadakke Vittil Mammad. Furthermore, Hitchcock's omission of the underlying tensions between Perapurath Ahamad Kutti and Vadakke Vittil Mammad inadvertently exacerbated the communal aspect of these events, deepening the schisms and antagonisms.

Hitchcock, therefore, deliberately tried to obfuscate the reprehensible atrocities committed by British colonial forces in the region. These actions showed a troubling lack of care, causing terrible harm to women and children during military operations. To rationalize these distressing occurrences, Hitchcock describes how the constant drumming in the mosque and the encouragement of Mappila women to men caused alarm. Hitchcock underscores the strategic importance of certain locales as centers of resistance, which was often attributed to the charismatic influence of figures like Ali Musaliar, who held sway over these regions due to their significant following. Notable among these areas were Kondotti, Tirurangadi, Irumpuzhi, Podiyat, Melmuri, Valluvambram, Nellikkuth and Ponmala, all of which emerged as crucial epicenters of resistance against the colonial forces.[43]

The historiographical examination of the events that transpired in the Malabar region warrants nuanced scrutiny. In numerous instances, the imperial administration tended to obscure factual accounts, opting to foreground alternate narratives and propagate fictitious accounts of Hindu–Muslim discord in the region, thereby advancing the policy of 'divide and rule'. District Magistrate on the first day of August, the constabulary tried to subject Mammad to an interrogation within the precincts of the *kovilagam*, yet the determined resistance offered by him, coupled with the resolute support extended by a substantial retinue of his adherents, compelled the law enforcement authorities to withdraw tactically. Noteworthy is the instance wherein Tirumalpad sought financial assistance from Muslim neighbors to resolve the vexing issue with Vadakke Vittil Mammad. This peculiarity beckons the question of how, if the milieu was entirely marked by communal strife and religious fanaticism, such an intercommunity financial transaction could be feasibly executed to mitigate a crisis linked to an individual deemed as the epicenter of these disturbances.[44]

13 August 1921: Hitchcock Collaborated with Collector Thomas

Hitchcock also collaborated with Collector Thomas to exacerbate the issues in the Malabar region. The prelude to the carnage was executed with Hitchcock's support, and his earlier correspondence clearly indicates his intention to foster strife in the region.[45] Hitchcock's attitudes and intentions are reflected on reading between the lines of a report dated 13 August from J.T.W. Filson, personal assistant to the inspector general of police. On his way back to Malabar, Hitchcock acknowledged the critical nature of the situation and anticipated trouble if the authorities acted against individuals with pending cases. The report, with extracts from a letter by Mainwaring and a letter by Hitchcock that was enclosed by Mainwaring, indicates that action was postponed to allow the excitement to subside, but this was only a temporary measure. Hitchcock expected to deploy troops in Malappuram, which he considered more necessary than during the war when a detachment was stationed there. He also expressed the need to be prepared for a very serious situation, suggesting that British troops and magazine rifles were necessary. This implies an expectation of disorder and chaos and the need for an armed force. Mainwaring also delved into strategies such as the idea of using airplanes against the people of Malabar, given the challenges of their terrain. He concluded by emphasizing that some among them were not ignorant of how to arrange effective resistance and that this attack would likely be better organized than ever before. He highlighted the difficulties that would need to be overcome if organized resistance were to succeed, including the need to remove obstacles like fallen trees from roads. He reassured his superiors that there would be no chance for even the smallest success for the people of Malabar.[46]

Evidently, Collector Thomas and Hitchcock were more than prepared to employ an unnecessarily hard-line with the native folk in Malabar, one that would ultimately result in the killing of unarmed people who had gathered at Tirurangadi Kacheri to discuss the release of their fellow citizens arrested by the forces. Hitchcock expected to have troops in Malappuram and created a general impression that highlighted a one-sided scenario.[47] Hitchcock also stated that he was not unnecessarily alarmist when asking that the regime should be prepared for a very serious situation.[48]

15 August 1921: Communication from the General Officer Commanding

The archival records from August 1921 reveal a significant telegraph correspondence between Calicut and Madras, culminating in a detailed dispatch sent on 15 August 1921. This communication confirms the allocation of three platoons from the First Battalion, Leinster Regiment (R.C.), equipped with Lewis guns, to reinforce Calicut on 14 August 1921. The primary objective of this deployment was to augment the Detachment's personnel count to approximately 200 individuals across various ranks. Furthermore, the statement underscores the readiness of the 81st Pioneers, an approximately 300-strong unit stationed in Bangalore, poised to mobilize to Calicut if necessitated by the unfolding circumstances. However, pertinently, the general officer commanding articulates reservations about the strategic decision-making process. He expresses concerns about the preemptive dispatch of troops in the absence of an imminent crisis demanding their intervention. He expresses dissent against the hurried deployment, emphasizing that such actions contradicted the sender's judgment. The report scrutinizes the ramifications of deploying forces hastily, cautioning that this proactive action, undertaken before the crystallization of a coherent plan for their deployment, could potentially negate the element of surprise and be misconstrued as an impulsive, panic-driven response. This historical document sheds light on the intricate considerations involved in military deployments, emphasizing the delicate balance between proactive keenness and the necessity for a meticulously devised strategy to ensure optimal utilization of forces while mitigating misinterpretations that could arise from rushed or reactive measures.[49]

The report further cautions against the unilateral movement of troops in circumstances where decisive civil authority action seemed imminent. A collaborative approach is called for, stressing the necessity for joint deliberation involving the chief magistrate and officers from Madras to comprehensively evaluate the situation from both civil and military perspectives before any troop mobilization. Additionally, it strongly advocates refraining from hasty decisions by civil authorities regarding military intervention. Instead, it proposes that in critical situations necessitating military involvement, the decision-making process should involve suggestions from military officers on-site, allowing them to determine the nature of the action required and the requisite troop numbers. Moreover, it highlights the logistical challenges during the current season in Malabar, particularly the restrictions on troop movements along specific routes. The report, acknowledging these limitations, provides recommendations to navigate these constraints effectively, emphasizing the importance of tactically handling the situation. Overall, this document underscores the significance of collaborative decision-making between civil and military authorities, stressing the need for meticulous planning, strategic evaluations and an acute understanding of the local terrain and logistical considerations to address emergent situations effectively.[50]

The report presents a nuanced depiction of the extensive deployment of military personnel to the region, highlighting the disproportionate allocation vis-à-vis the overall military contingent within the Madras jurisdiction. Notably, it articulates concerns about the substantial financial burden incurred by the government due to the premature mobilization of these forces. This underscores the imperative need of the district magistrate and the superintendent of police to secure comprehensive backing for their proposed military initiatives in the Malabar region, which mandated endorsement from the governing body of the Madras Presidency. Moreover, the report laments the absence of a conclusive report from the designated officer dispatched to confer with District Magistrate Thomas. It speculates that the envoy might discern the redundancy of augmenting troop numbers or deem a movable column from Bangalore more fitting than an Indian battalion for the prevailing circumstances. The report conveys an earnest aspiration for the resolution of the situation without additional military reinforcements.[51] The scenario outlined pertains to the response from Madras to the assertive stance taken by District Magistrate Thomas and Police Superintendent Hitchcock, who seemingly championed a confrontational initiative, potentially indicative of militaristic inclinations. Despite receiving counsel advising against instigating any form of conflict, these officials appeared resolute in pursuing their objectives. The populace's reaction to this assertive stance, particularly among informed circles or influential voices within the community, remains a subject warranting scholarly scrutiny.

16 August 1921: A.R. Knapp Disagrees with Thomas and Hitchcock

On 16 August 1921, following his return from Malabar, A.R. Knapp, a senior British civil servant in India, issued a remarkable official note of action that did not endorse the plans of Hitchcock and Thomas. The approved actions were as follows: (a) deployment of troops and police for a daybreak operation at Tirurangadi to apprehend Erikunnath Ali Musaliar of Nellikkuth, who was a teacher and leader; (b) arresting Lava Kutti, who had been accused of frequenting the memorial at Mambram that was dedicated to those killed in a previous conflict and (c) detaining Karadan Moideen, a Non-Cooperation Movement leader. The district administration was granted approval for these arrests under the Mappila Outrages Act, 1859 (Act No. XX of 1859) and to conduct searches for knives, as per Thomas's request. However, a notable directive in the approval explicitly stated that it was 'not intended to search in mosques'. On 16 August 1921, during a Cabinet meeting, discussions centered on the Malabar affairs, and it was agreed that action should be taken under the Mappila Outrages Act. Careful consideration was to be given to ensuring that no impression was created that this measure was directed against the Khilafat Movement. Importantly, the proposal of the district magistrate, Thomas, to wage war against the people of Malabar was not approved. There were no objections to the district magistrate taking action under Section 7 of the Mappila Outrages Act wherever there were sufficient grounds. The meeting concurred that the district magistrate should proceed as planned in Tirurangadi, and if further action was being considered, a definitive and detailed plan should be submitted. The meeting also stressed that any action should be limited to individuals for whom the district magistrate was satisfied that Section 7 of the Mappila Outrages Act applied.[52]

On 16 August 1921, E.F. Thomas, the district magistrate and collector of Malabar, sent a communication from Calicut. In this message, Thomas notes that A.R. Knapp had informed him that since he would be returning to Madras soon, there was no need for Thomas to wire the results of Hitchcock's inquiries. A.R. Knapp asked about what should be undertaken in various areas, including Tirurangadi, Tanalur, Pukkottur and Chembrasseri, which was further inland and had experienced issues in 1915. Thomas explains that there were approximately 170 soldiers at West Hill, and his initial plan was to focus on Tirurangadi. In this area, individuals were to be arrested under the Mappila Act, and a search was to be conducted to seize a number of war-knives. Those found in possession of such weaponry would be arrested and punished under the Malabar War-Knives Act, 1854.[53]

It was noted that Hitchcock and Thomas had previously presented a detailed plan to extend their operations to regions like Tanalur and

Pukkottur. However, the events in Tirurangadi indicate that these earlier plans were intended to conceal their true intentions, which seemed to be to create significant trouble and atrocities in Tirurangadi. This ran contrary to A.R. Knapp's directions and the Cabinet's decision not to search in mosques and to avoid declaring a war against the Khilafat Movement. Thomas states that if the actions in Tirurangadi yielded positive results, they would proceed to Pukkottur. Here, they would arrest both individuals subject to the Mappila Acts and those who had committed specific offenses. A British Detachment would be stationed in Malappuram for this purpose. If necessary, they would take a similar approach in Chembrasseri, as there were a few men there who needed to be brought under the Mappila Act and might not be found in the aforementioned places as they roamed.[54]

In his letter, E.F. Thomas enclosed a list of individuals prepared by Hitchcock. He states that, in addition to this list, it was uncertain how many people might be arrested for the possession of war-knives. Thomas also sought permission to transfer certain detainees to Coimbatore prison. He explains that some of those arrested were considered highly dangerous individuals, and it would be unwise to keep them custody in Malabar, even temporarily. He requests the government to issue instructions to the superintendent of Coimbatore Jail to receive remand and other prisoners that he might send. This request raises concerns about his intentions to facilitate events that could prove perilous for the Malabar region. A.R. Knapp had discussed the proposed implementation of Section 144 by Thomas, which he argued was absolutely necessary for Malabar. Thomas acknowledges that one objection to his report was the identified intention to declare war on the Khilafat Movement. He decides that this objection could be mitigated or removed by modifying the draft to charge the agitators with using the Khilafat as part of their activities:

> Mr. Knapp has discussed the proposed order under 144, which I think absolutely necessary. It occurs to me that one of his objections to my draft that it is a declaration of war on Khilafat, may be removed or minimized if the draft is so modified as to charge the agitator with using Khilafat, its volunteer uniform and badges as a cloak for cultivating the fanatical spirit and inciting to the familiar outrage.[55]

17 August 1921: E.F. Thomas's Role in the Carnage

It remains conspicuous that District Magistrate Thomas was among the British officers who were resolute in validating their positions, even at the cost of collateral damage, including the unfortunate loss of British officers' lives. His discontentment stemmed from the actions and sentiments expressed in the Khilafat and Non-Cooperation Movements, as well as the perceived 'disrespect' he encountered from both the general populace and local leaders. A pivotal juncture in this narrative occurred on 17 August 1921, when three prominent leaders of the Khilafat and Non-Cooperation Movements, namely Gopala Menon, Madhavan Nair and Moideen Koya, were released from imprisonment after serving a six-month term.[56] Their return was marked by a grand reception in Calicut, during which processions openly demonstrated derision when the district magistrate passed through the collectorate. The district administration, notably Thomas, the district magistrate, and Hitchcock, the police superintendent, deemed this display of unity as shameful. They accused a significant number of people from Tirurangadi of participating in both the protests preceding the leaders' arrest and the enthusiastic procession following their release. In response to this perception, they took measures that eventually led to the massacre in Tirurangadi shortly after these events. Hitchcock repeatedly points out the involvement of Tirurangadi in his book, accusing the people of being primarily responsible for Yakub Hassan's arrest. He also specifies that at the visit of Hassan, Ernad Mappilas were brought in. They cared little for his imprisonment, but a very grave situation was caused by their endeavors to force a procession.[57] The district magistrate's motivation was rooted in a determination to substantiate his initial stance to the governor, even if it necessitated heinous firing upon unarmed civilians and directing them to kneel in Tirurangadi—a stark and regrettable chapter in the historical record of the period.[58] The district magistrate's expedition to Tirurangadi to apprehend Non-Cooperation leader Ali Musaliar and his associates marked a watershed moment that set in motion a comprehensive military intervention. This development, in turn, ignited a substantial insurgency of notable proportions throughout the region. Consequently, individuals hailing from diverse geographical locales were galvanized into a collective mobilization, converging upon Tirurangadi in a conspicuous manifestation of unity and opposition.

Subsequently, Hitchcock attempted to construct a historical narrative that obscured their involvement and depicted the indigenous population negatively. To attain a comprehensive understanding of the Malabar events, it is imperative to distinguish the chronology of occurrences in the region from those associated with Vadakke Vittil Mammad. A meticulous analysis is warranted, wherein these incidents are systematically linked with contemporaneous reports and the actions undertaken by the district collector. The local police inspector, in a report submitted to the district magistrate, raised a matter of grave concern. According to his assessment, the Mappila community was actively engaged in the formation of volunteer corps while simultaneously engaging in the manufacture and accumulation of arms and weaponry. He articulated apprehensions regarding the potential eruption of a 'Mappila uprising', particularly in the Erand Taluk, if decisive and expedient measures were not taken.[59] District Magistrate E.F. Thomas concurred with this assessment and deemed the situation to be of utmost seriousness. Consequently, he petitioned the Madras governor for military intervention to restore and uphold 'peace' within the district.[60] Thomas's perspective was that the disarmament and apprehension of a substantial number of potential Mappila protestors necessitated a meticulously executed operation, entailing the systematic combing of villages across Malabar. A letter to the general officer commanding dated 11 August 1921, continuing from cipher telegram no. 257 dated 11 August 1921, specified that reports from propaganda press were utilized. For instance, the report included a copy of the district magistrate's letter regarding the situation, along with a cutting from the *Madras Mail* of 8 August, claiming that it provides a 'fairly accurate account of the facts'. This served to elucidate the ground-level situation, which indicated the potential for a 'serious outbreak'.[61] Therefore, a request was made to dispatch a detachment of British troops to Malappuram upon receipt of a telegraphic requisition.[62] In response to this earnest entreaty, the Leinster Regiment was dispatched to Calicut. However, the governor, in his response, explicitly prohibited the district magistrate from engaging in a comprehensive action against the populace. Rather, the authority granted was confined solely to the arrest of influential leaders with the primary objective of preempting any further disturbances.[63] Evidently, the district magistrate's sense of urgency and anxiety was not congruent with the perspective of the central government. A.R. Knapp, a member of the governor's executive council, embarked on a fact-finding mission to Calicut and, after his assessment, did not categorize the situation in Ernad as an immediate and severe crisis.[64]

Numerous reports issued by the highest colonial authorities had strongly advised District Magistrate Thomas against embarking on a military campaign against the Khilafat in the Malabar region.[65] These reports were founded on a contrasting portrayal of the region's peaceful coexistence, one that diverged markedly from the accounts provided by District Magistrate Thomas and District Superintendent of Police Hitchcock: The order from Madras, dated 17 August 1921, specifies that 'Khilafat must be kept out of proclamation under section 144', with a special note indicating that 'it does seem rather as Mr. Thomas and Mr. Hitchcock were against Khilafateers too much'.[66] This report notably underscores the pronounced personal aversions held by Thomas and

Hitchcock against the Khilafateers. The extent of these biases, it is noteworthy, elicited concern in the colonial administration.

18 August 1921: The Actions of Thomas and Hitchcock Promoted Atrocities

In the official records, a discernible disquiet was evident among the higher authorities regarding the pronounced actions of the Malabar district collector, Thomas, and the superintendent of police, Hitchcock. A letter addressed to E.F. Thomas, bearing the reference number 286-8 and dated 18 August 1921, specifically cautioned against the perception of a targeted campaign against the Khilafat. Such warnings were recurrent, originating from the colonial higher authorities, directed at these two officials responsible for the administration of the Malabar district. Their actions were perceived as instigating issues and promoting atrocities throughout the entire region:

> You will have got after you wrote that my telegram of the 16th, No. 276, telling you that Government approve of the Tirurangadi and Tanalur operations and await a report from you after these operations are over as to subsequent plans. As regards the use of section 144, Criminal Procedure Code, the Government do not wish, I am to say, to interfere with or to fetter your discretion except to the extent indicated in the concluding part of telegram No. 276, namely, that in all your proceedings you should at present avoid the appearance of a special campaign against Khilafat but should deal with the matter on the basis of a threatened Mapilla outbreak. Concerning the reception of your under-arrests at the Coimbatore Jail, action is being separately taken and I hope this will be arranged.[67]

On the same date, a supplementary memorandum pertaining to the Malabar affairs delineated the perceptible emotional perturbation of Collector Thomas after his exchange with Knapp.[68] Following an extensive discourse involving not only Hitchcock and Austin, subdivisional magistrate of Malappuram, but also a resident rubber planter in Ernad, Brown, noteworthy input was garnered.[69] Knapp, conspicuously, did not subscribe to the essentiality of military intervention within the region. He vehemently disapproved of any such measures directed against the local populace, as eloquently conveyed in the following terms:

> I say 'so far as local affairs are concerned' for I found some difficulty in making him realize that in such a matter as a deliberate declaration

> of war against Khilafat volunteers' local action must be decided by considerations of general and not merely local policy.[70]

In tandem with Thomas, Hitchcock also endeavored to persuade the higher authorities to endorse a more extensive military campaign in the Malabar region, as mentioned in a letter from Thomas, dated 10 August 1921:

> It is with full sense of responsibility, as it is with the deepest regret, that I inform Government that the situation is beyond the district officials. Mr. Hitchcock will not advise action by the Special Force and Reserve Police even if supported by the British Detachment, he will act if ordered, but the order I will not issue. We have to face the facts. We cannot go on as we are with peace only so long as we remain inert. Crime has been committed and remains unpunished. At any moment another and worse calamity may occur and we cannot move till we have sufficient force. I consider that we require one complete battalion of staunch Indian troops would prefer British if only because the Mappila traditionally prefers dispatch to a better world at their hands, but suppose that is out of the question-supported by detachments aggregating a double company of British troops with the two Stokes Mortars now at Calicut.[71]

His rationale for this advocacy was based on the premise that local communities would misinterpret restraint as a sign of fear on the part of the authorities, especially in the aftermath of the issues fabricated and presented by Thomas and Hitchcock.

A detailed report from E.F. Thomas, collector of Malabar, dated 7 August 1921, discloses 'a very ugly development in Ernad' along with the story that Inspector Narayana Menon was 'for some time in imminent danger of being murdered out of hand'. Thomas featured five important points to prove his arguments: (a) the organized collection of a number of men at short notice in the name of religion, (b) the spirit of fanaticism which was evoked and might have burst into flame at any moment, (c) the enlargement of the boundaries of fanaticism so that, perhaps, no part of Ernad was free, (d) the arming of the crowd and (e) the undermining of law and order as police action can be stopped by rallying in the name of religion.[72] However, these attempts at emotional manipulation did not yield the desired results, as reports from other officers and discussions with British planters settled in Malabar led Knapp to the realization that the perceived 'fanaticism' was a characteristic attributed to only a minority of Muslims, rather than a widespread issue. Contrary to the persistent efforts of the collector and the police superintendent to convince their superiors in

Madras, the situation did not present an alarming or widespread crisis as they had portrayed.[73]

The collaboration between the district magistrate and the police superintendent culminated in the generation of a report that erroneously characterized the utilitarian knives commonly employed by the indigenous population for various mundane purposes. Their report further insinuated that the manufacturing of swords and knives hinted at a premeditated outbreak of violence.[74] Nevertheless, the official investigation of Madras revealed that such artifacts were neither unusual to the region nor did the reported incidents possess any semblance of novelty. Knapp candidly averred his personal cognizance of these incidents dating back to 1894:

> A noticeable feature of this affair has been the manufacture of swords and knives in preparation for an outbreak. This however is not a novelty. It occurred to my personal knowledge in 1894 and also, I believe on earlier occasions. I could not get first-hand information regarding the larger swords which were said to have been introduced at Pukkottur and I should think that they were possibly temple swords of a harmless type.[75]

The first-hand intelligence concerning the purported introduction of larger swords at Pukkottur was found to be fabricated and was fully discarded after scrutiny. He assumed that these might be benign temple swords.[76] After procurement of a substantial Malabar knife, Knapp reported that while it was formidable in size, it did not warrant classification as a formidable military weapon.[77]

The objection to the idea of waging war against the Khilafat Movement, which would be symbolized by forbidding the wearing of Khilafat badges, is a matter of significant concern. Thomas was cautioned not to issue his general order until the government had thoroughly examined the issue. Knapp decided to send a draft of Thomas's order to the chief secretary and suggested that it be carefully reviewed. This way, District Collector Thomas could receive guidance on how far the government deemed it advisable to proceed in this matter. Knapp's opinion was that it would be better to minimize the use of the term 'Khilafat' in the prohibition orders issued in Malabar. This approach not only applied pressure to Thomas and Hitchcock but also compelled them to consider collaborative measures to overcome the decision. Nevertheless, the official investigation of Madras yielded policy. Knapp suggested that individual instances of lawlessness could be addressed without necessarily implicating the entire Khilafat Movement. In contrast to reports and fanatical narratives with a strong Muslim focus, Knapp pointed out an intriguing detail: the Khilafat

Movement in Malabar was predominantly led by a Hindu named M.P. Narayana Menon, who had adopted Mappila clothing. He emphasized that it would be incorrect to categorize the movement as purely religious, especially given its leader, M.P. Narayana Menon.[78]

Knapp diverged from the views espoused by the district magistrate and the police, countenancing the premise that while a congregation of one thousand individuals armed with these knives could conceivably encircle a hundred soldiers, the genuine threat of such a scenario posed remained minimal. Rather, he construed the proliferation of domestic knife production not as an imminent peril but as an indicator of economic and technological changes in the local landscape. Knapp voiced his dissent concerning the original blueprint advanced by Thomas. The latter envisaged a comprehensive sweep through the Ernad region, entailing a substantial troop presence tasked with arms confiscation and the apprehension of individuals implicated in the alleged agitation. Prior to his arrival in Calicut, Knapp's consultations with the colonel of the Leinsters informed him that a successful raid on Tirurangadi could be mounted with the available resources. Consequently, Knapp sanctioned the foray into Tirurangadi.[79]

The 1884 'upheaval', he posited, emanated from this very locale. The mosque proximate to Mambram, Tirurangadi, bore unique sanctity for the Mappila community. In consideration of these elements, the expedition to Tirurangadi was duly authorized. The Cabinet permitted a raid while strictly adhering to the provided instructions, which included avoiding entry into the mosque and refraining from engaging in hostilities against the local population. Knapp also confirmed that the raid would be executed on the following day.[80]

20 August 1921: Massacres of Civilians and Sacrifices of British Officers

In the early hours of the morning on Saturday, 20 August 1921, the district magistrate, E.F. Thomas, along with the superintendent of police, Hitchcock, and a team of 100 special police force officers, accompanied by a detachment of the Leinster Regiment under Captain McEnroy, departed from Calicut for Tirurangadi. This action was carried out with the approval of the presidency to conduct a search and effect the arrest of Ali Musaliar and other individuals whose names had been submitted and approved for custody.[81] Upon reaching Parappanangadi, the British police contingent paraded to Tirurangadi, where they established their base of operations at the *kacheri*, the courthouse (Fig. 1.3). The contingent's primary objective was to secure the vicinity of

Figure 1.3
Tirurangadi Kacheri

Photograph by author

Kizhakkepalli, and, accordingly, soldiers were strategically positioned on the Kottakkal Road to regulate the movement of the local populace. An additional special force, composed of sixty personnel, arrived from Malappuram, located at a distance of 12 miles, under the command of Assistant Superintendent Lancaster. Their mission involved conducting meticulous searches, a task shared between the police and the military forces. The civilian population, for its part, demonstrated full compliance with the instructions provided by the police, while the leaders of interest remained confined to their respective residences.[82]

Despite extensive search operations that spanned several hours, British narratives claimed that Ali Musaliar's primary deputy, Lava Kutti, managed to evade capture by discreetly leaving his residence via an upper-floor route.[83] Instead of following the directives of their superiors, the collector and the police decided to search within the mosque. Initially, they dispatched native Muslim officers for this task, with Head Constable Moideen Kutti and Deputy Superintendent Amu responsible for the thorough search within Tirurangadi Eastern Mosque, also known as Kizhakkepalli. Moideen, after washing his legs, entered the mosque and meticulously searched its shelves for any signs of swords or knives. Deputy Superintendent Amu, too, personally conducted an examination and inquired if anyone within the mosque possessed any weapons. However, they did not discover any weaponry within the mosque. K.M. Moulavi notes an alternative account suggesting that Moideen and a small contingent of non-Muslim soldiers entered the mosque without removing their footwear.[84] Furthermore, I personally observed the presence of religious books bearing dirty boot prints left by British soldiers in Muhammed Ali Musaliar's residence.[85]

The wanton destruction of the Khilafat office extended to the illegitimate dismantling of its infrastructure, which included looms, benches and other associated equipment. Furthermore, they desecrated the board and the flag that were emblematic of the office.[86] This wave of destruction also reached the extensive traditional granary owned by Pott Mummed Haji. Within this context, K.M. Moulavi's account, as articulated in his book, unequivocally affirms the absence of any weaponry among the individuals involved. Nevertheless, it should be noted that the local populace adheres to a long-standing tradition of carrying small knives, a cultural practice that has persisted across generations. Certain elderly members of the community still uphold this tradition by wearing such knives on their waist as an emblem of their cultural heritage.[87]

Within the mosque premises, they identified a small group of leaders and subordinates, designating Moideen Kutty and the village officer, Mussa Kutty, as liaison officers. The police contingent apprehended several volunteers associated with Ali Musaliar, and news of these developments rapidly disseminated throughout the region, especially in the areas of Kottakkal, Vengara and Tanur. In response, residents collectively mobilized and marched to Tirurangadi to safeguard the mosque and their revered leaders. According to the local narrative of the incidents, colonial officers dispatched unidentified envoys to the surrounding regions with news of the raid to gather people in Tirurangadi, creating a context for confrontation.[88] E.F. Thomas and Hitchcock had their own agenda, namely, to incite significant unrest in the region to support their request for sending additional troops to engage in conflict with the local population. Their initial mission involved searching for arms, as per the plan endorsed by the government after Knapp's visit to Malabar. However, the operations did not yield the desired results upon closer examination. The searches were conducted without significant resistance. They could only arrest three, namely P. Muhammed Haji, O. Muhammed and his son Moideen Kutty, and the arms found were quite limited, falling far short of Thomas and Hitchcock's expectations for the day in the region. In their accounts of the efforts to capture the listed individuals, Hitchcock also wove a narrative in their favor. According to their rendition, Lava Kutti narrowly escaped, leaving behind his uniform and sword when he fled from his residence. They accused Ali Musaliar of hastily hiding, further noting that his wooden sandals were discovered wet in his empty house at 8 a.m. Colonial authorities also accused Ali Musaliar of immediately sending messages to Tanur, Vengara and Kottakkal, claiming that the mosque was surrounded for the purpose of conducting a search. These stories, however, appear to be fabrications from Hitchcock, likely intended to shield their reputation, particularly to obscure the relatively peaceful atmosphere encountered in Tirurangadi during the raid. The news of the police raid swiftly disseminated throughout Tirurangadi and its adjacent areas, prompting the local populace to engage with the authorities to secure the release of those who had been unjustly arrested.[89]

Ali Musaliar and his associates Lava Kutti and Kunha Alavi arrived at the mosque to deliberate on their next course of action. Their discussions encompassed various facets of the situation, with a particular focus on the possibility of approaching the police to secure the release of their detained colleagues. Ultimately, they arrived at the consensus that employing force against the government would constitute an offense. Instead, they agreed that a collective appeal should be made to secure the release of those who had been arrested earlier in the day.[90]

Ali Musaliar and his followers went to the Tirurangadi police station to present a formal memorandum requesting the release of volunteers who had previously been apprehended. Near the station, a contingent of police personnel intercepted the group. The assistant superintendent of Palakkad, who happened to be present at the station, initiated a dialogue with the petitioners to discern the underlying motives and intentions of their visit. In response, Musaliar clarified that their singular objective was to secure the release of the detained individuals. After carefully reviewing the earnest appeal made by the petitioners, they were asked to be seated, and the group, as per Musaliar's direction, obediently complied. The situation took a drastic turn when, suddenly, officers were ordered to open fire. This act was part of a broader conspiracy designed to sow chaos in the region. Rowley, the assistant superintendent of police, unwittingly became a scapegoat, serving the interests of Collector Thomas and Hitchcock, who sought to vilify the area. This tragic episode resulted in the loss of numerous lives among the unarmed group who had accompanied Musaliar. In total, more than forty innocent individuals fell victim to the police firing. In response, a retaliatory confrontation unfolded. As per the colonial version of the events, about three thousand people from Tanur came to Parappanangadi station. Police supported by troops proceeded to disperse the crowd. They argued that the firing became necessary.[91]

The situation rapidly evolved into a sequence of atrocities, resulting in the loss of innocent lives and inciting an uncontrollable wave. A multitude of individuals hailing from diverse geographical regions swiftly assembled to condemn these grievous acts. Concurrently, a significantly larger assembly from the eastern areas launched an assault on a smaller British detachment that had been left in Tirurangadi. The British forces suffered casualties, notably the loss of Lieutenant Johnstone from the Leinster Regiment and Rowley, the assistant superintendent of police (Fig. 1.4). This unexpected outcome took colonial authorities by surprise, but it was a response to the massacre of innocent lives. In the aftermath of the massacre and the death of the primary operational commanders, Rowley and Johnstone, the leadership of the colonial force was transferred to McEnroy. After this distressing incident, some of the volunteers sought refuge in the mosque, while others congregated at the Panampuzha ferry to impede the entry of additional troop contingents into Tirurangadi.[92]

At approximately 2 p.m., the district magistrate's vehicle, accompanied by a motor bus carrying a complement of soldiers, reached the ferry location. The special force inspector, Reed Man, attempted to cross the river. Unfavorable weather conditions, from the colonial perspective, prompted them to seek shelter in a nearby shop. However, a confrontation

Figure 1.4
The Tomb of Rowley and Johnstone[93]

Photograph by author

ensued when the inspector engaged with the individuals present in the shop, resulting in the discharge of firearms. Subsequently, the officer attempted to escape in the direction of Tirurangadi. During this pursuit, the officer approached Chalilakath Ibrahim Kutty's residence, yet his efforts to ensure his safety were unsuccessful, ultimately leading to the officer's demise. This incident was perceived as a retaliation to the officer previously firing upon innocent individuals.[94] A similar fate befell the driver of the car and the bus when they encountered a group led by Odakkal Moideen Kutty Musaliar. In his book, Hitchcock details the killing of a lorry driver, allegedly perpetrated by Moideen Musaliar. Furthermore, he recounts the demise of the policeman Kunhali, attributing his death to Moideen Musaliar Urakam Kizhimuri. Hitchcock also mentions that Moideen Musaliar resided in Urakam Hill for a month.[95]

In an official report, Collector Thomas mentions that information was incomplete, and things only came to his knowledge piecemeal. This itself shows his inclination for being on the safe side of events and only articulating his own version of the story:

> The police at once fell in and advanced down the road to meet them led by Mr. Hitchcock, Mr. Lancaster, Mr Amoo and Mr. Mainwaring. About a mile and a half away from Tirurangadi the police met the crowd. Mr. Amoo called upon them to disperse. They came on steadily with shouts and war cries. The police at twenty yards distance charged with fixed bayonets. They continued to advance and met the bayonets with their clubs. The crowd did not give an inch but met the police with uplifted sticks and swords and brought them down with great clatter on the bayonets. The police then opened fire in self-defence without a word of command and indeed in the uproar no word of command would have been heard. The effect of the firing was to make the crowd retreat a few yards. The firing at once stopped.[96]

The massacre at Tirurangadi Kacheri was carried out using rifles and Lewis guns. That night, the troops were compelled to take refuge at the sub-magistrate's office. To save face, they resorted to taking numerous lives and sacrificing the lives of British officers, all to safeguard their pride and uphold their biases. The force stationed in Tirurangadi endured an anxious yet unmolested night. On the following day, Sunday, they made the decision to evacuate the area, eventually returning to the railway station at Parappanangadi. From there, they followed the railway line to Feroke, 15 miles away, and ultimately boarded a train for Calicut, reaching their destination by midnight. By Sunday evening, the railway line had been severed in several places between Feroke and Shoranur, effectively isolating Calicut from the rest of the Madras Presidency.[97]

The district magistrate's report stated that Assistant Superintendent of Police Rowley was just missing to suggest the list of casualties from the side of British may be lower than it was:

> Meanwhile 30 men left to make arrests Tirurangadi driven in about 14–25 by armed hostile crowd. estimated number some thousands from eastern amsams and local crowd. Cutcherry attacked. Attack driven off. Our casualties-one officer Leinsters, A.S.P. Rowley missing, also two constables. Situation extremely serious. Imperative despatch forthwith one battalion troops.[98]

Despite lacking official sanction to raid the mosque or search the Khilafat committee office, Magistrate Thomas and Police Superintendent Hitchcock exceeded their authority in Tirurangadi. Their actions culminated in lethal force being employed against the indigenous population, resulting in numerous fatalities. While contextual issues may be cited to justify such actions, the deaths of British officers further exacerbated the situation, necessitating accountability for the events. Consequently, the district magistrate of Malabar tried to suppress this information in the initial report.

Contrary to the colonial account, it becomes evident that Collector Thomas and Hitchcock were actively attempting to incite unrest to validate their earlier report, which had been submitted and subsequently rejected by the presidency. To connect these incidents with their prior objectives of waging war and deploying additional troops in the region, they tragically sacrificed numerous lives, including those of their colleagues. This drama also presented an opportunity to implement martial law in the region, effectively allowing them to conceal and counter the perspectives of innocent individuals who were arrested and sentenced under this draconian law. Additionally, they propagated a narrative suggesting a potential attack on Calicut itself on 21 August, which, they claimed, was prevented by the actions of Tottenham, the district superintendent of police, North Malabar.[99]

Due to the delayed transmission of news, the relatively calm response to the events in Tirurangadi, which had transpired as foreseen by Knapp (who had opposed Thomas's warlike stance against the Khilafat Movement), did not reach Madras until around midday on Sunday, 21 August. Subsequently, the deaths of several individuals, including high-ranking officers, prompted the general officer commanding of Madras District to dispatch reinforcements. The exact scale and composition of these reinforcements were left to his discretion, resulting in the deployment of the Dorset regiment from Bangalore.[100]

The ambitions of Thomas and Hitchcock were becoming more vibrant, and they found themselves in the situation they had long yearned for. On 22 August, they telegraphed the central government, requesting permission to proclaim martial law in the taluks of Ernad, Valluvanad and Ponnani. Thomas transmitted more alarming reports from the district, saying that the situation in Calicut was exceedingly grave, urging the government to telegraph for a warship. A telegram was dispatched in the early hours of 23 August to the naval commander in-chief, and the HMS *Comus* departed from Colombo on the same day, heading for Calicut.

24 August 1921: Martial Law Ordinance

On 24 August 1921, the authorities received a draft of the Martial Law Ordinance from the colonial Government of India accepting the proposal to temporarily exclude the provision for special tribunals and summary general courts martial. Concurrently, they formally petitioned for the inclusion of Calicut taluk within the purview of martial law. On the subsequent day, namely, 26 August, the district magistrate submitted a comprehensive report encompassing the expansion of the concerns to the taluks of Kurumbranad and Wayanad. This report also chronicled the tragic assassination of Eaton, a prominent planter, and how several other planters narrowly avoided harm. Simultaneously, an official request was dispatched to the Government of India, beseeching the incorporation of these two taluks into the martial law jurisdiction.[101]

Upon receiving reports of the Tirurangadi incident, leaders from the Khilafat and the Congress in Calicut orchestrated a delegation comprising a distinguished roster of individuals, including K.P. Kesava Menon, Muhammad Abdu Rahman Sahib, Thayyil Mammad Kutty Musaliar, K.V. Gopala Menon, E. Moidu Moulavi, U. Gopala Menon, Manikyath Gopala Menon, Ponmadath Moideen Koya, Kodungallur Shekhara Menon, Kunhammad, K. Madhava Menon, T.V. Chathukutty Nair, M.P. Moideen Koya and Madhuvanam Govinda Kurup. This delegation journeyed to Tirurangadi on 26 August 1921. The delegation was graciously received by volunteers at the Mambram ferry, after which they convened at the Khilafat Committee Office in Tirurangadi. The focus of their deliberations was the imperative of preserving peace as a means of averting further exacerbation of the conflict.[102]

Two days thereafter, on 28 August, the Martial Law Ordinance arrived via telegraph from the Government of India and was expeditiously disseminated to the district magistrate and other pertinent local functionaries. Subsequently, a divergence of perspectives emerged between the regional government and the Government of India about the date designated for the commencement of martial law in the taluks of Kurumbranad and Wayanad. The regional government ardently advocated for the alignment of the specified date with the overarching commencement date of 19 August, applied elsewhere in the region. However, under the weight of deliberation, they ultimately, albeit reluctantly, assented to the date being fixed as 24 August. This underscores the pivotal significance of the date 19 August within the context of district administration, particularly in terms of its potential implications for concealing their involvement in the events that precipitated the ongoing unrest.[103]

25 August 1921: Attempt to Attribute Responsibility to Deceased British Officers

It is incontrovertible that Collector Thomas and Hitchcock were cognizant of the calamitous event they orchestrated in Malabar. Subsequently, their endeavors shifted towards obfuscating the incident by crafting a narrative that cast them in a favorable light. In this endeavor, they fabricated accounts and leveled accusations against Ali Musaliar and the local populace. Collector Thomas, in particular, sought to deflect culpability by implicating the mob and linking the issues to the unfortunate demise of two British officers during the massacre. He meticulously composed a letter outlining the events in a manner conducive to his narrative, asserting that the constables stationed in the town were strategically positioned at the crossroads where three roads converged. Rowley, bereft of a uniform, ostensibly lingered at the deputy tahsildar's *kacheri*, their established base camp, and was apprised of the unfolding situation before assuming command.[104]

Thomas adroitly manipulated the narrative to impute responsibility for the firing on the two officers who lost their lives, portraying them as the principal instigators who acted without directives from his office. The narrative, downplaying the gravity of the situation, unfolds with Rowley encountering the advancing crowd with a limited contingent. In his missive, Thomas tries to foment communal tensions, alluding to a statement purportedly made by a member of the crowd, implying a sectarian bias. This calculated move aimed to construct a narrative of religious fanaticism, with the demise of Police Officer Moideen contradicting Thomas's allegations of sectarian groups perpetrating violence. Thomas expounded that, notwithstanding the crowd's insistence that Muslim soldiers depart, Moideen remained steadfast. This proves that those resisting colonial forces seldom scrutinized the religious affiliations of individuals but rather aligned their allegiance with either the British or the indigenous population. Such considerations underscored the events culminating in the tragic demise of Moideen and fellow officers on 20 August in Tirurangadi.[105]

Thomas blames the deceased officer for the firing, cognizant of his inability to counter the accusations. The narrative proceeds with Rowley's directive to load weapons at a juncture when, according to gathered information, the police contingent had received reinforcement. Within the same communication, Thomas ascribes the firing into the crowd to 'Mr Johnstone', insinuating that it was executed with his sanction.[106] The narration continues, detailing the dire circumstances in Tirurangadi that day, with the crowd ostensibly encircling the police party, leading to the officers' assumed demise, surrounded, incapacitated and subjected to violence.[107]

In contrast to the account presented by Collector Thomas on 25 August, Deputy Inspector-General N.E.Q. Mainwaring provides an alternative version of the events. Mainwaring emphasizes the lack of a highly dependable account detailing the circumstances under which Rowley and Lieutenant Johnstone became detached from the force.

> It is said that the Mapillas beckoned to them and indicated that they wished to talk and these young officers went forward attended by four or five constables and were immediately hit on the head and dragged away. Later on a search was instituted. This had evidently been anticipated by the Mapillas who had evidently laid the bodies in an exposed place beside the road so that they might be found as we advanced up the road towards Tirurangadi from the cutcherry. The bamboo fence between the scrub and the place the bodies were laid had been broken outwards, towards the spot, the bodies horribly mutilated were laid on their backs with arms extended.[108]

He expounded upon the revelation that a *jutkawallah*[109] had communicated pertinent information during the ongoing search, disclosing the proximity of the bodies near his residence. This informant specifically guided them to the deceased head constable, Moideen. However, a shift in narrative occurred after a two-day interval, initiated by Collector Thomas, wherein an alternative account emerged. Thomas attempted to shift all the blame for the firing on the innocent mob in Tirurangadi onto Rowley and Johnstone. This was noted in a report prepared after their deaths:

> Mr. Rowley held up his hand and told the crowd to stop. This man then said, if there were any Muhammadan constables, they had better go. It is unnecessary to say that they did not but stood by

> their officer and their fellow-constables. Mr. Rowley then ordered the men to load. By this time, so far as I can gather, the police had been reinforced by a lance corporal and four men who took post alongside the police: three on one side of them and two on the other. The crowd overflowed into the parambas on both sides of the road, tracking down the hedges, and outflanked and almost surrounded the party. Mr. Johnstone appears to have arrived about this time and ordered his men to load one round.[110]

This report from Thomas reflects his perspective, but the local populace was entirely against the narratives of Thomas and Hitchcock. There was no mention of the individual private actions of Rowley or Johnstone in their narratives.

30 August 1921: 'Musaliar King' Was Arrested

The colonial military column advanced towards the station, reaching it on 30 August. The mosque was surrounded by British forces. Official reports claimed that at 9:15 a.m., the people rushed out and charged the troops, but it was evident from local accounts that the military initiated the firing on the mosque.[111] In the old structure of the Tirurangadi Mosque, numerous bullet scars were evident, along with bullets lodged inside the wooden doors. During the seventy-fifth anniversary commemorations of the 1921 events, I had the opportunity to personally examine these marks and engage with individuals from the region who shared vivid memories passed down from their parents. A brutal massacre occurred in Tirurangadi on 30 August when the British opened fire on the people inside a mosque. British propaganda portrayed Ali Musaliar as the 'Musaliar King' and the 'Khilafat King', and he was often referred to as Ali Raja. In the judgment against Ali Musaliar, prosecution witness number 5, Pokker, alleged that Ali Musaliar referred to himself as the 'king' when Pokker was held and brought before him.[112] Additionally, there were reports of people calling Ali Musaliar the 'king' and Ali Muslaiar himself allegedly claiming the title of the 'king'.[113] The credibility of these statements is questionable and can be labelled as fabricated. The British authorities attempted to portray Ali Musaliar as a king through such questionable accounts to rationalize the brutal actions carried out by the British military against the local population. Colonial records claimed that the Jamat Mosque issued edicts declaring Musaliar as their king, which supposedly took place from 22 to 30 August.[114] This was an attempt to conceal the heinous acts of violence and frame them as part of a conflict against a fabricated kingdom. Hitchcock, in his book, titled the judgment against Ali Musaliar and his associates as the 'Khilafat king' on trial.[115] It is noted in the judgment of the special tribunal of Calicut on 2 November 1921 that following the withdrawal of troops on 21 August, Ali Musaliar, who had gathered volunteers and armed them, assumed the role of the king himself and briefly wielded authority.[116] This assertion is reiterated in another paragraph of the judgment, stating that Ali Musaliar claimed kingship within days and summoned people to the mosque to oppose British troops, culminating in the battle of the mosque. The intention behind highlighting these events is to depict the mosque as a site utilized for waging war.[117] In the incident, British forces tragically killed twenty-four people at the Tirurangadi Mosque. To prevent further loss of life, Musaliar came out from the mosque and was subsequently arrested.

This narrative claimed that two of Musaliar's supporters were responsible for the deaths of Rowley and Johnstone.[118] C. Gopalan Nair's book can also be seen as part of the broader colonial narrative, published under the 'native historian' category, much like Elliot did to tarnish the Mughal Empire and during Tipu's time when Khirmani was entrusted to provide another version.[119] French magazines presented similar narratives in their advertisements without altering the propaganda content.[120] The charges brought against Ali Musaliar, aimed at declaring him the Musaliar King, were an attempt by colonial propaganda to cover up the officers' shortcomings. This propaganda was also documented by the *Englishman's Overland Mail* on 13 October 1921 in an article titled 'Khilafat Rajah Installed in Mosque'. The report details the installation of Ali Musaliar as the Ali Rajah of Tirurangadi in the Tirurangadi Mosque with pomp and splendor.[121]

The arrest of Ali Musaliar, a pivotal figure in the Malabar district, garnered substantial attention both within Britain and internationally. On 2 September, a report disseminated by the Australian Press Association from Melbourne, titled 'Troops Restoring Order, Moplahs Flee to Jungle' unfolded a propagandistic account. Primary reports from Allahabad narrated the issues of Malabar, noting the strategic retreat of people into the jungles to evade advancing military forces. The report delineates the arrest of Ali Musaliar in Tirurangadi following a protracted confrontation by emphasizing the purported sanctuary within the mosque. Significantly absent from the report is any reference to the incursion by British forces into the mosque; instead, precautions taken to preserve the sanctity of the religious site are highlighted. In addition to detailing casualties, the report documents the loss of forty natives and two soldiers, alongside injuries sustained by four soldiers. Noteworthy in the report is the significant confiscation of munitions, arms and combat weaponry from the Moplah groups, coupled with an ultimatum demanding their surrender within a specified timeframe. The report exhibits concerning sectarian undertones, potentially exacerbating communal tensions. It alleges coerced conversions by insurgents, who presented Hindus with the grim choice of death or embracing Islam. Disturbingly, it recounts the death of two officers and the public exhibition of their severed heads in local marketplaces, contributing to a further escalation. The report concludes by highlighting ongoing disturbances in Madras, suggesting a broader continuum of societal discord beyond the confines of the Malabar District.[122]

The *Nottingham Morning Post*, on 5 September 1921, documented the aftermath of the arrest of Ali Musaliar and his group on the front page of the newspaper, shedding light on the British ultimatum issued to those opposing colonial rule. This report garnered widespread coverage not only in newspapers across England but also in those from America and New Zealand. The report highlights that many individuals sought refuge in the jungle to evade British troops. Ali Musaliar, identified as the 'rebel leader', and forty other 'insurgents' apprehended at Tirurangadi were transported to Coimbatore. The report mentions instances of looting at Cherpalacherry (Cherpulassery), attributing the act to both Moplahs and Hindus. It describes resistance activities, such as seizing funds from landlords, as acts of looting. Moreover, it details developments in nearby areas like Tanur, citing a Calicut telegram reporting the arrest of eighty-two Moplahs near Tanur. Field post offices were established in the disturbed regions for the convenience of British troops.[123]

The *North Star*, self-described as the eminent advertising and publicity platform of north-eastern England, likewise published the report under the title 'Ultimatum to Indian Rebels: Surrender Within 48 hours' on the same date (Monday, 5 September 1921). This report emerged after the arrest of Ali Musaliar and his associates from Tirurangadi, receiving prominent placement on the front page of the *North Star*.[124] Essentially, it mirrored the official dissemination without significant alteration. The news of Ali Musaliar's arrest was also prominently featured in the *Daily Mail* on Tuesday, 6 September 1921, as well as in the *Lincolnshire Echo* on the same date.[125]

Conclusion

In conclusion, the chapter illuminates a pivotal juncture in Tirurangadi's history of resistance, marked by the symbiotic rise of British authority and indigenous resistance. Collector Thomas and Hitchcock ascended to commanding positions, wielding a formidable military force that unleashed a brutal campaign against the local population. Martial law ordinance emerged as a dreadful tool, quashing dissent and shielding British officers amid tragic losses.

This chapter exposes a stark confrontation between colonial might and local resilience, painting a sobering picture of unchecked power, unyielding defiance and the dire consequences borne by the populace in the face of unrelenting force. The indigenous populace valiantly resisted encroaching colonial control, supported by influential leaders. In response, the colonial administration expanded martial law, employing ruthless guerrilla tactics that spared no one, not even women and children.

Mappila, Mappilla and Moplah

'Moplah' is a term employed to denote the Muslim community within the historical context of Malabar. Initially, this term encompassed both Muslims and Christians, yet differentiation in religious identity was achieved through the application of adjectival prefixes. The spelling of this term exhibits variations, including 'Mappila', 'Mappilla' and 'Moplah'. Notwithstanding its historical usage, the precise etymology of Moplah remains a topic of enduring scholarly discourse. One hypothesis posits that Moplah may be the composite product of two constituent Malayalam terms, namely, *Maha*, signifying 'great', and *Pilla*, signifying 'child'. This conflation conveys a nuanced implication of 'great child', thereby connoting reverence, nobility and high esteem. This interpretation is endorsed in the writings of scholars such as William Logan and C.A. Innes.[126] An alternative etymological derivation proposes that 'Mappila' may trace its origins to the lexical constituents *Ma* (mother) and *Pillai* (child), with the term denoting the progeny born to indigenous women in unions with foreign individuals, encompassing both Arabs and non-Arabs. Moreover, another interpretive strand posits that Moplah conveys the connotation of 'son-in-law' or 'bridegroom', a correspondence with the prevalent Tamil terminology designating the prospective bridegroom or husband-to-be. Notably, in some parts of Malabar, a unique marital practice was observed where husbands of younger women resided in the households of their wives. This practice is reflected in their designation as bridegrooms, even posthumously, with their tombs identified as *Puyyappla* or *Puthiya* Mappila, denoting the 'new bridegroom'. As astutely observed by Cathleen Gough, this usage reflects the customary role accorded to younger husbands as honored guests and, to some extent, outsiders.[127] In essence, 'Mappila' serves as an honorific title historically ascribed to foreigners integrated into indigenous families, and it retains its usage in contemporary contexts primarily to signify the 'bridegroom'. Notably, foreign researchers on Malabar Muslims are the principal cohort employing the term 'Moplah' in their discourse.

Ali Musaliar

The appellation 'Musaliar' holds a prominent place in the lexicon of Islamic scholarship, particularly among those who have successfully completed their education at Ponnani Graduate School. The term's etymology can be traced to its Arabic roots, where *Muslih* denotes 'cultivated' and *yar* signifies a title rooted in the vernacular tradition. In subsequent eras, 'Musaliar' evolved into a synonym for religious scholars. Born in Nellikkuth in the Malappuram District of South India, Ali Musaliar (1854–1922) hailed from a family with a notable legacy of philanthropic work. His father, Erikkunnan Palath Moolayil Kunhi Moideen Sahib, enjoyed regional recognition for his charitable activities, and his mother, Amina (d. 1935), was the daughter of Ottakath Mammad Kutty Musaliar, also from a lineage deeply entrenched in scholarly Islamic traditions. Young Mohammed Ali received his preliminary education under the tutelage of Kunhikkammu Molla of Karakkad Kunnummal and Nuruddin Musaliar, his uncle, before matriculating at Ponnani Graduate School. Following his graduation, he embarked on a scholarly journey to Makkah (Mecca) in 1880, where he pursued advanced studies. Upon his return to his homeland in 1905, Musaliar assumed the role of chief instructor at Kavarathi Juma Masjid in Lakshadweep, dedicating nine years of service to this institution. Subsequently, Musaliar's pedagogical pursuits led him to various locations, encompassing Wandoor in Ernad, Podiyatt-Parammal, Alathur-Melmuri and his hometown, Nellikkuth. In 1907, Musaliar relocated to Tirurangadi Kizhakkepalli, where he served for an extended period of fifteen years, ultimately culminating in his apprehension by British authorities from the mosque premises. Musaliar emerged as a prominent sheikh and a leader of the Tariqa[128], amassing a substantial following hailing from diverse strata, including scholars, the business community and the working class of the region. As the custodian of the mosque and Islamic education, Musaliar earned the honorific title 'Moilyaruppappa' (the grand Musaliar). Historically, the Musaliar family had been involved in anti-colonial resistance movements, notably participating in the 1886 leadership of Athan Kurikkal of Manjeri and the resistance efforts of 1891 in Mannarkkad. A number of Musaliar's close relatives made significant sacrifices for the cause, enduring imprisonment and exile to remote regions.

Chapter 2

'MOPLAH AMAZONS'

Catalysts for 'Feminist' Thought

The historical narrative pertaining to colonial endeavors often underscores a disturbing trend: the dehumanization and categorization of indigenous populations to substantiate egregious actions. This practice involved employing derogatory terms and, in some instances, associating indigenous individuals with fauna, for instance, the initial portrayal at the Australian War Memorial.[1] The classification of indigenous communities as 'uncivilized beasts' or their juxtaposition with animals serves as a tool to rationalize and justify the violence perpetrated against them. The case in point, specifically the British administration's portrayal of the populace in Malabar as uncivilized and the depiction of women's involvement in the conflict as a negative attribute—paralleling the historical denigration of feminism—is profoundly disconcerting. The deliberate manipulation of information in newspapers to depict indigenous groups as subhuman or inherently aggressive further perpetuated injurious stereotypes. An academic approach demands a critical examination and interrogation of these historical injustices, advocating for a reassessment of constructed narratives that served to rationalize oppression. Rectifying these misrepresentations within our collective historical memory is essential. Central to this endeavor is the acknowledgment of the inherent humanity and dignity of all individuals, irrespective of their ethnic or cultural background, thereby fostering a more equitable and just societal framework.

> 'Moplah Amazons', Madras, Oct. 28. It was brought out during the trial of Ali Musaliar for waging war against the King that Moplah women had been observed taking part in the battle of Pukottur and shouting the war-cry—of Allah hu Akbar. I have authority for adding to the fact that among the dead bodies found after the battle was that of a Moplah woman clad in male attire. Again, a number of Moplah women with prayer beads were moving about among crowds of Moplahs collected near Pukottur Kovilakam and were

> reciting and inciting little boys to join the men. Numbers of Moplah women and girls are even now going in the wake of the rebel bands as camp followers to help in cooking food, looting, carrying away loot, spying and so on. Several instances have also come to light of Moplah women tracking Hindu fugitives sheltering in thickets and jungles and out-houses and revealing the hiding places of these unfortunates to rebel gangs. Early in the rebellion Moplah women and children were seen actively collecting and bringing in fuel for burning out the woodwork of the railway bridge. Altogether it has been abundantly proved this rebellion has produced many feminists.[2]

This 1921 report from Madras, published on 3 November but dated 28 October, emerges as a strategically crafted attempt by the British authorities to rationalize and legitimize the extensive violence inflicted upon women and children in the region amidst the uproar over brutal massacres. The report's defense relies on the trial of Ali Musaliar for waging war against the king of England. It highlights the participation of Moplah women in the battle of Pukkottur, who were chanting the war cry of '*Allah hu Akbar*' (God is great). Rather than recognizing this as an act of solidarity in a dire situation, the report manipulates this information and cites their active involvement in warfare to justify the execution of these women. The assertion that these women were clad in male attire to evade identification is a baseless argument, contradicted by the report's own acknowledgment of Moplah women distinctively identified in the crowd, engaging in various activities. Moreover, the description fabricates allegations of Moplah women attacking Hindus, conveniently omitting the religious affiliations of the police officers involved in the massacres. This omission undermines the broader context of the conflict, disregarding the complexities of support or opposition to colonial rule among individuals regardless of their religious background. The report's conclusion reflects the imperial mindset of the early 20th century, particularly regarding their attitudes toward women's freedom and feminism. It erroneously associates the rebellion with the emergence of feminists.

This propagandist trend is observable in various statements in the same newspaper page, which showcases conflicting accounts that point to deliberate misrepresentations. These reports from Madras and Calicut attempt to portray communal divides, painting a skewed picture of the conflict between Muslims and Hindus and neglecting instances where both communities jointly resisted the colonial forces. Additionally, the report about the Moplah prisoners held at Bellary underscores the inhumane treatment by colonial authorities, who detained numerous individuals, including juveniles, under stringent security measures in the prison camp.[3]

This manipulation of information extended beyond newspapers, as reflected in Hitchcock's book, where he tried to obscure the inhumanities perpetrated by colonial forces in the region. These efforts collectively highlight a systemic agenda to distort truths, diminish resistance unity, and conceal the atrocities committed by colonial powers against the people of the region:

> In many respects the situation differed in no way from war with a savage enemy without conventions. To troops accustomed to such warfare, the situation in Malabar must have seemed incomprehensible, especially in places where they were sniped every time they went out from their posts. To be shot at by rebels from an ambush and yet not to lay waste the country in the vicinity—to allow the inhabitants to continue to live there though they must have known of the presence of rebels and never gave any information—to know that women and children were taking an active part in the fighting and yet to let them remain in possession of their houses and property—to know that a mosque was being used constantly as a shelter and a store and a meeting place for armed rebel, and yet to leave mosques standing, even to go further to find out what the local idea of pollution might be and to observe it—must have all seemed incongruous, yet it was in few places that houses were destroyed and action taken which might even indirectly affect the women and children, and those places were where ambushes were regularly prepared, such as Vadapuram and near Kalikavu, where in fact, military precautions necessitated it.[4]

The British administration orchestrated a comprehensive strategy using official channels and individuals masquerading as journalists, to produce a multitude of reports daily.[5] This information was meticulously crafted to manipulate and distort the realities of their actions in the Malabar region. Hitchcock, among other defenders, vigorously contested any dissenting voices that emerged domestically or internationally, dismissing them as altered accounts in a concerted effort to obscure the profound extent of the brutalities perpetrated.[6]

Despite the concerted effort to control the narrative, international press coverage managed to illuminate the atrocities committed by the British forces. Hitchcock's endeavors to discredit these accounts were evident; however, the weight of substantial evidence often made it arduous to repudiate the egregious acts carried out against women and children by the colonialist military. Most of the atrocities committed against women, children and the elderly by the British army were omitted from colonial historical narratives. The events at Melmuri-Adhikarithodi involved brutalities that violated even the most basic norms to be followed during war. Among the victims were two girls who were killed while trying to protect their beloved fathers. One of them was an eleven-year-old girl who was beaten with a gun and killed while attempting to shield her father. The other girl was specifically identified as Kadiyamu, the daughter of Areeppuram Parakkal Kunjeen Haji of Konompara Cheeranganthodi. Kadiyamu had come from her husband's house to care for her sick and elderly father. She tried to prevent the colonial army from dragging away her aged father, who was lying on a large wooden storage container called a *pathayam*. Kunjeen Haji was forcibly taken outside the house and forced to lie face down on the ground. Kadiyamu attempted to shield her father, but the colonial army brutally killed both.[7]

The official statements and correspondences made by the police superintendent were echoed in the press reports. Hitchcock's mentions can be used to compare the actions of a particular regiment that faced significant challenges during the resistance, suggesting they had tougher circumstances in the region. This juxtaposition aimed to cast a favorable light on the regiment, even amidst the broader narrative of documented British atrocities in the region, implying a significant debt owed to this regiment.

> Of one instance which occurred and of which many distorted account have appeared, it may be as well to relate the facts partly because it is still occasionally referred to in the press and partly because this isolated case is so constantly quoted against a very fine regiment which perhaps had a more trying time than any other Indian battalion throughout the rebellion, and one to which Ernad is greatly indebted.[8]

The tragic killing of women and their vulnerable children often lurked within the subtext of official justifications. Hitchcock himself, in his reporting, appears to justify the killing of boys. On 21 November 1921, the residence of Thallusseri Mammad Kutti, a loyal colonial mappila of Wandoor, was 'looted and severely assaulted'. Hitchcock acknowledges that this incident occurred close to the military camp. The question arises as to why they could not stop issues if it were so close to the camp. It would be easier to conduct a military raid to control the situation. Yet the 'assailants' vanished before troops could intervene. However, subsequent military actions, particularly on 24 November 1921, under the guise of a raid, escalated drastically. Hitchcock's acknowledgment of the burning of forty houses suggests a likely higher count, and he confirms the tragic death of a boy. This points to a callous military campaign indifferent to the presence of children or women. Hitchcock reports a woman being shot, emphasizing her survival, which, however, does not negate that the military operations relentlessly targeted women and children under the guise of martial law. The military gang's actions, raiding toward Pandikkad and Manjeri and subsequently vanishing, further underscore the erratic and uncontrolled nature of these operations, which left a trail of devastation in their wake.[9]

The Manjeri surrender of Kodinhi Pukoya Thangal and the subsequent events at Valiyora, where Maravakulath Abdulla Kutti Haji was reportedly located, is a harrowing account of violence and tragedy. According to Hitchcock's detailed report, on 23 December 1921, upon receiving information about Abdulla Kutti Haji's presence in a house at Valiyora, Sub-Inspector Rao Sahib Govindan, along with a company of the Malabar Special Police, took action. The report indicates that the house was initially found closed, and despite calls for those inside to exit, they allegedly responded with gunfire and cries of 'Kootu Bangu' (call to prayer made by a big group). Subsequently, the house was fired upon, leading to the emergence of Chittambalan Kunhalavi and Maravakulath Abdulla Kutti Haji, who were fatally shot by the military. Additionally, two others wielding swords were also shot outside the house, and three deceased bodies were discovered within. Notably, aside from the identified leaders, the individuals shot by the military remained unidentified, one among them being a young boy. This tragic account highlights a recurrent pattern in military actions during this period. Upon receiving information about resistance leaders, the military often resorted to excessive force, conducting operations that resulted in the loss of lives, indiscriminately targeting individuals in the vicinity, including women and children. In several instances, as in this case, the military failed to identify those they had fatally shot, emphasizing the indiscriminate and hasty nature of their actions during these confrontations.[10]

The perpetration of egregious acts unfolded within the jurisdiction of martial law, establishing an environment of perceived impunity wherein perpetrators operated free from anticipated scrutiny or legal accountability. This setting fostered a sense of assured immunity from interrogation, leveraging a judicial system that often tilted in favor of the authoritative powers rather than the aggrieved populace. Simultaneously, the press documented instances wherein dissenting officers, such as Arthur Rowland Knapp (1870–1954), opposed the endorsement of warfare against the region's inhabitants, only to be subsequently replaced.[11] This transition underscores a deliberate orchestration of propaganda strategies stage-managed by figures such as Thomas and Hitchcock.

30 August 1921: Special Tribunal under the Martial Law

On 30 August, the Madras government formally petitioned the colonial central government for the establishment of a special tribunal under the Martial Law Ordinance, aiming to address more severe cases. Subsequently, the Special Tribunal Ordinance was received on 5 September, though it encountered initial difficulties in its establishment, delaying its operational commencement until 23 September. Thomas submitted proposals on 7 September, following the reception of the Special Tribunal ordinance, seeking action under the Mappila Outrages Act, which received government approval for notification issuance concerning the distressing incidents in the region.[12]

The special tribunal, blaming all atrocities in Malabar on Ali Musaliar, found it convenient due to his substantial influence in the epicenter of resistance where his followers resided. The tribunal's judgment seemingly aimed to establish Musaliar as the pivotal figure responsible for the region's turmoil. This approach, however, appeared aimed at veiling the proactive involvement of Thomas and Hitchcock in instigating conflict. Notably, the special tribunal's judgment, under Case No. 7/21, outlines various incidents, purportedly implicating Ali Musaliar in these acts:

> But, it was not mere fanaticism, it was not agrarian trouble, it was not destitution that worked on the minds of Ali Musaliar and his followers. The evidence conclusively shows that it was the influence of the Khilafat and non-co-operation movements that drove them to their crime. It is this which distinguishes the preeent from all previous outbreaks. Their intention was absurd though it may seem, to subvert British Government and substitute a Khilafat Government by force of arms; in fact Ali Musaliar aunounoed that he bad become king, though be did not define his kingdom and exersised his authority for about a week. All their is borne out by the evidence, as will be shown later.[13]

The document details the affiliations among key figures such as Vadakke Vittil Mammad, Ali Musaliar, Kunhi Koya Thangal and Kunhi Kadir within the domain of the Khilafat Movement. This narrative encapsulates accusations, actions and the perceived role of Ali Musaliar in a series of events, emphasizing the authorities' construal of his involvement in Khilafat-related activities. Ali Musaliar's association with influential personalities and events is notably underscored, particularly in the context of propagating non-cooperation and advocating the overthrow of British rule, in collaboration with Gandhi and the Ali brothers. Accusations against Ali Musaliar include incitement of violence against government officials, despite the absence of weaponry during searches. The administration construed the accumulation of arms and recruitment of volunteers as a prelude to potential conflict. The text tries to deflect responsibility from British administration figures like Thomas, painting Ali Musaliar as the instigator of turmoil in Tirurangadi. It attributes various activities, such as the enlistment of Khilafat volunteers and the establishment of Khilafat committees in diverse locales, solely to his influence. Moreover, it delineates instances of communal harmony, joint initiatives against alcoholism and the convergence of Gandhian movements with anti-alcohol campaigns. It chronicles the establishment of Khilafat committees across diverse regions and fundraising efforts for 'Swaraj'. The report describes visits by eminent figures like M.P. Narayana Menon, Kattilasseri Muhammad Musaliar and Parambot Achuthan Kutti Menon, emphasizing their endorsement of Congress Khilafat committees under the guidance of Gandhi. In essence, the document constructs a multifaceted tableau of relationships, actions and ideological undercurrents within the Khilafat Movement. It aims to portray Ali Musaliar as a pivotal figure orchestrating various initiatives and endeavors, albeit acknowledging counterarguments that suggest a broader contextual framework beyond his singular influence.[14]

The historical records reveal an intriguing aspect where several non-Muslim individuals participated alongside Muslims in protests against colonial forces during the period. Among those initially listed for arrest by the colonial administration was M.P. Narayana Menon. Additionally, after Ali Musaliar's surrender, individuals such as M.P. Narayana Menon and Mozhikunnath Brahmadattan Namboodiripad were also listed among the convicts.[15] Moreover, the document G.O. No. 867, Judicial, dated 15 November 1921, references the governor in council's authorization under Section 196 of the Criminal Procedure Code. It sanctioned the prosecution of seven individuals for offenses under Section 121 of the Indian Penal Code (IPC). The prosecution was intended before the special tribunal constituted under the Martial Law (Supplementary) Ordinance, 1921. This historical record provides insight into the legal proceedings and the involvement of various individuals in the context of these events during that period.[16]

The list, comprising individuals such as Edachola Kutta Panikker, Chenampara Appu Panikker, Valia Vittil Appu Panikker, Perumanath Attu alias Ashtamoorthi Namboothiri, Verkoth Damodara Panikker, Appulli Kesavan Nayar and Vazhapalli Appu Kunhan alias Kelu Nayar, was forwarded to the district magistrate, Malabar, with a request to promptly initiate proceedings before the special tribunal. This inclusion of individuals from various religious backgrounds in this roster signifies the diverse and interreligious nature of the organizational structure involved in the resistance against colonial forces. This composition aligns with the demographic landscape of the region.[17]

The document underscores the establishment of the Congress Khilafat Committee as a pivotal event, portrayed within the report as a significant transgression associated with Ali Musaliar. However, a nuanced examination reveals a conspicuous absence of fanaticism in these initiatives, instead revealing communal accord through the active participation of influential leaders, both Muslim and non-Muslim, during these foundational events. Corroborative accounts from figures like Chembrasseri Thangal lend weight to this assertion, signifying collaborative efforts led by M.P. Narayana Menon and Kattilasseri Musaliar in launching Congress Khilafat committees in Karuvarakundu on 6 August.[18] On the events of the Tirurangadi raid on 20 August, a cloud of suspicion surrounds the purported surprise element of the troop movement. The failure to apprehend Ali Musaliar and his associates suggests a potential foreknowledge, hinting either at an administrative lapse or a deliberate concealment of information or a serious failure in military/security intelligence gathering. Koyatti Moulavi confirms that Muhammed Abdurahiman, general secretary of the Khilafat Movement, had sent a letter specifying that the military was ready to march to Tirurangadi or Pukkottur. He advised in the letter to handle the situation carefully to avoid any confrontation. This letter was received in Tirurangadi, and on the same night, the military departed from Calicut.[19]

Information purportedly originating from unidentified sources in neighboring regions such as Tanur, Kottakkal and Vergara forewarned about police actions in Tirurangadi.[20] These revelations sparked suspicions that the movement might have been orchestrated by colonial officials to instigate conflict, furthering their agenda and validating their reports on Ali Musaliar.[21] Testimony presented during the trial of Kunhi Kadir of Tanur seemingly corroborated this suspicion, indicating that an individual from Tirurangadi had arrived in Tanur early in the morning. That person reported the arrival of the troop, though the identities of this and other informants remained undisclosed. The imperial authorities attempted to contextualize the freedom struggles in the Malabar region through a religious lens. However, they grappled with acknowledging the significant involvement of non-Muslims in the resistance movement. While endeavoring to sow divisions along religious lines, they accused the Khilafat movements of handling arms, funds and resources, intertwining the slogans of 'Mahatma Gandhi' and 'Shaukat Ali' with the Islamic Takbir. This accusation underscores the colonial officials' intolerance and antagonism toward the idea of

Hindu–Muslim unity in the struggle for independence. Furthermore, the document G.O. No. 867 has a noticeable bias in the depiction of religious identities associated with individuals involved in various incidents.[22] Colonial authorities often accentuated the religious affiliations of Hindu landlords supporting the administration while conspicuously omitting or downplaying religious associations when Muslim landlords or officials were targeted or affected due to their connections with actions undertaken by the authorities, particularly in incidents involving colonial officers or residents.

The British authorities in India disseminated news reports that favored the colonial forces in the region, which received coverage in newspapers worldwide, notably in colonies such as New Zealand and Australia, as well as in England and America. These reports, primarily originating from India, were circulated through various newspapers after a brief period. For instance, a report dated 28 August from Shimla, published by the *Mercury* in Australia on 30 August, details the movement of a column dispatched from Calicut, indicating military intervention in the Malabar region.[23] Additionally, another report from Shimla on 29 August, carried by the *Mercury* on 31 August, is an official force report, stating 'troops in action with rebels in a five-hour fight, with four hundred Moplahs killed', albeit these casualty figures were contested by eyewitnesses on the ground. This account depicts the events of 26 August in a favorable light for the troops, ignoring those aspects that made the reality more akin to a massacre than a conventional war. It underscored the colonial force's purported retribution for the deaths of their soldiers and officers, emphasizing the use of knives and swords by the local populace to justify killings. Moreover, new reports highlighted animosity among the local population, suggesting the conflict was not against the colonial government but directed at non-Muslims. Throughout this episode, British news agencies disseminated such propaganda globally, reinforcing their perspective.[24]

One report in the *Belfast Telegraph* on 30 August 1921 attempts to define the term 'Moplah', referring to the inhabitants of Malabar. It claims that Moplahs were descendants of Arab traders who married low-caste or outcast women. This characterization aimed to categorize the tribe, potentially facilitating ethnic segregation for the ease of enacting British policies. The Irish report also emphasizes the commercial acumen of the Moplah community, attributing a significant portion of the economy of Malabar to their expertise, as they were considered traders by birth and heritage. Notably, certain reports and descriptions differentiated Muslims from Moplahs with a single sentence. The Moplahs were depicted as primarily matrilineal, described in some contexts as 'mother's sons', possibly alluding to the matrilineal communities prevalent in the region.[25] British officers, such as Charles Alexander Innes (1874–1959), viewed this practice as non-Islamic and sought to discourage it through legislative measures. Innes, a settlement officer in Malabar, disapproved of the matrilineal system, considering it contrary to Quranic principles. The British administration aimed to reform this traditional system by introducing Anglo-Muhammadan law, which restricted women's freedoms and altered property rights and inheritance practices.[26]

The colonial forces in Malabar resorted to linguistic warfare to justify their brutal actions against the local populace. Employing an 'othering' tactic, they branded the natives with distinct names and attributed different, often negative, characteristics to them. To bolster their portrayal of the Mappilas as dangerous adversaries, the administration propagated numerous falsehoods and exaggerated reports. Hitchcock, among others, details alleged Mappila activities and their weaponry used against the British forces, including claims that they possessed advanced armaments for the period. Notably, this includes a description by a police superintendent of the use of 'missiles' by the people of Malabar, later identified as road pebbles. This distortion magnified the significance of mundane objects, such as stones, to justify the severe repercussions inflicted upon numerous individuals from the region.[27]

Furthermore, on 31 August 1921, the *Western Daily Press* reported on the Moplahs, characterizing them as well-armed, ferocious and eager for death. It conveyed an impression that disturbances in the districts were gradually subsiding and anticipated a favorable turn in the situation shortly. These details aimed to paint the Moplahs as a formidable and inherently violent force, justifying the colonial forces' actions as a necessary response to quell a perceived threat.

> Reuter India Office has received further information regarding the disturbances in Malabar. The District Magistrate reports that the detachments the Leinster Regiment and special police which on Friday last left Calicut, to relieve Malapuram, was attacked about ll o'clock next morning large body rebel at Pukkotur a few miles from their destination. The Moplah insurgents were armed with sporting rifles, swords, and war knives, a s well some carbines captured from the police that, they had looted. They showed their traditional ferocity and eagerness for death. The fighting lasted five hours before that Moplahs were beaten off with casualties estimated at 400 killed. Two British soldiers were killed, and officer and five men wounded. Lancaster. Assistant Police, was also shot, and has since died of his wounds.[28]

The *Daily Herald*, in a publication dated 2 September 1921, covered the supposed war strategy in Malabar. As the situation grew increasingly critical, efforts were made to fabricate alternative narratives to mask the massacres and brutal killings, which had particularly targeted women and children in the region. The report asserts that the Moplahs were purportedly gearing up for trench warfare. The article suggests that they exhibited a resolute determination to engage in a fight to the death by reportedly digging trenches in various districts, particularly in the vicinity of mosques. This depiction aimed to portray a readiness for protracted conflict and a strategic preparation for battle among the local populace. Additionally, the same newspaper account narrates the reported death toll of 400 individuals in Pukkottur. This information was conveyed by a group of Congress workers who, as per an exchange cable announcement, had returned to Bombay (Mumbai) after visiting the areas affected by the ongoing conflict. Their reported observations indicated a substantial loss of civilian life in the Pukkottur region, further emphasizing the severity and casualties incurred within the conflict zone.[29]

The reports in the *New Britain Herald* and the *Washington Times* in August 1921 depicted a grave and tumultuous situation in the Malabar District of British India. The resistance against British rule is ascribed to Islamic mysticism and the influence of seditious agitators who allegedly manipulated religious fanaticism among the local population. The *New Britain Herald*, dated 24 August 1921, describes serious rioting, bloodshed and property destruction in the Malabar District due to the influence of agitators. It mentions military forces firing upon rioters, resulting in casualties, and highlights disruptions such as railway line cuts and robberies at post offices. The report emphasizes the perceived control of areas by Indian natives and ongoing disorders, portraying a grim situation where mob law seemed prevalent.[30]

Meanwhile, the *Washington Times*, in its 25 August 1921 edition, reports a death toll of over 1,000 individuals in clashes between Indian natives and British troops in the Malabar District. It highlights the tragic deaths of numerous children and continued disorder, suggesting that the Indians maintained control over certain areas. The report underscores severe fighting between troops and Indian locals, raising concerns about the threat posed to British rule in India.[31] It details occurrences such as murders of military officials and a superintendent of police, signaling the gravity of the situation. Both reports paint a distressing picture of unrest, violence and challenges to British authority in the Malabar region. They depict a scenario of chaos and confrontations between British forces and local Indian communities, illustrating a precarious and volatile state of affairs during that period.[32]

Militaristic Rhetoric and Biased Discourse

Exploring the reports featured in various Australian newspapers from 1921 to 1922 reveals intriguing perspectives on how they covered resistance movements on a distant continent. The majority of these reports emanated from British colonial authorities in India, swiftly finding their way into Australian publications within a day or so. Upon review, it becomes apparent that these primary documents initially functioned as tools of pro-colonial propaganda. They endorsed narratives that portrayed the indigenous population's revolutionary movements seeking freedom negatively. Often, these narratives employed aggressive language and were rife with religious bias. On 16 September 1921, the *Warwick Daily News* reported from Malabar, datelined from Allahabad. The report describes the defensive preparations underway in Nilambur and alarming instances of 'wholesale looting' in the region. It raises concerns about a potential attack on Palakkad, emphasizing the imminent threat. It details the arrest of a hundred individuals, including prominent non-cooperators, in Ponnani, with a total of 457 people reportedly sentenced during that period. Additionally, the report reveals the temporary suspension of operations on rubber and other estates in the unrest-affected area. Typically overseen by landlords or the British administration, this suspension aimed to protect British supporters while inadvertently impacting the lives of common workers, adding further turmoil to their livelihoods.[33]

The documented reports exhibit a discernible semblance to official colonial intelligence, meticulously chronicling both anticipated and executed events within the region. Emanating from media affiliates entrenched in the colonial apparatus, these reports conspicuously served as conduits for bureaucrats. They not only facilitated the coordination of imperial operations but also strategically aimed to captivate media attention for propagandistic purposes. Notably, these reports systematically underplayed or omitted instances of British atrocities in the region while robustly amplifying the colonial narrative regarding the indigenous populace, thereby actively sculpting narratives that overwhelmingly favored the colonial standpoint.

The British administration, to bolster their military actions and discredit the resistance in the region, sought support from certain Muslim factions, effectively using their denouncements to validate their own agenda. One report cites influential Moplah merchants in Calcutta (Kolkata) expressing sentiments that deemed it unjust to universally condemn all Moplahs for the actions of the 'Ernad fanatics', characterizing them as 'misled individuals incited by agitators', akin to 'mad dogs' deserving immediate elimination. Notably, the report lacks specifics in identifying these 'influential' figures, crucial information that typically warrants citation in credible reporting. Evidently, certain segments of the Moplah Muslim community aligned with the British either as part of their employment or due to landholding positions that allowed them to levy taxes on local farmers and merchants. The report's deliberate use of derogatory terms, such as *mad dogs* mirrors the lexicon historically employed by colonial forces to disparage regional fighters. The insinuation of justifying the mass execution by advocating to 'shoot at sight' conveys a dehumanizing rhetoric. Such reports strategically framed these individuals not as human beings deserving due process but as mere threats to be summarily disposed of. Furthermore, the inclusion of purported opinions from unidentified Moplah merchants originating from imperial headquarters in Calcutta seems orchestrated to fortify the rationale for escalated military actions in the region.[34]

On 1 September 1921, the *Observer* from Adelaide, Australia, published an official report attributed to the general staff concerning the unrest in the Malabar area. The report asserts that as of the statement's issuance, no conflict had transpired in Tirurangadi. It indicated the surrender of several Moplah individuals to the mobile column stationed at that location. Additionally, it mentions the dispatch of another column to address the situation in the Ernad district of Malappuram. Notably, the report indicates the cessation of naval assistance, implying a perceived alteration in the operational requirements or strategic assessment of the situation in the region.[35]

Australian newspapers participated in a similar vein, serving as conduits for disseminating official records, thereby presenting British reports intended for public consumption. The motive behind making these reports public through newspapers was multifaceted. The *Register*, another publication from the same region, echoed the news previously published in the *Observer*, retaining an unchanged copy of the official statement released two days prior. This synchronization in reporting across newspapers aimed to amplify the reach of British accounts.[36] Titled 'Malabar Revolt', these reports offer insights into the global recognition of the Malabar resistance while elucidating colonial efforts to manipulate anti-colonial struggles within a global context.

For instance, the *Argus*, a publication based in Melbourne, featured a report titled 'Moplahs Surrender to Gurkhas'. The significance of this coverage lies in the portrayal of the Malabar region's resistance, a matter of substantial importance, being reported from Lahore and subsequently printed in Australia. This news served to accentuate the supremacy of colonial forces, celebrating the success of the Gurkhas (Gorkhas) a military contingent notorious for its severe massacres, including of innocent women and children within the region.[37] The narrative indicates a deliberate allocation of specific areas to battalions of troops, granting the Gorkha military sweeping authority over the entire affected region—a domain predominantly inhabited by freedom fighters. This allocation essentially empowered the Gorkhas to conduct inhumane operations throughout the area under their purview.

Notably, the reports highlight the dissatisfaction of the leaders of the anti-colonial resistance, often referred to as 'the chief rebels', with the ongoing military actions. In the reports, these military actions are described in positively charged language such as 'progress'. Furthermore, these reports provide specific details from the region, indicating the involvement of embedded media operatives working in favor of colonial interests on a global scale. Specific locales like Areekode are highlighted as crucial centers where inhabitants displayed numerous white flags—a symbolic plea for peace and cessation of hostilities.[38] Despite the populace's calls for the cessation of shootings, the colonial forces seldom heeded these appeals. The reports also note the existence of a certain number of 'chiefs' yet to be confronted, anticipating a decline in their numbers. Notably, the reports reveal that around three thousand individuals surrendered to the Gorkhas across the entire region.[39]

The *Herald*, a publication from Melbourne, on 20 September 1921, published a report focusing on the issues faced by non-Muslims in the Malabar region. The narrative deliberately attributes communal colors to the native resistance. This report, originally dispatched from Shimla on 17 September and subsequently published in Australia on 20 September, describes the Malabar situation as persistently serious. Moreover, it highlights the perceived insecurity of non-Muslim lives, employing terminologies such as 'spirit of rebellion' and 'unsafe lives of non-Muslims'. Such deliberate language and selective portrayal in the media aimed to sow seeds of discord and apprehension among different communities, furthering the divide and rule strategy employed by the colonial powers to maintain their dominance in the region.[40]

In an account published by the *West Australian*, detailed military engagements in the region are highlighted, emphasizing significant losses endured by the native 'rebels'. The narrative depicts a series of engagements where a Burma battalion seized a substantial cache of eighty thousand pounds of grain. Subsequently, approximately 1,800 rebels, armed with 760 knives, surrendered at Melattur, followed by an additional 300 at Perinthalmanna. Notably, the 'rebels' inclined toward surrender gathered along the south bank of the Beypore River, with over 500 yielding at Mannarkkad on Saturday. Additionally, an incident occurred in Cannanore (Kannur) where natives attempted to escape from prison, resulting in an altercation with guards. The warders, under attack, resorted to firing, resulting in the death of six and injuries to several others, while two warders sustained injuries. As a response, a contingent of reserve police constables and Indian infantry was mobilized and dispatched to reinforce the prison. The report also notes ongoing arrests within the region, indicating a broader effort to apprehend individuals deemed as such by the colonial administration.[41]

The *Mercury*, a publication based in Hobart, on 30 August 1921, published a comprehensive report concerning the Malabar region, delineating the orchestrated actions of the colonial authorities in various localities. These publications underscored their forceful interventions against indigenous groups, casting these people as fanatical or rebellious. Dated 28 August and sourced from India, this report specifically references staff reports acquired the preceding evening from Malabar.[42]

The report published by the *Kalgoorlie Miner* on 31 August 1921, attributed to the Australian Press Association, conveyed a significant implication regarding the involvement of Indian policemen and ex-soldiers in the reported 'revolt'. This emphasis underscores their potential influence in shaping the narrative, juxtaposed against the critical perspectives of indigenous voices that vehemently opposed colonial authority and its associated atrocities in the region. The report tactically portrays the general religious identity of the populace while conspicuously omitting the religious affiliations of the officers aligned with the British administration. The British officials' selective approaches caution us to stress the importance of carefully reorienting our understanding of the 'Moplah rebellion'. Moreover, the report strategically highlights instances of 'outrages against Hindus by fanatical Moplahs', emphasizing how these events led to division between Hindu and Muslim communities, thereby weakening Hindu sympathy toward the Khilafat Movement.[43]

The *Maryborough Chronicle, Wide Bay and Burnett Advertiser* from Australia, in its report on 23 November 1921, chronicled the events in Malabar, depicting the native population as 'rebels' engaged in resistance—conveniently termed as a 'rebellion'—despite the British functioning as the brutal colonial administrators in the region. The report specifically highlights the casualties among the native 'rebels' at the hands of the colonial army forces, the number of prisoners captured and the inventory of firearms collected. Such detailed enumeration of casualties and armaments served as propagandistic tools in support of the colonial administration's interests.[44]

Letter from Colonial Prison

The turbulence during the insurrection brought forth a persistent challenge: the judicial proceedings under the Martial Law Ordinance.

By early September, these tribunals convicted 350 individuals, prompting concerns about overcrowding within prisons. To address this, the inspector general of prisons proposed establishing a specialized penitentiary for Mappila prisoners in Bellary. Despite its official inception on 24 September, it held around 3,000 convicted inmates, mirroring the overcrowding prevalent in conventional prisons. A poignant letter emerged from Areekkan Moideen, dated 22 May 1925, penned in Salem Jail, offering a vivid account of colonial prison atrocities (Fig. 2.1).[45] It vividly describes the anguish and horrors faced by prisoners, including witnessing daily hangings under the martial law's lawlessness. This historical manuscript, discovered during research on Vengara's vernacular history, illuminates the severe treatment meted out to Malabar detainees in South Indian prisons even years after the Tirurangadi incident. Moideen's letter reflects archaic language and customs, notably his salutation, '*Udakathodukoodi*', a humble and polite salutation now obsolete in modern Malayalam. The letter addresses landlord Edathola Kunhali, wishing him a better life in both this world and the hereafter. It uses archaic expressions and displays a level of deference uncommon in contemporary times.

Moideen writes of receiving a prior letter, confirming its receipt in prison, and mentions twenty-two fellow prisoners from Ernad and

Figure 2.1
Letter of Areekkan Moideen, Dated 22 May 1925, from Salem Prison

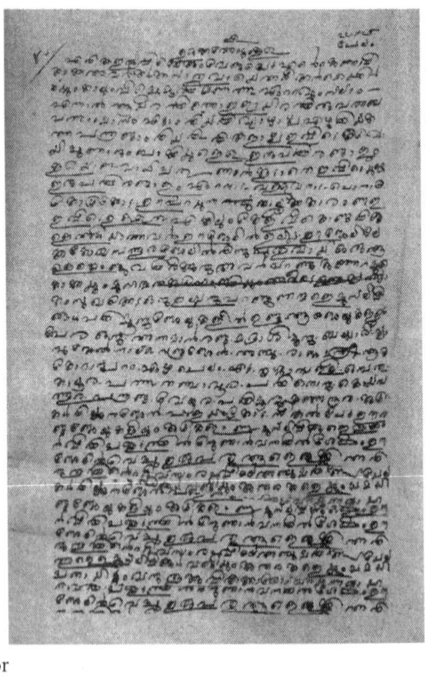

Photograph by author

Valluvanad, Ponnani and Kozhikode Taluks. He lists thirteen prisons where detainees from the region were incarcerated, including Bellary, Madras and Salem. Shockingly, Moideen notes the imprisonment of children in Palayamkode Sinkal Petta Prison, stressing the colonial forces' indiscriminate detention, even of minors. He heart-wrenchingly narrates the execution of twenty Muslims in Salem, recounting the arrival of Muslims from Salem in a decorated horse cart on the day of the executions. This bleak portrayal of the colonial prison system and the treatment of detainees, including children, sheds light on the grim realities faced by those imprisoned.[46]

'Khilafat King' Sentenced to Death

The historical record from November 1921 sheds light on the legal proceedings that transpired during the colonial era in India, particularly in the Malabar region. The *Englishman's Overland Mail*, dated 10 November 1921, reported the tribunal's verdict on Ali Musaliar and thirty-seven others accused of inciting 'rebellion' against the British administration and the murder of Private Williams of the Dorsetshire Regiment at Tirurangadi. The report indicates that twelve individuals, including Ali Musaliar, were sentenced to death, while the remaining twenty-five faced transportation for life along with property confiscation. Notably, three underage individuals were recommended for clemency by the court. The characterization of these legal proceedings differs significantly when viewed through an Indian perspective, revealing them as manifestations of colonial military authority suppressing individuals fighting for their freedom. The *Englishman's Overland Mail*'s portrayal of various stories on Indian resistance, though featured on page 3 of 10 November 1921, edition, appears to support colonial oppression and attribute crimes solely to the native populace.[47]

Another news piece details military intervention to thwart the coronation of a figure termed the 'Khilafat prince'. The report highlights the perceived danger in the 'Calicut-Wynaad' area, reinforcing the British military's strategy, which often exacerbated local dissent by apprehending those protesting against colonial oppression. One specific incident that is described was the timely arrival of military police, averting a potential conflict during the coronation ceremony of 'Mohamed', the proclaimed 'Khilafat prince'. The report mentions the involvement of specific individuals and groups in resistance activities. For instance, Parambati Koyapari and others attempted to join a 'rebel camp', while the capture of a boatman from Vayakad (Vazhakkad) by the Moplahs and subsequent release upon expressing willingness to 'convert to Islam' is detailed. Incidents of road blockades disrupting troop movement were also reported, painting the Calicut-Wynaad route as unsafe. The *Englishman's Overland Mail* extensively covered clashes between the military police and local inhabitants. Incidents near Areacade (Areekode) and the strategic positioning of British soldiers at the Feroke railway bridge were highlighted, depicting the resisting natives as 'rebels and bandits'. Furthermore, the publication reported incidents of violence against non-Muslims during resistance movements against landowners, showcasing the complexity of conflicts within the wider social hierarchy during this period.[48] An earlier report from 13 October 1921 details the Moplah trial, emphasizing substantial evidence against the secretary of the Khilafat Committee.[49] Additionally, an account dated 4 October 1921 in the same edition outlines the examination of 'Khan Bahadoor Amoo' (Amu), deputy superintendent of police, by the special tribunal.

> His evidence went to show that when a Lieutenant of Ali Musaliar was shot dead from the Mosque, the accused hoisted white flag and surrendered. The evidence of Amoo and two other witnesses examined today showed that Ali Musaliar preaching violence and openly saying that Amir of Afghanistan would invade India, that Mr. Gandhi and the Ali Bros would help the Amir and that every Moplah should help them. It was further in evidence that there was a regular conspiracy against the Government and arms had been manufactured in on a large-scale.[50]

Continuing the discourse in the *Englishman's Overland Mail* from the same page and dated 8 October, an additional report emerged from Palakkad, offering insights into the situation prevailing in Kumaramputhur near the Mannarkkad area. These reports likely depicted the events, conflicts or sentiments prevalent in the Mannarkkad region during that time. The report's context and specifics from Kumaramputhur near Mannarkkad in the Palakkad area needs detailed examination and cross-referencing with other contemporary sources to establish a more comprehensive understanding:

> Mr. V.H. Barve and two other members of the 'Servant of India Society' arrived in Palghat on Tuesday to investigate the cause of the Moplah rebellion and devise relief measures. They went round the town interviewing refugees from the disturbed areas. Information has reached here that in the action at Kumuramputhar near Manarghat nearly eight rebels were killed. Our casualties were nil.[51]

The colonial-era accounts starkly contrasted in their portrayal of casualties, revealing a distinct bias in the depiction of lives lost during conflicts. The narratives constructed by British authorities often portrayed the killing of natives defending their land against British forces as valorous encounters that highlighted the bravery of British officers. However, when British individuals succumbed to these confrontations, their deaths were framed as acts of rebellion or brutality committed by the indigenous population. This disparity in portrayal underscored a profound inconsistency in the valuation of lives. Indigenous individuals, engaged in resistance against rule and defending their territories, were denied the acknowledgment of their humanity and the recognition of their inherent rights.

An illustrative example of this biased reporting is discernible in the *Englishman's Overland Mail*, specifically in the headline 'Rebels Kill Villagers', published on 8 October. This report, originating from Madras, represented the British rendition of events in the region. It drew upon official telegrams received at Army Headquarters, Shimla, from the general officer commanding, Madras District, providing an account of the situation until the evening of 6 October 1921. The reporting methodology employed and the language chosen in these official reports cast the actions of the indigenous population in an unfavorable light, potentially overlooking or downplaying the contextual complexities that precipitated these conflicts.[52]

There are several telegrams in the public domain that are significant to the argument here. A telegram dated 7 October presents a supplementary account delineating the situation until 6 October in the specified region.[53] These telegrams, originating from the army headquarters in Shimla and relayed by the general officer commanding of the Madras District, served as primary documentary sources encapsulating the unfolding events during that period. These dispatches were likely intended to furnish a comprehensive situational appraisal to the colonial authorities, outlining troop movements, engagements with local populations and any instances of conflict or resistance encountered during the specified timeframe. The telegrams aimed to offer a meticulous record of the developments and occurrences within the region of concern. However, a critical evaluation of these telegraphic reports necessitates an understanding of their inherent biases. As products of military communication channels and subsequent transmission to colonial headquarters, these telegrams inherently reflect a perspective that aligns with colonial interests and agendas. The language, descriptions and interpretations contained in these reports are likely influenced by the prevailing British narrative and objectives in the region. A scholarly approach demands the triangulation of these telegrams with a spectrum of contemporaneous sources, which includes indigenous testimonies or alternative historical archives to foster a more nuanced comprehension of the events. Such an analysis seeks to discern and contextualize the biases ingrained in these telegraphic reports, contributing to a more multifaceted understanding of the intricate sociopolitical dynamics prevalent during that volatile epoch in colonial history.

The contrasting approaches adopted by the British military in the Madras and Malabar regions during the period of protest show a notable disparity in their treatment of the populace. In Malabar, the military and the police responded with a harsh and punitive stance, resorting to violent measures resulting in fatalities among the local inhabitants. Conversely, within the provincial headquarters, a more conciliatory strategy was seemingly employed, avoiding confrontations that led to human casualties. This distinctiveness in the military's response was mirrored in colonial reports. These reports, while documenting casualties, regrettably lacked the human considerations essential to understanding the plight of the people in the Malabar region. They portrayed incidents devoid of empathy or acknowledgment of the profound human toll exacted by such actions. For instance, a specific report detailing troop movements in Palakkad on 10 October exemplifies this dichotomy in the military's approach and subsequent reporting within the region.[54]

The historical records delineate a disturbingly casual enumeration of casualties, portrayed in figures and numbers that fail to capture the profound gravity of the loss of life. These reports, presented with a degree of indifference or pride, recklessly depict the tragic fate of individuals seeking refuge in the hills to evade military assaults in Malabar. The lack of consideration for fundamental human rights in the actions of the British colonial military and police is strikingly evident in the newspapers of that era. One such report elucidates the contents of a telegram dated 10 October, received at the Army Headquarters in Shimla from the officer commanding, Madras:

> On the 8th rebels were observed crossing the Manjeri-Pandikkad road to the north and collecting near Elankur. One platoon was sent in the evening to Tanur to deal with the threatened rebel activity in that neighbourhood. A bond of rebels was also observed near Tanur and bands north of Eddakkulam were reported out for looting. One company of 83rd Infantry left Cannanore for Eddakkulam yesterday. Section of the Armoured Car Company arrived at Tirur on 7th. Beyond a slight recrudescence of rebel activity in the area southwest from Malappuram to the railway there a nothing to report ... Oct. 10.

> A force of 200 special polite is being recruited at Calicut for the duty in connection with the rebellion. Palghat, in Friday night at 10 p.m. armoured cars motor vans, a Burmese battalion, a wireless set, and cavalry passed through Olavakkod to the disturbed area.[55]

The British report featured in the *Englishman's Overland Mail* on Thursday, 13 October 1921, offers insights derived from official telegrams, detailing military movements within the Malabar region. A separate telegram highlighted the situation in Madras as normal. This report reveals contrasting approaches employed by the police and military forces in addressing protests in Malabar versus Madras, particularly in instances of brutal military attacks targeting the general public, including women and children, in the former region.

The arrest of Ali Musaliar prompted British authorities to disseminate reports from the region that attempted to justify their actions in Tirurangadi and its vicinity. The military action executed by British forces in Tirurangadi Kacheri transpired when Ali Musaliar and his supporters sought to petition for the release of arrested individuals after a raid in the region. The sudden and unprovoked firing upon the people became the catalyst for the altercation at Tirurangadi Kacheri, culminating in the loss of British officers' lives and numerous innocent native casualties. On 5 September, the *Courier* published the British perspective on the situation. The report, headlined as 'Ultimatum to Rebels. Trouble Still Brewing in India', urgently requests military aid in the area:

> The situation in India, while quieter on the surface, is still far from satisfactory. A despatch from Palaghat (70 miles southeast of Calicut and on the mainline to Madras) says trouble is still at Mannaraghat. Hundreds of refugees are fleeing in the direction of Palaghat. Reports of dacoity, robbery, and plundering are coming in from Ponanni, where matters are apparently assuming an unpleasant aspect. The local police have telegraphed saying that the Treasuries at Ponanni and Chawghat are threatened and requesting urgent military aid. The Madras Mail understands that an ultimatum has been sent to the rebels demanding their surrender within 48 hours. Orders have been issued prohibiting the addressing of meetings by provincial delegates to the National Congress.[56]

Another telegram from Calicut reported the arrest of eighty-two Moplahs and highlighted forty-five reported incidents of dacoity in Ponnani.[57] A report in the *Englishman* depicts Ali Musaliar and his associates, arrested from the mosque, as 'the rebel Moplah leader' and the forty 'rebels' captured at Tirurangadi, portraying the people of the region as criminals involved in property confiscation. The report outlines that these 'rebels', attempting to evade the troops, sought refuge in the jungle. Published in the *Englishman* on 8 September titled 'Casualities in Wednesday's Fighting', it details an official telegram received from Madras on 1 September, providing further details from Tirurangadi on 31 August. According to the report, a group of 'rebels' had gathered in a mosque and were either killed or captured. The colonial invaders labelled the native people as 'rebels' and aggressively attacked and killed them without judicial processes. The report highlights the capture of Ali Musaliar, deemed an 'important rebel', confirming casualties on the British Dorset side as one death and four wounded. A detailed narrative of the British attack on Tirurangadi mosque is provided, portraying it as a necessary measure. It depicts the massacre of native individuals as mere 'casualties' while confirming the deaths of four European ranks and injuries to five others. The mosque incident was presented ambiguously, with some parts omitted or distorted to rationalize the brutal military attacks. The report describes the surrender of Ali Musaliar and forty-one 'rebels' with a white flag, while further characterizing Ali Musaliar as an elderly religious teacher from a hamlet near Pukkottur. It justifies British military and police actions by citing Musaliar's alleged refusal to comply with orders to appear before the divisional magistrate. Additional reports from the Calicut timeline centered on the events in Tirurangadi. These reports indicate that the engagement resulting in the capture of Ali Musaliar and forty-two others lasted for several hours, during which the 'rebels' fiercely resisted. These biased military propagandas sought to rationalize the invaders' brutalities in the region. Notably, the report misrepresents the use of traditional drums, called Nagara, in mosques, portraying them as military drums of the 'Musaliar king'. Typically, mosques have a single drum for ritualistic purposes. The report further alleges that a large mob took refuge within the mosque, beating drums and chanting war cries. It claims that about forty Moplahs were killed, while alleging that two soldiers were killed and four wounded. The natives were accused of using various weapons such as rockets with sharp spikes, explosive materials, hand knives and swords. The prisoners were then brought to Tirur as part of a military operation, drawing a large crowd to witness the event. Another Musaliar and two others were reportedly arrested and taken to Tirur.[58]

Reports in the same publication from diverse sources presented conflicting details, notably regarding the British assault on Tirurangadi mosque.[59] However, subsequent investigations post arrest failed to substantiate these claims, revealing merely a small collection of work knives common in rural areas.[60] A 3 September report from Calicut delves into the trial proceedings of thirty-five Moplah rebels linked to the Tirurangadi incident, presided over by Special First-Class Magistrate M. Krishnan Nayar.[61] These reports seem designed to bolster the image of colonial military authority, framing trials as performative endeavors for public consumption. However, these legal proceedings lacked judicial fairness, with colonial officers rendering verdicts in a dictatorial manner, ignoring legal principles and humanitarian considerations. The identification of accused individuals relied on assessments by the reserve policemen who were involved in their apprehension, employing terms like 'evidence' and 'witness' without true procedural depth. Additionally, instances arose where military officials assumed the role of both accuser and arbiter, unilaterally declaring verdicts based on accusations. Following the violent episode in Tirurangadi and the apprehension of Ali Musaliar, subsequent protests triggered the deployment of British forces to these locations. Furthermore, the postmaster-general authorized the establishment of field post and telegraph offices in disrupted areas, primarily for the convenience of military operations.[62]

On 3 September, reports emerged detailing the arrest of Kunhikoya Thangal (Sayed Ahmed Kunhi Koya Tancal in the report), leader from Malappuram, by K. Govinda Nair of Tiruvabadi (in the same report, this officer was also introduced as K. Govinda Nambiar). Charges against Thangal, a sixty-year-old figure, included his alleged presence during the altercation at Pukkottur. Recovered items such as a war knife, two additional knives and currency notes highlight the British portrayal of innocuous objects like the 'war knife' as perilous armaments, despite the prevalent use of firearms against women and even children in the region. Another allegation against Thangal was the possession of multiple Khilafat uniforms, leading to his remand in custody. The surrender and arrest of Ali Musaliar and his followers in Tirurangadi garnered varied interpretations and analyses in news narratives. These accounts aimed to disseminate false information and distorted analyses concerning their actions and philosophies, seeking to manipulate public perceptions of the events and strategies employed by Ali Musaliar and his adherents in Tirurangadi:

> The surrender of their venerable leader Ali Musaliar and rebels at Tirurangadi mosque is regarded as a great humiliation, for it never has been the policy of Moplah fanatics to surrender. They invariably fight and kill their wounded and prevent them from being taken prisoners alive.[63]

The British military provided misinformation on the people who resisted the terrible military actions. This report went on to state that Calicut was extremely quiet and the local Moplah shopkeepers and tradesmen were pursuing their daily avocations quietly and peacefully. This colonial mindset of the reporter is lucidly reflected between the lines of the story. It claims that people could no longer hear the bold claims of upcoming self-rule (Swaraj) and the elimination of the British (referred to as *firingi* or white man), which were frequently made just ten days ago. After the arrest of Ali Musaliar, the British relaxed, and they continued their atrocities against the people with a strong belief that they could rule the land for ever. The reporter writes about his experience of proceeding to Tirur, the base of colonial military operations.[64] Official reports blamed the common people for cutting the railway lines to prevent the military invasion in the region. The reports affirm that the railway lines were thoroughly rewired and regular train services were reinstated. The railway telegraph lines had also been put right, but as to government lines, the reporter expresses his personal fear that would take some time before they could be put in working order. The highlighting of the plight of Hindu refugees may also have been part of a wider strategy to stress the alleged Muslim communal agenda. This angle was also intentionally emphasized to give color to the British argument that Muslims were fanatics.[65]

The mockery of the martyrs of the Tirurangadi mosque was also seen in the newspaper reports. The *Dundee Courier*, for example, published such a narrative on 6 September under the title 'Three Days' Siege of Mosque. Moplahs' Scorn of Death'. This article describes the climate in August in the Malabar region, which caused uneasiness in the military side:

> The first party of sick, consisting of an officer and nine of the Dorsets, arrived at Bangalore yesterday from the Moplah country. Considering the long marches in a flooded country under a sweltering sun by day and torrential rain by night, the health of the troops is wonderfully good. The Dorsets are part of the column which had surrounded the mosque from which, after three days resistance. Ali Musaliar, the rebel leader, ultimately surrendered after they had hung a white shirt out of a window of the mosque, which was taken a token of surrender, and the investing force had ceased fire. What was left of the rebel band came out with hands up. A good many of those killed received number of rifle shots before they fell, their scorn of death being truly remarkable. There was a good deal of fighting before the rebels surrendered, and bayonet work of the closest description took place, the Moplahs making desperate efforts to get in with their knives even when impaled the bayonet. The mosque, which was surrounded at distance of one hundred yards, appears to have been very full of them, including women, and was rationed for a siege. The Moplah

dead were thrown into the river from the mosque walls during the night, and no accurate idea of the rebel casualties is possible. After the surrender a remarkable collection of arms was gathered, from the latest sporting express rifles to muzzle-loading shot guns. The rebels ran short of lead and melted down copper coins for bullets.[66]

Judgment: Special Tribunal at Calicut

The detailed judgment regarding Ali Musaliar and thirty-seven others, who were arrested and directed to the Tirurangadi Chantha, a weekly marketplace, where they were ordered to stay overnight. Subsequently, the army perpetrated atrocities in the region, resulting in widespread destruction and burning of houses and offices. The following day, the captives were transported to Calicut. On the 2 November 1921, the case (Code no. 7 of 1921) was adjudicated at the special tribunal in Calicut. Judges J.R. Huges, A. Edington and R. Narayana Ayyar presided over the case involving the thirty-eight individuals, including Ali Musaliar. Their decision favored the colonial army's stance on the matter.[67]

The following were arrested:

1. Palathum Mulayil alias Erikkunnan Ali Musaliar
2. Kokkapparambil Rayan
3. Chelupattath Kunhi Chekku
4. Kotasseri Ahmad
5. Chericheel Mammad Kutty
6. Mattath Saidalavi
7. Panakkal Unneen Kutti
8. Thekke Chekkingathodi Abdu Rahman
9. Pachengal Kunhammad
10. Chalil Pocker
11. Achippurakkaran Saidali
12. Annasseri Unneen Kutti
13. Kakkidipparambath Mammad Kutti
14. Kattusseri Sooppikkutti
15. Chembilakkal Eni Haji
16. Kondath Pallipparambil Ahmad
17. Nechimannil Ahmad
18. Koolippilakkal Athan Kutti
19. Nechimannil Kunhammad
20. Eruman Mammad Kutty
21. Kizhakke Peedikakkal Kunhali

22. Charath Saidali
23. Kalathil Mammad
24. Pallippatt Mayan Kutti
25. Paramban Koyakkutti
26. Kozhippurath Saidalikkutty
27. Kallan Alavi
28. Purakkat Hydru
29. Tenhilam Kunhi Moidu
30. Elampulaseri Moideen Kutti
31. Mattara Pokkai
32. Pattalathil Kuttasseri Ahmad
33. Urunian Ahmad
34. Palasseri Ittilakkal Kunheedu
35. Karimbil Ahmad
36. Nechimannil Kunheen
37. Chemban Ali Kutti
38. Kolakkattil Kunhalan Kutty

The offences of the prisoners were waging war against the king or Section 121 IPC; murder or Section 302 IPC and unlawful assembly or Section 149 IPC. Accused 1, 2, 3, 4, 5, 7, 18, 20, 30, 31, 32, 33 and 38 were sentenced to be hanged by the neck until they be dead:

Palathum Mulayil alias Erikkunnan Ali Musaliar (1)
Kokkapparambil Rayan (2)
Chelupattath Kunhi Chekku (3)
Kotasseri Ahmad (4)
Chericheel Mammad Kutty (5)
Panakkal Unneen Kutti (7)
Koolippilakkal Athan Kutti (18)
Eruman Mammad Kutty (20)
Elampulaseri Moideen Kutti (30)
Mattara Pokkai (31)
Pattalathil Kuttasseri Ahmad (32)
Urunian Ahmad (33)
Kolakkattil Kunhalan Kutty (38)

The court handed down varied sentences to the accused individuals. Accused 6, 8, 9, 10, 11, 12, 13, 14, 15, 16, 17, 19, 21, 22, 23, 24, 25, 26, 27, 28, 29, 34, 35, 36 and 37 were sentenced to transportation for life under Sections 124 and 302 of the IPC. Additionally, under Section 121 IPC, the property of each accused was forfeited to the government. A.V. Balakrishna Menon, appointed by the colonial army court, acted as the defense lawyer for the accused. The court's findings revealed that the 'rebellion', stemmed not from mere fanaticism, agrarian troubles or destitution but from the influence of the Khilafat and Non-Cooperation Movements. Unlike previous 'riots' in Malabar, the accused aimed to establish 'Khilafat rule' by force. The judgment elaborated on Ali Musaliar's connections with other Khilafat leaders, outlining his role in the Tirurangadi Khilafat Committee and his associations with various influential figures involved in the movement.[68] All the thirteen individuals, including Ali Musaliar, sent to Coimbatore Jail were hanged. Three others were deported to the Andaman Islands. Ali Musaliar, scheduled for execution on Saturday, 18 February 1922, prayed fervently to avoid the British gallows. Reportedly, he passed away in deep prayer during the Fajar prayer. Despite this, the British authorities claimed he was hanged. His funeral prayers were conducted, which were led by the elder pesh imam of Coimbatore, attended by Congress-Khilafat leader Yakub Hassan. Ali Musaliar and his associates were laid to rest in the Shukran Petai graveyard at Mettupalayam. A memorial building, inaugurated in 1958 by the minister Humayun Kabir, stands in Coimbatore as a tribute to their legacy. The building was formerly a religious school named Mambaul Khairat.[69]

Press Correspondence by Variamkunnath Kunhamed Haji

In the milieu of extensive global news reports that propagated a disparaging portrayal of the populace and leadership of Malabar, a response was initiated by Variamkunnath Kunhamed Haji. He composed a missive from Pandalur Hill to elucidate the authentic sociopolitical environment prevailing in the region and counter the misinformation. This epistle was disseminated via the *Hindu* on 7 October:

> Honoured Editor—I request you to publish the following facts in your paper. According to the press reports from Malabar which you will have got. Hindu Muslim unity in Malabar has thoroughly ceased to exist. It appears that the Hindus are forcibly converted (by my men) is entirely untrue. Such conversions were done by Government Party and reserve police men in Mufti mingling themselves with rebels (misunderstanding as rebels). Moreover, because of some Hindu brethren, aiding to the military, handed over to the military innocent (Moplahs), who were hiding themselves from the military, a few Hindus have been put to some trouble. Besides that, the Nambudiri, who is the cause of this rising, has also similarly suffered. Now chief

> military commander (of Government) is causing the Hindus to evacuate from these Taluks. Innocent women and children of Islam, who have done nothing and possess nothing are not permitted to leave the place. Hindus are compulsorily impressed for military service. Therefore, several Hindus seek protection in my hill. Several Moplahs too have sought my protection. For the last one month and half except for the seizure and punishment of the innocent no purpose has been achieved. Let all people in the world know this. Let Mahatma Gandhi and Maulana know it. If this letter is not seen published, I will ask for your explanation at one time.[70]

The sharp words that sometimes fell from his lips could not disguise the warm heart that beat beneath a masculine exterior. Addressing an esteemed editor, Haji advocates for the circulation of empirical facts, specifically concerning the intercommunal cohesion between Hindus and Muslims. Vehemently refuting the accusations levelled against him and his associates about coerced conversions, Haji unequivocally dismisses these charges originating from government sources as devoid of substance. Instead, he accentuates the complicity of government-affiliated entities, including officials and undercover police, in orchestrating conversions under the guise of insurgency. At the end of the letter, a fundamental order was given, both relational and ethical, that if this letter is not seen published, Haji will ask for an explanation at some point.[71]

Acknowledging instances of collaboration between select members of the Hindu community and the military, Haji concedes the resultant adversity faced by certain individuals within this demographic cohort. He emphasizes the calculated governmental strategy of displacing Hindus from the region, fueling antagonism toward Muslims and laying the groundwork for communal violence and ethnic cleansing. Central to his narrative is the plight of innocent women and children, held captive in an illustration of British tactics targeting even the most vulnerable segments of society. These stratagems, according to Haji, echoed the historical pattern of colonial powers fabricating narratives to justify atrocities globally. The boldness and psychological acumen of such material needs both indefatigable persistence and impudent bias. Propaganda of this magnitude must be popular, not elitist, and emotional, not logical. It must focus on plausible points repeatedly, especially through the utilization of crafty slogans. It must eschew objectivity and appeal primarily to emotions and senses, without any hesitation or reservation. Expressing concern over the dissemination of these fallacious narratives through official channels and embedded newspapers, Haji highlights the pervasive influence of governance over regional news outlets. He aimed to globally disseminate an accurate portrayal of the situation, particularly to reach influential figures such as Mahatma Gandhi and Maulana, pivotal leaders in the regional movement, to apprise them of the ground realities.[72]

In December 1921, the *Detroit Free Press* and the *Baltimore Sun*, American newspapers, prominently featured a communication received by the Friends of Freedom for India from Variamkunnath Kunhamed Haji in the form of a cablegram. Preceding this transmission was a categorical refutation of allegations of the Moplahs' involvement in the execution of numerous Hindus and the coerced conversion of others to Islam. These allegations were robustly repudiated as elements of a calculated British stratagem to undermine the legitimacy of the movement advocating for India's independence. The published article, titled 'Denies the Murder of Hindus—A Statement of Moplah says Report is British Propaganda', was dated 6 December and had a New York dateline. The substantive content, encapsulating the communication from 'Variyan Kunnath Kunhamed Haji', was delineated within the second paragraph:

> A few cases of conversion of our Hindu brethren have been reported to me, the message said. But after proper investigation we discovered the real plot. The vandals that were guilty of this crime were members of the British reserve police and British intelligence department, and they joined our forces as patriots to do such filthy work only to discredit our soldiers. There are Christians, Hindus and Moplahs amongst these British agents and spies. They have deservedly been put to death.[73]

In the *Detroit Free Press* from Michigan, a further report surfaced on Wednesday, 7 December 1921, under the title 'Denies Moplahs Forced Converts'. Accompanying this headline was a subtitle, 'Leader Says Report Is Part of British Plot'. Dated with a New York timeline of 6 December, this report had extensive coverage compared to its predecessor.

> We are at war with England. We are fighting for the independence of Indian, and we are doing exactly what the Americans did to free America from British domination. So, anyone giving aid and comfort to the enemy will be severely dealt with, irrespective of social position or religious affiliation. let the great people of the great land of Washington postpone Judgment until they have a chance to know the full truth about the present war in Malabar.[74]

Haji emphasizes in this report the conflict with the British as a strife for India's independence. Similar to the Americans' struggle to liberate themselves from British rule, Indians were engaged in a comparable pursuit. Anyone providing support to the opposing side would face severe consequences, irrespective of their social status or religious affiliations. He encourages the people of the land to reserve judgment until they have a comprehensive understanding of the ongoing war in Malabar. Conflicts often arose not solely on religious grounds but were intertwined with alliances either in support of or opposition to colonial powers, plus multiple economic and class issues.[75]

Variamkunnath Kunhamed Haji's leadership is noted in history, specifically in the case of the murder of Chekutty, a colonial police officer, which stemmed from Chekutty's alignment with the British. Certain affluent Muslims were known supporters of the colonial forces and subsequently became targets of political hostility. Figures like Kazhungum Thottathil Moosakkutty Adhikari, Chalilakath Ibrayan Kutty along with his son Ahmad, Vettilakkaran Kunhi Ahmad and Thrikkulam Marakkarthodi Marakkarutti were prominent among those seen as advocates for the British cause. On 28 October, Variamkunnath Kunhamed Haji planned a coordinated action involving approximately 200 individuals, targeting Kondotti. The operation involved deliberately burning official records housed in the sub-registrar's office and the local police station. Subsequently, the group moved towards the residence of Kondotti Thangul. Though reports indicate an incident involving a firearm resulting in an individual being shot, the overall scope and impact of the group's activities beyond this episode remained relatively restrained.[76] Instances also occurred where families like Achampatt in Parappanangadi aligned themselves with British troops and met with resistance from local populations. Notably, Nalalakath Kunhippocker, also known as Mullan Kunhippocker, who was the manager of Musakkutty Adhikari, a known British supporter, faced repercussions alongside Azhu Valappil Kunhi Ahmad. Moreover, certain Muslim landlords and officials actively backed the British, often causing disruptions in the Khilafat movements. This support came from individuals such as Kalappadan Ali Adhikari of Malappuram, Perappuran Ayamutti Adhikari of Pukkottur, Kadaliyil Moosakkutty Adhikari of Pandikkad, Kalladi Moidutty of Mannarkkad, the Parayil family of Cherpulassery and specific factions within the Kurimannil Valiya Mannil family of Anakkayam.[77]

The 17 November 1921 report from the *Englishman*, datelined Calicut on 8 November, is conspicuously biased in its depiction of religious identities amid instances of violence. The report notably underscores atrocities targeting Hindus while briefly mentioning the murder of Thoudiyil Hydru Haji, a physician, attributing his demise to Moplahs under allegations of assisting troops. An intriguing omission within the report is the conspicuous absence of acknowledgment of

Thoudiyil Hydru Haji's religious identity, notably his pilgrimage to Mecca, symbolized by the honorific title 'Haji' bestowed upon him. The deliberate exclusion of this religious facet, a significant and respected aspect in Islamic traditions, prompts scrutiny into editorial choices and the nuanced presentation or suppression of identities to align with the colonial narrative. While emphasizing the victim's purported assistance to the troops and his distress over his son's abduction during the troops' visit to Vettikattiri in Eranad, the report creates a narrative of conflict. This selective omission of critical contextual details underscores the calculated nature of colonial propaganda tactics within the media.[78]

Flawed Photo Descriptions

In the historical context of colonial narratives, a critical examination of certain publications, such as the *Sphere*'s depiction of the Moplahs in 1921, reveals significant inaccuracies and biased representations. An examination of a photograph titled 'A Typical Moplah—A Mahomedan Malabaree' (Fig. 2.2) that appeared in the paper exposes a fundamental discrepancy in the description's claim regarding religious identity. The assertion that the individual depicted was unquestionably Muslim contradicts the nuanced reality of diverse religious affiliations within

Figure 2.2
A Typical Moplah—a Mahomedan Malabaree, a Misrepresented Image

Source: Sphere, 15 October 1921, 6

the Moplah community. Such misrepresentations underscore how colonial media sources employed misattributed identities to propagate preconceived notions, thereby undermining the authenticity of their narratives.

Furthermore, the strategic utilization of an image depicting interactions involving a Christian denomination within the Malabar region to insinuate the perceived 'fanaticism' of the Malabar Muslims exemplifies a deliberate distortion of events. This journalistic approach aimed at associating unrelated occurrences to reinforce a biased portrayal of the native population. Additionally, the image description referencing 'A Delegate from the Patriarch at Antioch Amongst the Moplahs' presents a puzzling juxtaposition of unrelated elements (Fig. 2.3). The attempt to conflate the presence of the Patriarch of Antioch, a figure of significance in early Christianity, with the purported fanaticism and connection to Turkey of the Moplahs lacks substantive cohesion, further underscoring the dubious intentions behind the newspaper's narrative construction. This analysis illuminates the complex interplay between visual representations, textual descriptions and colonial agendas within historical media.[79]

Beyond the Amazon: Rich, Fertile Plains

The examination of historical news reports reveals a confluence of contrasting narratives pertaining to regions characterized as the Amazon and jungle landscapes, notably in the context of colonial

Figure 2.3
A Delegate from the Patriarch at Antioch amongst the Moplahs

Source: Sphere, 15 October 1921, 6

discourse. The portrayal of these areas, with vivid imagery and textual descriptions, challenges the prevailing colonial propaganda that idealized them as dense, impenetrable jungles devoid of civilization. Reports delineate a multifaceted terrain with dense jungles, meandering rivers and expansive fertile plains, suggesting a diverse ecological landscape contrary to colonial depictions. In the context of events in the Malabar region during the early 20th century, these reports present a mosaic of portrayals involving the Moplah community. These reports describe a complex series of events, notably actions targeting estates and plantations, accompanied by allegations of violent acts such as burning bungalows and religious conversions from Hinduism to Islam. Such representations potentially serve to vilify the Moplahs and underscore colonial narratives aimed at justifying intervention.

Moreover, the use of photographs alongside textual descriptions in these reports introduces a layer of complexity. Images of serene surroundings, the presence of a Muslim ruler of Arakkal kingdom with the governor-general of French India (Fig. 2.4) and scenes of daily life amid chaos seemingly diverge from the overarching narrative conveyed by the headlines. This duality within the visual and textual elements challenges the singular narrative of turmoil and presents facets of a civilized generation in Malabar. The juxtaposition of contrasting descriptions, photographic evidence and overarching narratives in these reports underscores the complexity and challenges in interpreting historical events through the lens of colonial-era media.[80]

Figure 2.4
The Ruler of the Arakkal Kingdom with the Governor-General of French India

Source: Graphic, 3 September 1921

Echoes from the Jungle

During the early 20th century, British colonial interests in regions like Malappuram prompted an engagement with local cultures and landscapes, often manifested through publications aimed at documenting and comprehending indigenous communities. Vincent Jos Ryder's work *Two Years in Malabar* encapsulated a periodical endeavor to delineate the *halilakkam* (frenzy) of Moplahs, as previously described by William Logan.[81] This portrayal featured a colonial inclination toward comprehending and potentially managing local societies and environments. In the introduction to the book, it is mentioned that the content in the book was earlier published as articles in the journal *Echoes from the Jungle,* a detachment journal published fortnightly from Malappuram, south Malabar, during the years 1905–1906. The title *Echoes from the Jungle* is an attempt to characterize the locale. Ryder appears to rationalize the selection of this title by suggesting a tangential connection: the military station or cantonment situated near the Kadalundy River's northern bank, adjacent to a fringe of jungle. This nomenclature seemingly combines elements of colonial perception and geographical attributes of the area.[82] These historical narratives, while providing insights into colonial viewpoints and administrative endeavors, necessitate a critical approach. Analyzing such texts warrants a consideration of the authors' intentions vis-à-vis the sociopolitical milieu of the time. This scrutiny allows for a deeper understanding of the colonial gaze and its implications for the studied regions and their inhabitants.

The official use of the term *jungle* in a specialized police journal in the colonial Malappuram region exemplifies a form of lexical imposition indicative of the practice of 'othering'. This encapsulates the Eurocentric tendency to categorize and define indigenous landscapes and communities through a lens shaped by external perceptions. The designation of the journal as *Echoes from the Jungle* suggests an institutionalized perception prevalent among the troops stationed there. It implies a preconceived notion and classification of the region as a 'jungle', predating any subsequent propaganda or persuasive narratives. This terminology's inclusion in official documentation amplifies its integration into the colonial discourse and bureaucratic apparatus, potentially reinforcing stereotypes and biases directed toward the local community and its geographical milieu. The act of naming, far from being a mere superficial label, assumes profound significance in the colonial framework. Such naming practices influence the perception, categorization and subsequent treatment of these communities within the administrative infrastructure, contributing to the perpetuation of hierarchical structures and entrenched biases. Vincent Jos Ryder, in *Two Years in Malabar*, offers his perspective on interactions within the region. Contrary to prevailing narratives prevalent at the time, Ryder's observations diverge significantly from the preconceived notions propagated by earlier British officers and prevailing propaganda. Notably, Ryder's firsthand experience revealed a marked absence of disrespect or animosity directed towards him during his extensive explorations through the villages and surrounding areas in pursuit of information.[83]

Ryder's documentation challenges the established discourse of the indigenous populace's bitterness toward British troops. His meticulous observations contest the prevailing narratives that portrayed the local community in an unfavorable light. He emphasizes the disparity between the negative portrayals and the civility he encountered, asserting that the earlier impressions, largely shaped by reports and prejudicial accounts, did not align with the reality he experienced.[84] Furthermore, Ryder eloquently refutes the prevailing mischaracterizations of the indigenous community as uncivilized or primitive. His personal interactions and observations with the community illuminated their commendable qualities, thereby underscoring the disparity between popular perceptions and the actual character of the community in Malabar.

Conclusion

This chapter makes it evident that the region faced significant and complex challenges, particularly in the context of British influence. The Muslim community of Malabar cannot be dismissed as an anomalous corner of the British Empire in India or as an abstract, idealized or symbolic bridge between East and West in a political or ideological sense. The history here is full of people, families and groups trying to understand and adapt to changing social ties and circumstances. The colonial portrayal of feminism as an integral part of daily life underscores the crucial role women played in personal, professional and societal spheres. The diary of a woman from Vergara, Thithachumma, the daughter of the poet Chakeri Moideenkutty, serves as a valuable historical artifact showcasing her independence in business and wealth management. Permit me a brief foray into the zone of red string and thumbtacks on the wall, but I see no difficulty in acknowledging that her diary illuminates her active involvement in various businesses, social endeavors and family life, providing a glimpse into the dynamics of the time. The family's support for British administration, leading to their escape to Parappanangadi during perilous times, highlights the tumultuous atmosphere of the era. The diary vividly depicts cultural events like the Malappuram *nercha* and reflects her autonomy in financial matters during her journey to Parappanangadi. These narratives, whether from supporters or opponents of colonialism, emphasize the empowerment of women in this context. Women's involvement in resistance movements, challenging traditional gender roles and indicating the intersection of feminism with societal change and political resistance during that period, seems to have surprised the British. The stories contained in these newspaper accounts provide excellent lessons about both the manipulation of historical facts and what constitutes proper leadership.

Variamkunnath Kunhamed Haji

Variamkunnan, also known as Chakkiparamban Kunhamed Haji, born in 1883 in Valluvanad, Vettikattiri amsam, hailed from a family deeply affected by the events of the 1894 resistance. His father, Moideen Kutti Haji, faced transportation for life during this tumultuous period when Variamkunnath was between the ages of eleven and twelve. Upon learning of the details surrounding the Pukkottur flight, Variamkunnath Kunhamed Haji journeyed to Karuvarakundu to procure additional arms and seek counsel from Thangal. Subsequently, accompanied by his followers and individuals gathered along the way, he traversed from Melattur to Angadipuram. The murder of Chekutty, while brutal, was perceived as an act of vengeance by Variamkunnath. It was a retaliatory response stemming from the painful recollection of the 1894 incidents, during which this inspector was involved in the killing of several members of Haji's family. Moreover, the inspector was regarded as being closely aligned with the British and often reported as their most loyal associate in the region. This act of retribution occurred on the morning of 30 August 1921.[85]

Chapter 3

UNVEILING THE IDENTITIES

An Exploration of Propaganda Film and Photography

> A portrait of Mohammed Ali, who was one of the main architects of the revolt.
>
> His capture and execution discouraged his supporters and led to their submission.
>
> On each side, two Moplahs who gave the signal for the uprising by murdering English settlers.
>
> —Captain Harry, 'Comment Fut Perimee La Revolt des Moplahs,' *Sciences et Voyages*, 10 August 1922

This caption accompanying photos published with an article on Malabar in a French magazine sparked significant controversy during the centenary celebration of the Malabar resistance. This chapter seeks to explore the contentious nature of photographic imagery in historical studies. A longstanding acknowledgment of significant deficiencies and issues in pictorial depictions prompts a critical examination of their role. The primary focus of this chapter lies in disclosing individual identities depicted in photographs used for British propaganda journalism. A meticulous investigation involves scrutinizing extensive documentation to identify recurring language employed in both advertisements and propaganda film production. Notably, two images featured in a French magazine, *Sciences et Voyages*, initially circulated in South India as depictions of the freedom fighter Kunhamed Haji, are scrutinized. The objective of this inquiry is to unveil the true identity of the individuals in these photographs. Widespread controversies were sparked in the region because of the incorrect identification of one of them as Variamkunnath Kunhamed Haji. Colonial narratives are invoked to suggest that Ali Musaliar and the Tirurangadi community were cognizant of the events of that day and attributed them to colonial strategies. Furthermore, this chapter undertakes an analysis of the killings of Rowley, Johnstone and

Moideen, along with an examination of the arguments posited by the colonial force.

A proliferation of articles in diverse newspapers and academic journals sought to legitimize the actions undertaken by British authorities in the Malabar region. The article 'How the Mappila Riots Were Suppressed', featured in the 10 August 1922 edition of French publication *Sciences et Voyages*, triggered extensive discourse and controversy during the centenary celebration of the 1921 resistance. Notably, one of the accompanying photographs was purportedly identified as Variamkunnath Kunhamed Haji, yet this identification lacked comprehensive academic scrutiny and substantial evidential support. During the centenary commemoration of the 1921–1922 Malabar resistance to colonial rule, the images highlighted in a French magazine sparked discussions about the pictorial representations of Variamkunnath Haji.[1]

However, the validation of these identifications was notably deficient in methodological rigor and empirical corroboration. It is easy for simple minds to deride this pursuit, this line of inquiry into the true identity of the individual in the photograph, as a kind of naive sentimentalism, but that would be a shallow analysis. Regrettably, the publisher of the book *Sulthan Variyamkunnan* refrained from releasing these visual materials alongside the published book, thereby maintaining ambiguity about their authenticity.[2] This omission led to disparate interpretations among the public, resulting in a dichotomy of acceptance and skepticism regarding the proposed identities of the individuals in question. In a critical analysis conducted in 2021, emphasis was placed on the need to release these images to the public domain alongside the comprehensive article from *Sciences et Voyages*. Such a disclosure would not only elucidate the identities depicted in the photographs but would also serve to authenticate the magazine's assertions. Furthermore, it was observed that the magazine, true to colonial propaganda, refrained from explicitly divulging the identities of the two individuals flanking Ali Musaliar (Mohamed Ali) in the disseminated visual documentation.[3]

In the context of the public availability of these images, I had underscored the absence of conclusive evidence in *Sciences et Voyages* to substantiate the assertion that the figure portrayed was indeed Variamkunnath Kunhamed Haji.[4] The centennial commemoration of the event primarily centered on the debate surrounding this photograph, triggering fervent discussions that, due to the sensitive nature of the issue, escalated into religiously charged discussions from opposing ideological factions. The description of the photo can be read as follows (Fig. 3.1): 'A portrait of Mohammed Ali, who was one of the main architects of the revolt. His capture and execution discouraged his

Figure 3.1
Sciences et Voyages Article Page

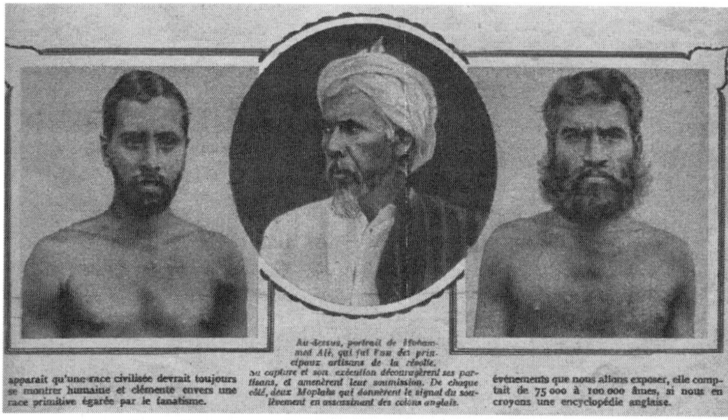
apparait qu'une race civilisée devrait toujours se montrer humaine et clémente envers une race primitive égarée par le fanatisme.

Au-dessus, portrait de Mohammed Alî, qui fut l'un des principaux artisans de la révolte. Sa capture et son exécution découragèrent ses partisans, et amenèrent leur soumission. De chaque côté, deux Moplahs qui donnèrent le signal du soulèvement en assassinant des colons anglais.

événements que nous allons exposer, elle comptait de 75 000 à 100 000 âmes, si nous en croyons une encyclopédie anglaise.

Source: Captain Harry, 'Comment Fut Perimee La Revolt Des Moplahs,' *Sciences et Voyages*, 10 August 1922. Photograph by author

supporters and led to their submission. On each side, two Moplahs who gave the signal for the uprising by murdering English settlers.'

My intent here is to scrutinize these figures using data and corroborative evidence that could shed light on the background of the image. The exploration of various facets in Malabar holds significance for me, transcending academic inquiry, as it intertwines with the timeline of my life experiences. I conducted further investigation by revisiting the British Library and prominent military archives of the United Kingdom in pursuit of identical copies of the images published in *Sciences et Voyages*.

It becomes evident from the composition and context of the article, coupled with insights into the author's background, that these images were officially supplied by the administrative apparatus of the British government in India. The specific intent behind the article was to persuade the French-speaking community that the actions undertaken by the British in Malabar were not unfamiliar or unconventional, implying that a similar response might be expected from the French in their colonial contexts. Additionally, the author draws parallels, highlighting that the atrocities witnessed in the Malabar region were not dissimilar to those carried out by Belgium and France in their African colonies.[5]

This article serves as a lens through which to comprehend the British assessment of the resistance in Malabar a century ago, illustrating their efforts to sway international opinion in their favor. It sheds light on how the British portrayed and presented the events in Malabar within and outside Europe to garner support for their actions. Additionally, it unveils the attitudes of the British officials toward the people of Malabar during and after the struggle, exposing the colonial narratives constructed by the West around the revolution and its participants. The article commences by attributing the primary cause of the 'civil war' in Malabar to 'Islamic mysticism'. This unearths the British endeavor to dismantle the integrated and indigenous fabric of Malabar society. Notably, the article underscores how the Malabar resistance against foreign incursion was labeled as a civil war within India itself, emphasizing the intrinsic connection of the conflict to the homeland of the British.

The adversities faced in Malabar were far from what the British had anticipated, despite their military might. The discourse in Harry's article employs terms such as *cannibalism* and *brutality* to vindicate the killing of civilians under British rule, which stretched across a spectrum from the United States to Fiji, encompassing both ends of the Pacific Ocean. This rhetoric aimed to justify the actions of the British administration as purportedly necessary measures against perceived barbarism and savagery among the local populace.[6] The widespread dissemination of news of the brutal assault by British troops in Malabar, which included attacks on children and women, created an international outcry. Captain Harry's article can be contextualized within a broader campaign to counter and mitigate such 'damning reports' and descriptions on such a 'damning scale'. His objective was to sway French readers by drawing parallels, suggesting that under similar circumstances, their authorities might have reacted comparably if faced with a series of assaults akin to those witnessed in British India. Captain Harry deliberately evokes the horrific massacres perpetrated in the Congo by Belgian forces, using these events as a benchmark to justify and draw parallels with the situation in Malabar. The article sought to equate these massacres as analogous endeavors to eradicate what was referred to as 'human predators', much like the actions witnessed in Central Africa.

By presenting this international context, the article endeavored to portray Britain's actions in Malabar as synonymous with the actions of other European powers such as France and Belgium in different corners of the globe. While the media portrayed the atrocities in Malabar as akin to the alleged brutal homicides in the Congo attributed to Belgium, Captain Harry criticizes most media outlets, excluding the *Times*, for failing to grasp the underlying facts about how Britain quelled the 'Moplah riots'. The *Sciences et Voyages* article purported a stance of impartial narration about the situation in Malabar. However, it paradoxically asserts that the Moplahs were the initiators of bloodshed in the region. The article justifies the British brutalities by attributing vulgarity, racism and religious fanaticism to the Moplahs. The author frames the nature of the Moplahs in a manner that questions the possibility of exhibiting humanity and empathy toward a misguided, primitive race.

The term 'Moplah' is elucidated for European readers, emphasizing that it does not denote a distinct race but refers to Indians who embraced Islam and resided along the Malabar coast in the southwest peninsula. This narrative aimed to portray the Moplahs as not ethnically distinct from the general populace of South India but accentuates that their ancestral adoption of Islamic practices rendered them physically and morally more dynamic than Hindus and Christians.[7] This portrayal of strength and vigor was crafted to counter British allegations of racial violence. Furthermore, the article sought to link the resistance in Malabar during the early 20th century with anti-Dutch and Portuguese struggles of the 16th and 17th centuries. However, the author's estimations of the Moplah population in the region as ranging from 75,000 to 100,000 indicates a lack of precise demographic data, revealing potential inaccuracies in the author's understanding of the community's demographic specifics. Kozhikode is prominently depicted as the focal point of the Malabar district, emphasizing its significance as a renowned city distinguished for its civilization and commercial prowess. The notion of 'community' can be slippery and elusive, fluid and porous, contested even. Despite being integrated into Malabari society for centuries and enjoying an ecumenical cosmopolitanism, the Muslims of the region have always preserved a philosophy of autonomy and distinction in their identity. This cosmopolitanism contradicts narratives casting the local populace as primitive and uncivilized, thereby challenging any inclination to annihilate them. The term *Calicut* even permeated language through the term *calico*, a form of cotton cloth, a testament to the wide production and export of this fabric from the region. This recognition underscores Kozhikode's stature as a bustling trading center and the significance of its associated ports, which held substantial regard in European regions well into the early 20th century. The city's historical renown as a hub for commerce and cultural exchange not only shaped its identity in the local landscape but also garnered recognition and acknowledgment beyond its regional boundaries, leaving an indelible mark on global trade networks.

The author's argument for European occupation is substantiated by referencing historical conquests, notably highlighting Alexander the Great's expedition in 327 BC. This period in Asia is characterized as the initial contact between the Indies (subcontinent) and the Western world, occurring over eighteen centuries following the Greek conqueror's temporary reign. Moreover, the article emphasizes centuries of Western intrigue and dominance over Kozhikode, providing European readers with a nuanced understanding of historical interactions. It specifically mentions the arrival of the Portuguese envoy Pedro de Covilha (1460–1526) at Calicut in 1487, signaling a pivotal moment in this historical narrative. Covilha, an earlier visitor to India, was also referenced for his role in expanding Portuguese trade ventures in the region, highlighting the longstanding Western interest and efforts to extend their commercial reach into the Indian subcontinent.[8] The voyage to Calicut was notably accompanied by a map of the Indian Ocean and the Middle East crafted by Fra Mauro (1400–1464), a Venetian cartographer. This mention of the story of the map is an intentional effort to depict the history of colonial occupation as a comprehensive narrative encompassing the broader history of the country. It aligns with a deliberate strategy to intertwine the colonial era within the overall historical fabric of the region, emphasizing the intersections of global exploration, cartography and colonial ambitions during that period.

The article, while justifying British atrocities in Malabar, also exalts the Portuguese occupation. It introduces Vasco da Gama as a figure initially perceived as virtuous but who became notorious for his unparalleled cruelty and aggressive actions within the maritime domain. The 'famous' Vasco da Gama, 'renowned' for his voyage from Lisbon to the Malabar coast, arrived at the port on 20 May 1498. Shortly thereafter, he established a treaty of friendship with the Zamorin's ruling dynasty of Calicut, marking the 'commencement of Europe's conquest of India'. Additionally, the article refers to numerous historical landmarks associated with the city and its environs, further contextualizing the rich historical and cosmopolitan tapestry of Kozhikode within the broader narrative of colonial encounters and conquests. This portrayal aligns with an overarching theme of glorifying imperialistic figures while intertwining them with the historical landscape of the region.

Captain Harry revisits the coastal history tied to the arrival of St Thomas. 'Modern accounts firmly establish the evangelization of the Malabar Coast by St. Thomas,' he recounts. He also mentions Vasco da Gama encountering a sizable Christian community exceeding 300,000 members along the Malabar shores, providing insight into the region's religious demographics. These narratives notably reflect the colonial agenda of religious segregation and its divisive, often violent, implications. 'It was observed that the Moplahs were perceived as industrious individuals among the pacifist Hindus,' he notes. Effectively, the author attempts to rationalize British atrocities by delving into the direct catalysts behind the 'bloody tragedy' in the Malabar region of the Indian subcontinent (Fig. 3.2). At the end of World War I, approximately seventy million Muslims in India supported the English course of action. The author suggests that the Hindu majority also

Figure 3.2
Picture Published in *Sciences et Voyages* on 10 August 1922

Source: Captain Harry, 'Comment Fut Perimee La Revolt Des Moplahs,' *Sciences et Voyages*, 10 August 1922. Photograph by author

favored these policies. The author points out a shift when British prime minister David Lloyd George (1863–1945) facilitated the disintegration of Turkey. 'All Muslims' in India protested this decision. The 'fanatical Moplahs' demonstrated a more violent response compared to their counterparts in the north and west. As early as 1919, they proclaimed allegiance solely to God, the caliph and the sultan of Turkey. However, Harry's reference ignored resistance in various parts of India, even preceding the World War I, while attempting to anchor the region's issues to problems with Turkey and the Caliphate.[9]

The article further emphasizes that the Moplahs were predominantly peasants working on large plantations owned by the British or Brahmins. In October 1921, agricultural strikes erupted in the Kozhikode region, demanding increased wages for workers and addressing grievances of harsh treatment by English and Hindu landlords. Notably, the protests targeted not only British or Hindu landlords but also Muslim landlords mistreating workers. Harry's narrative, however, excludes Muslim landlords in Malabar from this group. Primary sources from Malabar itself provide evidence of resistance against landlords, irrespective of their religious or linguistic affiliations.[10]

If you read between the lines, Harry's article hints at British apprehension about the labor struggle. They perceived it as a significant administrative threat. There is a suspicion about potential Russian involvement behind these Malabar protests, with Harry pondering whether they were orchestrated with support from the Soviet-backed Institute of Propaganda in Asia, based in Moscow. The discourse surrounding the Malabar resistance has been subject to historical scrutiny, particularly in assessing the representation of key figures like Ali Musaliar and the events that unfolded during this period. This analysis reveals elements of truculent colonial propaganda in the documentation of these events, which shaped the narrative to serve certain political agendas of the time. Harry's assertions about the alleged training of representatives from diverse Asian nationalities in revolutionary tactics by Moscow, alongside an association of Islamic mysticism with the Soviets as the catalyst for the Malabar resistance, remain unsubstantiated and lack cohesive explanation for their linkage to the resistance movement. Furthermore, the portrayal of the strikers' actions, purportedly involving the murder of several individuals in Malabar and Ali Musaliar allegedly orchestrating 'beheadings of plantation owners and their families', bears the hallmarks of biased representation to rationalize the imposition of martial law and the subsequent tribunal judgments.

The deployment of native police, predominantly Muslims with alleged connections to the 'rebels', suggests a complex interplay of loyalties and societal affiliations during the resistance. Lord Reading's (1860–1935) initially underestimated the seriousness of the 'rebellion'. He then tried to negotiate, but there were claims of a 'holy war' being declared by the people of Malabar. This shows how complex the conflict was and how different parties responded. Moreover, the use of derogatory terms like 'religious lunatics' to describe the natives possibly reflects the prevailing colonial attitudes and prejudices. The article's claim of the formation of an interim government led by Ali Musaliar and the proclamation of independence by the people of Malabar, purportedly under the rule of the Turkish sultan, suggests a dissimilar narrative. Local sources indicate that Ali Musaliar had significant influence in Tirurangadi between 20 August and 30 August. He took initiatives to prevent intruders and culprits from engaging in illegal activities in the absence of law enforcement. According to vernacular narratives, the claims about governance under the Turkish Sultan are baseless. Captain Harry's propaganda underscores the importance of carefully re-evaluating historical sources to fully grasp the complex nature of the resistance and the diverse roles played by various actors within the sociopolitical context of the time.[11]

The portrayal of the Malabar resistance in Captain Harry's accounts is conspicuously one-sided, focusing predominantly on the attacks on Hindu landlords while neglecting the challenges faced by Muslims, especially landlords and government officials, who were also targeted during the conflict. This one-dimensional representation serves to incite sentiments while disregarding the broader sociopolitical context and grievances of all parties involved. The reliance of the article on British reports, echoing the narrative of extensive bloodshed, particularly the deaths of Englishmen and Eurasians, reflects a replication of the colonial perspective that amplified the scale and impact of the natives' actions. These reports, likely influenced by the myopic biases and objectives of the British administration, paint a picture of widespread devastation, attributing looting and destruction solely to the 'Moplah' without contextualizing the underlying reasons or complexities of the situation.

Captain Harry's role in disseminating propaganda reports, potentially embellishing accounts of villages being plundered and set ablaze, aligns with the strategic use of exaggerated narratives to justify subsequent military actions and reinforce colonial authority. The mention of numerous refugees who fled to Kozhikode and coastal regions, having lost everything, further amplifies the humanitarian toll of the conflict, yet it remains framed within the prism of the British perspective, emphasizing the victims' plight while overlooking the root causes and motivations behind the resistance.[12] The portrayal of the Malabar events in this article, focuses on the valorization of British military prowess while glossing over their potential vulnerabilities and earlier defeats.

The emphasis on the defeat of the natives by ordinary British soldiers, without acknowledging the initial fears of British forces in Kozhikode, lionizes British military might. Moreover, the depiction of the Gorkhas, while acknowledging their historical clashes and victories against the British, appears to contrast their physical characteristics with their perceived martial abilities. The narrative contextualizes the Gorkhas as a formidable force that, despite initial victories against the British, eventually entered into a treaty and aligned with British forces. This narrative of military conquest and eventual collaboration dovetails with the historical complexities and power dynamics at play during the British expansion in India. However, the portrayal seems to oversimplify the multifaceted relationships between indigenous groups and colonial powers, presenting a somewhat romanticized view of the Gorkhas' history in the broader context of British expansionism.

The portrayal of the British alliance with Nepal and the depiction of the Gorkhas as loyal allies exemplify a strategic partnership that extended beyond geopolitical boundaries, serving British interests during critical periods, such as the so-called 'Sepoy Rebellion'.[13] The narrative appears to underscore the British perception of the Gorkhas as a formidable force, capable of ruthless and relentless actions in support of British objectives. The articulation of the British attitude toward Indians, as seen in the characterization of the Gorkhas, reflects a broader colonial sentiment that emphasizes the willingness to employ extreme measures to maintain control and vigorously suppress perceived threats to British authority. The author's note about the reliance on British protection and the warning about the consequences for the people of Malabar highlights the power dynamics at play, hinting at the impending repercussions for those who opposed or challenged British dominance.

The disturbing account of the atrocities committed by the Gorkhas following their alliance with the British presents a grim picture of indiscriminate violence against civilians, including unarmed individuals, women and children. The celebration of these acts in the article is a troubling glorification of brutality and the depiction of a 'war of annihilation', wherein even surrendering individuals faced the threat of extermination. Such actions, as described, indicate a disproportionate and merciless response by the Gorkhas under the support and guidance of the British forces. This portrayal raises significant ethical and moral questions about the conduct of colonial powers and their allied forces, showcasing a distressing chapter in the history of imperial rule in India.

In a series of telegrams from 12 to 15 September 1921, the British authorities attempted to prevent Gandhi from entering the Malabar region to conceal the true situation from him. A telegram from the general officer commanding, no. 347-S., dated 12 September 1921, indicated Gandhi's planned visit to Malabar around 15 September and expressed the government's strong objection to his presence in the martial law area. Another telegram from the general officer commanding, no. S. 250/233-G., dated 13 September 1921, revealed the government's intent to hinder Gandhi from visiting Malabar or taking any action against him if he entered the martial law area. A subsequent telegram from the officer commanding, Malabar, no. M.C./247, also dated 13 September 1921, enforced orders preventing Gandhi from staying or entering the martial law area and suggested serving him with this order at Tirur. Further, a telegram from the district magistrate, Malabar, dated 14 September 1921, reported the military commander issuing an order to prohibit Gandhi from entering the martial law area and recommended informing Gandhi of this order. On 14 September 1921, a telegram from the general officer commanding, no. S. 250/238-G, addressed to Madras and others, informed about the martial law order preventing Gandhi from entering or staying in the area, urging that Gandhi be notified of the order for military reasons. In response, a telegram to the general officer commanding, no. M. 101, dated 14

September 1921, conveyed the government's approval of the order and commitment to keep him informed about Gandhi's movements. Finally, a telegram from the general officer commanding, dated 15 September 1921, reiterated the government's approval of the order concerning Gandhi and instructed to intercept him at Tirur if he entered the area. It also directed to escort him out of the area and report his destination. It becomes clear that Captain Harry's claims are merely propaganda and do not align with the reality and truth of the situation.[14]

Captain Harry's depiction of Mahatma Gandhi as a 'famous Hindu agitator' advocating nonviolent resistance against British rule aligns with historical records of his advocacy for peaceful protests and civil disobedience. However, Gandhi's involvement in Malabar, specifically his interactions with authorities on behalf of the Muslim community, appears to be presented in a skeptical light.

The claim that Gandhi advocated for mercy toward religious fighters is questioned as it is believed to be fabricated to portray the conflict as purely religious. The article's description of the cessation of hostilities only after widespread devastation emphasizes the intensity and scale of the conflict before any resolution was achieved. Moreover, the arrest and execution of key leaders accentuate the punitive measures taken by the colonial authorities to suppress the resistance, indicating a severe crackdown on dissent and resistance.

The article talks of certain groups that sought refuge in the Nilgiris and allegedly perpetrated attacks on police forces and Hindu communities, which raises questions about the complexities of post-conflict dynamics and potential ongoing tensions in the region.[15] So, the conflict continued even after the cessation of major hostilities, which points to the enduring social and political ramifications of the Malabar issues. However, it is essential to critically assess the source and veracity of these claims, given the possibility of bias or propaganda in the historical documentation. Understanding the nature of historical events like the Malabar Rebellion requires a nuanced examination of diverse perspectives and a comprehensive analysis of available sources beyond monomythical narratives.

The language used to describe the paddy fields as 'Hindu fields' indeed suggests a discriminatory lens and could signify the divisive nature of the colonial administration, which often categorized land or plantations based on the religion of the owners. In reality, similar to residents in other Indian cities and regions, the people of Malabar had taken on multiple identities and loyalties over the centuries, representing various class, religious, political and social facets and frameworks. Underneath a thin veneer of allegedly monocultural uniformity, Malabari society has always been heterogeneous: multiple social units experiencing internal conflicts on a myriad of topics, from theological to theoretical disputes over faith, race and politics and so forth. Captain Harry's accounts of the loss of lives during the Malabar conflict suggest deliberate concealment of or uncertainty about casualty figures in what could be a concerted attempt to downplay the scale of atrocities.

The incident known as the Wagon Massacre, where prisoners died due to suffocation and thirst in packed train carriages, is a harrowing example of ignominious neglect and inhumanity.[16] The official explanation provided by Captain Harry, blaming the deaths on a repainted roof obstructing ventilation, appears to be an attempt to shift responsibility away from the authorities, revealing a stark disregard for the lives and well-being of the prisoners. This representation attempts to justify these massacres through manipulation of facts and language.[17] This instance underscores the hostile nature of colonial documentation, indicating potential discrepancies and partial representations within the historical narrative that warrant critical scrutiny.

Reel Deception: The Film of British Propaganda

The narrative surrounding the identification of individuals depicted in a photo during the Malabar resistance is significant in the historical discourses. A concerted effort was made to ascertain the identities of persons featured in a photograph that had been definitively identified by the writer of a Malayalam book *Sulthan Variyamkunnan* as Variamkunnath Kunhamed Haji. The photo is the exclusive cover image for the book.[18] This endeavor involved exhaustive research across esteemed repositories including war museums, the British Library's manuscript collections and exclusive archival libraries. The British authorities had launched a complex campaign, including articles, numerous news reports and even the production of a film to justify their actions in Malabar. This film, presented as an official record under the title *The Malabar Moplah Rebellion*, was specifically commissioned by the colonial Government of India. Structured in three parts, the film extensively showcases the ravaged regions of Ernad, Manjeri, Nilambur, Valluvanad and Malappuram.[19]

In this visual narrative, Ali Musaliar is prominently depicted as the 'rebel king' and 'arch conspirator' who was sentenced to hanging. Additionally, the film emphasizes the identities of the alleged murderers responsible for the deaths of Johnstone and Rowley. This deliberate focus on identifying these individuals in the film could be perceived as a strategic move to deflect attention from the unpleasant actions of District Collector Thomas and Police Superintendent Hitchcock.[20] The advertisement of the screening of the documentary film on 5 January 1922 in *Kinematograph Weekly* intriguingly portrayed the 'Rebellion', highlighting the affected regions and claiming that the film depicted the 'murders of Rowley and Johnstone' (Fig. 3.3). It depicts the victims and the perpetrators of violence, painting a complex narrative that intertwined acts of insurgency with efforts by the British authorities to establish control and order. Moreover, the film's screening before dignitaries such as Lord and Lady Wellington at Government House in Madras lent official gravitas to its content. This suggests a deliberate attempt by British authorities to not only document but also manage the narrative surrounding the resistance, possibly to mitigate the repercussions faced by officials and assert their authority amidst the tumultuous events of the time.

The use of media, particularly documentary film making, and its advertisements published in various parts of the world emerged as a pivotal aspect in fostering and shaping colonial historical narratives. Such media were wielded strategically to construct specific portrayals of events and individuals, thereby influencing public perception

Figure 3.3
Documentary Film Advertisement Published on 5 January 1922

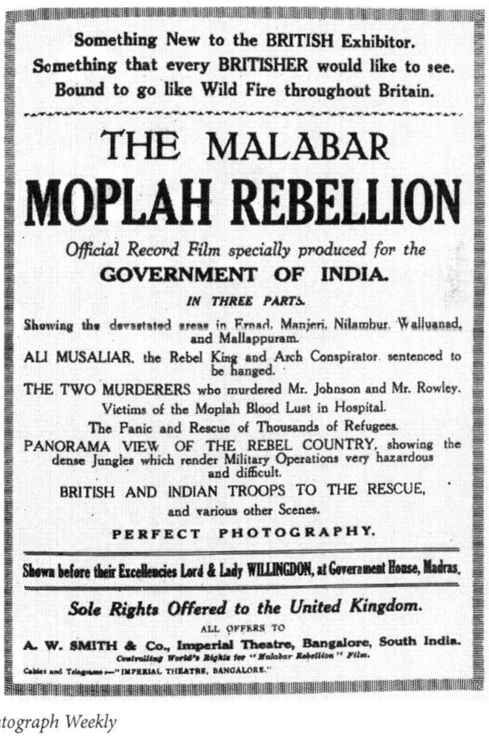

Source: Kinematograph Weekly

and potentially safeguarding the image of British authorities while attributing negative roles to natives.

This propaganda film sought to establish a clear narrative, positioning Ali Musaliar and the two highlighted figures as the primary instigators of the Tirurangadi events. Notably, official reports and correspondences indicated that the officers were killed by a mob, which complicated efforts to pinpoint specific individuals as the 'perpetrators'. The advertisement promoting the film revealed intriguing facets of its dissemination strategy. There was a deliberate effort to present the film as an asset, with A.W. Smith & Co., Imperial Theater in Bangalore, who had control over the worldwide distribution of this movie, offering sole rights to the United Kingdom. Along with advertisements, advertorials of this film were published widely. For example, a report on the film with almost all details was published in the Daily Herald.[21]

The narrative extended far beyond local boundaries, evident in its advertisement in the American publication *Motion Picture News*. The modified layout in the American edition, with captivating descriptions, targeted US exhibitors and audiences. It hints at the documentary's broad appeal and potential success to entice interest. This advertisement, featured in the January-February issue of *Motion Picture News*, hints at the propagation of a propaganda film to North America, likely to counter certain news reports about the Malabar atrocities. The urgency displayed by Thomas and Hitchcock in unveiling and publicizing the identities of those accountable for the deaths of Rowley and Johnstone emphasized a critical need within the colonial administration. They sought to absolve themselves of blame and construct a narrative that would pin responsibility on specific individuals lower down the social ladder. This move was crucial to safeguard the reputation and authority of the British administration, especially given the tumultuous events in Tirurangadi.[22]

During the centenary commemorations of the 1921 events, a photograph of Variamkunnath Kunhamed Haji sparked significant controversy. This unexpected portrayal of Haji became a focal point for certain groups aiming to leverage it for political gains and identity assertion. The full image was crucial for verifying the authenticity of claims made about the photograph. In that article of the magazine *Sciences et Voyages*, interestingly, the name of Variamkunnath Kunhamed Haji is not explicitly mentioned. The author of the book *Sulthan Variyamkunnan* (2021) attempted to decipher the name Haji from a caption that only contained the name 'Mohamed Ali'. Admitting to reading only these two words, the author speculates that 'Ali' could somehow relate to 'Ali Musaliar', insisting that 'Ali' was the sole name for Musaliar. This led to the claim of European articles attributing 'Muhamed Haji' to Variamkunnath. The author then lists several individuals who may have been involved in initiating the conflict, including Variamkunnath Kunhamed Haji, Chembrasseri Thangal, Seethi Koya Thangal, Konnara Muhamed Koya Thangal, Lava Kutti, Kunhalavi and Vadakke Vittil Mammad. Finally, the author concludes that the photo depicts Variamkunnath Haji, supported by the argument that Variamkunnath Haji was arrested on 5 January, brutally tortured on 6 January and ultimately shot dead on 20 January 1922.[23] However, a factual error emerges in the argument presented. The caption on the photo in question was affixed before Variamkunnath Kunhamed Haji was taken into the colonial custody. The advertisement of the film, claiming to have been shown before Lord and Lady Willingdon at Government House, Madras, published on 5 January 1922, in *Kinematograph Weekly*, serves as evidence that the film was produced before that date. The film capturing the image and its caption were finalized before 5 January, undermining the author's argument in this regard.[24]

The caption accompanying a pivotal image in the article describes three individuals who reportedly played significant roles in the resistance. The identification of 'Muhammed'—part of 'Muhammed Ali'—as Kunhamed Haji raises significant doubts about the accuracy of this identification. I had the opportunity to hear supporting testimony from Muhammed Ali Musaliar, the grandson of Ali Musaliar, affirming that his grandfather was named Muhammed Ali. This assertion resonates with the prevalent naming customs of that era, wherein grandchildren commonly inherited the names of their grandparents.

The caption in the propaganda article published by *Sciences et Voyages* solely mentions Ali Musaliar. In the magazine featuring 'the celebrated picture', the full photo caption reads: 'A portrait of Mohammed Ali, who was one of the main architects of the revolt. His capture and execution discouraged his supporters and led to their submission. On each side, two Moplahs who gave the signal for the uprising by murdering English settlers.' Examining materials specifically detailing the events of 20 August will be instrumental in identifying the individuals accused by the British of signaling the uprising through the murders of these two English officers. Investigating the roster of prominent individuals enlisted by the Malabar district authority and submitted to higher authorities for their alleged involvement in 'waging war against the British' is crucial. Additionally, delving into the list of individuals who were to be arrested by the British during the raid in Tirurangadi would provide valuable insights into the targeted figures and the extent of their perceived involvement in anti-British activities.

The following names were on the list of people deemed necessary for arrest under the Mappila Act of 1859. This list was put together by Hitchcock and included by Thomas as an enclosure.[25]

1. The primary figure listed was Palathumalayil Ali Musaliar, also recognized as Erikkunnan Ali Musaliar, originating from Payanad Amsam and in his sixties. His background encompassed a trajectory of religious education, transitioning from Ponnani to Podiyat in Melmuri Amsam and later relocating to Mankolam. Over the past decade, he had established his residence in Tirurangadi, occasionally visiting Nellikuth and Payanad. Hitchcock's reference to Ali Musaliar as a pivotal figure in congregating residents near the Tirurangadi *cutcherry* (*kacheri*) compound stemmed from rumors linked to a historical event—the annual commemoration of the Cherur martyrs through prayers. However, Hitchcock accused Ali Musaliar of leading processions with 'armed volunteers' every Friday and chronicled efforts to address the situation when Ali Musaliar and his adherents engaged with Retired Inspector Chekutty and the influential Jakeri (Chakeri) family. Nevertheless, according to Hitchcock's documentation, instead of resolving the matter, they persisted in recruiting additional members and fostering a combative ethos. Moreover, some members allegedly threatened the local ferry contractor at Panampuzha, expressing intentions to establish a competing ferry service in defiance of the government.[26]
2. Karadan Moideen, introduced as the principal aide to Ali Musaliar according to the colonial authority, initially pledged support in suppressing the movement during a discussion. However, Hitchcock observed that these commitments went unfulfilled, with no subsequent efforts made to honor them. Furthermore, Hitchcock pointed out Moideen's designation as the local representative of Muthu Koya Thangal, attributing to him significant influence.[27]
3. Kondachamparambil Kunhi Poker Haji was the third individual listed by Hitchcock. Similar to the previous accusations, Hitchcock noted a parallel accusation against Kunhi Poker Haji: despite being a person of influence, he had acknowledged the movement's danger but, despite assurances, continued to extend support to it. The report claimed that this man promised to help suppress the movement, but it was alleged that his promises were not fulfilled and that he had not made any attempt to fulfill them.[28]
4. Chenimathil Lava Kutti occupied the fourth position on the list and was identified as the leader of the volunteers. He was consistently noted as the first to be armed and described as an individual of lower social status yet deemed dangerous by the colonial police.[29]
5. Chittambala (Chittambalan) Kunhalavi[30]
6. Ossan Mammad[31]
7. Ossan Moideen Kutty[32]
8. Elambulasseri Moideen Kutti Haji[33]

9. Potta Mammad Maji is introduced as an elderly man. According to Hitchcock, there were around forty other volunteers whose arrest at that moment appeared unnecessary.
10. Kattillaseri Muhammad Musaliar, identified as Mangataparambil Vadakithodi Muhammad Musaliar from Valluvanad taluk, had studied for an extended period in Vellore. Hitchcock's records indicate this individual's continued involvement in the political landscape of Calicut, where he purportedly propagated a distinctive and contentious interpretation of these Khilafat movements within the Ernad and Valluvanad taluks. Recent reports emphasized Kattillaseri's notable focus on Chembrasseri and Kalikavu, regions where, as per the colonial documentation, he allegedly disseminated what was deemed as 'the most dangerous propaganda'.[34]
11. Muthal Puredath Narayana Menon, previously serving as the vakil of Angadipuram, consistently traveled alongside Kattillaseri, with their activities and whereabouts meticulously documented on a weekly basis. Notably, M.P. Narayana Menon was also listed by Hitchcock for arrest, linked to charges concerning non-cooperation and involvement in the Khilafat Movement. This underscores the diverse and interreligious complexion inherent in these movements.[35]
12. Thayil Mammad Kuty Musaliar, originating from Trikolam in Tirurangadi, shared a comparable educational background with Kattillaseri, having studied in Vellore. Hitchcock attributed to him Pan-Islamic ideologies. Prior to this report, around April or May, he was teaching at a private religious institution managed by Kiliyamannil Moidu in Kodur. Hitchcock portrayed his religious teachings as 'perilous'.[36] Thayil was initially cautioned and subsequently dismissed, following which he commenced roaming and disseminating what Hitchcock categorized as 'hazardous ideologies'.[37] The term *dangerous* within this context represents the viewpoint of the colonial administration, which saw expressions of patriotism and aspirations for peace and stability as 'hazardous'.[38]
13. Madambat Avaram Kutti Musaliar engaged in the Khilafat Movement around October or November 1920, assuming the role of an itinerant lecturer focusing on this specific topic. Hitchcock accuses him of fostering a 'fanatical spirit', holding him partially accountable for the prevalent disorder in Tanalur.[39] Notably, the absence of direct confrontation has so far forestalled any outbreak of violence.[40]
14. Aminummanthagath Parikutty Musaliar, hailing from Tanur, came under Hitchcock's scrutiny as a scholar with parallels to (Madambat) Musaliar. Parikutty Musaliar, too, began displaying a keen interest in the Khilafat Movement and authored pamphlets that Hitchcock alleged were instrumental in fomenting a 'fanatical spirit'.[41]

15. Valiyapeediakal Kunhamath Musaliar from Tirur drew Hitchcock's attention due to his role as a traveling lecturer. Hitchcock supported specific accusations, affirming that Musaliar delivered speeches in Tanalur advocating the rationale behind 'employing violence'. Crucially, Musaliar's advocacy of 'violence' aimed to address the colonial atrocities and injustices inflicted by local landlords in the area.
16. Ottagath Kunhi Koya Thangal from Chembrasseri, as Hitchcock alleged, was galvanized by Kattillaseri Muhammad Musaliar.[42]
17. P. K. Alavi Musaliar of Pangu.
18. M. Ahamathkutty Musaliar from Pangu, who was engaged in preaching alongside P.K. Alavi Musaliar, specifically at Vadakumpram in Kaipakancheri.[43]

Hitchcock, in his report, identified these eighteen individuals as highly dangerous figures. It should be noted that this list may require further elaboration, and the duration of their detention or deportation from Malabar may vary depending on their level of influence. He also noted that, behind these eighteen individuals, there were a few others who may or may not have been aware of the volatile sentiments they were inciting. Their speeches seemed to have a singular purpose: to agitate the Mappila community they addressed. In this context, they can scarcely claim ignorance of the disposition of their audience as a defense. Notably, these additional individuals included E. Moidu (who was to face prosecution for sedition), P.M. Abdul Qadir of Alleppey, Theyil Assan Koya Mulla of Calicut and Mulekandi Moidu of Calicut, as well as Umayandakath (Umayyathantagath) Kunhi Kadir of Tanur who were primarily regarded as locally significant figures.[44] In Hitchcock's account, there were variations in the spelling and family names, such as Thyil Avaran Koya Mulla and Makkad Moideen of Calicut.[45]

Hitchcock added another six people also after those descriptions.[46]

19. Karat Moideen Kutti Haji of Pukkottur.[47]
20. Kaladi Issup of Podiyat.
21. Manithodi Kunhalan of Valluvambram.
22. Kollapramban Abdu Haji of Valluvambram
23. Paradi Kunhammotti Haji of Pukkottur.
24. Khizhikat Kunhammotti Haji of Pukkottur.[48]

Hitchcock accused those individuals who were involved in the attempted Pukkottur incidents on 1 August 1921. On 16 August 1921, the report compiled by Thomas, which included Hitchcock's recommendations for the arrest of specific individuals, was formally submitted. Thomas's report highlighted the cases of Ali Musaliar, Lava Kutti, Kunhalavi, Ossan Mammath, Ossan Moideen Kutty and (Elambulasseri) Moideen Kutti Haji as subjects of particular concern. These individuals were identified as the most significant figures in the initial list that was presented to the higher authorities before the Tirurangadi raid. Thomas levied accusations characterizing them as 'dangerous' and purveyors of 'dangerous ideas'.[49] Notably, authorities from Madras had, at a prior instance, expressly cautioned Collector Thomas against any campaign targeting the Khilafat.[50]

Upon a comprehensive examination of the initial report formulated on 16 August, Variamkunnath Kunhamed Haji's absence from the list earmarked for police apprehension is conspicuous. This absence raises substantial doubts whether the man depicted in one of the photographs alongside Ali Musaliar is Variamkunnath Kunhamed, purportedly symbolizing the 'uprising' that culminated in the fatal actions against English officers on 20 August in Tirurangadi. Further scrutiny through subsequent reports and legal charges after the Tirurangadi incidents elucidated no potential connection between Haji's name and purported images in relation to these events. Notably, Variamkunnath Haji's name is absent from the roster of individuals slated for arrest in the initial list that distinctly focused on prominent figures. The specific events of 20 August, involving the tragic demise of Rowley and Johnstone, did not involve Variamkunnath Haji either. This omission highlights the lack of substantiation for identifying the man in the widely circulated image as Variamkunnan within this context.

Further, a meticulous investigation into the identities of the two individuals originally depicted on either side of Ali Musaliar in the image, designated as the two Moplahs responsible for signaling the 'uprising' by murdering British officers, emerges as a critical pursuit. Revisiting historical records through a decolonial lens reveals a narrative wherein the district magistrate and the police superintendent appear intent on attributing culpability for the killings to two specific individuals. Their primary motivations seem to revolve around avoiding scrutiny and inquiries into the events of 20 August, thereby avoiding potential repercussions and maintaining control over the narrative. My research indicates that the district magistrate's objectives were twofold: first, to establish these individuals as culprits to validate their suppression efforts, and second, to shield themselves from higher authorities' inquiries and potential consequences.[51] This emphasis led to the prominence of these two individuals, alongside Ali Musaliar, in propagandistic accounts and notably in films showcased to audiences in Britain and America. Examining British records becomes imperative to discern whom they labeled as the 'perpetrators' of the Rowley and

Johnstone killings and whom they labeled as 'instigators of the conflict'. Such an exploration is pivotal to comprehending the British perspective and the narratives constructed around these pivotal historical events.

The examination of the lists of charged individuals sheds light on crucial aspects of the Tirurangadi events. Notably, some influential figures implicated in these events are absent from the list of arrests but were purportedly involved according to the British narrative. To clarify discrepancies in attributions and understand the roles of all linked to the Tirurangadi incidents, this scrutiny involves both the initially arrested individuals and those accused but not apprehended. The absence of Variamkunnath Kunhamed Haji from these lists raises significant questions about his alleged involvement. This absence underscores the need to explore how an individual, neither associated nor accused by the British in connection to Tirurangadi, could be portrayed as an instigator responsible for the deaths of Rowley and Johnstone. Such historical inaccuracies challenge the identification of the image as Variamkunnath Haji and question its celebration during the centenary of the 1921 events. This discrepancy emphasizes the importance of a more accurate and comprehensive understanding of the historical narrative.

The publication of a list of individuals charged in connection with the Tirurangadi issues, after the arrest of Ali Musaliar and his associates marks a crucial phase in this historical context. This list highlights persons to be prosecuted under various Sections, including 121, 121-A and 122 of the IPC, as well as Section 196 of the Criminal Procedure Code. Such a publication signifies an axiomatic juncture in the legal proceedings related to the Tirurangadi events, shedding light on the severity and nature of the charges leveled against specific individuals involved in these circumstances. This development warrants a meticulous reevaluation of attributions and accounts to comprehensively understand the legal ramifications and implications for those charged in this context.

1. Palathum Mulayil alias Erikkunnan Ali Musaliar of Nellikuth
2. Kokkamparambil Rayan
3. Chelupatath Kunhi Chekku
4. Kotasseri Ahamad
5. Cheeichal Mammad Kutti
6. Mattath Said Alavi
7. Panakkal Unnian Kutti
8. Thekke Chekkingathkandi Abdu Rahiman
9. Pachengal Kunhammad
10. Chalil Pokkar
11. Achiprakaran Saidali
12. Annesseri Unnian Kutti

13. Kakkittiparambath Mammad Kutti
14. Katusseri Sooppi Kutti
15. Chembilakal Eni Haji
16. KondathPalliparambil Ahamad
17. Nechimannil Ahamad
18. Koolipulakkal Assan Kutti alias Athan
19. Nechimannil Kunhamad
20. Eeuman Mammad Kutti
21. Kizhakkepeetikakkal Kunhali
22. Charath Saidali
23. Kalathil Mammad
24. Pallipat Mayan Kutti
25. Paramban Koya Kutti
26. Kozhipurath Saidali Kutti
27. Kallan Alavi
28. Purakkat Hydru
29. Thenhilam Kunhi Moidu
30. Elambulasseri Moideen Kutty
31. Mattare Pokkayi
32. Pattalathil Kuttasseri Ahamad
33. Urunian Ahamad
34. Palasseri Ittikkal . Kunheedu
35. Karimbil Ahamad
36. Nechimannil Kunheen
37. Chemban Ali Kutty
38. Kolakkattil Kunhalan Kutty
    Section 121.

These accused surrendered at the mosque at Tirurangadi after fighting. The first thirty-eight names were modified here using the full surname from the judgment of the special tribunal.[52] The short version of surnames are used in the letter from E.F Thomas, district magistrate of Malabar District to the chief secretary to Government of Madras, dated Calicut, Magistrate, 19 September 1921, no. 410, requesting sanction for prosecution under Section 196 of the Criminal Procedure Code.[53]

1. Chembrasseri Kunhi Koya Thangal
   Section 121. He was waging war at Melathur. He was still to be captured.
2. Pulath Chek of Tiruvali
   Section 121. For waging war in Nilambur, Evidence to be collected after capture of Nilambur. He was strongly suspected of having led the band that murdered Eaton.

3. Mannazhikaran Unnian Haji, started the resistance at Karuvarakundu, was very active.
4. Elaya Nayar of Mannarghat, remanded for trial by the special tribunal.
5. Katalisseri Muhammad Musaliar.
6. Muthel Purath (Muthal Puredath) Narayana Menon. These two men must be dealt with under the 44.
7. Mozhikunnath Brahmadathan Nambudiri (Mozhikunnathu Brahmadattan Namboodiripad) collected men to assault at Cherpulcheri.
8. Umayandakath (Umayyathantagath) Puthen Veetil Kunhi Kadir of Tanur—Section 121 or 121-A. Waging war at Tirurangadi and conspiring before this (under sentence of two years). This man was charged of leading the mob at Tirurangadi which attacked from Parappanangadi and committing the 'first overt act of waging war'.[54]

The terminology of 'first overt act of waging war', 'signaling for rebellion' or 'signaling for war' stands prominently linked to the unfolding events of 20 August. Emphasizing the historical context of that day becomes pivotal in grasping the volatile climate of resistance that engulfed the region. This was largely attributed to the fervent advocacy of the Khilafat Movement, where Ali Musaliar held considerable sway in its dissemination. Notably, the report highlights the movement of Kunhi Kadir of Tanur, indicating his apparent mobilization with a force toward Ali Musaliar's relief, hinting at an intention to provide support.[55] However, the colonial report shifts the blame, attributing the outbursts to a foreseeable consequence of teachings propagated by Ali Musaliar. These events were framed as the anticipated signal for a broader resistance, strategically aligning with a narrative that positioned these occurrences as a catalyst for a widespread movement. The use of such terminology underscored the portrayal of these events as pivotal moments that heralded a larger revolution, shaping the perception of the August events as a critical juncture in the escalation of resistance within the region.[56]

Kunhi Kadir's 'Signaling for the War'

The historical document meticulously elucidates the pivotal role of Umayyathantagath Puthen Veetil Kunhi Kadir of Tanur in the resistance movement, specifically highlighting his leadership in orchestrating a 'rebel mob' in Tirurangadi. The potential legal ramifications of this action, possibly falling within the purview of Section 121 or 121-A, are underscored, particularly in Collector Thomas's report.[57] Here, Kunhi

Kadir's actions are deemed as the inaugural act in the alleged conspiracy of waging war, a perspective echoed in judicial verdicts concerning both Kunhi Kadir and Ali Musaliar.[58]

The document vividly portrays Kunhi Kadir's group as the instigators of the assault from Parappanangadi, indicating that they initiated hostilities. This portrayal seamlessly aligns with the colonial narrative, attributing Kunhi Kadir's faction's actions on 20 August as the inception of engagement with the colonial forces. Notably, there is a nuanced connection between the reported gunfire incidents, hinting at a contemporaneous sequence of events rather than discreet occurrences. This analytical interpretation presents a comprehensive view, attributing the actions of the group under the leadership of Kunhi Kadir as the commencement of the engagement with the colonial forces. This comprehensive exploration augments scholarly understanding of the sociopolitical fabric underlying this historical episode. The discourse surrounding Umayyathantagath Puthen Veetil Kunhi Kadir's involvement in historical events presents a dichotomy. Vernacular narratives contend that Kunhi Kadir and his associates were apprehended at Pantharangadi en route to Tirurangadi, absolving them of direct involvement in the incidents of 20 August.[59] Mozhikunnath states that people, under the leadership of Kunhi Kadir, surrounded the police and military to release the leaders.[60] However, British archival sources unequivocally ascribe the entirety of responsibility for 'initiating hostilities', including the engagement with 'law enforcement' and the military on that day, to Kunhi Kadir.[61]

This attribution of culpability is recurrently emphasized across a spectrum of documents, elucidating the narrative surrounding these events. Specifically, the judicial proceedings of the special court tribunal, dated 18 October 1921, prominently feature the introductory paragraph pinpointing the alleged instigation of the August confrontation by Kunhi Kadir. This initial exposition within the judgment underscores the significance placed on his purported role in the commencement of resistance during that historical period.

> It was the opening scene in the drama of the present Mappilla rebellion in Malabar and was the first of the event which have necessitated the enforcement of Martial Law. On the 20th August last the District Magistrate took troops from headquarters and surprised Tirurangadi with a view to search for concealed weapon the possession of which is forbidden by the Malabar War Knives Act, XXIV of 1845 [1854] and to effect certain arrest.[62] The case is that while the District Magistrate and troops were still at Tirurangadi the accused Umayyathantagathu Puthen Veetil Kunhi Kadir, who was

> the organizer of the Khilafat movement of Tanur, took a large armed force of Mappilla out to attack them and actually attacked the civil and military force of the Crown on the road between Parappanangadi and Tirurangadi.[63]

The judicial portrayal of the judgment as the 'opening scene in the drama' evokes a sense of irony, especially when considering the orchestrated nature of events by the district magistrate and police superintendent. This strategic maneuvering facilitated the imposition of martial law in the region. The raid conducted on 20 August, ostensibly a surprise search in Tirurangadi aimed at uncovering concealed weapons prohibited by the Malabar War Knives Act of 1854, yielded feeble results. The absence of weapons in the mosque, coupled with the conspicuous lack of protest or resistance during the raid, undermined the veracity of the district magistrate's assertions regarding the presence of such armaments in the locality. This initial setback stands in stark contrast to the subsequent narrative within the judgment. It unequivocally implicates Umayyathantagath Puthen Veetil Kunhi Kadir, suggesting his leadership of a substantial armed force in an attack against both civil and military authorities. This abrupt shift in the narrative, from a lack of evidence during the raid to an explicit accusation of armed aggression, delineates a puzzling dichotomy within the judicial discourse surrounding these historical events. The case of Ali Musaliar was notably perceived by the colonial administration as a significant trial of the Khilafat Movement figurehead. This case intricately interlinked events from the life of Umayyathantagath Puthen Veetil Kunhi Kadir to establish that his initial attempt to incite an attack served as the primary impetus behind the tumultuous events on 20 August. The judgment in the case of Ali Musaliar vividly portrayed the colonial disdain for the Parappanangadi group, portraying them as aggressors who attacked the military and police.[64]

From the colonial perspective articulated within this judgment, this event was construed as the initiation of war in Malabar, with Kunhi Kadir directly linked as the orchestrator of this incendiary act. This judgment methodically connected the preceding events with the subsequent altercation, resulting in the loss of two British officers' lives. Notably, prominent leaders and freedom fighters met with a harsh fate under martial law, among them Kunhi Kadir, the Khilafat secretary and chief of Tanur, who valiantly endeavored to aid Ali Musaliar at Tirurangadi. Kunhi Kadir's interception by troops between Parappanangadi and Tirurangadi marked his immersion into the resistance movement. Subsequently, he was apprehended, tried by a special tribunal and sentenced to hanging.

> Mr. Rowley and 2nd Lieutenant Johnstone went to meet a mob on the East of the *kacheri*. Then at the *kacheri* information was received that a large mob was coming from Parappanangadi side to attack the troops and the police. So a party of reserve constable under Mr. Mainwaring and Mr. Hitchcock left Tirurangadi about 11 o'clock to meet them. A small party of Leinsters went with them. Two miles from Tirurangadi they met a mob numbering more than 8,000, who were armed with knives and sticks. There was a standard beam with the Khilafat flag. Kunhi Khader was the leader. The Mappillas attacked the troops, who fired in return and some of the mob were killed and Kunhi Khader was captured along with others. The police and troops returned to Tirurangadi. The police party that was there being attacked by another mob which had also to be dispersed by fire. It was then learnt that Messers. Rowley, Johnstone, and head constable Mohi-nd-din had been killed by the mob and that another head constable and a constable were missing. In the evening the mutilated dead bodies of Messrs. Rowley and Johnstone were found on the public road and also the dead body of Mohi-nd-din.[65]

The colonial records linked the first and second attacks on the police party. The subsequent firings in response were deemed necessary to disperse the agitators, with little regard for the substantial loss of life incurred. Instead, the focus was directed toward the deaths of Rowley, Johnstone and head constable Moideen, which are prominently highlighted in the colonial documentation. The British asserted that the evening discovery of the mutilated bodies of Rowley and Johnstone, along with Moideen's corpse, on the public road was a result of the actions of the mob. A pivotal sensitivity emerged regarding who struck the initial blow on Rowley, a detail that had significant ramifications within the colonial administration. The colonial authorities meticulously aimed to specify the killers of these officers by their full names and provide intricate details. This selective emphasis on these two fatalities led to their prominence in earlier lists, presenting them as pivotal elements in creating a convincing narrative.

A report in the *Englishman* newspaper, dated 13 October, encapsulated the intricate nuances of the 'Moplah Trails'. Noteworthy in its contents is a specific focus on the legal proceedings concerning the secretary of the Khilafat Committee, marked by a distinct subheading underscoring the weight of the evidence presented. Originating from Calicut on 4 October, despite its eventual publication on 13 October, the report offers comprehensive insights into the legal corollaries faced by Kunhi Kadir.

> The special tribunal was renegaded today in hearing the case in which Kunhi Kadir, Secretary of Khilafat committee, was charged with waging war against the King Emperor under the section 121 (A) IPC. According to the prosecution the accused collected large number of Moplahs and preached to them to wage war against the King Emperor for the subversion of the government established by the law and replacing the same by a Khilafat Kingdom. With that object in view, he collected a large mob went to Tirurangadi on 20th August and joined Ali Musaliar's party and fought against our forces. The chief witness of the prosecution were Khan Bahadur E. V. Amoo, deputy superintendent of police and Mr. N. E. G. Mainwaring, D. I. G. at Police.[66]

In the comprehensive report, the testimony of the witness Amoo (Amu), the deputy superintendent of police, of the events that unfolded in Tirurangadi on 20 August was thoroughly outlined. Deputy Superintendent Amu's testimony notably specified the tragic deaths of the English officers Rowley and Johnstone, categorizing these killings among the array of charges brought against Kunhi Kadir. Additionally, the report underscores Kadir's alleged involvement in the manufacture of weaponry, alongside his apprehension from a mosque setting. Further strengthening the account, the report emphasizes Mainwaring's validation of Deputy Superintendent Amu's testimony, thus fortifying the case against Kadir. The report expounds on the motive behind the British officers' tragic deaths as integral components of the accusations levied against Kunhi Kadir. This narrative found resonance in not only British reports but also subsequent judicial determinations. Consequently, arguments propagated by certain individuals erroneously associating Kunhi Kadir's photograph with that of Variamkunnath Kunhamed Haji, while suggesting Kadir's arrest occurred before the Tirurangadi incident and before the deaths of Johnstone and Rowley, appear to lack substantive support in the primary sources highlighted in these reports.[67]

Lava Kutti's Initial Strike against Rowley

Hitchcock crafted a fabricated narrative to highlight the individuals deemed responsible for the fatalities of the two British officers. Employing a presentation style reminiscent of an eyewitness account, Hitchcock intricately details scenes that purportedly unfolded during these incidents. This narrative seems to draw heavily upon the district magistrate's preceding reports and communications with higher authorities. This use of established sources appears calculated, intended to bolster the official rendition of events. Hitchcock's narrative construction seems to serve a dual purpose: safeguarding the established authority's stance while placing the entire weight of responsibility for the events squarely upon the local populace of the region.

> Ali Musaliar and the Tirurangadi Mappilla knew that this was all the result of a lie they had started; now they must put into practice the theories they had so long taught, so they began by butchering an unfortunate constable. This was the work of Narakatil Kunhappa and Melothil Mammath, both of Tirurangadi. The rifle and the bicycle were taken into the Mosque. The Vengara and Kottakkal party wanted to press on too, and on the withdrawal of the 30 police to the courthouse marched to the mosque in a body where they were joined by the Tirurangadi party. It was then they saw Mr. Rowley coming. The Tirurangadi party had just tasted blood and it was their chief, Lava Kutti, who struck the first blow when Mr. Rowley went near with head constable No. 133, Moideen, a local Mappilla head constable who had been reporting on their activities for months and had for long been an object of hatred to the Khilafat party. Once the blow was struck it was not difficult to cut down Mr. Johnstone and head constable No. 728, Govindan Nayar, who rushed to Mr. Rowley's Assistance, it was only when firing started that they scattered, leaving behind the rifle taken from the constable recently murdered. A small party then returned to the Tirurangadi mosque; the main body collected at the Panampuzha ferry.[68]

The analysis of the statement about Ali Musaliar and the awareness within the Tirurangadi community presents contrasting viewpoints. One perspective suggests that Ali Musaliar and the local populace were knowledgeable about orchestrating events, diverging from the narrative that the entire incident stemmed from misinformation stage-managed by the district magistrate and executed by the police superintendent. In this alternate narrative, Hitchcock appears to deflect attention away from the actual circumstances, blaming Ali Musaliar and the community, thereby obscuring the genuine sequence of events. Hitchcock's narrative, anchoring the inception of violence on the unfortunate killing of a constable, faces scrutiny against divergent accounts sourced from various documents and local testimonies. Contrary evidence challenges Hitchcock's depiction, suggesting that the violence on 20 August originated from the British side. Eyewitness reports indicate that unarmed individuals, seeking information about those arrested, faced gunfire from British authorities, resulting in multiple casualties among the gathered crowd.[69]

Moreover, Hitchcock's account implicates specific individuals in the constable's demise, such as Narakatil Kunhappa and Melothil Mammath, elucidating discrepancies in attributing the initial act of violence and spotlighting individuals allegedly involved in the constable's death and ensuing events. In Hitchcock's narrative of Rowley's death, a comprehensive sequence unfolds: A larger assembly that included groups from Vengara and Kottakkal converged with the Tirurangadi party. This assembly's observation of Rowley, after the withdrawal of thirty police officers to the courthouse, forms a crucial juncture in Hitchcock's depiction. Notably, Hitchcock accuses Lava Kutti, identified as the purported leader of the Tirurangadi group, of initiating the fatal act. This portrayal aligns with a broader propagandist narrative that relied on photographic evidence to underscore the alleged involvement of specific individuals in pivotal events. However, an intriguing contrast arises in Hitchcock's narrative of Johnstone's death, where no individual is accused. While Hitchcock details the sequence leading to Rowley's demise and implicates Lava Kutti, a lack of similar specificity is evident in the account of Johnstone's fate. This discrepancy in specificity between the depictions of Rowley and Johnstone prompts scholarly curiosity, inviting a deeper examination into the selective emphasis and narrative construction within Hitchcock's rendition.[70]

Some reports added that Kunhalavi was also probably involved in Rowley's death. It is clear from the vernacular narrative that it was not easy to identify one person who killed Rowley or Johnstone. British accusations, cases and tribunal judgments were trying to identify a specific person so the district magistrate could evade responsibility. Tottenham, on 15 September 1921, raised the need to revisit Tirurangadi due to the rumors of a gathering again at Taurangadi, headed by Kunhalavi and Lava Kutti, adding that these people were probably responsible for Rowley's murder.[71] When there was an attack on Kunhalavi on 23 September 1921, Tottenham mentioned the probability of Kunhalavi's involvement in Rowley's murder.[72] Then, on 23 December, the colonial forces killed Kunhalavi and M. Abdulla Kutti along with five others. The possibility of Kunhalavi's involvement in Rowley's murder was raised to justify these killings without any chance of a trial. Abdulla Kutti's case was similarly justified by labelling him as a criminal who had been rescued from Manjeri prison.[73] The colonial administration under Thomas and Hitchcock did not allow these individuals any opportunity to appear in court, even under martial law.

Analysis of Transitions in Governance Structures and Power Dynamics

Thomas's account details the police opening fire in what is described as an act of self-defense, noting that no explicit command was given due to the tumultuous uproar. The firing caused the crowd to retreat a short distance. Subsequently, the firing ceased, and the police force proceeded to drive the crowd back, apprehending several individuals. As they were driven back toward Parappanangadi station, the crowd diminished in numbers, with some individuals evading capture by escaping into nearby fields. Thomas further describes the road conditions, noting the presence of cudgels, Khilafat caps and banners strewn along the route. A specific mention is made of a Khilafat banner, seized at the onset of the unrest, with the bearer reportedly wounded and later succumbing to the injuries. The manipulation in the death statement of the Khilafat flag bearer is noteworthy. It appears to have been carefully composed to substantiate the narrative that the firing was carried out in self-defense and that the actions taken by the police were a response to imminent threats:

> Before he died, he gave a dying statement to my Assistant Collector. Though the police opened fire in sheer self-defense without a word of command, I am satisfied having been present that no more force was used than was necessary to disperse this who had remained at Parappanangadi and whose conduct has been quite commendable, that the mob, probably the mob we had driven back, with additions from Parappanangadi had sacked the railway station.[74]

It appears that a purported statement ascribed to a flag bearer prior to their demise was accompanied by a body of evidence, a majority of which was purportedly fabricated within the administrative domain. This situation warrants a critical examination of the veracity and origins of the statement and accompanying evidence to highlight potential discrepancies between the claimed source and the administrative handling of the documentation. Further investigation into this matter may shed light on the accuracy and reliability of the information presented. The collector's discernment that the situation had gone beyond the capabilities of civil authorities to manage effectively led to the request for intervention from Captain McEnroy, entrusting him with comprehensive military control of the situation. This decision signifies an acknowledgment of the gravity and intricacy of the circumstances, which prompted the transfer of authority to a higher-ranking military figure. It reflects an understanding of the escalating unrest's complexity, necessitating a shift in leadership to address the escalating challenges.

Conclusion

The dissemination of a photograph purported to depict Kunhamed Haji has engendered pronounced schisms in communities, eliciting fervent support from some quarters and staunch opposition from others. Initially, the academic reception of this photograph was circumspect, primarily due to the unavailability of the original pages from the magazine in which it was formerly published. The opacity maintained by both the publisher and the author's team of *Sulthan Variyamkunnan* further compounded reservations regarding its authenticity. Subsequently, the emergence of a new photograph garnered substantial favor among a broad spectrum of the general populace, achieving virality across diverse media landscapes—both social and traditional. In response to this discourse, I initiated a discussion by publishing a comprehensive accumulation of all pages from the 1922 French magazine *Sciences et Voyages*. The incorporation of these photographs in the magazine appears intricately linked to a coordinated effort within British administrative and military spheres to construct a narrative aligned with vested interests. This narrative seemingly operated to shield the actual culprits responsible for the firing upon the public while also exonerating signal officers, thereby substantiating a rationale for initiating a conflict within the region. Within this context, it becomes imperative to ascertain the identities of the personalities in these images, given that the narratives they constructed were methodically formulated within administrative echelons and extensively propagated across a spectrum of propaganda channels. Unraveling the origins and motivations underlying these propagandistic efforts is pivotal to comprehend the manufactured narrative and its underlying objectives.

Notably, regardless of the photograph's authenticity in depicting Haji, its veracity does not detract from Haji's significant role in the freedom movement and his staunch advocacy within the Non-Cooperation Movement. His documented correspondences with the *Hindu* and American media endure as tangible evidence of his steadfast dedication to fostering intercultural and interreligious engagements. However, the incidents in Malabar and the context of the photograph did not derive from religious schisms but were entangled with the colonial strategy of sowing discord through their divisive 'divide and rule' policy.

Chapter 4

ENDURING LEGACY

The Significance of Hindu–Muslim Harmony Amid Struggles

This chapter elucidates the profound implications of the Non-Cooperation and Khilafat Movements in the Malabar region, delineating the intricacies of their influence. As these movements traversed Malabar, the colonial administration strategically accentuated issues of communal division, notably demarcating the Khilafat Movement as primarily a Muslim-centric affair, thereby dissociating it from the broader canvas of the Non-Cooperation Movement. Consequently, the involvement and contributions of other communities in the collective struggle against colonial subjugation were consistently sidelined in the official colonial discourse. Central to this analysis is an examination of the contextual exigency and relevance of the Khilafat Movement in Malabar, diverging from its implications in the northern regions of India. This comparative study scrutinizes the nuanced sociopolitical landscapes, dissecting the distinct regional exigencies within the broader tapestry of the Indian independence movement. Moreover, this chapter accentuates the harmony amid the turbulence of struggles in Malabar. Despite concerted efforts by the British administration to propagate discord along communal lines, this narrative elucidates instances of notable cohesion and solidarity that persisted amidst adversity. The exploration of this communal accord, juxtaposed against the backdrop of British propagandist disruption, serves as a critical focal point in this chapter. It unveils the resilience and collective unity exhibited by diverse communities during a pivotal phase marked by relentless resistance against colonial hegemony.

The Khilafat Movement: Prioritizing Political Dissent and Mobilizing Protest

In the crucible of Malabar's historical trajectory, we find the emergence of mass movements that fundamentally transformed the political landscape and posed formidable challenges to the colonial authorities. These sociopolitical developments were further catalyzed by the steadfast commitment of the local populace within the paradigm of the Non-cooperation Movement. Notably, this period witnessed the emergence of charismatic leaders such as Ali Musaliar, whose unwavering leadership endeavored to rally the general public toward a common cause. Of profound significance, the Malabar narrative also heralded a rare phenomenon: the harmonious convergence of Hindus and Muslims. This coalition was underpinned by a shared objective—to oust the oppressor—and a collective aspiration for peaceful coexistence in the region. Against this backdrop, the Khilafat Movement (1919–1924), a pan-Islamist political protest campaign led by such as Shaukat Ali, Maulana Mohammad Ali Jauhar, Hakim Ajmal Khan and Abul Kalam Azad in British India, assumed a peculiar and somewhat tangential relevance in the context of Malabar. Herein lies the essence of this discourse; in Malabar, the historical tapestry of anti-colonial resistance had been woven with threads of unity, binding Muslims and non-Muslims in a shared 'Jihad' to safeguard the throne of the Hindu king, the Zamorin of Calicut.

While the Khilafat Movement found fertile ground in the communal mosaic of north India, its transplant into the Malabar milieu appears incongruous. The Malabar narrative had long been punctuated by the resolute involvement of Muslim leaders and scholars in the struggle against colonial dominion, in concert with their non-Muslim counterparts. The pan-Islamic impetus, as epitomized by the Khilafat Movement, appeared misplaced in the Malabar narrative. Here, venerated Sufi leaders had already declared non-cooperation by withholding tax payments to the British government. Before the ascendancy of the Khilafat Movement, stalwarts such as Mamburam Thangal had waged valiant battles against the British, thus laying the groundwork for Muslim resistance. In the Malabar context, the restoration of the khalifa of the Ottoman Empire and the propagation of Muslim interests assumed marginal relevance and were scarcely articulated in the political agenda. The distinctive legal traditions of Malabar and the burgeoning influence of Sufi movements engendered an indigenized manifestation of Islam.[1] Here, the focal point remained anchored in the veneration of the Zamorin as the *amir*, obviating the imperative for a Muslim khalifa. This nuanced and distinct trajectory elucidates the intellectual merit of divergent narratives within the broader canvas of colonial resistance in Malabar.

British colonial historiography labelled the Mughal and Delhi Sultanates as Muslim rulers, but Sanskrit historical resources accepted those sovereigns beyond their religious beliefs. *The History of India, as Told by Its Own Historians*, which was prepared by Henry Miers

Elliot (1808–1853), a colonial civil servant who worked with the East India Company in India for twenty-six years, depicted the earlier invaders' political narratives as the history of Muslims. It was an official attempt by the British colonial power to show that their rule was better than their predecessors by showcasing repugnant actions by earlier conquerors. Their historical extracts, with the support of 'native historians', characterized rule by earlier conquerors as 'Musulman despotism' based on the religion of the head of state. This book tells the history of Islam in northern India only; southern Muslim communities are completely neglected in the text.[2]

The History of India, as Told by Its Own Historians overlooks the south, where Muslim communities thrived under the patronage of non-Muslim kings, enjoying various privileges. Muslim leaders considered Hindu kings as their protectors who ensured the preservation of Islamic law and Muslim culture. Surprisingly, the unique history of Malabar is largely absent from the narratives curated by Henry Miers Elliot. Nonetheless, a wealth of historical texts penned by local historians during the 16th century was available, with the British authorities collecting and preserving many of these manuscripts in the British Library. Furthermore, some of these texts were translated into English. So, it becomes evident that colonial historiography selectively disregarded these narratives to uphold their own hypotheses. The British habit of attributing plunders, burglaries and atrocities to earlier rulers based only on their religion was criticized by Romila Thapar, who observed that destructive activities and looting were always part of imperial conquest but seldom tied to the conqueror's religion.[3] This was expressed in the literature through Persian 'epics of conquest' and Hindi 'epics of resistance', the first intended for a Muslim audience and the second for a Hindu audience. Hence, there were epics of conquest and resistance in India before the coming of those labelled 'Muslim rulers'.[4] Sanskrit sources referred to invaders from the Iranian plateau not by their religion but by their linguistic identity and communal sentiments. Indo-Persian history specifically narrated the vernacular affiliations and traditions of the rulers of South Asia.[5] Even the British approach of considering the religion of the conquerors was not applicable to South India, where local kings ruled and provided privileges to various religious and cultural groups.

In the unique context of Malabar, pan-Islamism was not an absolute necessity for Muslim communities to participate in the Non-Cooperation Movement. It was a misunderstanding on the part of Mahatma Gandhi and Maulana Shaukat Ali, driven by their experiences in and expertise from northern India. When they extended the Malabar Muslims' participation to align with the broader pan-

Indian Non-Cooperation Movement, they introduced the Khilafat Movement to Malabar. Hindu and Muslim leaders from Malabar then united in the larger current of Pan-Indian non-cooperation efforts. However, in later times, the Khilafat Movement was exploited to brand Muslim leaders as fanatical. This narrative also shifted the focus away from the accounts of the challenges faced by Hindu landlords who supported the British, bringing Hindu–Muslim issues to the forefront while concealing the stories of Muslim landlords who endured similar hardships due to their support for the British administration.

The national background of Jamal al-Din al-Afghani (1838–1897) has been a subject of quite considerable historical controversy. According to his account, he was born in Asadabad, near Kabul, Afghanistan. However, some popular theories, supported by Nikki R. Keddie and accepted by a number of scholars, suggest that he was born and raised in a Shia family in Asadabad near Hamadan, Iran. Jamal al-Din al-Afghani's allegiance to the British has also been a topic of academic discussion. He initially received a home education and later pursued further studies in Qazvin, Tehran, and eventually in present-day Iraq. In books published in Afghanistan, he adopted names like 'al-Kabuli'.[6] It is believed that he later claimed an Afghan origin to better influence Sunni Muslims. There are numerous controversies surrounding the life of this pan-Islamist figure. Abdul Hamid II (1842–1918), the head of the Ottoman Empire, introduced a pan-Islamist agenda to safeguard the Ottoman Empire from internal and external threats. Jamaluddin Afghani, who was dedicated to the mission of Sultan Abdul Hamid II, was sent to India in the late 19th century, where he promoted pan-Islamic approaches among Indian Muslims. Abdul Hamid II sought to be recognized as the khalifa of the entire Muslim world. This idea of political Islam was promoted by the sultanate, and north Indian Muslims became subjects of this propaganda, which was in contrast to the earlier indigenized and integrated forms of Islam in Malabar.[7]

The Khilafat Movement is a subject of intense scholarly debate, eliciting a spectrum of opinions. In academic discourse, it is scrutinized both for its political underpinnings grounded in pan-Islamist and fundamentalist ideologies and its perceived detachment from the overarching Indian independence struggle. Concurrently, academicians of various orientations engage in multifaceted analyses that underscore the Khilafat Movement as a pivotal precursor to the Non-Cooperation Movement in India, emphasizing its role in fostering ameliorated Hindu–Muslim relations. Moreover, within the ambit of scholarly exploration, proponents of Pakistan and advocates of Muslim separatism recognize the Khilafat Movement as a seminal stride toward the eventual establishment of a separate Muslim state.[8]

Formation of Khilafat Committees

During World War I, the British government issued a proclamation designed to assuage the concerns of its Muslim subjects. This declaration entailed a solemn commitment to safeguard the sanctity of Muslim holy sites in Arabia and Mesopotamia and the crucial port of Jeddah. An additional facet of this pledge was the explicit assurance of non-interference with the Haj pilgrimage. This proclamation, while ostensibly an act of reassurance, instigated a complex conundrum for Muslims who were simultaneously legal subjects of the British Empire and devoted followers of Islam. This enigma can be distilled into a dichotomous predicament. On one hand, aligning with the Ottoman Empire, which was perceived as an act of support for the caliph, was fraught with accusations of treason. Conversely, opting to confront the caliph by siding with the British, despite the earnest assurances articulated by British prime minister Lloyd George regarding the preservation of Turkey's territorial integrity and the inviolability of Muslim holy sites, risked being construed as an affront to the Caliphate.[9] Within this historical context, it is conventionally held that these apprehensions of the Muslim populace significantly contributed to the genesis of the Khilafat Movement, ultimately resulting in a wave of organized agitation. However, meticulous scholarly inquiry has revealed a more nuanced narrative, characterized by a notable degree of British administrative involvement in the instigation and orchestration of this movement. Furthermore, subsequent events underscore how the Khilafat Movement was, in due course, deployed by British authorities to undermine the cohesion of Muslim–Hindu unity, particularly in disparate regions of the subcontinent. The case in point, the Malabar region, provides a salient illustration of this phenomenon.[10]

The Khilafat Conference convened on 22 September 1919 under the leadership of the Ali brothers, Maulana Abul Kalam Azad, Hakim Ajmal Khan and Hazrat Mohani and was presided over by Bengal leader A.K. Fazal-ul-Haque, who emphasized the need to secure the cooperation of Hindus to ensure the success of the Khilafat Movement.[11] The All-India Khilafat Conference, held on 19 November 1919 in Delhi made a crucial decision under the guidance of Mahatma Gandhi. It resolved to withdraw cooperation with the British government, a decision initially advised by Gandhi, and subsequently reaffirmed by Muslim gatherings in Calcutta and other locations, as well as by the Madras Khilafat conference on 17 April 1920.[12] To deliberate on the Khilafat question, a joint conference of Hindus and Muslims convened in Delhi on 23 and 24 November 1919. Mahatma Gandhi attended this meeting and presided over it on 24 November. During the proceedings, he staunchly advocated non-cooperation as a means to address the grievances related to the Khilafat issue.[13] At the Bengal Provincial Khilafat conference held in Calcutta, presided over by Abul Kalam Azad, Maulana Abdul Bari delivered a compelling speech and conveyed that the Muslims of India would renounce their loyalty to the British government.[14] The emergence of Gandhi as a leading figure in the national movement and his support for the Khilafat Movement breathed new life into nationalist aspirations. However, notably, the colonial administration strategically leveraged this confluence of movements to serve their own vested interests, using their influential media resources. Gandhi perceived the Khilafat Movement as an opportunity of uniting Hindus and Muslims, especially in the north Indian region.[15]

1 June 1920: All-Party Hindu–Muslim Conference

In June 1920, Mahatma Gandhi aligned himself with the prominent leaders of the Khilafat Movement, which culminated in the formulation of the agenda for non-cooperation. Two significant gatherings took place on 1 June 1920 in Allahabad: the All India Khilafat Conference and the All-Party Hindu–Muslim Conference. These gatherings focused on deliberations concerning the decisions of the Central Khilafat Committee. However, differences of opinion among Congress leaders created an impasse, hindering the achievement of a harmonious consensus about the Non-Cooperation Movement. In response to this challenge, the Indian National Congress resolved to convene a special meeting on 11 September 1920 in Calcutta. During this subsequent special session, support coalesced around Gandhi's proposal for non-cooperation with the British government until injustices in the Punjab and related to the Khilafat issue were redressed, and the aspiration for Swaraj was realized. As part of this strategy, people were encouraged to boycott government-run educational institutions, law courts and legislative bodies.[16] However, within the specific context of Malabar, a pertinent question arises: Why did nationalist leaders become enmeshed in the Khilafat Movement, which, in hindsight, appears to have been manipulated by colonial authorities to further their policy of divide and rule, effectively segmenting the nation along religious lines? This question underscores the complexity of the historical dynamics at play during that period and the multifaceted motivations and influences that shaped the decisions of leaders and movements in the broader struggle for Indian independence.

The British colonial administration in Malabar produced a series of reports that underscored the escalating influence of the 'Turky Khilafat' movement within the region. These reports held significant strategic value for colonial authorities as they provided a potential lever for stressing religious divisions among a populace where Muslims and Hindus had hitherto coexisted without confessional distinctions, owing to the region's integrated social dynamics. Notably, the emergence of 'the waves of Pan-Islamism' among traditional Sufi Muslims in Malabar was documented. This development, as articulated in a letter authored by F.C. Brown, a planter in the Malabar District, bore indications of being both misguiding and aligning with the broader colonial administrative strategy. This approach leveraged the Khilafat Movement, among other factors, to advance imperial objectives, thereby fostering an environment that ran counter to the prevailing ethos of interfaith unity and collaboration.[17]

The colonial administration astutely seized upon this juncture as a golden opportunity to impugn the loyalty of the Malabar region's Muslim populace to Turkey and, concurrently, to instigate a schism between them and the Hindu community. Charles Alexander Innes (1874–1959) reported a conspicuous episode in which the Muslim community in Malabar engaged in a continuous forty-day prayer at the Perinthalmanna Mosque, explicitly in solidarity with Turkey. It was a strategy to heighten religious sentiments, linking the Khilafat movement exclusively with mosques and highlighting the extended duration of the prayer, to foster aversion and alienation in the Hindu community and weaken their support for the Khilafat Movement. An antecedent British colonial official report concerning the Muslims of Malabar, predicated on the Political Conference of Malabar conducted in 1916 in Palakkad and the successive annual conferences held in Thalasseri, Vadakara and Manjeri, described a pronounced sense of communal cohesion and unity among the Mappila community. The British administration acknowledged the enduring support that the Mappila population had extended to their co-religionists, a sentiment that had been underscored in their earlier assessments.[18]

28 and 29 April 1920: The Manjeri Conference—Exploring Ideological Divides, Landlord Support and Annie Besant's Influence

The resistance to colonial powers in the Malabar region was based on a legacy of anti-colonial struggles passed down through generations, thereby ingrained in the collective consciousness of the populace. Contrary to the assertion of British propaganda, the substantial Muslim participation in these events, such as the Manjeri conference held on

28–29 April 1920, was not solely driven by external influences. Subsequent analysis has shed light on the motivations behind the pronounced Muslim involvement in the Manjeri conference. The British colonial authorities, recognizing the significance of the event, were apprehensive due to its diverse attendance, which represented a cross-section of society. Consequently, they formulated strategies aimed at eroding the communal unity, particularly between Hindus and Muslims.[19] R.H. Hitchcock's perturbation about the Manjeri conference was rooted in Manjeri's significance as the administrative hub of Ernad Taluk. This centrality attracted participants from a wide spectrum of societal strata.[20] Particularly notable was the key role assumed by Kasturi Ranga Ayyangar, the esteemed editor of *The Hindu* newspaper, who presided over the conference. These converging factors engendered a milieu of considerable complexity and consequence. Furthermore, the Manjeri conference witnessed pronounced schisms among prominent Congress leaders. On one end of the ideological spectrum, figures such as Annie Besant and Rama Ayer, frequently aligned with the vested interests of landlords, vociferously voiced their reservations regarding armed anti-colonial resistance. In contrast, a distinct faction, championed by luminaries such as K.P. Keshava Menon, Madhavan Nair, M.P. Narayana Menon and Ponmadath Moideen Koya, lent its unwavering support to the cause of tenants, laborers and the common citizenry. This intricate tableau not only underscores the diverse composition of the conference's attendees but also highlights the nuanced schisms within the overarching anti-colonial movement.[21]

In the discourse about the Khilafat resolution at the Manjeri conference, Annie Besant articulated apprehensions about to the potential infusion of religious dimensions into the broader context of the independence movement. Her reservations seemed to be influenced by what can be characterized as a regional bias with a 'North Indian hangover'. However, the support for the Khilafat cause transcended regional and religious boundaries among Congress leaders. This support was not merely rooted in personal motivations aimed at fostering interfaith coexistence and collaboration with Muslims in their respective regions. Furthermore, the Khilafat Movement did not originate naturally in the Malabar Muslim community; instead, it was introduced to the region through the efforts of Mahatma Gandhi as a complementary facet of the Non-Cooperation Movement. Most delegates at the conference demonstrated a pronounced inclination toward deliberating upon the Khilafat resolution. Notably, the responsibility of presenting the motion fell upon Komu Menon. In the resolution, a fervent call was issued to the government, beseeching it to address the Turkish question in alignment with the equitable and legitimate sentiments of Indian Muslims, as well as in adherence to the solemn commitments of British ministers. Furthermore, the resolution exhorted the populace to embrace a strategy of progressive non-cooperation with the government should it fail to resolve the issue in accordance with these principles.[22] Nevertheless, Annie Besant introduced an amendment that cautioned against advocating non-cooperation, characterizing it as an adventurous course of action. This stance faced staunch opposition from prominent leaders, including M.P. Narayana Menon, Moideen Koya and K.P. Kesava Menon, who delivered impassioned speeches in defense of the original resolution. Ultimately, the amendment was rejected, and the resolution, in its unaltered form, garnered overwhelming support. This episode underscores the spirited intellectual discourse and divergent perspectives within the conference.[23]

The Manjeri conference, a seminal event held in the Malabar region, notably espoused the non-cooperation resolution several months in advance of its formal adoption by the Indian National Congress. This proactive stance carried significant ramifications, particularly for the intertwined issues of agrarian tenancy and non-cooperation. It resulted in the withdrawal of substantial segments of the aristocratic class, commonly referred to as '*jenmis*', from active participation in the broader national movement. Concurrently, the conference resolutions on agrarian tenancy and the Khilafat issue played pivotal roles in mobilizing the natives, effectively integrating them in the fabric of the Congress movement.[24]

The earlier conference in Palakkad was mainly attended by landlords, but the Manjeri conference saw greater participation from the common people in the region. The significant number of attendees at the Manjeri conference, especially in the context of the Khilafat question, was highlighted. This perspective resembles the colonial narrative and aligns with the arguments advanced by Annie Besant. This narrative, in practice, tends to sideline the contributions of non-Muslim regional leaders who participated without necessarily foregrounding their individual agendas.[25] Beyond these intricacies, the Manjeri conference in Malabar serves as a testament to intercommunal unity, notably under the leadership of figures such as M.P. Narayana Menon and Kattilasseri Muhammed Musaliar.[26]

This event served as a catalyst for heightened scrutiny by the British administration of the Khilafat and Non-Cooperation Movements in the Malabar region, consequently giving rise to allegations and the propagation of colonial propaganda. In response to this heightened attention and as part of their strategic response, leaders of the Indian

National Congress tried to establish Khilafat movements in various taluks across the region.[27] Integral to the success of these movements was the active participation and support garnered from preexisting tenancy and non-cooperation committees. These committees, deeply rooted in local communities, played instrumental roles in organizing and disseminating the principles of the Khilafat Movement. Notably, many of these committees coexisted under the same organizational structure, fostering a cooperative and coordinated approach to advancing their shared goals. The leaders of these movements included figures representing both Hindu and Muslim communities, collectively engaged in propagating the ideals of Khilafat and non-cooperation. Furthermore, the translation and distribution of pamphlets emerged as a crucial mechanism for disseminating the principles and objectives of these movements. Particularly noteworthy was the translation of significant texts such as Abul Kalam Azad's *'Tarke-e-Muwalat'—Non-cooperation* and the fatwas issued by the central Khilafat Committee. These translated materials found their way into the public sphere, with mosques and Khilafat meetings serving as key distribution points. This concerted, collaborative and multilingual dissemination strategy contributed significantly to the widespread acceptance and integration of the Khilafat and Non-Cooperation Movements throughout the Malabar region.[28]

The vigorous distribution of such pamphlets during the conference conveyed several substantive messages. They underscored the illegitimacy of British army service, articulated the unlawfulness associated with government employment and stipulated tax payment as an illicit activity, while simultaneously promoting a boycott of government-supported institutions. Furthermore, the conference advocated for the unequivocal rejection of all honorary ranks and titles bestowed by the government, with the acceptance of such distinctions deemed inherently humiliating. The resolutions promulgated at the Karachi conference were translated and widely disseminated amongst the general populace. Prominent leaders representing diverse religious backgrounds convened and collectively resolved to instigate Non-Cooperation Movements. The cognizant dissemination of the Khilafat and Non-Cooperation Movements, concomitant with the burgeoning tide of anti-colonial sentiments and the cultivation of nationalist fervor, is inextricably linked to the dedicated endeavors of Kattilasseri Muhammed Musaliar and his intimate associate, M.P. Narayana Menon.[29]

In October 1921, discussions surrounding the Manjeri conference gained prominence when reports surfaced about the issues in Malabar. These reports shed light on the tactics employed by government missionaries, highlighting the propagation of inflammatory rhetoric and the use of linguistic warfare against the indigenous community. Notably, the characterization of the populace of the area as 'fanatical' was a common trope employed in these discussions. Surprisingly, the resolution and the speech both highlighted as the cause of the supposed 'fanaticism' of the Muslim community was not even presented by a Muslim but rather by a respected non-Muslim, Kasturi Ranga Iyengar, the editor of *The Hindu*. Colonial reports described his speech as emotionally stirring for the people in the region. Allegations were made about individuals visiting these perceived 'fanatical zones' and delivering provocative speeches, thereby contributing to the escalating tensions. Furthermore, the delineation between 'moderates' and 'fanatics' in the region was primarily based on allegiance to the landlords, rather than religious or regional affiliations. Those who aligned with the landlords were categorized as 'moderates', while others, irrespective of their religious or regional backgrounds, were often labelled as 'fanatics'. This characterization reflected the polarized sociopolitical landscape prevalent during that period.

> The success of their weak was demonstrated when they got in a very large number of fanatical Moplahs as delegates to the district conference May 1920, held Manjeri, passed a non-co-operation resolution by an overwhelming majority.[30] The President the countersense, Kastutiranga Iyengar, editor of the Hindu, Madras, made a fiery speech, which forcibly appealed to the emotions of the Moplahs. The day before the conference the agitators toured the fanatic zone, making inflammatory speeches, the chief among them being a prominent non-co-operation leader of Calicut. The Moderates also secured a large following, but they stopped propagandist work with the conference. The non-co-operators, however, followed their victory at the conference with an extensive and strenuous campaign in the Moplah taluqas, sweeping the fanatics into their camp by shoals. They had triumphal progress which left behind a lurid trail bitter hate of the Government, which was taken by the new organisation of Khalifat Volunteers, who carried the gospel of hatred into every hamlet. In their task the agitators were helped by Moplah priests and theologians, who are looked upon with pontifical veneration by the entire Moplah population. Among them was the son of a high priest. While the father sat on two stools, occasionally hobnobbing with officials and at the same time encouraging the pranks of his son, the latter joined the revolutionaries, going about spouting venom in an area where his father had a huge following. The fanaticism of the Moplahs reached the white heat point with

> Yakub Hussain and his comrades to prison by the district magistrate, Malabar. The agitators again went about the Moplah taluqas stirring bad feelings and attacking the good faith and intentions of the Government. [31]

The impact of this conference reverberated strongly among the team aligned with the landlords. Their efforts in supporting the landlords faced an unexpected challenge due to the joint initiatives of the Non-cooperation and Khilafat Movements. The fervent backing for these movements, coupled with their support for resistance groups, created significant upheaval and disruption, causing considerable distress and turmoil in colonial ranks.

18 August 1920: Confluence in Calicut—Visit of Mahatma and Maulana

To garner support for the national movement, Mahatma Gandhi and Maulana Shaukat Ali visited Malabar as part of their comprehensive tour across India. Despite vigorous efforts by the district magistrate to impede the presence of these national leaders, he failed to procure a prohibition order from the Madras government.[32] He expressed concern over the potential alignment of the Mappilas with the national movement and the confluence of religious and political dimensions, fearing that such a convergence could have detrimental consequences for the already volatile 'outbreak zone'. On 18 August 1920, the leaders arrived in Calicut to a warm and enthusiastic reception, which drew a substantial crowd of over 25,000 attendees for an evening public meeting on the Calicut beach. Subsequently, British authorities raised allegations regarding the composition of the audience, asserting a notable presence of Muslims. Pertinently, this gathering was not the result of a premeditated mobilization of Muslims from one location to another. Instead, it can be attributed to the unique demographic characteristics of the region.[33] During this gathering, Mahatma Gandhi delivered an address in which he expounded upon how the British administration had inadvertently wounded Muslim sentiments, particularly concerning the Khilafat issue. Furthermore, he highlighted the commendable display of self-restraint by the Muslim community and expounded on the virtues of non-violence and non-cooperation.[34]

The slogan 'Hands off the Turkish Calipha' constituted merely one facet of the broader appeal made by the nationalist leadership. In Malabar, the concerns and aspirations of both Hindu and Muslim peasants extended beyond this singular issue. A shared desire for emancipation from the burdensome yoke of bureaucratic oppression and the exploitative landlord class unified individuals from diverse religious backgrounds. I respectfully diverge from the assertion of Bipin Chandra that the Mappilas had a stronger inclination to align with the Congress and Khilafat movements than their Hindu counterparts. This viewpoint appears to emanate from a somewhat circumscribed understanding of the intricate societal dynamics characterizing the Malabar region and its historical resistance movements.[35] Bipin Chandra's perspective may have been shaped by his exposure to and experiences within the context of north India, which could have led him to overlook the distinctive contours of the anti-colonial struggle unfolding in Malabar. In light of the broader principles of justice and freedom, the advocacy of non-violence and non-cooperation by Indian Muslims in their pursuit of redress for the Khilafat issue indeed imposed upon every Hindu the moral obligation to extend cooperation to their Muslim compatriots. The struggle for liberty, autonomy and agency transcends confessional demarcations and serves as a unifying force for all denizens of the Indian subcontinent.

The Khilafat Committee of 1920 exhibited a remarkable degree of inclusivity with active participation from both Hindu and Muslim leaders. This organization exerted a considerable influence, particularly in the Malabar region. The formal establishment of the Khilafat Committee occurred in Calicut, with M. Kunhikoya Thangal as the president. Serving as secretaries were U. Gopala Menon, T. Hassan Koya Mulla and Melekandi Moidu. Consequently, the people were encouraged to actively strive for India's freedom. The Khilafat Movement also lent its full support to the tenancy agitation in Ernad and Valluvanad, aligning itself with the cause. Notably, M.P. Narayana Menon, after resigning from his post as an advocate at the Perinthalmanna court, dedicated himself full-time to the cause of non-cooperation and freedom. Alongside Kattilasseri Mohammad Musaliar, he embarked on tours across the taluks, actively championing the movement.[36] Hindu communities were actively engaged in the non-cooperation campaign. However, colonial sources contended that these movements were primarily motivated by the Khilafat spirit.

The Nagpur session of the Indian National Congress in December 1920 assumed considerable significance in the broader framework of the national movement due to its pivotal role in shaping critical strategies for attaining Swaraj or self-governance. This conference drew a substantial delegation from the Malabar region. The pervasive spirit of nationalism that had permeated the minds of these delegates found resonance in their home villages upon their return from the conference. Khilafat committees were systematically established in nearly every village, reflecting the widespread mobilization during this period.[37] Notable protest meetings took place at Pookottur, Areacade and Mankada-Pallipuram on 24 January, 5 February and 6 February, respectively. In certain meetings, there were instances of rather inflammatory speeches. Prominent leaders such as U. Gopala Menon, K. Madhavan Nair, K.P. Keshava Menon, M.P. Narayana Menon and Kattilasseri Muhammed Musaliar were actively involved in advocating for and participating in the Non-Cooperation Movement. The speakers from both the Muslim and Hindu communities consistently emphasized the paramount significance of non-violent means in their collective agitation efforts. By 30 June 1921, approximately 200 Khilafat committees had been established across a wide array of localities, including Kondotty, Tanur, Tirur, Tirurangadi, Manjeri, Kottakkal, Malappuram, Ponnani and Ottappalam. These committees served as a noteworthy embodiment of intercommunal harmony between Hindus and Muslims.[38]

15 February 1921: A Pivotal Visit and the Non-Cooperation Movement Integration

Yakub Hassan emerged as a prominent figure in the context of India's struggle for independence and made a significant visit to Malabar on 15 February 1921 as an integral component of the Non-Cooperation Movement in the Malabar region. This visit was a part of a broader initiative undertaken by leaders of the Non-Cooperation Movement, including Mahatma Gandhi, primarily to galvanize the local populace for an impending campaign of anti-British resistance. Yakub Hassan, a prominent figure in the Khilafat Movement and a former member of the Madras Legislative Council from 1916 to 1920, was invited by the leadership of the Congress-Khilafat alliance to address two significant public gatherings. These events were scheduled to take place in the towns of Tanur and Calicut in the Malabar region. The presence of Yakub Hassan in Calicut precipitated a sense of hesitation among British administrators, prompting them to implement stringent measures designed to impede his ingress into Malabar and the dissemination of the principles underpinning the Non-Cooperation Movement. Prior to the official launch of the Non-Cooperation Movement in Malabar, a legal notice was issued to Yakub Hassan and other influential leaders, notably K. Madhavan Nair, U. Gopala Menon and Moideen Koya, invoking Section 144 of the Criminal Procedural Code.[39]

This issuance marked a watershed moment, representing the inaugural instance of a prohibitory order directed against a political leader in Malabar. Nonetheless, Yakub Hassan chose to defy this legal notice and ventured into Malabar, thereby culminating in his apprehension on 16 February, pursuant to a warrant issued by the district magistrate. Subsequently, he was incarcerated for six months. Yakub Hassan's arrest triggered a widespread and fervent wave of protests across Malabar, including active participation by students who organized protest meetings and demonstrations. Notably, despite the strenuous efforts of the British administration to suppress these developments, Yakub Hassan's visit to Malabar and the subsequent legal action against him played an instrumental role in disseminating the fundamental tenets of the Non-Cooperation Movement amongst the local populace. Upon Yakub Hassan's arrival in Calicut from Madras, he, along with his wife, was handed the letter of prohibition, which was also served to local Khilafat leaders. This development led to the suspension of the planned meeting in Tanur, and the sizable gathering that had assembled there had to be dispersed. The situation in Calicut was marked by a sense of urgency and concern. In response to the prohibitory orders, the leaders found themselves compelled to defy the directives. They instructed Yakub Hassan to limit his discourse during the meeting to the imperative of non-violence.[40]

The very next day, 17 February, Calicut witnessed a complete strike in response to the arrests. The apprehension of Yakub Hassan and other leaders elicited profound concern among the populace, prompting them to express their dissent through various means such as processions and public meetings held throughout the Malabar region. This fervent reaction resonated beyond Malabar, gaining national attention. The impact of these events was felt far and wide, leading to the closure of shops, the withdrawal of students from educational institutions and a notable absence of several lawyers from court proceedings. Additionally, public gatherings and meetings convened in numerous locations in and outside Malabar to condemn the heavy-handed tactics employed by the authorities in dealing with the Khilafat leaders. K.P. Keshava Menon, in his observations, underscores the widespread and passionate response that these developments ignited across the country.[41] District Magistrate Thomas appears to have played a significant role in exacerbating the situation, contributing to its hostility and increasing tension. He also attempted to disrupt the unity among the various communities involved.[42]

On 17 February 1921, District Magistrate Thomas wrote a communication to the chief secretary to the government, indicating that he had gained a clear understanding of the situation's true nature. His assessment was based on a copy of a telegram issued by Madhavan Nair to the press. This telegram revealed Yakub Hassan's decision to address the public meeting despite the issued prohibition order. It is evident from District Magistrate Thomas's actions and bellicose communication that he not only played a role in intensifying the atmosphere but also sought to exploit divisions among different communities involved in the events.[43] Contemporaneous British accounts reported these events with a decidedly negative bias, and certain historians, influenced by the colonial narrative, construed the episode involving Yakub Hassan as a pivotal juncture within the Khilafat Movement.[44] This period witnessed a discernible shift toward a more belligerent and confrontational posture among Khilafat groups in Malabar, thereby marking a transformative phase in their approach to the larger struggle for independence.

The detention of a prominent individual served as a catalyst for a substantial public demonstration and ensuing waves of agitation. This event unveiled the fortitude and organizational prowess of a populace galvanized under the leadership of Ali Musaliar, a notable influencer across diverse domains in the regions of Malabar and Lakshadweep. Participation in the protest was robust, with an estimated 10,000 to 12,000 individuals hailing from Tirurangadi and its contiguous environs. In this context, Hitchcock's narrative introduces a pejorative dimension, recounting confrontations between demonstrators and military personnel along the coastal thoroughfare in proximity to the collectorate office. Notably, these confrontations were marked by the vocalization of the phrase '*Allah hu Akbar*' to give communal color to the event.[45] Dale, in his analysis, delves further into the religious aspects of the protest. He observes that Muslim participants congregated after deliberations held within the precincts of the local mosque. This observation emphasizes the punctilious performance of daily prayers, implemented five times daily within the mosque, serving as a strategic emphasis to portray participating Muslims as individuals profoundly devout and unwavering in their faith.[46] Hitchcock's narrative further partitions the Muslim demographic into distinct categories, spotlighting their affiliation with the Khilafat Movement. His exposition underscores a contrived narrative propagated by colonial authorities, highlighting the conspicuous absence of Congress leaders in Calicut. This absence was employed as a propagandistic tool to underscore the Congress leaders' unwavering commitment to non-violence, inadvertently perpetuating a portrayal of Muslim communities as fanatical.[47]

M.P. Narayana Menon played an active role in the agitation during the mentioned period. However, subsequent historical accounts have often marginalized his involvement, characterizing him as a singular exception among Congress leaders. These historical narratives have, in a broader sense, dichotomized the participants into distinct groups, aligning Muslims with the Khilafat Movement and non-Muslims with the Congress and Non-Cooperation Movements. This contextual framework assumes particular significance in light of the natives' unwavering commitment to non-violence during their confrontation with imperialist powers. It elucidates the intricate political dynamics and divisions that characterized the prevailing milieu during that epoch.[48]

The correspondences exchanged by the district magistrate offer valuable insights into the disposition of the British administration about the Khilafat Movement. These archival materials appear to have functioned as conduits for the dissemination of propaganda, with the underlying intention of sowing discord among various confessional communities and folk groups. The administrative apparatus made concerted efforts to diminish and marginalize the Non-Cooperation Movement, characterizing it as an inconsequential endeavor, while conspicuously magnifying the significance of the Khilafat Movement. Furthermore, the official reports disseminated the perception that the notion of Hindu–Muslim unity lacked substantive basis. Considering these propagandist undertakings, it becomes apparent that the colonial administration harbored a deliberate strategy to destabilize the foundation of Hindu–Muslim unity, which, notably, constituted the fundamental underpinning upon which the Non-Cooperation and Khilafat Movements were launched. This strategic manipulation of perceptions and sentiments underscores the nature of colonial governance during this historical epoch.[49]

26 April 1921: Ottappalam Conference—A Watershed Moment

In April 1921, the inaugural All Kerala Provincial Conference of the Congress convened in Ottappalam, Kerala, marking a seminal moment in the chronicles of the freedom movement in Malabar. This momentous assembly attracted a substantial gathering, with the participation of approximately 4,000 delegates hailing from diverse regions. At the helm of this consequential conference stood T. Prakasham, who was its presiding authority. The convening of the conference was in accordance with the resolution adopted during the Nagpur Congress in December 1920, which called for the establishment of district Congress committees organized along linguistic lines. As a result of this resolution, the Provincial Congress

Committee, comprising 100 members and with K. Madhavan Nair as the secretary, was formed.[50] Within the framework of the conference, a tripartite division was orchestrated, comprising distinct sessions that addressed the imperatives of Khilafat, tenancy and students. Remarkably, these sessions were held concurrently under a single roof. Distinguished leaders Sayed Murthaza Sahib, K.P. Raman Menon and George Joseph, the editor of the *Independent*, presided over these respective sessions, lending their intellectual and leadership prowess to the proceedings. Notably, the Khilafat volunteers, bedecked in distinctive uniforms, embarked on an ardent procession from the Ernad and Valluvanad Taluks to participate in the conference. This spectacle underscored the fervent engagement and unwavering commitment of these communities to the causes and ideals that were championed within the auspices of this significant gathering.[51]

The initial three days of the conference unfolded without serious incidents. However, on the fourth day, during the student conference session, a noteworthy confrontation transpired. Several Khilafat volunteers were apprehended by the police and subsequently subjected to physical abuse. In response to these distressing developments, the participants, adhering to their commitment to non-violence, maintained a steadfast and dignified silence.[52] Subsequently, when Ramanunni Menon, the secretary of the reception committee, and Hamid Khan, secretary of the Madras Khilafat Conference, sought to investigate the police assault, they, too, were subjected to physical violence and humiliation. Prominent figures such as Prakasham, K.P. Keshava Menon, M.P. Narayana Menon and Kunhikoya Thangal also experienced similar mistreatment at the hands of the colonial authorities. Leaders of considerable stature, including Kattilasseri Muhammed Musaliar, Ali Musaliar and Sayyid Alawi Koya Thangal, vociferously advocated for the unwavering adherence to the principles of non-violence as the most effective response to the provocations orchestrated by the authorities. These episodes serve as poignant exemplars of the unyielding commitment to non-violent resistance demonstrated by these leaders and participants, even in the face of significant adversity.[53]

The Ottappalam conference indeed stood out as a notable event that wielded substantial influence over the colonial administration, drawing significant focus in subsequent news reports dedicated to the prevalent issues of the period. Its importance and far-reaching consequences were consistently underscored in subsequent historical records, highlighting its lasting impact on the structural dynamics of colonial governance. Moreover, within such reports, the categorization of the community through a broad-brush label of 'ignorant' was a recurring tendency. Such generalizations were often used to validate predetermined assertions, contributing to a misrepresentation intended to substantiate the biased perspectives held by colonial entities.

> The finishing touches were given at the Ottapalam Conference May last, since which preparations were made for an outbreak on an extensive scale, fact known to the district officers, and which led them to adopt strenuous measures to curb the rebellious tendency of the Moplahs. They were, however, handicapped by countermeasures adopted by the agitators and the apathy of the loyalists, the licence enjoyed by the agitators to hit the Government right and left with impunity being attributed by the ignorant Moplahs to fear of the agitators by the former.[54]

Even the typically pro-government publication, the *Madras Mail*, conceded that the assault upon Ramunni Menon was a most regrettable incident, acknowledging the gravity of the situation. Furthermore, it lauded the comportment of the conference leaders within the pandal, deeming it praiseworthy.[55] A committee comprised of notable figures such as T. Prakasham, L.A. Subhramayyar, Murthaza Sahib, George Joseph and K.P. Keshava Menon was duly constituted to conduct a comprehensive inquiry into the events transpiring at Ottapalam. This committee demonstrated exceptional diligence in its investigative endeavors, which culminated in the expeditious preparation and public dissemination of its findings within the span of a single month.[56] The principal observation and conclusion drawn from the committee's reports and resolutions are of particular significance. It highlighted compelling evidence indicating that the police had engaged in a calculated conspiracy aimed at instigating a breach of the peace and the undermining of non-violent principles among non-cooperators.[57] Subsequently, the authorities resorted to retaliatory measures and sought to impute responsibility for the ensuing discord to the Non-cooperation Movement itself. Notably, the authorities responded to these findings by taking the exceptional step of proscribing the report's dissemination.[58] Paradoxically, the subsequent implementation of repressive policies by the administration had unintended consequences. Rather than quelling the nationalist fervor among the populace, these measures served to mobilize and unify individuals around the shared tenets of non-violence and non-cooperation. This, in turn, bolstered the resolve and commitment of those advocating for the ideals of independence and self-determination. Such developments bear witness to the lucid interplay of events during this critical period of the national struggle for autonomy.

29 July 1921: Abdurahiman Sahib Presented Translations of Resolutions

The events of 29 July were significant developments in the Khilafat Movement. During a meeting in Calicut, Mohammed Abdurahiman Sahib presented translations of resolutions from the All-India Khilafat Conference. These resolutions emphasized the imperative of upholding the sanctity of holy places in accordance with Sharia law. It staunchly stated that until this preservation was assured, Indian Muslims would neither find peace nor tolerate colonial administration. Authorities took note of the burgeoning advocacy for civil disobedience and non-payment of taxes among Khilafat groups across different regions of Malabar, recording over 101 meetings convened with identical agendas. Concurrently, congregational Friday prayers were strategically utilized to disseminate information about the Khilafat Non-Cooperation Program. On the same date, Ali Musaliar relayed the resolutions of the Karachi Conference to the congregation at Tirurangadi Mosque, marking a pivotal moment in galvanizing support. These views flagged him as one of the most significant and curious figures in Malabar history. These activities significantly contributed to the establishment of Khilafat committees in nearly every village, fostering a well-structured Khilafat volunteer corps at both district and taluk levels. The structuring and coordination within the Khilafat Movement proved to be remarkably efficient, evident in its widespread and systematic outreach. The authorities also noticed the call for civil disobedience and non-payment of taxes among the Khilafatists in different parts of Malabar.[59]

The Khilafat Movement later became a tool for the British to instigate the non-Muslims' aversion to Muslims. The colonial administration was able to create negative narratives surrounding the movement. In this scenario, Haji wrote in the letter to media that the existence of Hindu–Muslim harmony should be known to the Mahatma and Maulana.[60] The colonial administration caused a major tragedy. They manipulated the situation in their favor and stoked hatred between communities in the region based on religion and social status. Hitchcock highlighted that the Friday congregational prayers were also utilized to gather the masses on the Khilafat Non-Cooperation Program.[61]

Entwined Histories: Bonds with the Ottomans before the Indian Khilafat Movement

On perusing the Ottoman archives, a fascinating historical narrative emerges, delineating the intricate precepts of association between

Malabar and the Ottoman Empire that predate the formal Khilafat Movement in the region. Within these archival annals lies an array of documents indicative of a profound entwinement between the two entities. This symbiotic relationship precedes the stewardship of Sayyid Fazal, marked by the exchange of emissaries and ceremonial offerings that served to fortify the bridge between these geographically distant realms. However, these ties experienced a marked deepening during the tenure of Sayyid Fazal, exemplified in a compelling correspondence originating from M. Moideen Musaliar of Kalpankacheri Tirur, Malabar district, directed toward the esteemed grand vizier of Constantinople (Fig. 4.1).[62]

Dated 25 April 1913 and crafted in the formal lexicon characteristic of official English correspondences, this missive from Kalpakancheri, Tirur is a testament to the unified solidarity of the 'Muhammedans' of Malabar. It commences with a respectful plea as a representative of this community, enclosing a cheque numbered 125/13, amounting to 72 pounds. This monetary contribution was expressly designated for the relief of war sufferers in Turkey, underscoring a profound

Figure 4.1
Letter of M. Moideen Musaliar from Malabar to the Ottoman Sultan

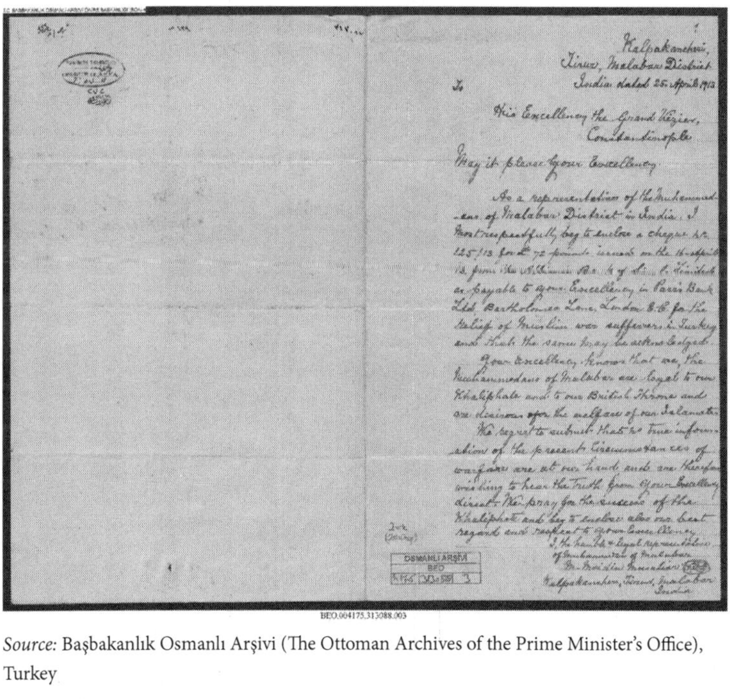

Kalpakanchery,
Tirur, Malabar District
India dated 25 April 1913

To

His Excellency the Grand Vizier,
Constantinople

May it please Your Excellency

As a representative of the Muhammedans of Malabar District in India, I most respectfully beg to enclose a cheque No. 125/13 for £ 72 pounds issued on the 16 April 13 from the [illegible] Bank of [illegible] Limited as payable to your Excellency in Parr's Bank Ltd, Bartholomew Lane, London E.C. for the relief of Muslim war sufferers in Turkey and that the same may be acknowledged.

Your Excellency knows that we, the Muhammedans of Malabar are loyal to our Khaliphate and to our British Throne and are desirous of the welfare of our Islamatis.

We regret to submit that no true information of the present circumstances of warfare are at our hand and are therefore wishing to hear the truth from Your Excellency direct. We pray for the success of the Khaliphate and beg to enclose also our best regard and respect to Your Excellency.

I, the humble & loyal representative of Muhammedans of Malabar
M. Moideen Musaliar
Kalpakancheri, Tirur, Malabar
India

OSMANLI ARŞİVİ
BEO

BEO.004175.313088.003

Source: Başbakanlık Osmanlı Arşivi (The Ottoman Archives of the Prime Minister's Office), Turkey

allegiance to both the Caliphate and the British throne. Amidst the tumultuous atmosphere of conflict, there was a sincere yearning for direct, unadulterated information from His Excellency about the prevailing circumstances of warfare. Embedded in the discourse were fervent supplications for the triumph of the Caliphate, coupled with expressions of deference. The epistolary conclusion, signed by M. Moideen Musaliar, evoked sentiments of reverence and unwavering fidelity, echoing the enduring support and fraternal bonds linking the Muhammadans of Malabar with their counterparts situated across distant seas.[63]

Moplah Rifles: Accepted Fez Caps

It is evident from earlier chapters that the Moplahs were unjustly labeled as 'illiterate fanatics'. This region was also misrepresented as a jungle or an unknown territory to outsiders. Prior to the Non-Cooperation Movements, there existed a distinct division of Moplahs in the British force. They played an active role and bravely fought in several wars on behalf of the British authorities. An example is the disbandment of the 77th Moplah Rifles on 31 August 1907, an event detailed in a report by the *Sphere*, where they ceremonially yielded up their colors to the bishop of Madras (Fig. 4.2).

> The impressive ceremony of receiving the colours of the late 17th Madras Infantry, under which the 77th Moplah Rifles, now on the eve of disbandment were raised, was performed on July 12th at St. Marks Church, Bangalore, by the Bishop of Madras. The regiment was first formed at Fort St. George in 1777 and was designated the 17th Carnatic Battalion. It served with distinction in the Carnatic against Hyder Ali and specially distinguished itself at the battle of Sholinghur. In 1793 it formed part of a force of about 10,500 men which besieged and captured the French settlement of Pondicherry. In 1806 it was disbanded but was raised again in 1807 as the 2nd Battalion 24th Madras Native Infantry. In 1817, during the Mahratta war the regiment took a distinguished part in the operations against the Rajah of Nagpur.[64] In 1885 the regiment saw active service in Burma. From 1777 till 1899 the regiment was composed of Madrasis of the same type as the men who formed the old coast army but in 1899 a number of Moplahs were enlisted and in 1902 it became the 77th Moplah Rifles.[65]

The 77th Moplah Rifles held a significant position in the annals of the British Indian Army. Its inception can be traced back to the

Figure 4.2
The Officers of the Disbanded 77th Moplah Rifles

Source: Sphere, 31 August 1907

establishment of the 17th Carnatic Battalion in 1777. This regiment played a pivotal role in various conflicts, notably the Carnatic Wars and the pivotal Battle of Sholinghur during the Second Anglo-Mysore War. Its nomenclature underwent successive transformations, evolving from the 17th Carnatic Battalion to the 16th Madras Battalion in 1784, subsequently becoming the 2nd Battalion, 5th Madras Native Infantry in 1796, and culminating in the appellation of the 77th Moplah Rifles in 1903. In 1902, a paradigm shift in recruitment strategy occurred, transitioning from the enlistment of Madrasis to a concentrated focus on the Moplahs, a Muslim community hailing from Malabar.

This strategic shift in recruitment strategy was underpinned by the British acknowledgment of the martial prowess exhibited by the Moplahs. Consequently, deliberate efforts were made to integrate them into the army fold. While the 77th regiment was stationed in Madras, predominantly for garrison duties, the 78th Moplah Rifles was deployed for active service on the Northwest Frontier in 1905. This alteration in recruitment strategy and military deployment was also mirrored in distinct uniform changes. Notably, the adoption of the red fez cap, an unconventional element in the British Indian Army's uniform repertoire at that juncture, marked the transition. The 77th Moplah Rifles wore dark green serge uniforms complemented by scarlet facings, while the 78th regiment inverted this pattern, sporting scarlet jackets with green facings. This nuanced evolution in recruitment practices and uniformity symbolized a substantive transformation in the composition and visual identity of these regiments in the broader framework of the British Indian Army.[66]

Conclusion

The regional landscape was fraught with a distressing sequence of events characterized by numerous massacres, notably targeting women and children, devoid of any humanitarian or human rights considerations. The prevailing circumstances severely limited any benign strides toward the reconstruction imperative. The persistence of martial law until 25 February, coupled with the deployment of an additional battalion of Indian infantry tasked with quelling the populace, prolonged the phase of reestablishment. Notably, the execution of remedial measures remained dormant until the revocation of martial law. Scholars and biographers often debate the precise role Variamkunnath Kunhamed Haji played directly in the series of events during this era, but the historical evidence and narrative presents him as an extremely significant figure in the region, closely associated with Ali Musaliar and actively engaged in the Khilafat Movement. Haji played a multifaceted role, declaring himself the 'Raja of the Hindus, Amir of the Muslims, and Colonel of the Khilafat army', effectively establishing himself as a dominant authority in the Ernad and Valluvanad regions.[67] His actions encompassed the appointment of officers, the issuance of passports, measures to curb looting, restitution of looted assets, anti-British edicts and the provision of sanctuary to diverse communities. Furthermore, other leaders like Ali Musaliar and Chembrasseri Thangal directed their associates to safeguard Hindu families. Notably, Kunhamed Haji, in a large congregation comprising Hindus and Muslims, explicitly instructed against violence toward Hindus, discouraging any attempts to coerce them into adopting Islam. He emphasized the repercussions of harming Hindus, foreseeing their potential alignment with the government, which he perceived as leading to the defeat of the movement. Additionally, he clarified their lack of animosity toward the Hindu community while asserting punitive measures against those aiding the government.[68]

Following the resistance in August 1921, prominent individuals such as Abdurahiman Sahib, K.P. Kesava Menon and M.P. Narayana Menon reinitiated efforts toward reconciliation by approaching Ali

Musaliar. Their plea for Musaliar surrendering to the government aimed to mitigate further calamity. Ali Musaliar asserted his commitment to non-violence, denying his involvement in any violent acts. He recounted an incident where his attempt to inquire about the unwarranted arrests led to a confrontation with the authorities, resulting in subsequent repercussions. This historical account underscores the complex dynamics of leadership, conflicting ideologies and efforts to mitigate violence during a turbulent period in the region's history. This chapter discussed the complex dynamics of the Non-Cooperation and Khilafat Movements in Malabar, exposing how colonial authorities deliberately fueled communal divisions and sidelined diverse community contributions. Despite these obstacles, it unveils a narrative of enduring harmony amid struggles, showcasing instances of remarkable cohesion and solidarity among communities. This exploration illuminates the resilience and collective unity witnessed during a pivotal period of resistance against colonial rule, providing valuable insights into the sociopolitical landscape of the Indian independence movement in Malabar.

Khalifa and Khilafat

The term 'Khilafat' is etymologically derived from the root word Khalifa, signifying the appointment of a successor, lieutenant, vicegerent or deputy.[69] In the context of Islamic jurisprudence, 'Khalifa' came to encompass the notion of a successor to Prophet Muhammad, bearing both temporal and spiritual authority. Within Islamic law, such a successor assumes the honorific title of 'Amir-ul-Momenin', denoting their exclusive legal authority. They possess the power and prerogative to institute political, legal and social reforms, provided these align with the precepts and mandates of the Quran.[70] The Khalifa must seek counsel from experts in Islamic jurisprudence. Opinion on this historical legacy—personal, communal, public and scholarly—is like a pendulum throughout the generations, constantly swinging in one direction or another.

A salient facet of the Holy Prophet's life was his multifaceted role as both a spiritual guide and the head of the state. This dual leadership underscored the comprehensive nature of his authority. The term 'Khalifa' finds multiple mentions in the Quran and has been construed by Muslim jurists to connote the headship of the Islamic state. Other titles such as 'Imam' are also considered synonymous with 'Khalifa', especially in the context of supreme leadership in matters of worship. Islam, as a complex social and political system, operates under theocratic principles, which permeate and regulate every facet of human activity. The khalifa's authority extends beyond religious affairs to encompass temporal allegiance, as they inherit not only religious but also temporal power. Consequently, the khalifa serves as the highest executive officer within the Islamic legal framework. Following the demise of Prophet Muhammad in AD 632, Abu Bakar, the newly elected ruler of the Islamic state, adopted the modest title of 'Khilafa Rasul-Allah' (successor of the apostle of God). Subsequently, Umar Faruq, who succeeded Abu Bakar in AD 634, referred to himself as 'Khalifah al Khalifa Rasul-Allah' (successor of the successor of the apostle of God). This designation was later streamlined to 'Kalifah' (vicegerent) or 'Amir-ul-Mueminin' (leader of the believers) due to its conciseness.[71] The initial four successors of Prophet Muhammad are collectively termed 'Khilafat-u-Rashida' or 'pious Caliphate' (AD 632–661). Subsequently, the Islamic world saw the rule of Umayyad rulers (AD 661–750), the Abbasids (AD 750–1258) and the Ottomans (AD 1517–1924), who held dual roles as temporal and spiritual leaders of Islam. Notably, the Mamluks of Egypt were an exception to this lineage. The Abbasid Caliphate met its demise with the Mongol invasion under Halagu in 1258, accompanied by the tragic destruction and massacre of the Abbasid family. However, an uncle of the last caliph survived and sought refuge in Egypt, where he was received hospitably and later instated as the caliph under the title 'Al Mustansir Billah' by the Mamluk ruler Baibers (1260–1277). This marked the commencement of a period during which the Abbasid Caliphate coexisted with Mamluks of Egypt in Cairo (1261–1517). In 1517, Sultan Salim I of the Ottoman Empire conquered Egypt, taking control of the holy cities Mecca and Medina. Subsequently, the nominal Abbasid Caliph, Al-Mutawakkil, was compelled to transfer the Khilafat to Salim I, who declared himself as the caliph of the Islamic world in 1518. This period saw the establishment of the Ottoman Caliphate (1518–1524). Traditionally, the custodians of the two holy cities, Mecca and Medina, have been revered as the caliphs of Islam. Presently, the king of Saudi Arabia bears the title of 'custodian of the two holy cities' or 'servant of two holy cities' (Khadim-ul-Haramain-i-Sherifain). The Caliphate movement ultimately dissipated by late 1922, as Turkey, having achieved a more favorable diplomatic standing, gravitated toward nationalism. In 1924, Turkey formally abolished the institution of the Caliphate.[72]

PART 2

PORTUGUESE AND BRITISH: 1498–1900

Chapter 5

PATHWAYS OF FREEDOM

Pre-First War of Independence in India

The Indian Ocean was a thriving hub of global trade, its ports bustling with the exchange of spices, goods and ideas. Among these busy ports, the Malabar region was a beacon—a crossroads where diverse cultures intersected in the vibrant tapestry of international commerce. Ibn Battuta (1304–1377), in awe of its safety and prosperity, lauded it as a haven unmatched by any other route.[1] However, the tranquility of this region was disrupted by the arrival of the Portuguese, which triggered a seismic shift in the lands and waters of the Indian Ocean. Their intervention unleashed turmoil, challenging the established order and threatening the sovereignty of indigenous communities. Despite the upheaval, the resilient spirit of the region prevailed. Rulers, leaders and scholars united in a formidable front, staunchly resisting the colonial onslaught. This chapter delves deep into the chronicles of the anti-colonial struggles—from the arrival of Vasco da Gama (1469–1524). This historic confrontation is a testament to the unwavering resolve of the people, where communal harmony created an alliance that defeated the Portuguese in the pivotal Chaliyam encounter, affirming the strength found in unity. This is a journey through the turbulent waters of colonial invasion, exploring the valor, resilience, and triumphs of those who defended their lands and cultures in the face of foreign domination in the region.

1498–1571: Vasco da Gama to the Chaliyam Encounter

The challenges of resisting colonial invasions along the Malabar Coast of the Indian Ocean were compounded by European powers aiming to disrupt the region's peaceful coexistence and lucrative trade. Although the arrival of Vasco da Gama did not mark the first European contact with the region, it catalyzed a tumultuous period on both land and sea, aimed at establishing European trade supremacy.

The inherent characteristics and dynamics of the natural monsoon winds assumed a crucial role in both the facilitation and sustenance of trading relations. Despite an absence of specific temporal markers delineating the revelation of the monsoon winds' characteristics, trajectory and strength, extant historical documentation accentuates the paramount significance of these climatic phenomena in configuring maritime trade.[2] While the attribution of the nomenclature of the monsoon wind to Hippalus by the Greeks is documented,[3] a broader consensus recognizes the flourishing of robust trade along the Indian Ocean littoral well before Hippalus became traditionally associated with the formal recognition of these winds in Europe during the first century.[4] The monsoon season significantly influences optimal sailing schedules for navigation in both eastward and westward directions. Ibn Majid (c. 1421–1500), a prominent maritime explorer, extensively detailed monsoon navigation in his renowned work, *Kitab al-Fawa'id*. This treatise provides profound insights into the experiential and technical dimensions of navigating during the monsoon season. Voyages to Malabar heavily relied on the monsoon, known as '*mawsim al-kaws*'. The seasonal wind pattern begins along the East African coast in March, reaching the Malabar region by late May. Arabian dhows and Chinese junks dominated the coastal regions, owing to their sophisticated comprehension and adept utilization of the prevailing winds. Celestial navigation along India's west coast typically concludes in June, coinciding with the onset of the monsoon's full force in July. This period is characterized by copious rainfall, gale-force winds and tumultuous waves.[5] Sebastian Prange expounds upon the paradigm of monsoon as a foundational concept. This theoretical framework posits that the socioeconomic development of the Indian Ocean region was principally orchestrated by the agency of mercantile actors, as opposed to being predominantly influenced by the authoritative mandates of ruling sultans. It underscores the pronounced impact of commercial imperatives over martial endeavors in shaping the regional milieu, thereby accentuating the nuanced experiences of Malabar.[6]

During the 14th century, the economic ties between the Western and Eastern worlds thrived, with Calicut gaining comparable renown to the port of Alexandria. Evidencing the vitality of the region, Ibn Battuta arrived in Calicut, en route to China, to a bustling port teeming with maritime activity. His accounts describe more than one hundred vessels at the port, with thirteen hailing from China. Notably, Battuta extolled the safety of the routes, the protective measures in place and the multicultural, cosmopolitan character of the area—all contributing factors to the brisk commerce that transpired.[7] The Malabar coast distinguished itself as a hub of spice trade, celebrated for its production of a diverse array of seasoning, including the highly prized pepper, thereby earning its moniker as the 'pepper country' due to its central role in the trade of this 'black gold'. These port cities embody a narrative of resistance, with a noteworthy instance being the 1571 confiscation of the Portuguese Fort at Chaliyam. This achievement was the result of intense warfare waged collaboratively by Muslims and Hindus to safeguard the tranquil and harmonious way of life under the rule of the Hindu monarch, the Zamorin.[8]

The ideological foundation of anti-colonial resistance rested firmly on the concept of Hindu–Muslim harmony. This theme is eloquently illustrated in primary documents related to the Malabar region by esteemed scholars, and the answer to these questions on Hindu–Muslim harmony shed new light on the intersection between ideas and pragmatism the decision-making processes were often a product of both improvization on the periphery of the kingdom and directives from the center. It is especially important to confront the prevailing colonial narrative and engage in lively discussions about regional nationalism, political chauvinism and propaganda. Such dialogue often wrongly suggests that various social factions are equally responsible for the destruction of each other's unique religious or cultural architecture, buildings, heritage and monuments. The Malabar freedom struggle was rooted in the principles of communal harmony, as exemplified in the following lines from Qadi Muhammed ibn Abdul Aziz's *Fat'hul Mubin*:

> All Muslim soldiers,
> touching the Qur'an,
> take an oath to sacrifice their lives first.
> Upon hearing this,
> Nair soldiers took offense,
> declaring that Muslims, being a minority,
> should not fight and die alone.
> They vowed to fight and march together to the fort.[9]

As a poet, the Qadi subtly suggests that inflexible ethical codes could evolve into burdensome baggage, despite his resolutely positive stance. Fearless in his intellectual discourse, he asserts that the combined wisdom in the Quran and Islamic monotheism espouses both egalitarianism and pacifism. This pivotal period witnessed Muslim and Hindu soldiers effectively uniting to repel Portuguese incursions. An elaborate analysis of the intricate interplay among social hierarchy, colonialism, gender dynamics, historical context, religious sectarianism and politics, viewed through the lens of power shifting between societal groups, unveils the significance of the Arabic term *jihad* (signifying 'struggle' in classical Arabic) in Malabar's historical archives. Its inclusion served as a catalyst, fostering interfaith harmony and peaceful coexistence. This linguistic addition carried a broader implication, signifying a collective commitment to safeguard not only the Hindu monarch's rights but also the inherent rights of all individuals, regardless of their caste or creed.[10] This ideological transformation from communal unity to a universal commitment to human rights marked a critical turning point in Malabar's history, resonating significantly in its freedom movement trajectory.[11]

Shaykh Zayn al-Din I's poem is a bold and open declaration against the Portuguese, articulating the necessity of war as a means of self-defense and the protect religious and cultural identity under the reign of the Zamorin of Calicut. His work adheres to the structural distinctions of medieval Arabic poetry, integrating thematic and linguistic elements to underscore the urgency of combatting foreign subjugation. Through this poetic form, Zayn al-Din I offers a critical overview of the Malabar context, marked by the violence and exploitation brought by European interlopers, notably the Portuguese.[12] Shaykh Zayn al-Din II was instrumental in the legal unification of the region, notably through his significant contributions to history and law. He authored the *Tuhfat al-Mujahidin*, a seminal book on Malabar.[13] His *Tuhfat al-Mujahidin* is particularly renowned for its detailed account of the confrontations with the Portuguese from 1498 to 1583, the atrocities committed by the Portuguese and the local resistance against them.[14] This work has been translated into not only several European languages, including Portuguese, English, Spanish, Latin and French, but also many Indian languages like Malayalam, Urdu, Kannada and Tamil, highlighting its widespread significance. Shaykh Zayn al-Din II's work was translated by Lt. M.J. Rowlandson to English in 1833 and another by S. Muhammad Husayn Nainar, who published his version through the University of Madras.[15]

Contrary to the portrayal of figures like Da Gama as exploratory heroes in some European narratives, Indian perspectives, including that of K.M. Panikkar, cast these figures in a villainous light for their role in extending the reaches of slavery and oppression. This critique extends to the broader discourse on colonialism's alleged benefits, challenging the glorification of industrial and technological advancements at the expense of indigenous development and autonomy.[16] Qadi Muhammed ibn Abdul Aziz's poem also delves into the profound spiritual dimensions of martyrdom, portraying it as a noble sacrifice for a just cause, with martyrs longing for the paradisiacal bliss promised in the afterlife. Scholars such as Ashin Das Gupta underplay the persecution faced in Malabar, thereby highlighting the poem's significance as a multifaceted document of resistance, spiritual ideology and historical testimony.[17]

10 May 1857: Shifting the Historical Lens and Recalibrating Perspectives

The echoes of this freedom struggle found poignant expression in a historically significant event—the substantial blow dealt to British colonial authority by the resistance in Malabar and Conolly's death before the seminal events of 10 May 1857. Evoking the politics and voices of the subaltern, I seek to address previous gaps in the available literature on this era and geography as an integral component of Indian identity, autonomy and agency. While these later events are widely recognized as the beginning of India's enduring struggle for independence, British narratives have often obscured the profound and sustained resistance exhibited by the southern regions of the Indian subcontinent. These territories consistently displayed unwavering defiance in their protracted confrontations with colonial forces, establishing a tradition of resistance dating back to the 16th century.

An exemplary instance of pre-1921 resistance movements can be seen in the sustained struggles against colonial forces in the Malabar region following Vasco da Gama's arrival. Da Gama's efforts to undermine regional sovereignty and disrupt coastal trade routes sparked formidable resistance movements. These early conflicts against colonial powers aimed primarily at preserving the autonomy of Hindu monarchs and fostering religious and cultural harmony in the region. These pre-1921 resistance movements against colonial powers witnessed the convergence of a diverse array of freedom fighters, transcending societal boundaries and discriminations, thus laying the foundation for subsequent efforts toward self-determination. These demands became especially intense in those mixed ports and coastal regions during times of economic upheaval or political agitation. Therefore, the conventional historical account of the events of 1857, often considered the principal catalyst for India's overarching struggle for independence, requires a nuanced and comprehensive reassessment. Such an evaluation must systematically consider the substantial and enduring efforts originating from the Malabar region, affording due recognition to the multifaceted nature of India's protracted journey toward self-determination.

One illustrative episode occurred during the reign of the Zamorin, the king of Calicut, when the king's mother convened a meeting in a mosque to garner the support of Muslim leaders with a shared objective: resisting Portuguese incursions. Hindus also played an indispensable role, steadfastly refusing to allow Muslims to bear the burden of defending the kingdom alone. This sentiment was rooted in the belief that Muslims constituted a minority, and accordingly, Nair soldiers willingly declared their readiness to sacrifice their lives before Muslims, epitomizing extraordinary harmony between religious communities. This historical collaboration underscores the shared commitment of both communities to preserve their land, safeguard its rich cultural heritage and maintain religious pluralism in the face of external threats. Sheikh Zainuddin's narratives also vividly depict the resolute resistance against Portuguese incursions across the diverse regions of Malabar. Among these narratives, Tirurangadi emerged as a significant non-coastal trading hub that played a pivotal role in supporting and contributing to resistance efforts against colonial forces in the 16th century. This highlights Tirurangadi's central position in the struggle against colonial powers.[18]

Tirurangadi's prominence in the resistance movement·testifies to its unwavering dedication and steadfast commitment to countering the encroachments of external forces. The town's active participation underscores its determination to protect the land from colonization, secure its inhabitants from enslavement and preserve the integrity of peaceful trade and coexistence. By taking a principled stance against malevolent forces, Tirurangadi not only demonstrated its resilience but also symbolized the collective spirit shared by the region's populace. The region's contribution to the resistance efforts underscores its historical significance as a bastion of resilience and unity, where the local populace united to thwart the ambitions of those seeking to subjugate and exploit both the land and its inhabitants. Its role in countering colonial domination highlights the indomitable spirit of communities united against adversity and their unwavering commitment to upholding their heritage, trade and harmonious way of life. When examining the broader panorama of historical struggles against colonial subjugation, it becomes unequivocally apparent that the multilayered resistance and resilience, intertwined with the spirit of Mamburam, significantly predates the temporal boundaries attributed to the 1857 struggle. This recalibration of historical perspective serves to elucidate the intricate and interconnected nature of India's quest for liberation—a narrative fundamentally informed by the valiant struggles and sacrifices of diverse regions and communities across the subcontinent.

4 March 1776: Evolution of Tellicherry Factory—Transforming into a Residency Hub

William Logan's official records offer a colonial perspective on the fundamental causes underpinning the conflicts between the British and the kingdom of Mysore. These contentious matters primarily revolved around intricate financial considerations and vested business interests as the principal drivers behind the enduring rivalry between the two entities. The imperative to reinstate authority over Malabar within the British dominion emerged as a pivotal objective within this multifaceted historical context:

> The Tellicherry Factory became a Residency on the 4th of March 1776, the Company's trade having greatly diminished after Hyder Ali's occupation of the country. But on the 27th of January 1784 the Chiefship was reestablished and continued down to 1794 when it was abolished.[19]

Thalasseri was one of the preeminent European trading hubs in the region.[20] The corporate headquarters of the British East India Company endeavored to augment trade and commerce through this strategic port. Noteworthy is the presence of a fort that served as the focal point for the trading company's activities. Thalasseri, on the other hand, emerged as a prominent port town in the Malabar region, distinguished by its brisk trade in spices, hill-produced commodities and timber. Subsequently, a significant development occurred when the British East India Company acquired a site from the de facto ruler of Kolathunad, culminating in the establishment of a factory in Thalasseri in 1708. To ensure the safety of their trade ventures, an intricate fortification was meticulously erected encompassing the periphery of the hills, with the indispensable support of the Kolathiri *raja*. The French occupation of Mahé in 1725 precipitated the imperative for the British East India Company to reinforce their fortifications and establish an impregnable stronghold along the Malabar coast. The British assumed control over Dharmadam Island in 1736. From 1776 to 1784, Thalasseri served as host to a formidable British military presence. The year 1781 marked a significant historical event when Hyder Ali, the ruler of the kingdom of Mysore, launched an unsuccessful campaign to capture the fort, as part of his broader strategy to exert dominion over the Malabar region. The Thalasseri fort was constructed from laterite blocks and has robust, round-holed walls and formidable flanking bastions directing a commanding view of the sea. It attains an elevation of ten meters and boasts an oblong structural design.[21]

The year 1792 marked the commencement of British colonial administration following the Seringapatam (Srirangapatna) treaty. This shift from the rule of Tipu Sultan (1751–1799) to British governance brought about significant sociopolitical changes in the region. The transformation in the administrative landscape resulted in noticeable tension between the local population and those who aligned with the new colonial authorities. This ideological and systemic shift led to a series of struggles across Malabar, collectively initiating a period of intense anti-colonial agitation that foreshadowed the significant Indian independence movement of 1857. Malabar became a crucible where resistance against colonialism burned fiercely, setting the stage for the broader fight for independence.[22]

22 February and 18 March 1792: Diplomatic Milestones—Unraveling Treaties of Seringapatam

The transfer of Malabar to British authority through the Treaty of Seringapatam in February and March 1792 revealed a region composed of numerous princely territories. However, it is crucial to scrutinize the colonial perspective articulated by figures like Logan, who displayed a critical view of the region. William Logan highlighted what he saw as 'intolerance' exhibited by the previous 'Muslim conquerors', the abandonment of the region by its primary landholders and pervasive issues of predation and avarice attributed to the 'Mappila bandits'.[23] The use of terms like *intolerance*, *Muslim conquerors* and *plundering and greed of Mappila bandits* in colonial discourse underscores the inherently biased nature of their portrayal of the Malabar region and the people.

> At the cession of Malabar, in the manner above related to the British by the Treaties of Seringapatam, dated 22nd February and 18th March 1792, the country was found to be split into a number of kingdoms and principalities, a prey to the bigotry of its late Muhammadan conquerors, abandoned by its principal landholders, and distracted by the depredations and rapacity of the Mappila bandit.[24]

William Logan conducted a colonial analytical examination of the factors contributing to the discord between Hindus and Muslims in the region. He posited that these tensions might have inclined the Muslim population to favor Tipu Sultan over the British, citing the issue of coerced conversions to Islam. Logan notably emphasized the perception of these conversions as being forcibly imposed. Importantly, Logan observed that religious tensions were not as pronounced when there existed harmonious relations with Muslim landowners and revenue officers.[25] This observation stands in contrast to allegations of coerced conversion, positing that the underlying dynamics of the conflict were not predominantly rooted in religious affiliations. Rather, the focal point appears to revolve around individuals' alignment with or opposition to the colonial power's presence in the region. Logan's historical account extends to the occupation of Kannur:

> It was done, however, under the strictest secrecy; two officers (Lieutenants Lewis and Munro) proceeded to Cannanore by sea and landed secretly there and obtained the Bibi's signature to it. The terms were that she was 'whenever called upon' to admit the company's troops to garrison the fortress of Cannanore and to give as hostages for such performance the husband of her eldest daughter, and one of her ministers. On these and other conditions, which it is unnecessary to detail, as they were never carried out, the Bibi was to be considered as an ally of the Honorable Company 'in the same manner as the other Malabar princes, their allies'.[26]

The British forces strategically leveraged their influence over the *raja* of Cochin, persuading him to renounce allegiance to Tipu Sultan and align with the British. Logan underscored that Tipu Sultan's Mysorean army possessed superior equipment, presenting a challenge for General Medows, who struggled to engage them.[27] In response, the British forces captured Kannur. However, Arakkal Bibi's ambivalent stance raised suspicions about her true intentions.[28] The British grew uncertain as to whether Bibi intended to side with Tipu Sultan against the company. Taylor, the British chief of Tellicherry (Thalasseri), in response, sought approval from the Bombay authorities to initiate a siege on Cannanore. Consequently, on 22 October, the colonial company commenced a naval blockade of the region. On 5 November, frustrated by Bibi's apparent evasion of engagement with the colonial company, the Bombay Government resolved to lay siege to her domain.[29]

Logan's narrative reveals the colonial perspective, where Colonel Hartley's request on 13 November urged Major Dow to be stationed at Ponnani, south of the river. However, the Bibi's persistently hostile stance rendered Taylor unable to fulfill this request. The British encountered Tipu Sultan's forces, joined by 4,000 Mappilas, on the plains of Tirurangadi in Ernad taluk on the morning of 10 November. Following a fierce engagement, Colonel Martab Khan and the right wing of the enemy were defeated. Having decided to besiege Cannanore on 5 November, the Bombay Government, under General Abercromby, embarked on vigorous preparations for the operation. On 25 November, they dispatched a regiment to Thalasseri.[30]

The formal siege was initiated on 14 December, with the critical outworks Forts Avary and Carlee falling to the British on 16 December. On 17 December, the Bibi, the besieged ruler of Arakkal, capitulated. Notably, her husband, who had consistently led opposition against the English, had passed away earlier in the siege. So, their plans and relationships appear to have all gone awry at the same time. Consequently, her minister and her heir apparent were sent as hostages to the English camp. The British forces seized all military and naval supplies, vessels and grain. They also claimed possession of Bibi's personal property and household effects, which were later made available to her and the palace inhabitants. The British flag was ceremoniously hoisted from the fortifications.[31]

28 May 1792: Sherborne Mercury Report—Unveiling Historical Chronicles

Colonial embedded journalists produced essential reports to satisfy the needs of both the public and ruling classes in their respective countries. Numerous reports on various events were published in prominent newspapers within their countries. For instance, the *London Gazette* featured a report dated 20 May, Sunday, covering the Malabar region.[32] This report detailed the 'violence' in the region, as described in the copies and extracts received by the East India Company. The report offered a firsthand account of the situation in the area. Due to the challenging climate and geographical conditions, the campaign's progress had been significantly delayed, presenting numerous extraordinary difficulties. This comprehensive account also chronicled Tipu Sultan's defeat and outlined the strategies employed by the colonial forces.[33]

Scholars of colonial history have rigorously reexamined the British perspectives on the conflict in the Malabar region. Their research suggests that religious dynamics, particularly the complex interplay between the *jenmis* (landlords) and the *kudiyans* (tenants), commonly referred to as *pattakkaran*, served as the primary catalyst for these tumultuous events. Scholars worked to contextualize religiosity within the spectrum of resistance movements in Malabar, using the term *Moplah* to encompass religious group.[34] However, 'Moplah' was not exclusively used historically to denote Muslims but also included Christians and Jews living in the region.

Conversely, R.E. Miller presented an alternative narrative that linked the Mysorean period with a temporary liberation for the Muslim populace from deeply entrenched feudalistic structures in Malabar.[35] However, this perspective requires refinement as it inadvertently overlooks the coexistence of numerous peasantry and tenants who lived harmoniously with their landlords, regardless of religious considerations. In this context, religion did not hold precedence over personal affiliations that fostered climate of religious coexistence among both the peasantry and the landlords. William Gamul Farmer, Jonathan Duncan, Alexander Dow and Charles Boddam, as part of a joint commission from Bengal and Bombay, were tasked with inspecting the state and condition of Malabar. Their report, submitted in 1792–1793, delves into various aspects of Malabar, including its history, culture, economy and geographical structure. This joint commission report revealed a noticeable shift in the mindset of the Muslim population about their land rights during the Mysorean era. Gradually, there was a growing inclination toward embracing the concept of autonomous land tenure, departing from the traditional feudal model, signaling a transition toward a more autonomous and individually oriented approach to land ownership and administration.[36]

It is important to approach this observation with nuance, as historical records show the presence of steadfast Mappilas who remained loyal to their landlords (*jenmis*), irrespective of their religious backgrounds.[37] This complex societal dynamic during the Mysorean period highlights the non-uniform and multifaceted nature of the evolution of land relationships, influenced by diverse factors. It becomes evident that, during Tipu Sultan's rule in Malabar, support for his administration did not solely revolve around religious affiliations. Instead, his tenure reflected the intricate and multifaceted political landscape. Opposition to the rule of the Mysore sultan was not exclusively rooted in religious sentiments, even among the Muslim populace. Hydrose Kutty Mooppan of Manathala, Chavakkad, fought against Mysore alongside the Zamorin. His tomb is well protected, and people observe *nercha* to commemorate his martyrdom.[38] Tipu Sultan moved against the Kurikals in support of the Manjeri Raja when Kurikal, a revenue official for Mysore, overreached in a 1784 attack on the *raja*'s home and the local temple. Manjeri Kurikal's family history highlights the complex political dynamics of the period, demonstrating that conflicts were often driven by political and personal motives rather than solely by religious or confessional differences.[39] Various political considerations played a significant role in shaping the dynamics of allegiance dynamics. Support for Mysore often stemmed from shared political objectives rather than religious affiliations.

The British colonial administration made deliberate efforts to portray those who supported Tipu Sultan's rule in Malabar as driven by religious fanaticism. However, Tipu Sultan, as a ruler, granted land to numerous temples in the Malabar region, highlighting the nuanced interplay of religious dynamics during his reign. Also, the religious orientation of political leaders was scrutinized primarily when examining the Muslim population. Conversely, certain Muslims who aligned with the British cause did not have their religious proclivities as a significant consideration. Additionally, the British authorities sought to enlist specific leaders who had previously been allies of Tipu Sultan, offering concessions and influence in tax collection within their respective regions. (A comprehensive analysis of the case of Unni Mutha will be conducted in this section to illuminate this intricate aspect of the political landscape.) The colonial administration implemented stringent regulations for revenue collection in collaboration with loyal landlords.[40] Figures like C.A. Innes argued that these regulations, seemingly involving consultations, exhibited a pronounced bias favoring revenue maximization for the colonial government, often at the expense of the welfare of the peasant class.[41]

In its early stages, the British administration displayed a notable inclination toward favoring landlords, resulting in a discernible bias against the tenant population. This pro-landlord stance significantly contributed to unrest in the region and had deep historical roots dating back to the era of the Mysorean sultans. The characterization of tenants as inherently untrustworthy fostered an environment conducive to their unfavorable treatment by the British administrative apparatus.[42] Consequently, the visible disparities in treatment among different communities during the early phases of British colonial governance in the region can be directly attributed to this systemic bias.

Reports by figures such as Logan shed light on earlier instances of resistance in locations like Mannarkkad, Tamarasseri (Thamarassery), Vettattnad (Vettathunad), Chernad (Cheranad) and Ernad (Eranad). These events were often depicted as conflicts between adherents of Hindu and Muslim faiths, but during this period, Hindus and Muslims coexisted harmoniously, and religious affiliations were not the primary drivers of these disputes. William Logan, as part of his official colonial duties, concluded that these 'upheavals' fundamentally stemmed from economic issues related to land ownership, which exacerbated hostilities between the two religious communities, eventually leading to what were colloquially termed 'banditry events' within the specified regions.[43]

The historiography of K.P. Padmanabha Menon draws extensively from colonial data, and his narrative aligns with a perspective where Muslims, having experienced a significant reduction in their once considerable influence, harbored deep animosity in response to this curtailment. In contrast, Nair adherents, backed by the British East India Company, sought retribution against their former oppressors. The convergence of these volatile forces culminated in a dire and significant outcome. The colonial data sources played a crucial role in this historical analysis, as exemplified in Menon's posthumously published book, which adhered to a similar narrative. Menon's view on the nomenclature of the region, where Malayalam was commonly used and Kerala was considered an oligarchical term, is a noteworthy aspect of his work. However, it has often been overlooked in subsequent historical accounts. He wrote his book at a time when common castes did not yet have the freedom to access public spaces or enter temples. Consequently, in earlier writings, the term *Hindu* primarily denoted the oligarchical class or landowners, with the common peasantry rarely finding representation in the historical narratives of the region during that period.[44]

The implementation of colonial measures, ostensibly to establish control and governance, generated resentment and indignation among the populace. Consequently, this era witnessed the emergence of early forms of resistance in the Malabar region, born out of shared dissatisfaction and opposition to colonial rule. These resistances were a direct response to the discriminatory policies and practices enacted by the British administration.

31 January 1794: Colonial Conquest—Unpacking British Looting in Mysore

Historical literature is not merely a bullet-point list of dates and dull facts, names and events. Usually, it is a lucid and vivid competition between different characters and their emotions, between contrasting interpretations and narratives of the past. There are rigorous debates about what aspects should be more pronounced. It is a complicated intellectual discipline that absorbs multiple comprehensions of the past. After each attack, the British engaged in looting in Mysore, even raiding their granaries. These actions were officially reported to incite a group of warmongers who consistently sought financial gain from these stolen goods. The reports describe the distribution of valuable items seized from Tipu Sultan, which was referred to as 'prize money'.[45] This distribution seemed to function as an incentive to garner public support for British colonial rule. The reports provide intricate details about the allocation of these valuables among various groups that supported the British during the war. It explicitly notes that these items were confiscated and looted after the war.

> The honourable company having been pleased to relinquish to the Army, its right to that Moiety of Military Stores and Grain, captured from the Enemy, during the late war with Tippoo Sultan, the value whereof had been retained, and to direct that the Amount should be issued for the purpose of being distributed and the Honourable the Governor in Council, of Fort St. George, having in consequence, being pleased further to direct, that the value of the Military Stores and Grain, retained, together with tie Sums lodged in the Treasury,

> which had accrued from the sale of other captured property, should be issued to the Prize Agents of the Army on the 15th day of February next, ensuing: Prize Agents do therefore hereby give Notice, that so soon as the Amount of the above Funds shall have been trued to them Government, they will forthwith proceed to distribute the same as follows: viz The shares of the Commissioned Officers will be paid to tie Officers individually, or to their Agents, or Representatives. The Shares of Native Commissioned Officers, of European and Native Non-Commissioned Officers, of Soldiers, Sepoys, and Persons classed as such, will be paid as was authorized, and practiced at the distribution of the former dividends of Prize Money, for the late War, to commanding Officers of Corps, or their Agents.[46]

The report was followed by detailed distribution records, specifically noting the amounts on various war dates: 31 July 1791 and 24 February 1792. The report also mentions that 'prize money' was distributed in 1790 and 1791. Not all precious items taken by the British from Tipu Sultan were included in these public lists. Some of these precious diamonds, ornaments and special gadgets were not publicly accounted for; instead, they were looted and taken by war-mongering officers. From a colonial perspective, plundering and looting were viewed as significant events and were celebrated as 'prize money' when they occurred against resistant groups opposing colonial administration. However, when such actions were committed against colonial administration or those loyal to it, they were considered grave crimes. This distinction was reflected in the newspaper reports and colonial administrative records of that era.[47]

9 April 1798: Colonial Complexities—Navigating Allies and Adversaries of Imperial Rule

Unni Mutha, a prominent agrarian figure known as a distinguished *kanamdar*[48] within the territorial boundaries of Valluvanad during the reign of the Mysorean rulers, is a noteworthy historical character. However, a pivotal moment in his life occurred following the events of 1786–1787. During this crucial period, he, along with a devoted cohort of a hundred followers, decided to pledge their allegiance and offer their services to the esteemed sovereign Tipu Sultan.

The complex historical circumstances that led to his transition from a respected agriculturist to a devoted adherent in Tipu Sultan's service underscores the nuanced nature of the sociopolitical landscape during the Mysorean rule. Unni Mutha consistently advocated for the sultan's endeavors, notably during the confrontations with the English East India Company in 1791. These substantial contributions propelled him into a position of conspicuous influence, to the extent that he dared to challenge the established authority of the colonial power. Leveraging his newfound ascendancy, he embarked on the construction of a fortified and bastioned residence, strategically positioned at the base of the Western Ghats. The establishment of such a robust dwelling underscored his resolute readiness to directly confront colonial forces and highlighted the strength of his position.[49]

The defeat of Tipu Sultan seems to have triggered Unni Mutha Moopan's heightened assertiveness, which was evident in a significant incident involving a British officer who interfered with his tax collection activities in a specific area. In response, Unni Mutha Moopan promptly communicated his strong disapproval of the intervention and insisted on the restoration of the previous status quo. The tone of his message exudes a blend of defiance and self-assuredness, with Unni Mutha Moopan firmly expressing his stance and hinting at his willingness to take direct action if his demands were ignored. He made it clear that he had no fear of the officer, his contingent or his entourage. Furthermore, Unni Mutha Moopan emphasized the officer's responsibility for the safety of himself and his associates, which included Nairs, head Chitties, other Chitties and customs personnel. This emphasis underscored the potential consequences of any harm that might befall them, thereby intensifying the gravity of the situation.[50]

This communication serves as an excellent example of Unni Mutha Moopan's audacious determination and unwavering resolve in protecting his vested interests and maintaining his authoritative position within the regional context. Furthermore, it sheds light on the complex power dynamics and individual personas during a historical period marked by the aftermath of Tipu Sultan's downfall and the subsequent establishment of colonial rule in the region.[51] The accusations of 'fanaticism', 'militancy' and 'jihad' were set aside in the case of Unni Mutha Moopan, when he joined hands with the British. William Logan also played a strategic role in documenting the fluid nature of loyalties.[52] His narrative encapsulates the power dynamics and acts of resistance during an era characterized by heightened geopolitical tensions and shifting fidelities. Unni Mutha Moopan's close affiliation with Tipu Sultan undoubtedly played a pivotal role in shaping his subsequent actions and the dynamics of power and influence in the region during this transformative historical phase.

Conrad Wood and Stephen F. Dale also took a strategic approach in narrating Unni Mutha's stories and the British approaches to him at different stages. Unni Mutha's unequivocal and self-directed leadership style within the region vividly illustrate his determination to assert his dominion, aligning with the principles and interests championed by Tipu Sultan. The colonial interest in him stemmed from his potential to control the region and collect revenue for the British authorities. His insurgency showcased a level of individual agency and political autonomy, setting him apart from being a passive subordinate under colonial jurisdiction. Consequently, colonial historians refrained from launching an aggressive linguistic war against him due to the double standards of colonial authorities, who sought to exploit the situation in favor of the colonial administration. The acknowledgment of his close association with Tipu Sultan, combined with his proactive and politically motivated policies, offers a multifaceted perspective on his position and actions during an era marked by regional turmoil and the fluid realignment of political loyalties.[53]

The striking contrast between Unni Mutha's ostentation and the restrained demeanor typically associated with colonial governance underscores the dynamics of power and the cultural disparities characterizing this historical period. The reported unease among British officials indicates that his behavior and actions were perceived as a blatant defiance of colonial norms and were a prominent manifestation of his autonomous and assertive stance. This interpretation highlights the complexities in the relationship between colonial authorities and indigenous leaders like Unni Mutha, characterized by a blend of collaboration and contention as they navigated the evolving sociopolitical landscape of the era. The conceptualization and manifestation of obedience by Unni Mutha can be inferred through a careful examination of his methodologies. Notably, his use of symbolic elements such as flags, the Nekareh (a ritualized drumming salutation) and the Nobit (a ceremonial musical instrument) collectively signifies his unwavering insistence on securing loyalty and allegiance from his followers. These emblematic gestures underscore his strong emphasis on soliciting unswerving loyalty and acknowledgment of his authoritative stature.[54]

The British aversion to Unni Mutha can be attributed to factors like his extravagant lifestyle rather than the fanaticism that British often associated with Muslim resistance against them. As documented by the joint commission report of 1792–1793, Unni Mutha's flamboyant character and lavish way of life caused discomfort and irritation among British officials. His penchant for extravagant displays and opulent practices seemed to deviate from the expected norms of British propriety, leading to a sense of unease within the official ranks. This stark contrast between his extravagant lifestyle and the more reserved conduct expected from colonial subjects emphasized his deliberate assertion of power and authority, challenging the influence of the colonial administration in the region. Unni Mutha gained favor with the colonial authorities due to his alliance with them. Previously aligned with Tipu Sultan, his governance exhibited a distinct sovereign character, indicating a significant degree of autonomy and authority. This attribution of sovereignty finds support in various aspects that collectively illustrate the extent of his dominion and the strength of his influence in the region. These practices underscore Unni Mutha's deliberate efforts to strengthen his authority within the intricate fabric of the regional milieu.[55] Together, these stories show how Unni Mutha had a lot of power and control in the region. He was good at gathering information and getting support from religious leaders. This shows how influential and effective he was as a leader within his territory.[56]

By advocating strongly for a pension to sustain his retinues, Unni Mutha aimed to secure their economic well-being and, consequently, ensure their unwavering loyalty to his leadership. This insistence on financial support underscores his determined commitment to preserving his autonomy and authoritative position, even in the face of shifting political paradigms. His calculated demand for a pension serves as a prime example of his astute understanding of the crucial role played by safeguarding the welfare of his supporters in maintaining his stature and resisting the encroachments of the newly established ruling authority.[57]

In 1793, a coordinated British military expedition led by Major Dow was launched to subdue Unni Mutha, which ultimately ended in failure. Subsequently, command was assumed by Captain Burchall, who meticulously planned a siege on Unni Mutha's fortified residence. Despite the determined and concerted efforts of the British forces, Unni Mutha responded with agility, launching a counteroffensive that allowed him to successfully evade and escape from the encircling grasp of the British troops. This historical episode stands as a vivid testament to Unni Mutha's shrewd military acumen and his adept maneuvering in thwarting the British attempts to capture him. The strategic advantage provided by his heavily fortified residence allowed him to withstand the prolonged siege and orchestrate an effective retaliatory campaign. The outcome of this engagement underscores the formidable challenges faced by the British military apparatus in their efforts to assert dominance over assertive and resourceful local leaders like Unni Mutha. This historical period was marked by a volatile political landscape characterized by shifting allegiances and competing interests.[58]

The failure of the British forces to apprehend Unni Mutha serves as a clear illustration of the intricate layers inherent in the paradigm of colonial rule in the specific region under examination and the serious limitations to the imperial project. Authorities assumed the prerogative to dictate the play of communal politics—the melange of actions endowed with swirling sociopolitical significance. This episode highlights the resolute resistance mounted by indigenous leaders against external incursions.[59] Unni Mutha's determination and resistance prompted the British forces to reassess their operational strategy. Recognizing the formidable challenges intrinsic to containing Unni Mutha's insurgency and seeking a resolution to the protracted conflict, the colonial authorities opted for a path of negotiation. On 8 May 1794, a formal agreement was reached between the colonial administration and Unni Mutha. As a key component of this agreement, the British authorities agreed to reinstate Unni Mutha's domain, Elambulasseri, thereby validating his dominion over the defined region. Additionally, Unni Mutha was granted an annual stipend of ₹1,000, signifying official acknowledgment and monetary compensation for his cooperation. This pivotal accord illustrates the delicate balance between coercive strategies and diplomatic channels employed by the British administration to quell the 'uprising' while appeasing the 'insurgent leadership'. The accord reached between the colonial administration and Unni Mutha shows the pragmatic approach embraced by the former, as they chose diplomatic reconciliation over prolonged conflict. The restoration of his estate and the provision of a monetary stipend can be seen as a deliberate strategy employed by the British authorities to pacify the influential leader.[60]

At the heart of Unni Mutha's demands was his persistent request for a share of the revenue generated from his place. The colonial administration's inability to meet this specific demand played a crucial role in prolonging his resistance. In their efforts to intensify their pursuit of his capture, the British authorities even issued a bounty of ₹3,000 for Unni Mutha's apprehension and to assert their dominance, British forces under the command of Captain MacDonald launched an offensive campaign. Their strategic efforts culminated in encircling and dismantling Unni Mutha's fortified stronghold in the Pandalur Hills near Malappuram. This military operation resulted not only in the destruction of his fortified residence but also in the dismantling of the dwellings and fortifications associated with his followers. In the final analysis, British protection and collaboration proved conditional, tentative and illusory. Following the swings and roundabouts of the victories of Muslim and native princes across southern India, most of the men involved in the resistance were gaoled and some murdered.

In either case, their reputation and latent motives were tarnished by a deliberate obfuscation of the history, often mired in lucid accusations of atrocities. The limited paperwork available and the demise of most participants has left modern scholars with limited options for accurate research. Indeed, there remains a serious paucity of information.

Following this British military incursion, Unni Mutha was forced to seek refuge in the depths of the Wayanad jungles, eluding capture and continuing his insurgency from a more secluded position.[61] This historical episode underscores Unni Mutha's committed determination to protect his vested interests and his resolute pursuit of what he perceived as his rightful share of revenue. This also underlines the role of energetic human agency—men like Tipu Sultan and Unni Mutha mattered. The intractable gyrations of their ambitions and experiences before, during and after the conflicts—their pious sense of individual responsibility, their competency and failures, plus their personal passions and philosophies—all contributed significantly to particular developments and policies and the overall triumphs and disappointments of the wider enterprises they were associated with. Moreover, this narrative highlights the British authorities' determination to consolidate control and establish dominion over local leaders who challenged their determined rule. The intriguing historical narrative unfolds as Tipu Sultan, under the lens of colonial historiography, is cast as adopting a fanatic stance. In stark contrast, Unni Mutha navigated away from the confines of such ideological categorizations, engaging with colonial powers for a finite duration. This dynamic invites scholarly examination, urging an exploration of the mechanisms influencing the construction of these historical representations and the nuanced interactions between individuals and colonial forces.

Conclusion

The Malabar region is a testament to a remarkable history of colonial resistance, where the preservation of communal harmony and interreligious coexistence formed the backbone. Through centuries, this land saw a remarkable union between Muslims and Hindus, united in their fight to safeguard their Hindu king. The cultural integration that evolved over time became the cornerstone of this unity, fostering celebrations that bound people together, transcending religious boundaries. This integration was not merely superficial; it ran deep, as Muslims embraced local traditions, leading to the indigenous adaptation of their practices and beliefs, thereby nurturing a vernacularized form of religion in the region. This rich cultural fabric and strength of the south found its roots in the longstanding Indian Ocean trading connections, which further fortified its resilience. The resistance against British colonial forces was not an isolated event but rather a continuation of this longstanding cultural resistance—a testament to the enduring spirit of unity and strength that characterized the history of Malabar. This history exemplifies how communal harmony, cultural integration and shared resistance have been integral to the region, serving as an inspiration for generations to come.

Chapter 6

THE LEGACY OF MAMBURAM

Communal Harmony and Anti-Colonial Resistance

In the tapestry of my early childhood days, Mamburam stood as a celestial beacon, a sanctuary woven into the fabric of coexistence. Like a lighthouse in the dark and wild sea, Mamburam Thangal steadfastly guided the region through the labyrinth of life's defining moments, his captivating charisma permeating every thread of the collective consciousness. Cherished by Muslims and embraced by people of all faiths, Sayyid ʿAlawi Thangal—widely known as Mamburam Valiya Thangal—served as a haven for all, transcending barriers of religion and caste.[1] Our neighbor Cheru Chakki always relied on Mamburam for her personal and family matters. Cheru Chakki's unwavering calls to Thangal resonated through the atmosphere, forming a harmonious melody of devotion and solid trust that transcended time. Mamburam Thangal's sacred aura exceeded the mortal realm, casting an eternal glow upon our lives. Even as generations passed, his ethereal flame continues to burn brightly, an ever-present guiding star, unextinguished by the sands of time. To our community, he is more than a memory or a distant figure of the past; he remains an inexhaustible source of solace, a spring of inner peace. Like a tranquil oasis in the vast desert of life's trials, Sayyid ʿAlawi Thangal's benevolence provides respite and nourishment. We seek refuge in his spiritual embrace, finding comfort and fulfillment in his blessings, which flow abundantly, like a sacred stream nourishing our collective spirit. Truly, Mamburam Thangal was a celestial anchor, tethering us to the divine, transcending the realms of morality and instilling in us an unswerving faith. His legacy, like a spiritual sphere, even in his physical absence, continues to shape lives, guide journeys and provide the sanctuary of the heart.[2]

The shrine of Sayyid ʿAlawi Thangal in Mamburam holds great significance both academically and spiritually. It serves as the symbolic starting point for newborns during the auspicious *Yaram Mudal* ritual.[3] Wrapped in a verdant green silk mantle infused with the alluring scent of attar from Thangal's holy sepulture, infants were embraced by the sanctuary's aura. While personal recollections of these moments elude me, the vivid memory of an eventful childhood day has become intertwined with a pilgrimage to the Mamburam Shrine. In our family, every joyous occasion and significant event began with a blessed visit to Mamburam. The shrine brimmed with captivating narratives, like the enchanting tales of Kizhakkepalli and Ottakkal Palli (mosque), where my father revered his own Sufi sheikh. The stories about the inception of all the mosques in the villages adjacent to Mamburam continue to carry the influence of Thangal's legacy. 'Irukulam Palli' translates to 'mosque of two ponds', but after the mosque was constructed, only one pond remained. According to a story that has been passed down for generations, this alteration took place because Mamburam Thangal, the key figure in the establishment of the mosque, advised the local community to build the mosque on the site where the second pond had previously existed. During our early childhood, we used to participate in the Friday congregational prayers at this mosque. Like several other mosques in the vicinity, this mosque remains a testament to the enduring legacy of Mamburam Thangal. These stories unfold like ancient manuscripts, intertwining mysticism and tradition. Mamburam's sanctuary serves as a revered integrated gateway, where we sought guidance, protection and a deep sense of belonging. Its hallowed embrace nurtures empathies, cultivating a profound connection to heritage and an abiding reverence for spiritual lineage.

Thangal's protection extends beyond all boundaries, as people from all walks of life and diverse religious and caste backgrounds tell countless adventurous stories from villages and their personal experiences. The festival of Kaliyattakkavu is a testament to the communal harmony fostered by Mamburam Thangal, who facilitated peaceful worship for downtrodden Hindus in the region. As the last among the farmers' festivals of the region, Kaliyattakkavu marks a moment of unity, where people put aside their quarrels and resolve year-long troubles before commencing new paddy cultivation after *Edavappathi*.[4] Thangal's influence is evident in this harmonious gathering, where festivity becomes a catalyst for reconciliation and collective growth. Thangal supported a lower-caste Hindu in establishing her own place of worship, exemplifying a spirit of inclusivity. The oral history of Kaliyattakkavu reflects the social system prevailing until the 19th century, marked by untouchability for those from the lowest caste. The chance to worship and host festivals signified great esteem. To this day, during the anniversary celebration at Kaliyattakkavu, a ceremonial effigy march upholds traditions, paying homage to the holy shrine of Thangal for his profound support. In these narratives and celebrations, Thangal's legacy shines brightly, transcending barriers and fostering a sense of unity and reverence among the diverse communities that share the same sacred land.

Sayyid ʿAlawi Thangal (1752–1844): A Beacon of Anti-Colonialism and Social Reform

The Thangals of Mamburam, most notably Sayyid ʿAlawi, played pivotal roles in the resistance against colonial forces during a significant historical period. They were affiliated with the Ba'Alwi Sufi order, an institution whose origins in the region can be traced back to Shaikh Jifri (1727–1807) of Calicut.[5] Shaikh Jifri, who bore the distinguished family name Ba'Alwi, introduced this Sufi tradition to the region and wielded substantial influence. People from various backgrounds continue to approach the shrines of Shaikh Jifri in Calicut and Sayyid ʿAlawi in Mamburam, seeking spiritual and worldly guidance. During my research visit, they graciously shared with me manuscript copies of the books that have been preserved as part of the sacred tradition in this revered place in Jifri house.[6]

The Ba'Alwi Sufi order, while well known, is fundamentally a subsidiary of the Qadiri Sufi order. Originally from Tarim in Hadhramaut, southern Arabia, Sayyid 'Alawi arrived in Mamburam in 1770. His uncle, Sayyid Hasan Jifri (1720 –1764), had occupied a distinguished position as a religious educator and community leader in Mamburam. Sayyid ʿAlawi Thangal married Hasan al-Jifri's daughter. His profound spiritual contemplation and mysticism quickly earned him recognition in the societal milieu. Individuals hailing from diverse religious backgrounds sought his wisdom for the resolution of dilemmas. Consequently, Sayyid ʿAlawi earned great esteem, ascending to the role of a spiritual authority and emerging as a prominent political figure, widely acknowledged as Mamburam Thangal.[7]

The fluctuations in transoceanic trade and the Zamorin's relatively successful state-building endeavors were significantly impacted by prolonged conflicts and the challenges posed by European invasions in the area. The historical documentation of Mamburam Thangal in the colonial records of Malabar in 1817 is found in a letter authored by District Collector and Magistrate Vaughan, dispatched to the Madras authorities. The communication delineates an incident involving an 'assault on government property'. In this correspondence, James Vaughan, who served as the magistrate of Malabar during that period, explicitly identifies Sayyid ʿAlawi Thangal as the instigator and leader of the 'attack'.[8] The report encapsulates a significant juncture in the interaction between Mamburam Thangal and the colonial administration, shedding light on the prominence of the Sufi Sayyid[9], whose widespread acceptance in Malabar society epitomized the reconfiguration and assertion of 'Islamic sovereignty'. Following the arrival of the inaugural British commissioners tasked with assessing Malabar's revenue potential and instituting an interim government, the East India Company encountered a succession of dissenting voices and resistance. This multifaceted resistance served as a testament to the layers of sovereignty characterizing the dynamics of power and authority. The specific episode that provoked Vaughan's response held deep-seated roots in Malabar's enduring resistance against the transformative governance introduced by the East India Company. Recorded by colonial officials in varying terms, ranging from acts of resistance to instances of disorder, this resistance had an extensive and nuanced historical context within the region.

In the original document, Thangal's name is written as Taramalle Coya Tangal, and he is described as an Arab by birth who has settled in the province for 40 years. It mentions the British perception that the 'Moplah Mussulman in Malabar looks to him almost as a Prophet'. The first summons issued for him to attend in person before Vaughn was not delivered to Thangal. The document notes that 'the Peon who was sent with the summons might be maltreated or even murdered'. This highlights the administration's propaganda, suggesting that the officials did not know what happened to their peon who carried the summons to Thangal. The second summons was sent with a 'small party of armed Colkars' to prevent any resistance. The summons to appear before Vaughan could not be delivered because Sayyid Alawi Thangal was unavailable; the peon and his party could not reach him in Mamburam. Upon receiving information about his reappearance in Calicut, Vaughan issued a subsequent summons, this time dispatching only a messenger without an armed escort. Vaughan had been informed through his sources that any fears of 'violent resistance' from Sayyid ʿAlawi Thangal was unwarranted. Despite these efforts, Sayyid ʿAlawi Thangal remained elusive, evading any direct interaction with the emergent authorities. Thangal's deliberate avoidance of even a simple encounter with the new claimants to authority carried significant implications.[10] His stance in refusing to acknowledge British authority was a resolute rejection, akin to leading an armed resistance, a perception that swiftly circulated as anecdotes surrounding his actions. These speculations persisted as an inherent part of his legacy, which encompassed both the inheritance of resistance and the responsibility for the broader Muslim community and its collective actions. Vaughan's persistent attempts to summon Sayyid ʿAlawi Thangal were countered by petitions from prominent personalities of the region. However, Vaughan remained steadfast in his decision, noting that he deemed it inappropriate to entertain their plea as long as Thangal persisted in refusing, or rather, abstaining from attending his office.[11]

Mamburam Sayyid ʿAlawi Thangal's pervasive influence and extraordinary stature restrained the magistrate from hastily resorting to coercive measures. Recognizing Thangal's eminence, Vaughan sought mediation through the esteemed qadi of Calicut, acknowledging the layers of sovereignty and jurisdictional complexities inherent in the situation. Engaging in a private conference, Vaughan summoned the town qadi, a figure of considerable repute. During their deliberations, Vaughan expounded upon the potential consequences of Thangal's persistent refusal to adhere to the summons. While expressing reservations regarding Mamburam Sayyid ʿAlawi Thangal's conduct, Vaughan assured that any interaction with Thangal would be conducted with utmost respect and dignity. This report serves as a testament to the profound influence wielded by Mamburam Sayyid ʿAlawi Thangal, elucidating how his stature significantly influenced decision-making processes and diplomatic engagements within the jurisdictional landscape.[12] Magistrate Vaughan's perspective implies that the confrontation with Thangal necessitated substantial support from Madras owing to Thangal's formidable influence. Vaughan astutely recognized that quelling and regulating an emerging popular movement would exact a considerable toll, potentially encumbering his professional trajectory. Vaughan, in his assessment, categorized Thangal and his adherents as 'fervent zealots', forewarning his dearth of resources to manage the repercussions.[13]

In Malabar, Sayyid ʿAlawi Thangal played a seminal role in instigating anti-British sentiment. His discerning comprehension of the profound implications of the colonial British administrative changes paralleled that of Umar Qazi of Veliyankode (c. 1757–1856). Umar Qazi journeyed to Mamburam Thangal, accompanied by his associate Aoukoya Musaliar. Umar Qazi experienced a profound intellectual transformation, influenced by the complexities surrounding his acceptance of Thangal as his sheikh. Consequently, Umar Qazi resolved this ambiguity by acknowledging Mamburam Thangal as his spiritual guide. This popular encounter is mentioned in the records of Mamburam Mala.[14] This shared perspective was conspicuously evident through their close affiliation, particularly in Umar Qazi's unwavering support for Thangal across various circumstances. K.N. Panikkar has mentioned this transformative process in his research on Malabar.[15]

Colonial historiography offers divergent perspectives on the engagement of Sayyid ʿAlawi Thangal in armed resistance vis-à-vis the British colonial administration and local landlords. Nevertheless, a prevailing consensus posits that Thangal actively aligned himself with the Cherur 'uprising' to uphold the ethos and prestige of the agrarian community in the region. In the process of bolstering colonial ideological constructs, Stephen Dale discernibly casts the armed conflict as a dual-frontal struggle, pitting the insurgents against both British forces and the broader Hindu societal milieu. Notably, while Dale meticulously delineates the religious affiliation of local landlords, he conspicuously omits reference to the religious orientation of the colonial actors, thereby emblematic of a nuanced colonial historiographic strategy.[16]

Richard Eaton questions the colonial bipolar stance on the history of Islam in India with ample evidence from modern texts and more intuitive sensibility. The transformation from an unbiased view to this bipolar stance has more often been asserted than studied or elucidated:

> Although sixteenth century Spaniards justified their conquest of Mexico in religious terms, modem texts never speak of a 'Christian conquest' of America; nor is the post-1492 period ever called America's 'Christian Era'. Rather, one hears of a 'Spanish conquest' of Central and South America, and of 'European settlement' in North America. How, one might then ask, did the notion of an 'Islamic' conquest of India find such a secure hold in the historiography of South Asia?[17]

In his work, Eaton describes the 'Muslim' conquest as the Persianate age and explains how textile manufacturing and other industrial development flourished in the region, stating that the era also witnessed India's emergence as the world's industrial powerhouse based on the export of manufactured textiles. This methodology of an Islamic conquest of India is so consistent and common that it is still usually overlooked by contemporary researchers who ignore the practice without really considering the concrete consequences at the grassroots level of society. The notion that India merely stood still for eight centuries is, to say the least, mistaken.[18]

This colonial historiographical paradigm becomes clearer when contextualized within the prism of potential consequences entailing a forcible seizure of Thangal. Contemplation of such an action elicited trepidation, as it portended the instigation of a widespread 'uprising' among the populace, each denizen equipped with a 'ubiquitous and perilous knife'—a prospect deemed profoundly disconcerting by colonial authorities. Thangal's pronounced antipathy toward British colonial authority was evident in his writings and actions, as he lent his sacred authority to support movements against both the British and local landlords within the contemporary milieu. The archival record unveils the inaugural trace of Sayyid ʿAlawi Thangal's involvement through his association with the apprehension of Manjeri Athan Kurikal and his entourage, including 'armed retinues', during an 'insurrection' spearheaded by Unni Mutha Moopan, Manjeri Kurikal and Chemban Poker, staged within the precincts of the Mamburam Mosque. Notably, British colonial administrators were reluctant to arrest Thangal, a posture ostensibly conceived to preempt potential public dissent. In this vein, Collector James Vaughan, in April 1817, transmitted a missive to the Madras Government, emblematic of this subjective evaluation and circumspect stance.[19]

The British authorities discerned a noteworthy association between the Kurikal family and the Mamburam Thangal. They possessed differences and rifts that occasionally spilled over into the public domain, but they usually cooperated to foster traditions and create new cultural and social activities. They shared political considerations that often brought them together. Although not a unified group in the modern sense, these actors singled out similar issues and problems in Malabari Muslim society, proffered analogous solutions and tapped into the same spiritual and cultural imagery. This connection became particularly apparent when the offspring and kin of Manjeri Athan Kurikal sought to reclaim their ancestral land, which had been confiscated.[20] Even in the aftermath of the quelling of the resistance in 1817, the collector expressed apprehension that Thangal's continued involvement could have enduring repercussions.[21] The British administration's concerns led to the adoption of a novel stratagem: infusing religious undertones in Thangal's actions. Notably, Thangal had the unique legacy of establishing the Kaliyattakkavu temple. Conrad Wood, in his work *Early Mappila Rebellion 1800-1802*, underscores how ʿAlawi Thangal's opposition to colonial exploitation of society engendered a moral foundation.[22] Colonial historians emphasized that Tirurangadi had long served as a focal point for 'fanaticism', with the Mamburam or Tharamal Thangal assuming a prominent role as its spiritual leader.[23] Nearly seventy years ago when 'Mappila outbreaks' first began in Malabar, it was at Mamburam that 'Mappila fanaticism' was focused and the *halilakkam* (religious frenzy) had its origin. Sayyid Fazl, the Thangal, frequently preached from the text that it was no sin, but a merit, to kill a landlord who evicted his tenants, and Shaheeds or martyrs, before embarking on their desperate enterprise, usually prayed at the shrine and sought his blessing.[24] For advocates and defenders of the British administration, history and the production of history came to manifest a didactic purpose: to foster loyalty to the Empire and bolster its power, hegemony and legitimacy. Furthermore, Stephen Dale attributes the emergence of the concept of 'suicidal Jihad' to this context.[25] Colonial officers like William Logan and C.A. Innes also tried to elucidate the colonial dimension of animosity directed at Thangal, concurrently attributing a religious facet to the resistance.[26] In K.N. Panikkar's examination of 'Alawi Thangal's anti-colonial stance within a regional context, he posits that Thangal's advocacy for a jihad against British colonial forces should not be misconstrued as indicative of a hostile attitude toward non-Muslim communities.[27] The trajectory of Muslim leadership in Malabar was structured by a plethora of imagined communities and social environments that Muslims had at their disposal, being part of the British imperial context but also being Malayalam speakers and members of the universal community.[28] Thangal, as Panikkar elucidates, maintained harmonious relations with the Hindu populace, among whom he enjoyed a substantial following of friends and admirers.[29]

During the period of British colonial governance in Malabar, there existed a categorization of Muslims as 'the worst race', a designation that emerged devoid of consideration for their intrinsic qualities or characteristics. This classification was starkly influenced by their perceived loyalty or opposition to British authorities. Citing Madras Governor-General Thomas Munro, Conrad Wood highlights the portrayal of Muslims as 'the worst race in Malabar' and the 'most hostile to British dominion'.[30] This selective adoption and rejection of certain aspects is key to colonial practices of marginalizing and damaging specific communities. In Logan's work *Malabar Manual*, an incident dated 26 November 1836 is recorded: Kallingal Kunhalan of Pandalur killed a Chakku Panikkar, an astrologer, injuring three others before absconding. Subsequent events saw his encounter with a police party under the leadership of the tahsildar on 28 November in Valluvanad Taluk, culminating in his demise during the ensuing confrontation. On 15 April 1837, Ali Kutti of Chengara amsam, Kalpetta desam, inflicted numerous severe wounds on Narayana Mussat. William Logan specifically highlighted Mussat as 'a Brahmin janmi'. According to the report, Ali Kutti then took refuge in his own shop, where he was attacked by the tahsildar and taluk peons and shot by the taluk police the following day. Another narrative, dated 5 April 1839, describes how Thorayampolakal Attan and another person from Pallipuram amsam killed Kelil Raman, set fire to a Hindu temple and then took refuge in another temple. They were subsequently attacked by the tahsildar and his peons and shot by a taluk peon. The British authorities highlighted these incidents, which involved Muslims against landlords, framing them as religious hostility. They emphasized the setting fire to the temple, and many of the accused were shot dead by the police without any formal judicial process.[31]

13 November 1841: Muttiyara Resistance—Unveiling the Collaborative Actions of the British Administration and Local Landlords

The Muttiyara Resistance is a significant historical event. The comprehensive references found in the India Office records shed light on the collaborative endeavors between the British administration and local landlords, their joint actions serving as catalysts against the peasantry within the region. This event forms the bedrock for a prolonged and complicated dispute. On 13 November 1841 in Mannur village near Pallipuram of Valluvanad Taluk, pivotal figures such as Kaidotti Padil Moideen Kutty, Pathyl Valia Kunhalan and others were involved in a consequential incident that resulted in the loss of lives, notably Tottesseri Thachu Panikkar and a peon. The circumstances preceding this resistance were meticulously recorded in a note authored by Kunhalan, directly addressing the tahsildar.[32] Originally acquired on a lease basis from Tottesseri Thachu Panikkar, Kundachenakkal Parambu underwent a series of developments. In 1820/1821, the landscape witnessed the establishment of a *kanom* (leasehold arrangement), followed by the construction of a tank and a shop, alongside the dutiful payment of government taxes. Subsequent years saw the excavation of a well in 1821/1822, with the formalization of landlord rights in 1822/1823. These sequential events significantly shaped the trajectory leading up to the Muttiyara Resistance and its aftermath.[33]

In 1841, escalating tensions arose from a dispute linked to the construction of a mud wall around the mosque, triggered by a false complaint registered by Tottesseri Panikkar at the taluk *kacheri*. The tahsildar acted swiftly without a comprehensive assessment, dispatching a *choondan* (peon) accompanied by several others. Their directive was to apprehend the nine individuals involved and bring them to the taluk *kacheri*. On the 28th day of the fast in the month of Ramzan, just before sunset, the *choondan* arrived at the mosque. He engaged the individuals verbally, demanding their immediate presence outside. Although these individuals expressed their willingness to comply after breaking their fast, the situation intensified when Panikkar forcibly restrained Moideen *Ikkakka*[34], the mosque's administrator, near the well. This altercation resulted in increased tensions. The eight individuals then armed themselves and waited for Panikkar to return from the taluk office.[35] According to colonial records, these individuals refused to surrender to the army and received support from a significant number of local inhabitants. The report indicates that they resisted arrest, motivated by a desire for martyrdom. All eleven were ultimately killed. The colonial administration demonstrated racial discrimination and inhumanity by burying their bodies alongside a dog. This action elicited 'outrage' among an estimated 2,000 Mappilas, prompting them to forcibly reclaim the bodies, reinstating them at the Muttiyara Mosque for an honorable martyr's burial. Consequently, twelve Mappilas faced apprehension, conviction and subsequent penalties imposed by the authorities in the aftermath of these events.[36]

19 October 1843: Exploring the Interplay of Religion and Social Grievances in the Cherur Resistance

The Cherur Resistance of 1843 was a culmination of deeply rooted religious, economic and social grievances among the people of the region. On 19 October 1843, five Muslims, led by Kunnancheri Ali Athan, murdered Kaprat Krishna Panikkar, an *adhikari*. Panikkar, empowered by the British administration, had affronted the sentiments of the predominantly 'low-class converts'.[37] These aggrieved individuals presented their grievances to Sayyid ʿAlawi Thangal, seeking his blessings to confront Panikkar. The issue of insult toward the newly converted had already been brought to the attention of the district collector, and Panikkar was subsequently found guilty and removed from his post. Unfortunately, the natives were unaware of this development and proceeded to kill Panikkar and another *adhikari*. They sought refuge in the residence of another Nair in Cherur, and later, another joined their ranks. On 24 October, a contingent of Native Infantry, led by Captain Leader, was dispatched to quell the defense. However, when the Muslims charged out, the sepoys were overwhelmed with fear and fled the scene. It is believed that Sayyid ʿAlawi Thangal himself led the battle on horseback. During the confrontation, three sepoys and one subahdar were killed, while Captain Leader and five sepoys sustained injuries. Additionally, seven peons were wounded, three of them seriously. Although all seven Mappilas who participated in the 'rebellion' were killed, the engagement marked a significant failure for the British forces and administration. Local historians estimate British casualties to be as high as twenty. During the defense, military authorities sought to cremate the martyrs' bodies, triggering resistance from the people. The bodies were reclaimed and buried at Mannathiparamba near Tirurangadi by the Mappilas, despite initial prohibitions by the authorities. It is believed that the injury sustained in this battle led to the demise of the Thangal (Fig. 6.1).

The revered seven Mappila martyrs were Poovadan Moideen, Punadakkapuram Moideen, Punthirundi Ismail, Pattarakkadavil Husain, Mussakkutty, Ali Hassan and Cholakkal Bukhari. Their valor

Figure 6.1
Mamburam Maqam Houses the Tomb of Sayyid ʿAlawi Mawla al-Dawilah al-Husayni Thangal

Photograph by Ajeeb Komachi

became the subject of commemorative songs that circulated widely, inspiring the natives in their struggle against colonial oppression.[38] These ballads, intrinsic to Malabar tradition, served as a catalyst for subsequent resistance, reigniting the memory of ancestors who sacrificed their lives for a noble cause. William Logan provides a detailed narration of these events, specifically noting the incident on 19 October 1843. He references individuals like Kunnancheri Ali Athan and his associates, who were involved in the killing of Kaprat Krishna Panikkar Adhikari. Logan recounts the death of the seven Mappilas, who later joined them and took refuge in a Nair's house in Cherur, declaring their determination to fight until the end. Logan details the involvement of a British detachment, led by Captain Leader, comprising various military ranks and personnel, in the subsequent operations. The conflict resulted in casualties among the British forces and local combatants. Logan's description of the events labels the native fighters as 'fanatics', highlighting their deaths at the hands of taluk peons and villagers. Their deaths triggered significant local protests against the biased and brutal actions of the British.[39]

There was controversy about the treatment of the deceased combatants by the British forces. Logan mentions the attempted burning of the fighters' bodies, which was eventually abandoned, leading to their burial far from Cherur near Tirurangadi Kacheri.[40] Differing narratives emerged among the locals, particularly concerning the deaths of all individuals involved in the conflict. Accounts of injustice and bias by British officers are prevalent in the popular stories of the Cherur region, which hold historical significance.[41] Logan references the district magistrate's report to the government (No. 29, dated 4 November 1843), highlighting the controversial perspectives and ongoing controversies surrounding the events: 'The military 1 detachment who had misbehaved were called into Calicut the next day and their place taken by a fresh body of 35 men, whom I thought it essential to keep in the disturbed locality until tranquility was more secured.' [42]

The locals argued that the military injustices during the Cherur event can be read between the lines.[43] ʿAlawi Thangal's significant support and substantial backing for non-Muslim communities is evident from the fact that non-Muslims still visit the shrine of the Mamburam Thangal and the nature of the celebrations of the local temple festival at Kaliyattakkavu and its ceremonial procession. Thangal's documented interactions and actions display a consistent pattern of fostering amicable relationships and providing substantial assistance to individuals and groups outside the Muslim community. His advocacy for inter-communal harmony and tangible support toward non-Muslim communities are evident in various historical sources.[44] It is discernible from field research with available local sources that Thangal engaged the services of a Hindu individual as his manager, showing his commitment to inter-communal cooperation. Thangal espoused the doctrine of Jihad-al-nafz[45], which places a distinct emphasis on self-purification as an integral facet for the progression of the community. He endeavored to purify personal practices and foster a cohesive sense of solidarity.

Sayyid Fazal Pookoya Thangal—Sayyid Fazal Pasha (1825–1900)

Upon Sayyid ʿAlawi Thangal's demise in 1844, his son, Sayyid Fazal Pookoya Thangal (1825–1900), assumed leadership and continued the legacy of anti-colonialism. He provided staunch support to those afflicted by colonial injustices. Against the backdrop of British-imposed evictions of farmers from their ancestral lands, leading to their loss of livelihood, Sayyid Fazal Pookoya Thangal advocated defense against landlords who had evicted peasants from their lands. The British administration misinterpreted this stance as an incitement to violence against all landlords.[46]

Fazal Thangal promulgated fatwas to catalyze social reform, particularly during a period marked by a notable influx of conversions to Islam among lower-class individuals. Among these edicts, three specific injunctions emerged, each of which provoked unease in the 'Hindu oligarchy community', as documented by the district collector.[47] In essence, Thangal's directives encompassed several critical facets of his mission for social reform. First, he mandated the abandonment of the usage of aristocratic titles when addressing individuals belonging to higher social strata. This edict was deliberate in its intent to challenge and disrupt established social hierarchies and prevailing norms. Second, Thangal discouraged the consumption of leftover food (referred to as *echil*) from the households of higher social strata. This directive served a multifaceted purpose: it not only instilled a sense of self-respect among individuals from the lower castes and new Muslims but also contributed to the preservation of distinct self-esteem and identities. The district collector later elucidated Thangal's stance as a deliberate and calculated effort to curtail practices.[48] This underscored Thangal's unwavering commitment to fostering and safeguarding religious and cultural distinctiveness, thereby contributing to the consolidation of a distinct socio-religious identity. Lastly, Thangal advocated for the cessation of coerced agricultural activities on Fridays to create time for congregational prayers. This was particularly relevant for farmers residing in the nearby villages of Mamburam, who had to journey some distance to attend the Friday congregational prayer. This observation, documented by the district collector within the annals of historical records, serves as a testament to the impact of reformist agenda on the broader socio-religious landscape of the period, and this engrossing and sympathetic study portrays the man as a highly competent and reliable person possessed of significant political and spiritual talents.[49]

K.N. Panikkar emphasizes that Sayyid Fazal Thangal played a crucial role in guiding the newly converted Muslims, particularly those from lower castes. Despite embracing Islam, many of them clung to their preexisting customs and practices without significant modification. Sayyid Fazal's efforts to bring about these changes presented a significant challenge to the authority and social standing of influential landlords and officials in the region.[50]

Thursday, 14 August 1851: Fabrics of Media Narratives—Traditions, Identity and Sociopolitical Transformations

In 1851, an article in the *Morning Advertiser* provided a detailed sketch of the 'Moplahs' of Malabar. The report portrays them as a tribe of Arabian descent who had settled on the coast of Calicut, where they predominantly remained. However, the report also contains offensive remarks and inaccuracies about the people. It claims that the Moplahs were 'Muslims of the most fanatical kind' and had little learning. It also states that they were primarily engaged in commerce and shipping, conducting a significant trade, especially with Arabian ports. These statements are contradictory and misleading and can be viewed as British colonial propaganda to undermine the influence of the local population on trade and commerce in the region.[51]

The report concerned the philanthropic works of the queen of Kannur, whose trading permits were more renowned than her regal manners. She profited from sending ships to Makkah (Mecca) with religious pilgrims. The British authorities respected her, and her family had acquired the principality from the Dutch. This succession was hereditary and exclusively in the female line. The report also describes the Moplahs in the interior as 'more fanatical' than those on the coast and depicted a 'Hindu–Muslim rivalry', emphasizing a feudalistic society and clan-like behavior among them. It suggests that Muslims in the interior were in constant feuds with Hindu landlords and farmers, who were looked down upon. These narratives contributed to the broader colonial strategy of divide and rule. The report portrays every dispute with Hindu neighbors as a religious feud, often exacerbated by spiritual chiefs.[52] However, there is evidence to suggest that these conflicts were not purely religious but driven by the loyalty of landlords to the colonial forces, while 'Moplahs' resisted British rule. Thus, there was no religious discrimination as claimed by the British but rather actions based on the behavior of landlords.[53]

The report falsely alleges that Tipu Sultan had employed these tribes to convert non-Muslims to Islam, leading to widespread violence and forced conversions. It also wrongly claims that every Moplah carried a dagger and frequently shed blood, creating fear among Hindus. These narratives served the colonial agenda of divide and rule but did not reflect the ground-level reality of harmonious coexistence among the local population. These reports emerged after the assassination of a British collector in Calicut, an incident discussed in the next chapter. The report also exaggerates the guerrilla warfare capabilities of the Moplahs, suggesting that they could field a hundred thousand armed fanatics. This negative portrayal of the region was used to justify brutal actions against them. In one instance, when the English resident requested assistance to apprehend a murderer, it was suggested that such interference would be impolitic, indicating a reluctance to provoke conflict in the region. However, the report does not provide the names of the individuals involved, raising questions about its accuracy and whether it was part of British propaganda against the local resistance.[54]

22 August 1851: The Controversy—Targeting Hindu Landlords

The British initiated biased religious reports from Malabar, widely circulated worldwide, regarding the killings of Hindus before 1921. On 22 August 1851, six Mappilas murdered Kottuparambath Komu Menon, the karyasthan of the Valluvanad *raja* and a wealthy landlord. Following this, they proceeded to Ittunni Ramu Menon's house, about two miles away, where they murdered him and Kadakkatil Nambudiri, an oligarchical landlord presents at the time. The 'insurgent group', numbering 19 by then, marched approximately 13 miles to Kolathur, where they attacked and killed Kolathur Warrier, a prominent local landlord. Two distinct patterns emerged in the actions, as noted by the special commissioner who described them as fanatics. First, they targeted the landlord; no other family members were harmed. At Kolathur Warrier's residence, women and children were instructed to vacate the premises. Second, they consistently burned account books. Notably, these '19 fanatics', supposedly seeking salvation by targeting Hindus, traversed about fifteen miles through a predominantly Hindu-populated region yet only targeted and murdered four affluent landlords. This discrepancy suggests that religious fanaticism might not have been the primary driving force behind their actions. The individuals of note, namely Komu Menon, Ramu Menon, Kadakkatil Nambudiri and Kolathur Warrier, held significant sway as landlords within the region. Komu Menon's demeanor, marked by a penchant for intoxication, was reportedly domineering and abusive, particularly evident in his interactions with tenants. Ramu Menon was reputed for his relentless usurious money lending practices and avaricious tendencies, while Kolathur Warrier faced accusations of land confiscation and encroachment upon religious institutions.[55]

The *Newcastle Guardian and Tyne Mercury* chronicled the incident in Kolatoor (Kolathur), Malabar, on 22 August. This occurrence, the fourth in the area, served as a focal point in reports designed to foment discord between the Hindu and the Muslim communities. These accounts provided purported justification for colonial interventions in the region. The incident portrayed 'Moplah fanatics' as a manifestation of a belief system centered on the perceived 'virtue of eliminating idolaters, purportedly securing a distinct reward in the afterlife'. The report presents a narrative steeped in fantasy, where 'fanatics' gathered, intent on achieving saintly status through the sacrifice of a wealthy high-caste Hindu near them. Allegedly, these individuals 'executed these beliefs by targeting such individuals, perpetrating murders and setting ablaze their residences'. These accounts, albeit sensationalized, achieved global circulation, painting the populace of Malabar as zealous and monstrous. The underlying motivation behind these reports lay in discrediting defenders resisting colonial incursions within the region. Significantly, these narratives often obscured the identities of victims, rendering them anonymous entities referred to vaguely as 'one Hindu' or 'another Brahmin'. The report extends its narrative, detailing the alleged killing of another Brahmin and the incapacitation of the village head, lacking specific temporal or crucial contextual details. Instead, it recounts two further fictitious events: one where they moved to a neighboring village, three miles distant, and killed the village head and seven others and another incident where they besieged the fortified house of a high-caste Brahmin.[56]

Criticism is leveled at the 39th Native Infantry for their purported inaction in stemming subsequent violence until 24 August, despite the presence of a detachment from the 39th Native Infantry, commanded by Major Wilkinson. The report's bias appears aimed at concealing British setbacks during this period within the region. Notably, civilians, lacking the sophisticated weaponry of the British colonial forces, resisted these colonial atrocities. Various detachments were deployed to the area and engaged unarmed individuals. The report delineates the overwhelming strength of the British forces deployed:

> The detachment continued firing at the house from two to four, with no effect. The Moplahs then charged the Sepoys, who panicked and fled, many abandoning their muskets. They incurred casualties of two men and a drummer. Subsequently, Major Wilkinson requested support from Her Majesty's 94th (a detachment of 50) and another company from the 29th stationed at Calicut, approximately 40 miles away. These forces arrived at Kolatoor on the 27th of August, augmented by Ensign Turner's detachment, totaling 220 men.[57]

The report further details the resistance force's estimated size: 'Numbering 17, the Moplahs engaged the troops.' The 94th detachment's initial volley proved ineffective, yet the subsequent volley claimed seven enemy casualties. Subsequently, as the Moplahs charged, they faced retaliatory fire from the Sepoys stationed on the Europeans' left flank, which momentarily staggered them. Before they could recover, the 94th had reloaded and discharged another volley.[58]

The indigenous populace, lacking formal combat training or access to armaments comparable to those of the colonial regiments, utilized small knives and sticks in their defense. Those knives were commonplace among the region's peasants and were traditionally carried at the waist for daily tasks, such as cutting areca nuts for consumption with betel leaves, and various personal uses, distinct from agricultural implements. The report asserts that those small personal knives became the impromptu weapons wielded by the surviving fighters during the confrontation with the colonial troops, leading to their swift subjugation—however, not before resulting in the killing of four individuals from the 94th regiment and a subedar from the 39th. Additionally, the report mourns the loss of Captain Mylne, blaming his death on the Arab tribes who hid the murderer, making it difficult to apprehend him. The report contemplates the practicality of acknowledging this affront as an unavenged transgression, considering the investment, both in terms of human lives and financial resources.[59]

The simultaneous publication of this report in both the *Tyrone Constitution* on 24 October 1851 and the *Newcastle Guardian* implies a coordinated orchestration in the realm of public relations and colonial stratagems, evidently designed to quell burgeoning resistance movements. This synchronized dissemination is palpable evidence of a concerted endeavor to stifle potential external support for these resistance factions. Aligned with antecedent reports, this document seemingly functions as a strategic instrument fostering discord within the populace, strategically calibrated to induce a sense of disillusionment and dissuasion. Moreover, the report tries to incite animosity toward the Malabar resistance, employing derogatory rhetoric to denigrate their actions and erode the legitimacy of their cause.[60]

The report featured in the *Morning Post* on 18 October 1851 echoes a consistent narrative without deviations in incidents or descriptions. Noteworthy is the newspaper's multifaceted coverage on the same page, with reports from various parts of the country alongside updates from China, as well as excerpts from the London Gazettes. The reporter expresses an apprehension about a prior occurrence in 1849, located near the current site where a contingent of Europeans had been permanently stationed following the initial 'outbreak'. Implicit within the report is a suggestion that proactive measures might have forestalled or mitigated the ensuing disaster.[61]

Saturday, 14 February 1852: Bombay Gazette, *the Definitive Perspective*

The *Bombay Gazette*, in its Saturday edition dated 14 February 1852, featured a correspondence from their representative stationed along the coast. This correspondence offers a more comprehensive insight into the Malabar region and its unique conditions and provides valuable suggestions for resolving the situation there. What makes this report particularly intriguing is the absence of similar accounts in newspapers from other parts of the world, many of which functioned as mouthpieces for colonial powers. Considering these circumstances, the following assumes significant importance:

> Things are now coming to a crisis now in Malabar and I much fear, if steps are taken to pacify the Moplahs, by removing the Nairs from office, a general rising will take place; the press (in extreme ignorance) represents the Moplahs as a cowardly, blood thirsty race; such, however, is far front the truth. Smarting under grievous wrongs, which they have borne till they became quite unbearable, their rage has at length burst its bounds and it is not the wrongs of a day, but the wrongs of years gone by, that they are redressing; and can we wonder at it? Have we not in our own civilized(?) Ireland instances of atrocities which quite throw Moplah outbreaks into the background, and for partly imaginary grievances? Are we, then, to be surprised that men who have suffered the grossest wrongs should, when no redress can be obtained by the laws, seek it at their own hands? People may prate about fanaticism, and Government may willfully shut their eyes against what is every day becoming more apparent; but the truth cannot much longer be concealed; the men are grossly oppressed, and they will no longer hear it. It may be all very well to talk of disarming the Moplah race, but would such a proceeding be practicable? And let me ask, is it not more than questionable policy to race over these men their bitterest enemies. Even supposing that we could secure the weapons of 20,000 desperate men, how long is it likely they would remain without others, when they manufacture them themselves, and have only to dig for materials? Remove all Nairs from office in Moplah districts, and place there instead the oldest and most trustworthy East Indians, who can talk their language, and with Mr. T. W. Goodwyn (Now Acting Resident at Tanjore) for Collector of Malabar, I will guarantee in three months this would be the quietest and happiest country in India. This is not intended as an attack on the esteemed Collector, there are many situations open for him, which he can have the pick of; but under existing circumstances change of air would do him good, and the country.[62]

The report in question recommends the removal of Nair individuals, alongside a steadfast emphasis on the need to pacify the populace. Delivered dispassionately and with ice-cold detachment, this marvelous effort certainly tried to eliminate skewed propaganda, uncritical journalism, popular prejudice and misconceptions and constituted a welcome endeavor toward a more integrated examination of the subject. The response—or lack thereof—well summed up the profound ambivalence and indifference toward popular grievances. These recommendations were evidently and conspicuously not implemented or incorporated into policy frameworks. Paradoxically, these proposals were systematically disregarded, seemingly eclipsed by the colonial force's unwavering pursuit of military preeminence over the indigenous populace.

In 1852, a special commission led by T.L. Strange was convened to investigate a series of outbreaks in Malabar. Rather than attributing these disturbances to agrarian discontent or economic deprivation, Strange's findings diverged, highlighting religious fanaticism catalyzed by influential religious leaders. Notably, the Mamburam Fazal Thangal of Tirurangadi, a prominent figure, was compelled to depart Malabar. Subsequently, in 1854, responding to Strange's recommendations, the legislative apparatus introduced the Moplah Outrages Acts, XXIII and XXIV. These legislative measures aimed to address the situation by empowering authorities to implement stringent policies. The first act granted authorities the ability to levy substantial fines on the populace, seize the assets of those found culpable and deport individuals suspected of involvement. The second act specifically prohibited the possession of the Moplah 'war knife'. To enforce these provisions, a specialized police force was established in Ernad. This period in colonial history emphasizes the administrative responses and legislative interventions implemented to address 'social unrest and violence' in Malabar during the 19th century.[63]

Nonetheless, when the British administration conducted inquiries into the root causes of the 'uprisings' that occurred in the region, they placed considerable emphasis on the influential role played by Sayyid Fazal. Consequently, they advocated for his deportation from the Malabar region to address the 'unrest and perceived instability'.[64] Meanwhile, the district collector H.V. Conolly forced Sayyid Fazal to migrate to Arabia, a decision that was executed on 19 March 1852. However, Connolly's actions infuriated the community, which had already experienced suppression and humiliation due to the enforcement of stringent regulations. Following Sayyid Fazal's exile, the British administration identified a potential ally in Sayyid Abdulla Koya Thangal (d. 1908), who utilized the platform of his journal, *Hidayat al Ikhwan*, to promulgate the value of British-centric education. His editorial stance within this publication aimed to persuade the Muslim populace to actively collaborate with British authorities.[65]

The colonial authorities remained apprehensive about the influence wielded by Sayyid Fazal in the region, even after his expulsion in 1852. Their pursuit and active obstruction of Sayyid Fazal's endeavors to return to Malabar exemplified their concerted efforts to curtail his potential impact. British interventions extended beyond mere pursuit, encompassing strategic involvement in areas like Dhofar, where Sayyid Fazal held considerable sway, often garnering support from local factions. Despite Sayyid Fazal's substantial roles in Arabian territories and his esteemed position within the Ottoman Empire in Istanbul, his persistent yearning to return to Malabar was consistently thwarted by calculated hindrances orchestrated by the colonial power.[66]

The correspondences between Jeddah and Madras reflect the colonial administration's meticulous scrutiny of Sayyid Fazal's movements in Arabia and their efforts to deter his re-entry into India. In a missive penned by Charles J.D. Cole, Her Britannic Majesty's vice consul and the East India Company's agent stationed in Jeddah, addressed to T. Pycroft, secretary to the Government of Fort Saint George, received upon Cole's arrival in Aden from Egypt on 24 December 1852, it was documented that Sayyid Fazal had departed from Arabia for Constantinople. Notably, while Sayyid Fazal had relocated, individuals associated with him, namely his family and followers, remained situated in the Hejaz. This correspondence illuminates the British administration's active endeavors to glean information on Sayyid Fazal Thangal's whereabouts. Subsequent directives from Pycroft mandated the transmission of this letter for the attention of the magistrate of Malabar, thereby directly disseminating this intelligence report to the magistrate and the collector in Malabar. Additionally, another correspondence originating from Charles J.D. Cole, addressed to T. Pycroft, dated 29 June 1853, reported Fazal Thangal's recent arrival in Constantinople approximately ten days prior. Learning of Thangal's intent to re-enter India, Cole conveyed to Thangal, via a communiqué, that the colonial government's position regarding his return remained unaltered. Emphatically, Thangal was reminded that re-entry into India necessitated prior explicit permission from the colonial authorities.[67]

The authorities used the count of attacks preceding and following Sayyid Fazal's expulsion to substantiate their actions, citing a reduction from eight attacks in the three years preceding his departure to only two in the subsequent three years. This statistical correlation was employed to bolster the rationale behind his exile. Sayyid Fazal's trajectory post-1852 exhibited substantial engagement in Makkah and the adjacent town of Ta'if, actively participating in Ottoman–Arab politics. Reports from 1856 indicate an alleged conflict wherein Sayyid Fazal purportedly clashed with the governor of Makkah during proceedings in a religious court. Sayyid Fazal assumed leadership in an eastern Arabian principality, Dhofar, potentially at the behest of local tribes, establishing his capital in Salalah. Field research in this region provided valuable insights, including discussions with Sheikh

Abdurrahman, who claimed familial ties to Sayyid Fazal. Notably, observations were made of the dilapidated former residence of the governor adjacent to their dwelling in Salalah, where a venerated portrait of Sayyid Fazal was displayed prominently. However, Fazal's tenure in Dhofar was terminated following a tribal uprising, leading to his expulsion.[68] Subsequent attempts to regain control of Dhofar were met with formidable resistance and thwarted by British intervention. Consequently, the latter phase of his life transpired in the Ottoman region of Istanbul.[69]

Bridging Continents and Advocating Anti-Colonial Values

During my research expedition in Turkey, I had the privilege of engaging with numerous scholars and researchers. The exploration of the extensive archives held by the Ottoman Empire revealed a treasure trove of documents pertaining to Sayyid Fazal.[70] This wealth of archival material remains largely unexplored, holding immense potential to unveil critical aspects of Sayyid Fazal's life, his influential role in intercontinental connectivity and his ideological stance against colonialism. These resources possess the promise of unveiling nuanced perspectives on the sociopolitical dynamics, diplomatic networks and cultural exchanges prevalent during Sayyid Fazal's era. Bringing these documents to the fore could foster a deeper understanding of historical interconnections between India and the Ottoman Empire, shedding light on the significant role played by Sayyid Fazal in bridging continents and advocating anti-colonial values. Sayyid Fazal Pasha played quite an illustrious and influential role in the Ottoman Empire. His receipt of honors and awards from the Ottoman ruler, including the Nişan-ı Osmani in 1881, signifies his esteemed position (Figs. 6.2 and 6.3). The original documents in the Ottoman archives, dating back to the Hijri dates 14-03-1298, are a rich historical record of his activities and involvement in various diplomatic positions across continents.[71] The numerous documents at the Osmanlı Arşivi Daire Başkanlığı in Turkey showcasing his power and influence implies that he held significant sway within the empire and likely had a wide network of connections. His engagement in diplomatic roles underscores his global reach and involvement in international affairs on behalf of the Ottoman Empire. Furthermore, the document recording the request for one of Sayyid Fazal Pasha's sons to travel with a sizable contingent of around eighty men in 1884 (dated Hijr i17-09-1301) hints at his family's prominence and

Figure 6.2
Seyyid Fazıl (Fazal) Pasha Was Awarded the Nişan-ı Osmani

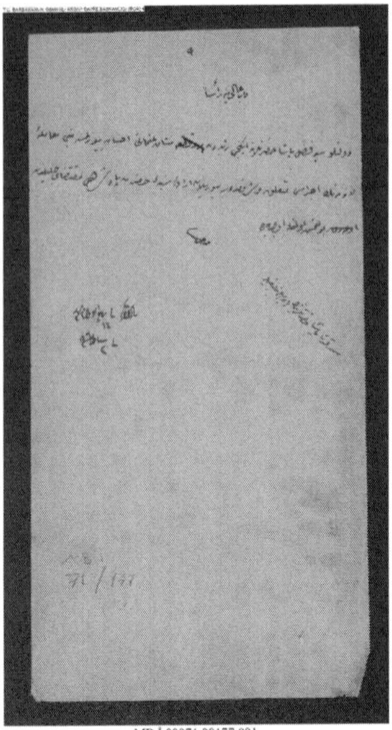

MB.İ.00071.00177.001

Source: Alaeddin Tekin, Department of History, Social Sciences University of Ankara, Turkey

the ability to mobilize a considerable retinue for travel or other purposes.[72]

One document reveals that Sayyid Fazal, in his commitment to the Ottoman reign, prohibited the publication of a pamphlet describing the miracles of Sayyid ʿAlawi bin Muhammed.[73] This decision shows Sayyid Fazal's prioritization of the political context in Turkey and the Ottoman Empire at that time, suggesting that the publication was deemed unnecessary. Another official document (H-18-04-1320) states that Sayyid Fazal's family, residing in Medina, was relocated to Istanbul, further highlighting the administrative actions taken during that period.[74] A report from Gazi Ahmed Muhtar Pasha (H-29-10-1312) details the hospitality extended to Sehil Pasha, brother of Sayyid Fazal Pasha, who was a guest in Egypt.[75] This underscores the favorable treatment of Sayyid Fazal's family within the Ottoman headquarters. There are documents specifically on salary allocations, with Omer Bey, the son of Sayyid Fazal Pasha, and distributing portions of his salary to his sister, mother, and brothers, Mustafa and Mehmed Bey (H-27-09-1317).[76] These

Figure 6.3
Darüssaade Ağa Hafız Behram Was Given the First Rank Nişan-ı Osmani, Seyyid Fazıl Pasha Was Given the Second Rank Nişan-ı Osmani and Kurena-yı Hazret-i Şehiryari Mahmud Bey Was Given the Mecidi Medal

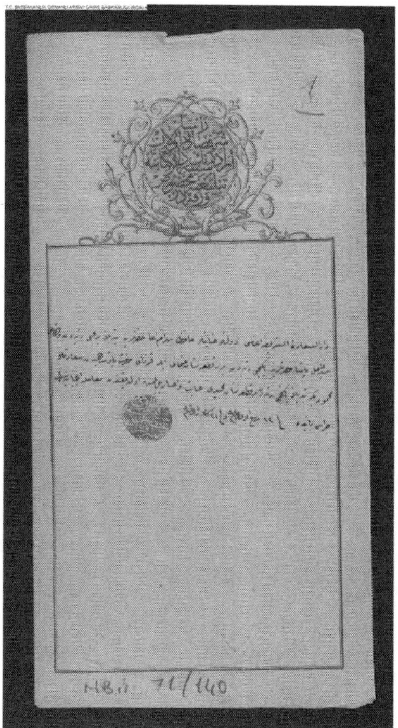

MB.İ.00071.00140.001

Source: Alaeddin Tekin, Department of History, Social Sciences University of Ankara, Turkey

archival records meticulously outline payments to Sayyid Fazal's family and descendants, including increased allocations to Suheyl and Hasan Pasha, sons of Sayyid Fazal Pasha, and Mehmed, Ahmed, and Omer Bey (H-06-07-1316).[77] There is a request for the payment of Sayyid Fazal Pasha's accumulated salaries and the allocation of new and additional salaries to his sons and grandchildren (H-19-01-1316).[78] Another document (H-24-03-1313) specifies the salary increase for Serif Suheyl Pasha, affirming Sayyid Fazal's prominence in the Ottoman Empire after his exile from Malabar.[79] During my presentation in Ankara on the subject 'Sayyid Fazal Pasha: Bridging Continents with Harmony and Anti-Colonial Values from India to the Ottoman Empire', I showed a photo of Sayyid Fazal's residence in Malabar and the huge mansion in Istanbul allocated by the Ottoman Sultan for him and his family.[80] This stark difference indicates that

Malabar played a crucial role in shaping such a leader and providing him with the unwavering energy to confront significant challenges. Documents related to the allocation of furniture and valuables to his mansion show Sayyid Fazal's elevated position and influence during his time with the Ottoman Empire. It is evident that the other facets of his life were vibrant and prestigious, involving interactions with diverse continents and communities worldwide. His progeny continued this legacy, assuming leadership roles in various places.[81]

The archival document marked H-01-05-1275 delineates a significant historical event, highlighting an invitation extended to Sayyid Fazal Efendi, identified as a leader in the Malabar community in India and a resident of Makkah. This invitation, dated 1858, summoned 'Sayyid Fazal Efendi' to the headquarters of the Ottoman Empire in Istanbul, a distinct honor. This documented summons signifies a pivotal recognition of Sayyid Fazal Efendi's leadership and stature in the Malabar community, as well as his residence in the revered city of Makkah. The invitation to Istanbul, the heart of the Ottoman administration, denotes a concerted effort by the Ottoman authorities to engage and establish relations with esteemed individuals from diverse regions under their purview. The inclusion of specific details such as Sayyid Fazal Efendi's identity as a leader in the Malabar community and his residency in Makkah in this archival record accentuates the meticulousness of Ottoman record-keeping and their deliberate efforts to foster connections with influential figures across varied geographies. This archival documentation serves as a testament to the transcultural interactions and diplomatic engagements orchestrated by the Ottoman Empire, showcasing their proactive approach in engaging with leaders like Sayyid Fazal from distant regions, thereby contributing to the broader tapestry of historical intercontinental relations.[82]

The documented care and support extended by the Ottoman sultan toward Sayyid Fazal Thangal's family underscore the depth of their relationship and the sultan's recognition of their contributions. Specifically, documentation in the Hijaz Railway archives, marked as 256974, illuminates a notable event where Sayyid Fazal and his family were granted the privilege of free passage from Haifa to Medina. This gesture signifies a manifestation of the sultan's support, providing them with royal facilities and the means for seamless travel across regions. The utilization of the Hijaz Railway, a pivotal infrastructure project, as a conduit for their journey underscores the sultan's intent to ensure the well-being and dignified treatment of Sayyid Fazal Thangal's familial lineage. This archival evidence accentuates the sultan's commitment to honoring and safeguarding the interests and welfare of those associated with Sayyid Fazal Thangal, reinforcing the enduring bonds between the family and the Ottoman administration.[83]

Sayyid Fazal Pasha's contributions to literature and scholarly discourse encompass a series of articles focused on Arabia. These writings delve into multifaceted aspects, notably encompassing the geographical landscape, political dynamics and the intricate relationships governing the administrative structures within the region vis-à-vis their allegiance to the Ottoman Empire. His articles constituted a comprehensive exploration of Arabia's geographic terrain, delineating its topographical features, geographical boundaries and the inherent diversity that characterized the region. Furthermore, Sayyid Fazal Pasha's writings provide nuanced insights into the intricate political landscape prevalent in Arabia during that epoch. He meticulously documents the various power structures, governance mechanisms and the sociopolitical fabric that defined the administrative entities within the region. A pivotal aspect elucidated in his writings pertained to the affiliations and loyalties exhibited by the administrative echelons of Arabia. Sayyid Fazal Pasha details the nuanced relationships, alliances and the nature of allegiance that governed the ties between the local administrations and the Ottoman authority. His articles likely provided a profound understanding of the interconnectedness, dependencies and diplomatic intricacies prevalent in the geopolitical milieu of that era. The depth and breadth of Sayyid Fazal Pasha's writings on Arabia not only contributed to the scholarly discourse surrounding the region but also served as invaluable sources shedding light on the historical, geographical and political dimensions of Arabia's relationship with the Ottoman Empire. His works remain a testament to his erudition, offering a rich repository for understanding the historical narrative and interwoven connections between the Ottoman Empire and the Arabian territories.[84]

Within the corpus of archival materials, a document of substantive import designated as 1883 (H-15-03-1300) delineates an intriguing proposal forwarded by Sayyid Fazal Pasha. This proposal articulates an intent to extend recognition and commendation to eminent dignitaries spanning Zanzibar, Muscat, Sihr and Hadramout, notably including Zanzibar emir Seyyid Bergis, Muscat emir Seyyid Terki, Sihr emir Molla Abdullah el-Kaiti and Hadramout emir Mansur bin Galib. Its submission to the sultan for deliberation underscores an orchestrated endeavor by Sayyid Fazal Thangal to fortify diplomatic ententes and potentially forge closer alliances with influential entities. Such endeavors, by their very nature, wielded substantive influence on the Ottoman Empire's geopolitical prowess, encompassing the consolidation of trade networks, cultivation of diplomatic amity and the strategic alignment of interests. This archival artifact testifies to the proactive role played by individuals like Sayyid Fazal Thangal in knitting together divergent regions and fostering cross-continental connections. Its examination enriches the comprehension of the rich tapestry of global powers, underscoring the symbiotic relationships that characterized that epoch.[85]

Robinson, who served as the acting magistrate of Malabar following Conolly's assassination, was in Istanbul in 1855. He reported to Pycroft on 18 November 1856 that Sayyid Fazal was well known and regarded as a remarkable personality in the region.[86] Of particular interest is a documentation denoted as 'Finance; ID/106' within the records, dated H-06-11-1340, which illuminates the allocation of salaries designated for Sayyid Fazal Pasha's soldiers, and it was after two decades of his demise. The meticulous archival record-keeping unveils the deliberate allocation of financial resources, emphasizing the Sultan's commitment to sustaining Fazal Pasha's cohort and adherents, thereby solidifying their loyalty and support. This allocation underlines Fazal Pasha's stature and esteem, accentuating the reciprocal relationship between his leadership and the Ottoman administrative machinery. These archival documents, specifically detailing the salary allocation to Sayyid Fazal Pasha's soldiers and followers, provide empirical evidence of the Ottoman Empire' s structured approach in honoring, sustaining and solidifying relationships with influential figures like Fazal Pasha, elucidating the nuanced dynamics of patronage and support within the historical context of the era.[87]

A noteworthy archival record details the bestowment of the distinguished title of Mirimiran upon Sayyid Abdurrahman Zahid Efendi, the son-in-law of Sayyid Fazal Pasha, on 29 April 1883.[88] This honor was a prominent rank in the Ottoman system and shows the high regard and status held by Sayyid Abdurrahman Zahid Efendi in the framework, reflective of his esteemed connection to Sayyid Fazal Pasha. Additionally, the archival records delineate another significant event dated 2 December 1899, wherein the prestigious title of Rumelia Beylerbey was bestowed upon Mehmed Bey, the son of Sayyid Fazal Pasha.[89] This designation elevated Mehmed Bey to a prominent position in the Ottoman administrative structure, accentuating the reverence and privilege accorded to him as the offspring of Sayyid Fazal Pasha. The Ottoman archival resources meticulously preserve significant milestones in the life and career of Sayyid Fazal Pasha, exemplified by two notable events of historical import. First, the documented engagement ceremony of Seyyid Suheyl Efendi, the son of Sayyid Fazal Pasha, is cataloged within the Ottoman archives under H-25-11-1299.[90] This archival record is a testament to the familial occasions and societal customs prevalent during that epoch, illuminating the engagement ceremony of Seyyid Suheyl Efendi as an esteemed event, reflecting the family's stature and social connections.

Second, a pivotal moment in Sayyid Fazal Pasha's career is encapsulated in an archival document dated Ramadan month of 1297, corresponding to 28 August 1880, marked as H-23-09-1297. This document meticulously chronicles the conferral of a prestigious title upon Sayyid Fazal Pasha, specifically the title of vizierate, a position of considerable significance in the Ottoman administrative hierarchy.[91] These archival records not only encapsulate personal milestones of Sayyid Fazal Pasha's family but also shed light on the strategic elevation and official recognition of his status in the Ottoman administrative apparatus. These documented instances within the Ottoman archives illustrate the Ottoman system's practice of recognizing and honoring esteemed lineages through the bestowment of titles and ranks. Sayyid Fazal Pasha's astute political acumen and international awareness are evident in an official request dated 22 July 1891, cataloged under H-16-12-1308. This archival record delineates an official plea submitted by Sayyid Fazal Pasha, shedding light on his proactive engagement with geopolitical affairs, particularly concerning the Yemeni region. The contents of this documented request underscore Sayyid Fazal Pasha's profound interest and involvement in matters concerning Yemen. His official appeal likely delineated pertinent issues, policies or interventions required for the welfare, stability or strategic interests of the Yemeni territories under Ottoman purview. Additionally, this archival record holds special significance as it provides specific intelligence regarding the appointment of an Islamic consul by the Russian State in Jeddah. Sayyid Fazal Pasha's attention to such international diplomatic appointments highlights his vigilance and awareness of external influences encroaching upon regions pertinent to the Ottoman Empire, illuminating his dedication to monitoring and potentially mitigating geopolitical developments that could impact Ottoman interests. This meticulously preserved archival document not only accentuates Sayyid Fazal Pasha's adeptness in international affairs but also underscores his proactive stance in safeguarding and navigating the geopolitical landscape, offering invaluable insights into his strategic foresight and engagement with the complexities of international politics.[92]

The preserved archival documents also offer intriguing insights into the diplomatic gestures and exchanges orchestrated by Sayyid Fazal Pasha in his interactions with other heads of states. One such remarkable instance is documented in an archival record detailing a presentation made by Sayyid Fazal Pasha to other dignitaries. Specifically, on 3 October 1880, in a gesture of sincere appreciation, a chest of dates and a ball of wool were presented to the Yemeni Sheikh on the occasion of Seyyid Fazal Pasha's ministry. This offering symbolizes the strong ties and mutual respect between the regions. The dates, symbolizing nourishment and prosperity, along with the wool, representing warmth and comfort, convey heartfelt gratitude and recognition of the Yemen Sheikh's support and the significant relationship fostered under Seyyid Fazal Pasha's distinguished leadership. Such diplomatic exchanges served as nuanced expressions of goodwill, fostering amicable relationships and alliances, while also honoring cultural traditions and practices. These meticulously preserved archival documents not only showcase the diplomatic finesse and strategic rapport cultivated by Sayyid Fazal Pasha but also highlight the cultural diplomacy inherent in such exchanges, offering a glimpse into the ceremonial gestures and symbolic importance attached to diplomatic relations during that historical epoch.[93] Sayyid Fazal Pasha's demise was extensively reported in Turkish newspapers, and the front-page coverage became a testament to his immense prominence in the region. Even after his death, he was honored with a royal burial at the Sultan Mehmed Mausoleum Compound in Istanbul, Turkey, where he rests in peace (Fig. 6.4).[94]

Figure 6.4
The Tomb of Sayyid Fazal Pookoya Thangal at Sultan Mehmed Mausoleum Compound in Istanbul, Turkey

Photograph by author

Conclusion

The historical landscape of Mamburam stands as a testament to the resilience of communal harmony in the face of multiple divisive narratives perpetuated by external forces. The central questions underlying this discussion have been: First, to what extent has Mamburam shaped the nature of the Malabari political system and state organs, and second, what role has Mamburam played in legitimating regional governments and political leadership? The answer to the former conundrum is that Mamburam was a contributory factor in building a harmonious society and a decisive one. Notably, the people in Malabar sought to construct a fully harmonious society. The vivid tapestry woven from shared celebrations, joint festivities and the veneration of the revered Sufi saint Mamburam Thangal illustrates a profound unity that surpasses religious delineations. Despite the pervasive dissemination of misrepresentative stories, the enduringly harmonious culture of Kaliyattakkavu and Mamburam persists, serving as a stronghold against discord. Noteworthy is the tradition of venerating effigies from the Kaliyattakkavu Bhagavati temple at the shrine, an act symbolic of prior interreligious engagements fostered by community leaders. Notwithstanding the propagation of divisive rhetoric by British media, the harmonious culture of Kaliyattakkavu and Mamburam endured and resisted, standing resolute even in contemporary times.

The convergence of marriages, *nercha*s and *utsava*s (festivals) as communal celebrations open to friends and neighbors without scrutiny of religious affiliations starkly contrasts with the misrepresented 'Hindu–Muslim' animosity propagated by British news stories. The testimonial account provided by an individual, Cheru Chakki, whose reliance on Mamburam Thangal for personal and familial affairs reflects a broader sentiment prevalent within the community. The resounding calls of support and solidarity from non-Muslim acquaintances for Thangal echo a prevailing sentiment steeped in devotion and unwavering trust, transcending temporal boundaries. This narrative encapsulates a poignant melody of communal devotion and unyielding faith that has endured through epochs, defying attempts at discordance and division.

Chapter 7

CONOLLY'S DEATH

Pinnacle of Anti-Colonial Struggles

Preserved within the confines of Palamadathil Puthupparambil house in Kuttur, Vengara, is a tangible relic—a traditional turban belonging to Mamburam Thangal—that is a silent testament to a pivotal moment in Malabar's history. This turban is connected to the conspiracy of the killing of Henry Valentine Conolly (1806–1855), whose death epitomizes the multifaceted and often conflicting aspects of colonial resistance.[1] This chapter embarks on a journey through the obscured corridors of historical narration to dissect the dichotomy surrounding Conolly's development strategy and death portrayal. Renowned as an East India Company official operating in the Madras Presidency during the 19th century, Conolly's tenure as a magistrate and collector in Malabar is shrouded in divergent accounts. Colonial historical records extol his contributions, such as the establishment of teakwood plantations to meet the demands of shipbuilding and the dedication of a waterway in his name, as hallmarks of progressive governance.[2] Yet, a closer examination unravels a stark contrast between the glorified administrative achievements and the disruptive repercussions of Conolly's policies on the indigenous populace. This narrative unfolds against the backdrop of Conolly's controversial actions—his role in the exile of Sayyid Fazal and the imposition of stringent laws that upset the tranquility of the inhabitants. The dichotomy between his celebrated developmental initiatives and the harsh realities faced by the locals unveils a nuanced tale of colonial governance, fraught with contradictions and obscured narratives. Through scrutinizing historical fragments and reconciling conflicting accounts, this chapter endeavors to unravel the complexities and resolve the discrepancies in the depiction of Henry Valentine Conolly, shedding light on colonial agendas and their impact on indigenous communities in Malabar.

In the retrospective examination of the fatal retaliation by the indigenous population, it becomes evident that this occurrence aligns with a historical phase marked by transitional periods. Such epochs typically witness the confrontation of established societal frameworks with transformative shifts, often resulting in sociopolitical upheavals and evolutionary trajectories. The parallels between these synchronous resistances and the revolutionary perceptions from the 18th century onward invite a critical exploration. Analyzing these resistances within the vernacular historical framework, particularly in proximity to the demise of the district head, introduces a novel perspective to their significance. This specific event can be construed as a prominent and consequential revolutionary movement akin to those observed across diverse geographical regions since the advent of the 18th century. These defenses, pervasive and multifaceted in nature, traversed varied territories and were often driven by aspirations for sociopolitical restructuring and challenging established power paradigms and societal norms. Engaging with the historical narrative through this interpretative lens serves not only to contextualize these events within the expansive canvas of global historical transformations but also invites deeper investigations into the motivating factors, catalytic elements and discernible parallels inherent within these movements.[3]

Conolly's analysis of the Malabar region reveals an imprecise understanding of the political, economic and religious dimensions. His astuteness is particularly evident in the recognition of the transformative trajectory of figures such as Sayyid Fazal, who evolved from reformists into symbolic leaders. This metamorphosis not only engendered a recalibration of their identities but also positioned them as emblematic figures embodying revolutionary ideals. Conolly was trying to feed a closer understanding of the intertwined political, economic and religious claims of different classes in the region to his higher officers. Embedded within the colonial discourse on 'fanaticism' is the complicated relationship between various societal strata, delineated as the 'commoners' harboring aspirations for perceived freedom and venerated religious figures sanctifying these aspirations. Conolly perceptively discerns the transcendent authority vested in Sayyids beyond the purview of the colonial state, which thereby posed a palpable threat to the colonial political structure. His regular reporting and analyses of supplementary statements played a seminal role in reshaping the colonial understanding of this complex power dynamic. However, Conolly's assessments encountered intermittent scrutiny from the Madras government, particularly about Sayyid Fazal's alleged involvement. Despite sporadic challenges, by 1852, Conolly's perspectives on the connections between fanaticism, violence and the ʿAlawi's garnered unanimous acceptance, marking a paradigm shift in colonial comprehension. This evolution in understanding, significantly informed by Conolly's insights, solidified his interpretations as the prevailing narrative in the apparatus of colonial governance.[4]

Conolly dealt with opposing opinions on Mamburam Thangal's role. Despite Thangal's conspicuous divergence from colonial administrative authority, colonial officers contested and dismissed his dissenting stance, maintaining his inability to disregard established colonial authority. Contrary to these assertions, Conolly steadfastly contended that the presence of Mamburam Thangal in Malabar held pivotal, if not predominant, significance in either catalyzing or exacerbating sociopolitical disruptions colloquially referred to as 'outbreaks'.[5]

The district administration grappled with alternative forms of sovereignty, recognizing them as genuine and immediate threats that warranted careful consideration. Partiçularly illuminating is Conolly's contemplation on Thangal's mental state, where he underscores the influence of spiritual exercises on the Thangal's extraordinary sway over the sentiments of the populace.[6] Conolly's contributions underscore his acute observations on the sociopolitical dynamics within the context, his adept engagement with the colonial archive and his contemplation on non-state sovereignty, religious authority and their profound implications within the colonial framework.[7]

11 September 1855: Assassination of Henry Valentine Conolly

Conolly, the Malabar magistrate from 1840 to 1855, played a significant role in shaping the colonial perspective on Mamburam Thangal and in orchestrating the departure of Fazal Thangal from India. In Conolly's documented correspondences, a distinct portrayal appears about Fazal Thangal's perceived involvement in the unfolding events. Conolly's correspondence speculates upon the extent of Thangal's awareness of the intentions of certain visitors who sought his blessings for their undertakings. There is an implicit suggestion that while Fazal Thangal ostensibly bestowed blessings for the advancement of the faith, he might not have been fully cognizant of the grave implications of the actions he inadvertently endorsed. Despite this, Conolly articulates that such purported lack of awareness does not absolve Thangal of his moral responsibility. Conolly proposes a more benevolent interpretation, positing that Thangal, given his experience in these matters, might have been misled or unaware of the concealed malevolent intentions behind the zealous individuals seeking his endorsement. This narrative accentuates Conolly's argument that influential individuals like Fazal Thangal should exercise utmost caution in granting their blessings and be cognizant of the potential far-reaching consequences of their actions.[8]

Conolly's administration in the Malabar region undertook a categorization of its personnel based on religious and caste affiliations.

This effort aimed to quantify the composition of Hindus and Muslims within the administrative, police and military sectors. Notably, positions of lower rank, such as peons, were predominantly occupied by lower-caste Hindus, while higher echelons of the bureaucracy and the judiciary were notably dominated by Nair tribes and other higher castes. In the early 1850s, Conolly published statistics detailing the composition of the native workforce under his administration in the Malabar region with categorization of their religion and castes. Out of the 330 higher-grade appointments in the Malabar administration, an exceedingly limited representation of Muslims, specifically seven individuals, was evident.[9] Correspondingly, J.F. Thomas, during this temporal frame, observed that native judges were predominantly Hindus.[10] Furthermore, Conolly, alongside contemporaries, endeavored to classify geographic regions in the Malabar as either amenable to colonial governance or resistant thereto. Notably, Conolly corresponded revealing that within the so-called 'fanatic' taluks, the police force exhibited a notable religious division, comprising 72 per cent Hindus and 28 per cent Muslims.[11] This strategic segmentation of the populace along religious lines was a discernible facet of colonial policy.

This data shows that Collector Conolly's role extended beyond mere developmental pursuits and involved a deliberate demographic categorization along religious lines. Moreover, Conolly's categorization extended to portraying all victims of various resistance movements as exclusively Hindu, overlooking instances where Muslim landlords and officers were targeted during regional insurgencies. This misrepresentation was further perpetuated by British reports, incorrectly asserting that all victims in the twenty-nine outbreaks were Hindus.[12] Primary source materials from the Malabar region illuminate that these circumstances affected not only Hindus but also those Muslims who aligned themselves with the British colonial administration.[13]

During the colonial era, there were instances where the local populace, particularly in the Malabar region, faced punitive actions for possessing traditional small knives used for agricultural activities. This phenomenon, documented by William Logan, highlighted the government's interventions, often portrayed as positive measures.

> In December 1854 Conolly proceeded on a tour to collect the war-knives through the heart of the Mappila country, and brought in 2,725, and by the 31st of the following month of January 1855 (the latest date on which the possession of a war-knife was legal) the number of war-knives surrendered to the authorities amounted to the large number of 7,561.[14]

Before Conolly's intervention, the use of personal working knives by the Malabar peasants was an accepted and customary practice. His enforcement of restrictions against these tools disrupted the established social and cultural fabric, significantly impeding the ordinary peasants' ability to engage in their agricultural tasks. This imposition not only undermined their traditional practices but also obstructed their fundamental daily activities.

This strategic maneuver of Conolly's removal can be construed as a conspicuous manifestation of overt resistance against British hegemony in the region, thereby symbolizing a resolute stance against colonial presence and control. H.V. Conolly's assassination of constituted a retaliatory response to significant transgressions orchestrated by him, particularly the expulsion of Mamburam Fazal Thangal, who held substantial spiritual and political influence in the region, transcending caste and religious boundaries. The impetus for this solemn undertaking stemmed from the considerable suffering inflicted upon the region's inhabitants by the British colonial machinery. In a seminal assembly marked by gravity and deliberation, unwavering resolutions were formulated to seek retribution for the forced exile of their leader. On 11 September 1855, Henry Valentine Conolly, then serving as a magistrate and collector in the Malabar District, met his demise.

G.B. Tod, the assistant collector in Malabar, penned a communication addressed to the chief secretary to the government, dated 12 September 1855, describing an incident or series of events:

> It is my melancholy duty to inform you, for the information of the Right Honorable the Governor in Council, that Mr. Conolly, the Collector of this district, was most barbarously murdered this evening, between eight and nine o'clock, in the presence of his wife. He received seven wounds, one of which at least was mortal. So far as the details at present are ascertained, the perpetrators were three Mappilas, who rushed into the verandah and completed their deadly work before assistance could be called. In the present state of Mrs. Conolly, it is impossible to gather further particulars of the tragedy of which she was the sole witness; but immediately that I am able to do so, I will furnish more complete information.[15]

The significant assembly where the decision to kill Conolly took place at the residence of Palamadathil Puthupparambil Kunhali, known for his strong family bonds and philanthropic efforts, hailing from Kuttur near Vengara. During my research visit, I had the privilege of observing the original turban worn by Mamburam Thangal, which is preserved as a sacred relic in their home in a perpetual tribute to the memory of the great leader. This enclave where the turban is preserved, intrinsically interwoven with the Mamburam

Mosque, a bastion of profound sociocultural significance, has traditionally served as the locus for deliberations of considerable import. The elaborate plan to assassinate the colonial collector was carefully planned out near Vengara under the leadership of Palamadathil Puthupparambil Kunhali. Prominent figures like Mandayappuram Mammadunni Mooppan and Veeranunni Mooppan were actively involved in this gathering, solidifying the visible unity formed in direct opposition to Conolly's actions and the subsequent exile of Sayyid Fazal. This gathering, symbolizing united determination and a model of intelligent investigation, highlights the unwavering spirit of resistance.

Significantly, the planned execution of Conolly occurred a century before the assassination of Michael Francis O'Dwyer (1864–1940) in retaliation for the Jallianwala Bagh massacre on 13 April 1919. O'Dwyer, a vocal supporter of Reginald Dyer's (1864–1927) decision to open fire on the gathered crowds, met his fate at the hands of Udham Singh (1899–1940), an Indian revolutionary and proponent of independence, on 13 March 1940. Reginald Edward Harry Dyer (1864–1927), an officer who initially served in the Bengal Army and later in the British Indian Army, earned notoriety as 'the Butcher of Amritsar' due to his directive to fire upon a substantial assembly of civilians, resulting in the tragic demise of a minimum of 379 individuals and injuries sustained by over a thousand others. Examining the imposition of martial law in Punjab on 15 April, retrospectively activated from 30 March 1919, reveals attempts to mask involvement in the massacre.[16]

5 November 1855: Sheffield Daily Telegraph *Report*

The resistance movement against colonial authority garnered substantial attention from various media outlets, which notably emphasized the demise of the district collector. Numerous newspapers featured correspondents' letters originating from major urban centers such as Bombay and Calcutta, presenting retrospectives on the events several weeks post-occurrence. These correspondences not only offered analytical insights but also elucidated the causes and repercussions intrinsic to the resistance movement against colonial dominance. The comprehensive dissemination of information across diverse newspaper platforms played a pivotal role in chronicling and diffusing the evolving events and their implications within the colonial framework. An illustrative report from Bombay underscored the transmission of intelligence to the local government, facilitated through telegraphic communication from Madras. This specific report delineated the demise of Conolly, serving as the collector of Malabar and concurrently a provisional member of the council at Madras. According to this account, Conolly met his tragic end at the hands of a group seeking retribution for what they perceived as his brutal actions against them and their revered leader.

> Bombay, Oct. 3.—On the 20th of last month intelligence reached the Bombay government, by electric telegraph from Madras, that Mr. H. V. Conolly, collector of Malabar and provisional member of council at Madras, had been murdered on the 11th a party of Moplahs. On the evening of the day in question Mr. Conolly was seated with his wife in the verandah of his house, near Calicut, when five men, armed with the long and heavy Moplah knife, rushed in and commenced a violent attack upon him. Mrs Conolly ran into the house, calling upon the servants to come to the assistance of their master. Two of them, who were near the spot, immediately came forward, but were kept at bay by the assassins, who cut off the hand or several of the fingers of one and inflicted a severe wound upon the other. Then, their work accomplished, the murderers disappeared in the darkness. Mr. Conolly was earned into the house, and medical assistance sent from Calcutta, but before it could reach him, he had expired. His injuries are described as being of the most frightful character. No fewer than 27 wounds were found upon his body, which was almost literally hacked to pieces. His poor wife sat by his side covered with the blood of her husband she had seen murdered before her eyes, stunned and tearless under the weight of a blow so sudden and so terrible. Immediately on hearing of the murder a party of the 74th Highlanders was dispatched to the spot, but before they had reached it the Moplahs had decamped. On the 17th, however, the Highlanders fell in with them at Manjerry, when, as on previous occasions of similar nature, it was found impossible to take these desperate fanatics alive, and they fell to a man by the bayonets of the soldiers. One of the 74th was killed in the affray, and another badly wounded by a cut in the throat, dealt him by a Moplah whom he had already transfixed with his bayonet. Mr. Conolly was an able and energetic magistrate and had lately succeeded in rooting out of the country a most dangerous vagabond of the Moplah tribe. He had also been actively employed in carrying out the act for disarming that part of the population of his collectorate. These proceedings no doubt made him obnoxious to the Moplahs, and his murder may be merely the result of the feelings so excited.[17]

The *Sheffield Daily Telegraph* vividly recounted the incident involving Conolly, detailing how, while he was with his wife in the corridor of their house near Calicut, five armed men wielding knives rushed in and initiated a ferocious attack. Conolly sought refuge inside the house, desperately calling upon the servants for aid. Despite the attempts of two nearby servants to intervene, they, too, fell victim to the fighters. The report remains uncertain about the extent of the injuries, mentioning one servant possibly having a hand severed or multiple fingers lost, while the other sustained severe wounds, adding to the distressing scene. Conolly's body bore a staggering 'no fewer than 27' wounds, an act described as almost rendering him 'literally hacked to pieces'. Notably, it is striking that the fighters focused their attack solely on Conolly, sparing his wife who was present during the incident.[18]

The report, however, portrays a biased colonial narrative that aims to solicit sympathy from readers in Britain. As commonly found in colonial accounts, the suffering and injuries inflicted upon the native people were disregarded. The report describes Conolly as an adept and vigorous magistrate, lauding his success in eliminating what they term as a 'dangerous vagabond of the Moplah tribe', thereby perpetuating the stereotypical 'othering' of an entire community. These narrative shapes a notion that certain individuals are destined to be targeted or eradicated, portraying Conolly's actions as instrumental in achieving this end. Such incidents were often glorified as heroic actions of the British administration. Ultimately, the report suggests that Conolly's actions made him widely detested in the region, framing his murder as a consequence of the resentment his actions had stirred among the local populace.[19]

Interestingly, the Irish newspapers presented a more nuanced tale. The same report appeared in the *Cork Constitution* on Tuesday, 6 November 1855. It provided additional details about the actions of the British forces regarding the murderers. The report accused the fighters of being driven by religious motivations and retaliating against the exile of their leader from the country. The report also shed light on how colonial authorities handled the bodies of those who had killed the collector. Upon hearing of the murder, the Madras administration immediately invoked a recent legislative act, stipulating that the bodies of Moplahs slain in action should not be buried but instead cremated, with their ashes scattered to the winds.[20]

10 November 1855: Kendal Mercury—Shaping Perspectives, Sparking Discourse

On 10 November 1855, the *Kendal Mercury* reported an incident tying the collector's assassination with disparaging remarks directed at Muslims. This report outlined a belief held by the British colonial administration that they could stop the deceased from attaining paradise by cremating their bodies.[21] The premise behind this belief stemmed from the misconception about Islamic tenets that martyrs' bodies would not ascend to heaven following their sacrifice if they were cremated. This perception often stems from viewing the religion through a materialistic lens. In Islamic doctrine, martyrs are not deemed to merely succumb to death; instead, they are regarded as living in the divine presence of almighty God. The British endeavor to dissuade martyrdom through the cremation of bodies was grounded in the erroneous notion that this act could impede resurrection during the Day of Judgment. Nonetheless, in the Muslim theological framework, martyrs occupy an exalted status in paradise, wherein the material body, its afflictions, or even its complete dissolution do not detract from their celestial standing.

The report proves that British officers endeavored to cremate the bodies to dissuade martyrdom. Nevertheless, this initiative proved ineffectual, as subsequent reports documented numerous additional instances in the region after the incidents and body incineration. These measures evidently failed to dissuade individuals from engaging in acts of martyrdom. The consistent and uniform reporting of the event across multiple publications served to reinforce the British stance. These news reports were propaganda against the indigenous population, highlighting their brutalities. Notably, in the *Durham Chronicle* on 9 November 1855, a striking absence of disparities or editorial modifications is evident among the various accounts in the paper. This observation underscores that the news disseminated in newspapers worldwide largely originated directly from the colonial administration, lacking significant editorial intervention.[22]

10 November 1855: The Bolton Chronicle *Narrative*

The *Bolton Chronicle*'s coverage of the 1855 murder of a government official in Madras provides valuable insights into communication constraints during the era. The report underscores a significant nine-day delay in transmitting crucial information from Madras to Bombay, signaling the challenges of timely dissemination across regions. Beyond the tragic event itself, the report describes the life of the victim, Conolly, in detail. It notably emphasizes aspects such as his domestic milieu, interactions within his surroundings and other minutiae, aligning with a pattern observed in contemporaneous accounts. Moreover, the portrayal of Conolly's wife, detailing her struggles during the assassination, appears strategically designed to elicit empathy from a British readership dispersed across various locations. The striking uniformity in narratives across multiple publications is noteworthy, suggesting a coordinated effort, possibly orchestrated by the colonial administrative apparatus. The consistency in content, encompassing specific details and linguistic style, hints at a deliberate endeavor to shape public perception through a standardized depiction of the incident.[23]

The report delineates the efforts undertaken by authorities to apprehend the assailant responsible for the tragic demise of Conolly. It explicitly notes the dispatch of the 74th Highlanders to the area for this purpose. However, the report indicates their inability to apprehend the 'perpetrator' within the specified timeframe, as upon their arrival, it was reported that the 'Moplahs had decamped'. Furthermore, the report offers detailed accounts of the confrontations between the military forces and the native fighters. It corroborates the toll taken during these encounters, confirming the loss of one soldier from the 74th Highlanders while another sustained a severe injury, specifically a throat laceration. This narrative highlights the intensity and peril of the engagements between the military and the local fighters:

> On the 17th, however, the Highlanders fell in with them at Munjerry, when, on previous occasions of similar nature, it was found impossible to take these desperate fanatics alive, and they fell to a man by the bayonets of the soldiers. One of the 74th was killed the affray, and another badly wounded by a cut in the throat, dealt him by a Moplah whom he had already transfixed with his bayonet. With the death of the murderers is probably lost the secret of the murder.[24]

The report, a copy of the other one in the *Kendall Mercury*, implies a strategic approach by colonial officials, suggesting a deliberate delay in providing information to the British newspapers until the native fighter responsible for the incident was eliminated. This tactic hints at a calculated narrative construction aimed at shaping the perception of events in favor of the colonial authorities. The concluding statement, 'With the death of the murderers is probably lost the secret of the murder', suggests a pivotal loss of crucial information. This inference might serve as a strategic maneuver to veil the potentially severe and oppressive administrative measures enforced by Conolly upon the local populace. It insinuates that the demise of the assailants might have erased any chance of uncovering motives or grievances against the administration, thus obscuring the underlying causes of the conflict.[25]

10 November 1855: Bicester Herald *Report: Strikingly Rhythmic—Murder in Madras*

The *Bicester Herald*'s report, dated Saturday, 10 November 1855, adopted a strikingly rhythmic and attention-grabbing subtitle, 'Murder in Madras', drawing focus to Conolly's role as the provisional member of council at Madras. The deliberate choice of words and the details about Conolly's position mirrored other reports. However, the *Bicester Herald*'s editorial touch was evident in highlighting Conolly's status as provisional member of council, aiming to provide regional context and captivate readers' attention through the evocative headline. The report vividly depicts the tragic scene of Conolly being carried into his house, with urgent medical aid sought from Calicut, but regrettably, his demise occurred before help arrived. Notably, this narrative strategy serves to amplify the sense of brutality, particularly when attributed to retaliatory actions from the natives of the region. These narratives are monotonous, exhibiting minimal variation due to their affiliation with various newspapers.

> His injuries are described as being of the most frightful character. No fewer than 27 wounds were found upon his body, which was almost literally hacked to pieces. His poor wife sat by his side covered with the blood of her husband she had seen murdered before her eyes, stunned and tearless under the weight of a blow so sudden and so terrible.[26]

The report's depiction of Conolly's wife witnessing the murder unfolds a harrowing and distressing scene, portraying her as being profoundly affected by the sudden and terrible nature of the attack. The narrative strategically amplifies the gravity of the incident, emphasizing her shock and helplessness, likely aiming to evoke heightened sympathy from readers.

Interestingly, from the native perspective, there is a specific mention that the fighters refrained from causing harm to the lady.[27] This contrasts starkly with the broader narrative of the colonial administration's disregard for the well-being and safety of ordinary Malabar residents, especially women and children. These dual narratives underscore the significant disparity in treatment between the privileged position of colonial officials and the harsh, indiscriminate measures imposed on the local populace. The characterization of the region and its people as mere subjects, devoid of basic human rights considerations, and the disregard for the lives of women and children exposes a deep-seated colonial mindset, portraying women as expendable casualties and dehumanizing the local population.

The widespread coverage of the incident in various publications like the *Reading Mercury*, *Oxford Gazette*, *Newbury Herald* and *Berks Country Paper* on 10 November 1855 attests to the profound impact and significance of the murder of Malabar District Collector Conolly. This synchronized dissemination of information through multiple newspapers, each carrying an identical report, serves as a testament to the shock it caused within the colonial administration in India.[28]

The extensive coverage and simultaneous publication in various newspapers suggest not just a local event but one of broader importance, potentially shaking the established order and prompting considerable deliberation and response within the apparatus in the Indian subcontinent. The British portrayal of Conolly as a capable and dynamic magistrate, celebrated for allegedly eliminating a perceived threat by rooting out a 'dangerous vagabond' from the Moplah tribe, overlooked or downplayed the derogatory and racially oppressive nature of their actions toward the people of Malabar. The characterization of certain individuals or tribes as inherently dangerous or criminalized contributed to a biased and discriminatory narrative that perpetuated racial stereotypes and oppression. The colonial propaganda machine, which disseminated these narratives globally, was likely oblivious to the discriminatory and damaging impact of their portrayals on the indigenous populations. The constructed image of Conolly as a valiant enforcer of order failed to acknowledge the complexities of the local social fabric and the systemic biases inherent in colonial governance, which often marginalized and oppressed indigenous communities under the guise of maintaining control and security.

Colonialism in Vernacular Heritages

The advent of British colonial dominion ushered in a mosaic of narrative perspectives that disrupted the prevailing ethos of harmonious coexistence in the region. Central to these narratives was the conceptual framework of 'fanaticism', a colonial accusation against Mamburam, which was blamed for disseminating 'divisive ideologies'. This construct was strategically elevated in the annals of colonial historiography, serving as a rhetorical device to obscure prior episodes of British-inflicted atrocities that occurred in the region. Subsequently, colonial historiographical interpretations have heavily influenced local historiography. In the case of Conolly's death, vernacular history and culture have developed narratives aligned with the British perspective, a phenomenon notably seen even in the discourses of the Calicut Heritage Forum.

The Heritage Forum commemorates the British collector of Malabar as an emblem of the reformist ethos, while the freedom fighters who played a role in his demise are marginalized and considered emblematic of zealous extremism. The audacious endeavor undertaken by the freedom fighters, culminating in Conolly's elimination, assumes the mantle of a significant retaliatory gesture, a stage-managed response to the repressive maneuvers orchestrated by the collector and the administrative apparatus under his purview. Conolly's assassination serves as a metonymic embodiment, representing the zenith of long-suppressed collective grievances and an unwavering determination of the local populace to exact retribution for the transgressions committed during the era of British colonial dominance.

By targeting the collector, a conspicuous symbol of British authoritative ascendancy, the freedom fighters sought not only to challenge the hegemonic regime but also to emphasize their unequivocal dissent against the yoke of British dominion. This act of revenge is significant as it marks the beginning of broader movements for dissent across different times and places in the Indian subcontinent. Similar sentiments were seen after the Jallianwala Bagh massacre. The pivotal historical junctures marked by the deaths of Conolly and Dwyer concurrently underscore the profound depths to which indigenous populations were willing to descend to counterbalance the dominion of colonial despotism and assert their resounding imperative for autonomy and self-sovereignty.

Historical Examination and Comprehensive Analysis

The narrative surrounding Conolly's assassination has conventionally been framed within the parameters of the British historiographical lens, which portray it as a manifestation of overt aggression directed toward an English individual. Deconstructing Conolly's assassination compels a nuanced inquiry that transcends facile categorizations and delves into the intricacies of its motivations and ramifications. At its core, the act of assassinating Conolly signified the inaugural instance of a calculated reprisal aimed at a high-ranking British functionary within the district. This stratagem, which bespeaks a discerning and premeditated mode of resistance, indicates a discernible shift from spontaneous insurrection to strategic orchestration. The astute choice to target the paramount British authority within the regional echelons, situated within his official sanctum, underscores a dimension of tactical sagacity that belies any inclination toward impulsive or reckless aggression. The calculated decision to safeguard Conolly's spouse not only manifests a keen awareness guiding their intentions but also elevates the episode beyond the realm of indiscriminate violence. Indeed, the event in question was more than a mere assault. It was spurred by deeply entrenched grievances, which had crystallized in response to colonial administrative policies and practices.

The act of assassinating Conolly assumes greater clarity when regarded as a calculated execution, rather than an outburst of fanaticism. This episode serves to illuminate an undercurrent of profound discontent and resolute determination within the local populace, driven by a yearning for justice and an impetus to resist the injustices perpetuated by the British colonial administration.

Conolly's stint as the collector of Malabar coincided with a phase of pronounced turbulènce, wherein the region was steeped in relentless anti-colonial agitations. As an unwavering proponent of British dominion, Conolly assiduously endeavored to quell the insurgency in the region. His tenure was notably marked by a zealous pursuit of identifying and penalizing. The assassination of Conolly thus reverberates within the broader canvas of colonial antagonisms, encapsulating the charged dynamics between the proponents of imperial authority and those who ardently sought to contest its dominion. In sum, the assassination of Collector Henry Valentine Conolly, situated against the backdrop of the 19th-century resistance, emerges as a consequential episode meriting profound scholarly scrutiny. C.A. Innes also observed that the forced deportation of Sayyid Fazal of Mamburam served as a significant motivating factor behind the assassination of Conolly.[29]

On the Verandah *of West Hill*

Within British circles, Conolly's assassination itself became a focal point of protracted contemplation. Executed by Valasherry Jamal, Poly Kunjathu Theni, Chempan Moithinkutty, Veluthedathu Parambil Moithin and Osan Aydrum (known as Osan Koya), the act held a central position in discussions, resonating with lasting significance. The plan was to bring capable people from prison to execute revenge on the district magistrate and ensure its success. Preceding the assassination, the group arrived in Vettathunadu Taluk, seeking shelter in the residence of Moideen, who was Osan Koya's brother. Their journey continued through Kozhikode taluk to the village of Vengara and further traversing Pandalur and Payyanad, crossing rivers and delving into the forested regions near Banglavu in the West Hill. The deliberateness of their intent manifested in their choice to execute the assassination during the evening prayers. Opting for this moment of spiritual significance, the fighters sought to infuse their act of retribution against the oppressive British administration with symbolic weight.

In the early hours of twilight, the scene was set: Conolly sat on the *verandah* of his residence in West Hill, while Mrs Conolly was nearby. A faint glow emanated from a lamp placed inside a teapot, creating an atmosphere of subdued light. Unbeknownst to Mrs Conolly, the warriors launched the attack. With decisive and forceful strikes, they incapacitated Collector Conolly, inflicting a barrage of twenty-seven wounds. He almost lost his left arm, and other injuries included a deep gash on his right knee. Mrs Conolly's desperate entreaties for assistance were regrettably ineffectual, as the retinue of household attendants, seemingly ensnared by trepidation or indecision, impelled her toward a safer sanctuary in an adjacent precinct. District Magistrate Conolly succumbed to the gravity of his injuries, his vitality extinguished precisely at 9:45 p.m. Having executed the assassination, the assailants expediently retreated toward Thamarassery. They arrived at Manjeri, where they rendezvoused with a village office peon stationed on the Kondotty side. This peon, having forged an alliance with their fellow jail escapees and sympathetic collaborators, convened in a united endeavor to extend support to the fighters.[30]

Rapidly informing the authorities about the incident, the peon triggered the dispatch of *adhikari*, leading a contingent of roughly twenty personnel tasked with investigating the matter. This inquiry confirmed Conolly's tragic demise, yet apprehending the natives posed formidable challenges. Despite subsequent efforts involving a larger force of nearly 300, which included figures like Arimbra Adhikari, the fugitive perpetrators deftly evaded capture. The involvement of local partisans and escaped prisoners added another layer of complexity, complicating the British colonial administration's quest for retribution. The fighters reportedly arrived armed with pilfered weapons—knives and swords taken from their prison confines—granting them a tactical advantage in evading capture. Their ability to access additional armaments through a network of collaborators bolstered their elusive nature, making their capture an extremely challenging task. To mitigate the escalating situation, the governing authorities implemented a reward system, aiming to incentivize cooperation from the local populace. The efforts of the authority and its allies encountered only a limited degree of cooperation from the locals. Continuing their journey toward Manjeri, the fighters engaged in another hard-hitting episode. They besieged the residence of Jenmi Moosath, restraining him with a rope and then dragging him through an adjacent orchard toward a nearby field. Moosath's strategically situated and substantial domicile, nestled among vast plantations with diverse crops, provided them with a secure vantage point, shielding them effectively from external scrutiny. When the police contingent arrived, the natives adeptly navigated intricate paths of evasion. The fate that awaited the other members of the group captured in the encounter unfolded within the confines.[31]

The vernacular decolonial narrative provides a nuanced portrayal of the sociocultural and religious contexts that underpinned the motives and responses of the local populace. It accentuates the surge of communal sentiments, resistance fervor and unity following the assassination. Notably, it highlights the cultural observance of the annual Mawlid[32] ceremonies, where the architects of the assassination were celebrated as champions. Their actions were commemorated by the community during these events, suggesting the emergence of a symbolic narrative around their deeds. Moreover, the vernacular narrative critically evaluates the biased portrayal evident in the British report. It proposes an interpretation of the attack as a retaliatory act by the followers of Mamburam Thangal against the British administration for the exile of their revered leader, Sayyid Fazal. The absence of their esteemed leader and subsequent exile are posited as primary provocations for the action against Conolly. The aftermath of the assassination is meticulously detailed, outlining the fate of the implicated individuals and their confrontation with British forces in Morayur, leading to their demise. Additionally, it underscores the accidental deaths of two individuals during this encounter—one due to British gunfire and the other presumably caught in the crossfire. This passage constructs a multifaceted historical narrative that intertwines elements of resistance, cultural significance, communal sentiments and the far-reaching repercussions of anti-colonial activities within the Malabar region during the colonial epoch.[33]

The architects of H.V. Conolly's assassination found an unexpected degree of empathy in the local community, receiving honors, lavish feasts, public parades and being escorted to the mosque for prayers—an emblematic site of sanctity and communal unity. In response to this serious incident, the British authorities invoked the 1854 Act (Clause XXIII) for the first time. This legislative statute included provisions that mandated punitive actions against communities or villages involved in violent acts against colonial officials or the broader administrative structure.[34]

While the direct involvement of only three villages was evident in Conolly's murder, a sweeping 719 individuals across nine villages faced fines imposed by the authorities. The cumulative fines amounted to approximately ₹38,331 and 8 annas. Additionally, as compensation, the widowed Mrs Conolly received a disbursement totaling ₹30,936 and 13 annas, 10 paisa. Logan's historical account presents a microcosm of the intricate dynamics characterizing colonial governance in India during that period.[35]

Colonial Misrepresentations: Economic Perspectives

British authorities approached the attack on Conolly from a colonial perspective, primarily focusing on economic considerations. Their assessment revolved around the financial aspects and wealth of the individuals involved. In Special Commissioner T.L. Strange's report on Malabar dated 25 September 1852, a comprehensive analysis of the socioeconomic status of the participants in the struggles was provided. The report highlighted that the main contributors to the events were wage workers, destitute tenants and individuals with limited economic resources.[36] These assessments fall short of capturing the intricacies of regional contexts. Money was not the predominant motivator or defining factor in the region, particularly among those who fought for the region's freedom. If wealth held significant sway, landlords with financial power could have more easily quelled such movements. A noteworthy observation from the report emphasizes that this specific group was unique in their lack of property ownership. This accentuates the socioeconomic profile of the active participants in these struggles as economically disadvantaged people. It thus delineates the economic dynamics that shaped the landscape of conflicts during that period.

H.M. Winterbotham's narrative from May 1885 reveals an intriguing discrepancy regarding the reported sum of ₹205 levied on a dozen participants in a specific incident. The observation made by Winterbotham in 1896 offers critical insights into the social strata of the freedom fighters, portraying them as 'field laborers, porters, timber-floaters, and others of the lowest class, living from hand to mouth'. This characterization underscores a potential misrepresentation in colonial narratives regarding the socioeconomic status of those engaged in the struggle for independence. Such descriptions could be interpreted as part of a deliberate strategy of linguistic warfare, aiming to distort the reality of the individuals who protested British oppression and atrocities. This pattern of generalization and potential misinformation in documenting the socioeconomic backgrounds of those involved in resisting British rule raises pertinent questions regarding the accuracy, authenticity and inherent biases within colonial accounts.[37]

Empowering Landlords and Engaging Loyalists

Conolly's activities as a collector were highlighted by the British, framing his efforts as a means of empowering and advancing the communities by collaborating with local landlords. In 1851, Conolly deliberately presented himself as a supporter of indigenous development and a patron of Muslim interests by highlighting the relatively small number of Muslim landlords who held positions as agents within the colonial administration. For instance, in the taluks of Ernad, Shernad and Valluvanad, out of a total of eighty-one *adhikari* positions, twenty-two were occupied by Muslim landlords from the region. This selective portrayal aimed to underscore Conolly's purported efforts in involving Muslims in administrative roles, projecting an image of inclusivity and support for native interests.[38]

The conflict between British loyalists and proponents of the independence movement precipitated a societal schism, impacting individuals aligned with the colonial establishment irrespective of their religious or caste identities. Notably, Muslim landlords who supported the colonial administration faced severe reprisals from proponents of the freedom struggle. In stark contrast, the predominant demographic of Hindu landlords, constituting 81 per cent, underscores that religious demarcations were not the focal point; rather, allegiance to colonial authorities determined their positioning within the conflict.

An attempt was made by the British to propagate the image of Collector Conolly as a supporter of the Muslim populace. Upon Conolly assuming control of Malabar in 1840, records indicate a nominal presence of only two confirmed and eight acting Moplah *adhikaris* across the three taluks. However, during Conolly's tenure, this number notably rose to twenty-two—a statistically significant upsurge. It was widely construed as a strategic maneuver employed by the colonial powers to streamline tax collection mechanisms.

The assertion made by William Logan, the district magistrate overseeing the disarmament of taluks in 1885 amidst protests contradicts the factual account: 'The risks run by the party employed in suppressing the Trikkallur gang from the firearms used by the fanatics made the Government decide to disarm three taluks of the district (Calicut, Ernad and Wallu-vanad).'[39] Evidently, affluent individuals were also active participants in opposition to the British colonial forces.[40]

Conclusion

The pivotal event of Conolly's assassination stands as a watershed moment in India's struggle for independence. Despite the glorification of Conolly's administrative accomplishments, a comprehensive analysis reveals a divergence between the celebrated achievements and the adverse consequences of his policies on the indigenous populace. While his initiatives such as teakwood plantation development and infrastructure dedications are lauded, a closer inspection unveils the disruptive implications of his decisions, including the exile of figures like Sayyid Fazal and the imposition of oppressive laws, significantly disrupting the tranquility in Malabar. This incongruity in the narrative underscores the complexities inherent in historical evaluations, where glorified administrative successes clashed with tangible repercussions experienced by the indigenous community. It underscores the complicated relationship between historical interpretations shaped by colonial influences and the necessity for a nuanced reevaluation of figures like Conolly, acknowledging both their celebrated achievements and the adverse consequences of their actions on indigenous populations.

CONCLUSION

Lineages and Leverages of Coexistence in the Post-Resistance Era

The Malabar region stands as a testament to remarkable communal coexistence despite the historical undercurrents of colonial propaganda that often fomented community discord and precipitated widespread suffering. Malabar was a land of pluralism, interfaith engagements, intercultural understanding and social cohesion long before any of these abstract phrases were fashionable. This region witnessed cohabitation between Muslims and Hindus in shared villages where communal resources such as water wells were jointly utilized. The intermingling of their children in play and the collective celebration of festivals were emblematic of a profound societal harmony. Evidently, the enduring bonds formed among individuals and families in this region transcended religious and caste boundaries, fostering a strong cross-confessional fabric across generations. Such an organic fusion of relationships flourished, based on personal interactions, mutual experiences with neighbors and noble aspirations, underscoring the resilience of social unity irrespective of religious affiliations or societal stratifications. This communal integration and solidarity served as a catalyst, fostering a thriving movement against colonial oppression. Leaders such as M.P. Narayana Menon teamed up seamlessly with Muslim friends, their collective efforts directed toward liberating the region from the shackles of colonial dominance. This collaborative spirit, rooted in shared experiences and a commitment to freedom, epitomized the movement in the region.

The exploration of local history unveils a rich tapestry interwoven with narratives of the fervent anti-colonial struggles. Concurrently, accounts of communal harmony and coexistence within the region surface prominently. A poignant anecdote relayed by a Nair family sheds light on them being sheltered by a neighboring Muslim household during times of insurgency.[1] Evidently, targeted attacks on landlords aligned with the British administration instigated a pervasive fear among the affluent, fostering an atmosphere of apprehension and subsequent flight from the region to ensure personal safety. The historical annals of this region offer a distinctive perspective on the events characterizing the resistance movements against British rule. Subsequent tribulations ensued for those involved in these movements, marked by targeted pursuits, profound familial losses and the unjust detainment of innocents. The socio-geographical fabric of the community underwent profound metamorphosis in the aftermath of the tumultuous events of 1921–1922. The deleterious aftermath of these events profoundly impacted the vulnerable segments of society, particularly women and children in the region. Notably, a dissonance surfaces between the colonial historical accounts and the vernacular histories prevalent in the region, unravelling stark disparities in perspectives. Such an elucidation reveals much about the wider Muslim experience and the evolution of Islam in a largely Hindu society. The narrative of interfaith harmony, although predominantly flourishing, occasionally encountered disruptions at the grassroots level. Nevertheless, Hindu denizens continued to revere Mamburam as a sanctuary, while effigies venerating Kaliyattakkavu pervaded households irrespective of religious demarcations, transcending sectarian divides.

The lived experiences after the insurgencies in the region effectively repudiate the reports of communal discord disseminated by the British colonial press and its representations. The current ethno-religious mosaic in southern India cannot be methodologically analyzed and understood without an in-depth study of the peculiar social system whereby Muslim and Hindu folk groups interacted—this was the very bedrock of Malabari society and statehood. This monograph has endeavored to provide the readers with a comprehensive analysis of the establishment and main pillars of this social structure. Furthermore, one will find information on the main dynamics of the integration of Islam in the region and on the complex geopolitical wrangling that followed the advent of the colonial era. The impact of conflict and the resulting unrest in the ethno-religious landscape is also given considerable space in this book. Lastly, the analysis describes the discrepancy between the policies adopted and enforced by the East India Company and their successors and the impact of those on the remote provinces and regions where the power of the imperial authority was limited or, even in some cases, only nominal. I have relied heavily on primary sources, such as contemporary newspaper articles, official reports, personal diaries and letters collected during field studies. Even in the wake of decades since these turbulent events, the allegations propagated by external entities failed to permeate the grassroots level. Relationships forged in childhood persisted, demonstrating that religious affiliations posed no barriers to communal engagement or collaborative economic pursuits within the local milieu. Notably, both the Hindu and Muslim communities defied conventional societal divisions, establishing an exceptional camaraderie that transcended religious delineations. Their collective involvement in religiously significant events like *nercha* and *utsavam* serve as markers of their harmonious cohabitation within the local terrain. The experience of Muslims and Islam in South India is different from the experience in north India, and this is not trivial.

The tradition of preserving piggy banks among both village boys and girls in anticipation of the eve of Kavilattu remains a cherished cross-confessional practice.[2] This ritual is undertaken to break these piggy banks to procure their favorite toys for boys and bangles for girls. Concurrently, round jaggery candies are customarily prepared, and children anticipate enjoying the playful tricks performed by conjurors during this celebration. Distinctly, Muslim families in our native community participate in the *utsavam* festivities and return bearing bags filled with jaggery candies, an assortment of balloon toys and colorful bangles. This cultural observance underscores a shared enthusiasm for these celebrations, albeit with subtle variations in the selection of souvenirs, emphasizing the spirit that persists amidst cultural diversity within the village.

The primary contention levied against the resistance in Malabar by the British was their characterization of its participants as 'fanatics' and the region as anarchic and even labelling the women involved as 'feminists'. Despite the passage of numerous decades since Independence, the lingering shadow of these allegations persists, exploited by contemporary right-wing factions on both sides of the religious spectrum for their vested political gains. The resistance against colonial forces was a concatenation of causal forces. Every act of learning is simultaneously the demise of some preconceptions. Adhering to the principles of decolonial historiography, this pursuit aimed to shed light on the regional milieu from the standpoint of a native, cantering on indigenous contexts and experiences. Within this framework, I directed attention toward the flourishing vernacular culture, which remarkably thrived amidst the turbulence of invasions.

The forefront of the resistance movement in Malabar featured a heterogeneous composition of individuals from diverse spiritual communities. Eminent personalities such as M.P. Narayana Menon, Kattilasseri Muhammad Musaliar and Parambot Achuthan Kutti Menon notably espoused the principles of the Congress Khilafat Committees under the tutelage of Mahatma Gandhi. This documentation endeavors to present a multifaceted tableau of relationships, actions and ideological undercurrents intrinsic to the fabric of the freedom movement. M.P. Narayana Menon, recognized as a prominent figure in the struggle for independence, consistently championed the cause of fostering communal harmony. His regular association and coordinated activities with Kattilasseri were meticulously documented on a weekly basis.

Hitchcock's records cited Menon for impending arrest, citing his alleged involvement in Non-Cooperation Movements and association with the Khilafat agitation.[3] This underscores the diverse and interfaith complexion inherent in the fabric of these sociopolitical movements. Notably, despite his Hindu background, Menon faced arrest and imprisonment under the controversial Moplah acts. The charges leveled against Menon bore a distinct interreligious connotation, remarkably the accusation of inciting Muslims gathered in a mosque to defend British authority.[4] I have tried to contextualize the cultural and social setting of the lives of such men and women, highlighting their interests outside the faith organizations. Notably, non-Muslims attending mosque events or engaging in discussions within the premises was not an anomaly. An intriguing facet emerges from the testimony of a Muslim individual, Hussain, who was a prosecution witness. Hussain attested to M.P. Narayana Menon's speech, reporting it to Inspector Karunakaran Nair, who then informed Inspector Narayana Menon. This incident underscores a notable absence of exclusive religious roles; instead, it delineates a clear demarcation between those who supported the British colonial regime and those who opposed it. The religious affiliation of the prosecution witness, Hussain, illustrates the diverse stance within religious communities during pivotal movements such as the Khilafat or Non-Cooperation Movements. Not all individuals adhered to or supported these movements. Law enforcement documentation presents evidence of Menon's speech in the Pandikkad mosque, accurately pinpointing meeting venues and speech locations. However, the accusations seem contrived, fabricated by police entities to amplify the significance of his cases. Menon, along with Ali Musaliar and Variamkunnath Kunhamed Haji, were accused of leading the community in opposition to British rule. The underlying subtext within the court proceedings for these cases vividly illustrates the collaboration between Hindus and Muslims in their collective resistance against British colonial forces. As should become obvious, the notion of a simple Muslim–Hindu rivalry does not suffice to explain in depth the complex mechanisms at work.[5]

In the initial British portrayal, the Pukkottur area held significance as an early indicator of rising tensions. However, this narrative evolved, with the killing of two British officers becoming the pivotal catalyst for the sequence of events in 1921 and 1922. Prevailing studies predominantly adhere to settler narratives, interwoven with a vibrant colonial backdrop. Prevailing studies mostly follow settler narratives within a colonial context. The Tirurangadi incidents are seen as a continuation of these events, remaining within this colonial framework. Altogether, intra-Muslim communal competition, the reshaping of social solidarities and Islamic identities across the region, and variegated political discourse have generated loyalties and differences that go well beyond one-dimensional ethnic conditionalities. This further reminds us that the British Empire was, in truth, somewhat chaotic and not a monolithic leviathan rigidly following a strict linear program of subjugation. It was a mass of competing contingent interest groups (economic, military, police, religious and so forth). The adoption of decolonial historiography presents an opportunity to unveil and illuminate the authentic historical narrative of the land.

The imposition of the colonial administrative structure in Malabar significantly disrupted the established framework of land settlements. Feudalism had cultivated distinctive relationships between *jenmi*s and *kanakkaran* (tenants), governed by informal agreements and customary practices concerning land usage and shared reliance. In this traditional agrarian society, landlords and peasants maintained a symbiotic rapport, mutually benefiting from the produce based on a foundation of mutual understanding and interdependency. Notably, there was a trend to emphasize the religious identity of landlords who suffered or were targeted by resistance groups, particularly when Hindu landlords were attacked. However, incidents involving Muslim officers being killed are often overlooked as they did not align with the colonial narrative of religious fanaticism. This selective portrayal underscores the biased nature of colonial propaganda, emphasizing confessional affiliations solely in certain instances to serve their agenda.

During the rule of the Mysore kingdom, the surplus from cultivation was collected from *jenmi*s, reimbursing the *kanakkaran*. An examination of these historical facets yields a deeper comprehension of the intricate nature of land settlements and interactions among diverse social classes in colonial Malabar. Moreover, beyond religious affiliations, whether an individual supported the British administration held paramount importance. Hence, not only landlords but also others aligned with the British faced retribution. During the colonial era, British officials investigating land tenures in Malabar framed the traditional ownership structure as follows: the *jenmi* held the main role as the landholder, while the *kanamkkar* were positioned as tenants. This construction was significantly influenced by the overarching colonial ideology and administrative norms that consistently favored consolidating the authority of the landed aristocracy (*jenmi*s).[6] This stance concurrently marginalized the rights and status of tenant communities, among whom a substantial portion was composed of the Muslim population. However, it is crucial to approach such historical narratives with discernment, acknowledging alternative perspectives, to enables a more comprehensive understanding of the dynamics of land tenure prevalent during that era and the complex interplay between different landholding classes. Ultimately, the book invites readers to navigate the complexities of Malabar's history beyond conventional colonial narratives, fostering a deeper appreciation for the intricate socioeconomic structures and the interplay of power dynamics within the epoch. In examining the resistance to colonial rule in Malabar, a critical evaluation of established interpretations becomes imperative. During the trial of Ali Musaliar for alleged insurrection against the king, testimonies unveiled a noteworthy facet of the conflict detailed in Chapter 2, 'Moplah Amazons'. This account delineates the active involvement of Moplah women in the 'battle of Pukottur'. They notably engaged in combat, vocalizing the cry '*Allah hu Akbar*'. The cry did not signify a call to 'battle' or 'war-cry' as alleged by the British, but rather echoed the despairing cries of vulnerable women who found themselves bereft after the ruthless annihilation of their entire family.

Women in Malabar were accused of donning masculine attire, symbolizing their deep involvement in the resistance. In one notable case in Melmuri, the British military brutally killed women who were not disguised as men. However, in the news stories, they created propaganda about disguises to justify their brutalities against women and children. The British, however, struggled to acknowledge this era's women empowerment in the region. They disregarded and systematically dismantled matrilineal communities by enacting laws against them. Historical records detail instances of women, some holding prayer beads, navigating through gatherings near Pukkottur *Kovilagam*.[7] Reports described them encouraging young boys to join male combatants.[8] This underscores the significant role of mothers in the resistance, preparing their children to fight for freedom. Moreover, the colonial administration accused women and girls of maintaining strong ties with fighting groups. These women were branded as feminists due to their multifaceted engagement, which included supporting their father, brother and husband in various capacities. The comprehensive evidence unequivocally substantiates the emergence of a notable cohort of feminists within the community. Their multifaceted involvement, encompassing both combat and logistical support roles, constitutes a pivotal and intricate dimension of this historical episode, warranting scholarly scrutiny and examination. Adopting a decolonial historiography approach prioritizes indigenous perspectives and delves deeper into the multifaceted historical context beyond religious or caste-based frameworks. By transcending reductionist views, a decolonial lens facilitates a nuanced analysis encompassing socioeconomic, political and cultural dimensions, revealing the authentic motivations driving the resistance.

In an era marked by the absence of women's rights, particularly evident in the limitations imposed on British women, including their exclusion from university education and the right to vote, an interesting and noteworthy exception was visible in Malabar. Notably, Muslim women serving as educators were referred to as *Mullachis* and were prevalent in all villages. In Britain, the period from 1916 to 1917 saw a significant development in women's rights, particularly, when James William Lowther, the Speaker of the House of Commons, chaired a conference on electoral reform. The conference recommended a form of women's suffrage, paving the way for incremental progress in acknowledging women's political agency. Subsequently, in 1918, the Representation of the People Act was enacted, ushering in a transformative change in women's right to vote. This legislative milestone granted voting rights to women over the age of thirty, provided they met certain property qualifications. Although 8.5 million women met this criterion, it was only about two-thirds of the total population of women in the United Kingdom. It was not until the Equal Franchise Act of 1928 that women over twenty-one were able to vote and women finally achieved the same voting rights as men. This act increased the number of women eligible to vote to 15 million.[9] Such legislative strides marked a departure from the historical disenfranchisement of women and reflected the evolving societal attitudes toward gender justice. At this historical juncture, investigating both the voting rights of women and the admission processes of universities will unveil the reasons behind the British labeling women from Malabar as feminists in 1921.

The controversies about specific historical artifacts, particularly contested photographs and the identities attributed to those depicted in them, underscore the imperative of empirical validation and meticulous scrutiny in historical inquiry. This emphasis on rigorous examination is fundamental in crafting an accurate representation of events and personalities within the historical narrative. The convergence of eminent national leaders Mahatma Gandhi and Maulana Shaukat Ali in Malabar is a pivotal juncture in historical exploration. Their visit not only underscores the interplay between the national movement and the local sociopolitical milieu but also offers profound insights into the region's aspirations and challenges during that epoch. Of significant note is the inclusive nature of the Khilafat Committee and the collaborative endeavors of individuals hailing from diverse religious backgrounds. Amidst the varied debates and disparate perspectives presented by historians, the pursuit of a decolonized comprehension of the Malabar resistance and its multifaceted character remains paramount.

This era witnessed a confluence of religious, political and colonial dynamics. Notably, scholarly exploration underscores the constraints inherent in historical interpretations influenced by colonial vantage points. This prompts a call for a historiographical paradigm shift, one that prioritizes indigenous perspectives, transcending the confines of religious or caste-centric frameworks. Particularly noteworthy is the persistence of pejorative lexicon in latter-stage historiography, manifesting terminologies forged by colonial historiographers to disparage the image of the freedom fighters. Terms such as *Kalapam*, *lahala*, *rebellion* and *Moplah* persistently denote the resistance and community, perpetuating colonial-era narratives even post-Independence. Significantly, vernacular historians, while preserving the identities of the Muslim and Marxist narratives, inadvertently perpetuated these derogatory connotations. This phenomenon underscores the enduring legacy of colonial biases in post-Independence historiography. Remarkably, official records following Independence, including commemorative publications recounting massacres, continued employing terms like the 'Wagon tragedy'. Even the municipality used the name for their memorial—Wagon Tragedy Memorial Municipal Town Hall. This term, originally propagated by colonial administrations and propaganda media to justify inhumane actions during the massacre, endured within post-colonial historical accounts.

Viceroy Reading addressed some of the issues raised by Europeans against Indians in his speech to the Council of State in Simla (Shimla), as reported by the *Liverpool Daily Post*. Referring to racial antagonism, Viceroy Reading stated that he did not assert that all the fault was on one side. He pointed out some cases of violence and discourtesy by Europeans towards Indians. Neither could it be said that the trial of certain Europeans in some criminal cases satisfied public conscience.[10] During the period of scrutiny surrounding the Malabar events in 1921, a discernible pattern emerges indicating Collector Thomas and Hitchcock's excessively stringent approach when dealing with the indigenous populace of Malabar. This approach tragically culminated in the killing of unarmed civilians who had congregated at Tirurangadi Kacheri to seek resolution for the detention of their compatriots by colonial authorities. Given the gravity of these circumstances, a judicious and impartial review of these incidents by an unbiased judicial body, analogous to the judicial investigation conducted into the actions of the Apartheid regime concerning the case of Imam Haroon in South Africa, posthumously, becomes imperative.[11] Such a comprehensive examination would serve multifaceted objectives, namely, the elucidation of ambiguities, the prosecution of the true perpetrators and the illumination of the foundational causes behind the demise of the initial two British officers. These fatalities were blamed on the leaders of the resistance in Malabar, subsequently resulting in retaliatory measures and the widespread massacre of thousands in the region during that historical epoch. Highlighting instances like the first event at Tirurangadi, where a 'Muslim police officer' (Moideen) was among the initial casualties, while the focus was not on religion but rather affiliations with the colonial regime, adds depth to the narrative.

The exploration of Malabar's history through the lens of decolonial historiography has unveiled a tapestry woven with intricate threads of cultural integration, interreligious harmony and sociopolitical complexities. Throughout this study, it became evident that vernacular cultures flourished on the foundations of intercultural engagements, fostering a sense of communal enjoyment amidst tumultuous periods. The indigenized nature of religion in the region emerged as a central theme, juxtaposed against the selective emphasis on religious affiliations by colonial powers to suit their narratives. Moreover, disruptions during the British colonial period significantly impacted the rich cultural fabric of the region, disrupting the inherent harmony and integration. Yet, amidst these challenges, the imperative to reinstate and strengthen cultural integration, interreligious harmony and coexistence becomes paramount in contemporary times. A crucial aspect stressed in this exploration is the need to confront extremist elements across diverse religious backgrounds that exploit religion for political gains. Struggling against such extremism is crucial to foster an environment conducive to coexistence, mutual respect and societal progress. In this era, the role of decolonial historiography stands pivotal. By offering a nuanced, inclusive and comprehensive understanding of Malabar's history, it provides a foundation for building a society that celebrates diversity, respects differences and values coexistence. This study seeks not only to uncover the historical complexities but also to ignite a collective endeavor toward a more unified and tolerant society, rooted in the lessons and nuances of the past. The attempt to foster a narrative that transcends religious divides and embraces the richness of cultural integration remains essential for a more harmonious and inclusive future.

NOTES

Introduction

1 *Kacheri* is a judicial venue where legal matters are adjudicated, either by a judge, a jury or a magistrate. The term *kacheri* was historically spelt as *cutcherry* in British primary sources.

2 Mambram, Mamburam and Pukkottur were the spellings used in primary sources of the time; however, more vernacularized spellings such as Mampuram and Pookkottur are now commonly used. To prevent confusion, this study opts to use the historical spellings Mambram, Mamburam and Pukkottur.

3 The Eastern Mosque in Tirurangadi, distinguished by its nomenclature and historical significance, is situated within a centuries-old riverside settlement, as corroborated by various historical documents. Tirurangadi (Tiruwarankad) is mentioned just before Tanur and Fannan (Ponnani) in *Tuhfat al Mujahidin*, highlighting the settlements in the region. It is also noted for its resistance against the Portuguese in 1524. See Shaykh Zayn al-Din II, *Tuhfat al Mujahidin*, translated and edited by M.H. Hussayn Nainar (Madras: Madras University, 1942), 51, 65. The term *Eastern Mosque* serves the purpose of distinctly identifying it amidst the numerous mosques in Tirurangadi.

4 During a visit to Muhammed Ali Musaliar's residence, the scholar personally exhibited his collection of traditional texts and Ali Musaliar's personal manuscripts, marked with the dirty boot prints of British officers, offering a tangible testament to historical events and interactions.

5 'Qiṣṣat Shakrutī Farmāḍ,' MS. IO Islamic 2807d, British Library, London.

6 'Qiṣṣat Shakrutī Farmāḍ,' MS. IO Islamic 2807d.

7 Shaykh Zayn al-Din II, *Tuhfat*, 35–41.

8 This Arabic word means 'land', and the Persian word denotes coast or country.

9 William Logan emphasizes the etymology of the word *Malabar*, attributing it to the combination of *Mala*, a Malayalam word meaning 'hill', and the Persian word *bar*, signifying 'country', rendering it as 'Hill Country'. William Logan, *Malabar Manual* (Madras: Government Press, 1887), 1–3.

10 Shaykh Zayn al-Din I, *Tahrid Ahlul Iman*, manuscript, Madin Academy Library, Malappuram.

11 Shaykh Zayn al-Dīn II, *Tuhfat*.

12 British records indicate that Ali Musaliar was taken to the Jakeri (Chakeri) family, where a discussion took place with Chekutty, who represented the British side. Ali Musaliar, as per the colonial version, was requested to refrain from participating in the voluntary activities associated with the Khilafat Movement. This situation will be further explored in the first

chapter. See R.H. Hitchcock, *A History of the Malabar Rebellion, 1921* (Madras: Government Press, 1925), 45.

13 *Nercha* is a religious and cultural festival observed at the tomb of a Sheikh or *Shaheed*, often combined with local folk festivities. It serves as a significant platform for the integration of religious rituals with indigenous local culture. *Sheikh* is a title literally meaning 'elder'. It commonly designates a Muslim scholar, chief or Sufi leader. *Shaheed* commonly means 'martyr', though it literally translates to 'witness' in Qur'anic Arabic. In Islam, it refers to someone who has died while fulfilling a commandment, including jihad. See Abbas Panakkal, 'Transformation of Admiral to the Sainthood and Sacred Stories of Chinese Sanctum Sanctorum from Malabar Coast,' in *Sacred Sites and Sacred Stories Across Cultures*, edited by D.W. Kim (New York: Palgrave Macmillan, 2021).

14 From the personal diary of Chakeri Thithachumma.

15 Personal interviews held in Pukkottur, Melmuri and Adhikarithodi.

16 Hitchcock, *History*, 9.

17 C. Gopalan Nair, *The Moplah Rebellion 1921* (Calicut: Norman Printing Bureau, 1923). The tribute published on 1 May 1923 is included before the table of contents.

18 Nair, *Moplah Rebellion*, 30.

19 Nair, *Moplah Rebellion*, 10–31.

20 K. Madhavan Nair, *Malabar Kalapam [Malabar Chaos]* (Calicut: Mathrubhumi Books, 2022). The book was written in the vernacular language of the region, Malayalam. Interestingly, the title of the book itself reflects a colonial hangover of the event, being a direct translation of the colonial aversion toward it.

21 Preface by K. Kalyanikutty Amma, in Nair, *Malabar Kalapam, vii–viii.*

22 Preface by K. Kalyanikutty Amma, in Nair, *Malabar Kalapam, vii–viii.*

23 Nair, *Malabar Kalapam,* xi–xiii.

24 Mozhikunnath Namboodiripad, *Khilafath Smaranakal* [Reminiscences of Khilafat] (Calicut: Mathrubhumi Books, 2015), 15–16.

25 Namboodiripad, *Khilafath Smaranakal.*

26 K.P. Keshava Menon, *Kazhinja Kaalam* [Yesteryear] (Kozhikode: Mathrubhumi Printing and Publishers, 1969), 117.

27 D.N. Dhanagere, 'Agrarian Conflict, Religion and Politics: The Moplah Rebellion in the Nineteenth and Early Twentieth Centuries,' *Past and Present* 74 (1977): 141.

28 Robert L. Hardgrave, Jr, 'The Mappila Rebellion, 1921: Peasant Revolt in Malabar,' *Modern Asian Studies* 2, no. 1 (1977): 57–99.

29 M. Gangadhara Menon, *Malabar Rebellion 1921-1922* (Allahabad: Vohra Publishers and Distributors, 1989).

30 M.N. Roy, *India in Transition* (Bombay: Nachiketa Publications, 1971), 88–92.

31 Soumyendranath Tagore, *Peasant Revolt in Malabar* (Bombay: People's Publication, 1937), 2.

32 This was brought up during the field study and is clearly reflected in his work.

33 E.M.S. Namboodiripad, *A Short History of the Peasant Movement in Keralam* (Calcutta: National Book Agency, 1985), 75.

34 Tagore, *Peasant Revolt in Malabar,* 53–64.

35 E.M.S. Namboodiripad, *Keralam Malayalikalude Mathrubhumi* [Keralam: Motherland of Malayalees] (Thiruvananthapuram: Chintha Publishers, 2009).

36 *Lahala* means noisy quarrel or mutiny.

37 K. Koyatti Moulavi, *1921-le Malabar Lahala* [Malabar Mutiny of 1921] (Kozhikode: IPB Books, 2020).

38 Conrad Wood, *Moplah Rebellion and its Genesis* (Delhi: People's Publishing House, 1987), v.

39 'A largely illiterate population like the pre-1922 Ernad Moplahs leaves little written record of which the historian can make use.' See Wood, *Moplah Rebellion and its Genesis,* v.

40 Interview with Muhammed Ali Musaliar, the grandson of Ali Musaliar.

41 Conrad Wood, 'The Moplah Rebellion of 1921-22 and its Genesis,' PhD thesis, University of London, 1975, 22–23.

42 Stephen Frederic Dale, *Islamic Society on the South Asian Frontier: The Mappilas of Malabar 1498–1922* (Oxford: Clarendon Press, 1980).

43 Information from field work and interviews in various regions where Musaliar worked.

44 Dale, *Islamic Society*, 180–183.

45 K.N. Panikkar, *Against Lord and State: Religion and Peasant Uprisings in Malabar, 1836-1921* (Delhi: Oxford University Press, 1989), 122–125.

46 This will be discussed in Chapter 7.

47 Panikkar, *Against Lord and State*, 125

48 Kathleen M. Gough, 'Peasant Resistance and Revolt in South India,' *Pacific Affairs* 41 (1968): 526–544.

49 A letter written by Haji, published in the *Hindu* on 18 October 1921, and interviews conducted during my research also corroborate this account.

50 Captain Harry, 'Comment Fut Perimee La Revolt des Moplahs', *Sciences et Voyages*, 10 August 1922.

51 Ramees Muhammed, *Sultan Variyam Kunnan* (Calicut: Twohorn Creation, 2021), 359.

52 Abbas Panakkal, 'The Unknown Photo, and British Construction of History: Revisiting Captain Harry's Article,' *True Copy Think*, 18 November 2021.

53 Personal interview at his house in Nellikuth in 1997.

54 Moulavi, *1921-le Malabar Lahala*; Nair, *Malabar Kalapam*.

55 The wagon massacre, referred to by colonial historiographers as the 'Wagon Tragedy', was an incident during the Malabar resistance against British colonial rule in India. It resulted in the deaths of a number of people.

56 Mahal (*mahallu* in vernacular language) refers to the regional Islamic community, centered around a main congregational mosque (Juma Masjid).

Chapter 1: Musaliar King

1 'Letter from M. Narayana Menon, Acting Inspector, D. Division, Malappuram, to the Superintendent of Police, South Malabar, Calicut, dated the 2nd August 1921,' in G.R.F. Tottenham, *The Mapilla Rebellion, 1921-22* (Madras: Government Press, 1922), 13. This incident was highlighted as 'Prelude of the Rebellion'.
2 R.H. Hitchcock, *A History of the Malabar Rebellion, 1921* (Madras: Government Press, 1925), 20–21.
3 Hitchcock, *History*, 21.
4 Ali Musaliar was mentioned as the elected provisional government chief and was attributed with the title of 'Musaliar King' by Captain Harry in the French magazine *Sciences et Voyages* on 10 August 1922. The *Englishman's Overland Mail*, dated 10 November 1921, highlighted the tribunal's verdict on Ali Musaliar with a headline reading 'Khilafat King Sentenced to Death'. In the propaganda film released under the title *The Malabar Moplah Rebellion* by the colonial Government of India, Ali Musaliar was depicted as the 'rebel king'.
5 *Uppapa*, meaning grandfather, is a term rooted in the rich tapestry of local vernacular culture and oral history. This understanding is drawn from interviews conducted as part of this study, with a particular emphasis on the perspectives of the natives of Tirurangadi and Vengara.
6 The Cherur battle will be discussed in greater detail in Chapter 6 in the second part of the book.
7 Hitchcock, *History*, 29.
8 On 2 November 1921, the special tribunal incorporated this accusation into its judgment against Ali Musaliar and thirty-seven others. See Hitchcock, *History*, 246.
9 Hitchcock, *History*, 29.
10 'Moplahs of Malabar,' *Madras Mail*, 27 July 1921, 3.
11 'Moplahs of Malabar,' *Madras Mail*, 9 February 1921, 6; 'Moplahs of Malabar,' *Madras Mail*, 27 April 1921, 8.
12 These incidents were documented in reports gathered during my local history collection in Vergara.
13 K.P. Keshava Menon, *Kazhinja Kaalam* [Yesteryear] (Kozhikode: Mathrubhumi Printing and Publishers, 1969), 98.
14 Hitchcock, *History*, 26.
15 Conrad Wood, 'The Moplah Rebellion of 1921-22 and Its Genesis,' PhD thesis submitted at School of Oriental and African Studies, University of London, 1975, 260.
16 The continuous reporting of the Malabar knife was dismissed by Knapp, who provided reports on the requests from Malabar administrative authorities. See Tottenham, *Mapilla Rebellion*, 33. A common aspect of rural life throughout Malabar is the frequent use, distribution and production of knives and small tools. In the Malabar tradition, the previous generation always carried a knife on their hips.
17 Tottenham, *Mapilla Rebellion*, 16.

18 Khilafat has been explained in Chapter 4. For more details and study, see Gail Minault, *The Khilafat Movement: Religious Symbolism and Political Mobilization in India* (Columbia: Columbia University Press, 1982).

19 Hitchcock, *History*, 45.

20 The British used the term *bands* to denote the resistant groups aligned with Ali Musaliar. These groups lacked equipment but occasionally wore uniforms. The term *band* was also cited in the verdict of the special court in Ali Musaliar's case, indicating it was an evident preparation for war. The primary accused was engaged in assembling the bands, referred to as Khilafat volunteers. See Hitchcock, *History*, 28–29. See 'Special Tribunal Malabar, Calicut, Judgment 2 November 1921', in Hitchcock, *History*, 244–254. See 'Note on the Rebellion by Mr. F. B. Evans,' in Tottenham, *Mapilla Rebellion*, 42–45.

21 Hitchcock, *History*, 29.

22 A *kovilagam* is the primary manor or palace of princely Kshatriya lineages such as Thampuran, Koyi Thampuran, Thirumulpad or Samanthan. This serves as the residence where family members who do not ascend to the titles of *raja* (king) or *rani* (queen) are overseen by the eldest male or female member of that specific branch of the family.

23 Thirumulpad, which means Samanthan, a person from the royal family, is the modern vernacularized spelling. British records used Tirumalpad. The ladies belonging to this caste are known as Kolpad or Koilamma.

24 Tottenham, *Mapilla Rebellion*, 13.

25 'Letter from M. Narayana Menon, Acting Inspector, D. Division, Malappuram, to the Superintendent of Police, South Malabar, Calicut, dated the 2nd August 1921,' in Tottenham, *Mapilla Rebellion*, 13.

26 Tottenham, *Mapilla Rebellion*, 13–15; Hitchcock, *History*, 29.

27 'M. Narayana Menon, Acting Inspector, D. Division, Malappuram, to the Superintendent of Police, South Malabar, Calicut, dated the 2nd August 1921,' in Tottenham, *Mapilla Rebellion*, 13.

28 Tottenham, *Mapilla Rebellion*, 13.

29 C. Gopalan Nair, *The Moplah Rebellion—1921* (Calicut: The Norman Printing Bureau, 1923), 21–22; Robert L. Hardgrave, Jr, 'The Mappilla Rebellion, 1921: Peasant Revolt in Malabar,' *Modern Asian Studies* 11, no. 1 (1977): 57–99.

30 Tottenham, *Mapilla Rebellion*, 13.

31 Tottenham, *Mapilla Rebellion*, 13–14.

32 *Adhikari* is the village head, responsible for collecting taxes and overseeing government-related matters in the village.

33 'M. Narayana Menon, Acting Inspector, D. Division, Malappuram, to the Superintendent of Police, South Malabar, Calicut, dated the 2nd August 1921,' in Tottenham, *Mapilla Rebellion*, 13.

34 Tottenham, *Mapilla Rebellion*, 13–14.

35 *Kariastan* is a term used in the Malayalam language to refer to the caretaker or manager. During the era of landlord systems, individuals were appointed to oversee and manage various properties, aiding owners in conducting business operations with workers and tenants. '*Kariastan*'

is the spelling used in British records, and now the vernacularized spelling 'Kaaryasthan' is also commonly used.

36 A *munsif* is a civil authority with local jurisdiction in the designated area, which includes presiding over a court of small causes.

37 'M. Narayana Menon, Acting Inspector, D. Division, Malappuram, to the Superintendent of Police, South Malabar, Calicut, dated the 2nd of August 1921,' in Tottenham, *Mapilla Rebellion*, 13. This document is sourced from official British records. The alternative narrative is provided by Kunhalan Kakka, who witnessed the incidents in Pukkottur and was interviewed by me during the seventy-fifth anniversary of the events.

38 This story is specific to the letter dated 2 August 1921 written by M. Narayana Menon, acting inspector, D. Division, Malappuram, to the superintendent of police, South Malabar, Calicut. See Tottenham, *Mapilla Rebellion*, 13.

39 K.N. Panikkar, 'Peasant Revolt in Malabar in Nineteenth and Twentieth Centuries,' in *Peasant Struggles in India*, edited by A.R. Desai (New Delhi: Oxford University Press, 1979), 617.

40 K.N. Panikkar, *Against Lord and State: Religion and Peasant Uprising in Malabar, 1836-1921* (Delhi: Oxford University Press, 1989).

41 This clarification is derived from field studies conducted in the region.

42 Hitchcock, *History*, 28.

43 Hitchcock, *History*, 29.

44 Tottenham, *Mapilla Rebellion*, 13–14.

45 Hitchcock, *History*, 29.

46 Tottenham, *Mapilla Rebellion*, 26.

47 '*Demi-official*—from J.T.W. Filson, Esq., Personal Assistant to the Inspector General of Police, dated Madras, the 13th August 1921,' in Tottenham, *Mapilla Rebellion*, 26.

48 '*Demi-official*—from J.T.W. Filson, Esq., Personal Assistant to the Inspector General of Police, dated Madras, the 13th August 1921,' in Tottenham, *Mapilla Rebellion*, 26.

49 '*Demi-official*—from the General Officer Commanding, dated Wellington, the 15 August 1921, No. (Secret) S. 250/13/G,' in Tottenham, *Mapilla Rebellion*, 30.

50 Tottenham, *Mapilla Rebellion*, 30.

51 Tottenham, *Mapilla Rebellion*, 30.

52 From the telegram drafted by A.R. Knapp, approved in Cabinet to be dispatched to the district magistrate. In the note on proposed action in Malabar by A.R. Knapp, Lava Kutti's name was written as Lavarkutti, and Karadan Moideen was specifically Mohideen. See Tottenham, *Mapilla Rebellion*, 27.

53 'Demi-official—from E.F. Thomas, I.C.S., Collector of Malabar, dated Calicut, the 16 August 1921,' in Tottenham, *Mapilla Rebellion*, 28–29; Also see Hitchcock, *History*, 29–31.

54 Telegram with the detail of the notes of discussion at Cabinet meeting on 16 August 1921, drafted by Knapp and mentioned that it was approved by

cabinet to send District Magistrate No. 276. Reproduced in Tottenham, *Mapilla Rebellion*, 27.

55 'E.F. Thomas, I.C.S., Collector of Malabar, dated Calicut, the 16th August 1921,' in Tottenham, *Mapilla Rebellion*, 28.

56 Madhavan Nair, U. Gopala Menon and Moideen Koya were greeted with enthusiasm by a jubilant Congress-Khilafat procession in Calicut upon their release from six months of imprisonment. This event underscored the power of unity within the region and portrayed an image of relentless resistance. I obtained anecdotes regarding these incidents during my interview with P.P. Ummer Koya, a Congress leader and former minister of education in 1997. For more details, see Hardgrave, 'The Mappilla Rebellion,' 84.

57 Hitchcock, *History*, 26.

58 This excerpt is from a personal interview with Muhammed Ali Musaliar, the grandson of Ali Musaliar.

59 'M. Narayana Menon, Acting Inspector, D. Division, Malappuram, to the Superintendent of Police, South Malabar, Calicut, dated the 2nd August 1921,' in Tottenham, *Mapilla Rebellion*, 13.

60 'E.F. Thomas, Collector of Malabar, dated Calicut, the 7th August 1921,' in Tottenham, *Mapilla Rebellion*, 23.

61 The *Madras Mail* was a propaganda mouthpiece of the colonial administration, and it assisted the officers to create false notions on the region to execute their brutal actions. This was linguistic warfare to support the colonial force. Number of post-colonial studies quoted these reports to prove Malabar populace were fanatic and war was unavoidable. See Conrad Wood, *The Moplah Rebellion and Its Genesis* (Delhi: People's Publishing House, 1987); Stephen Frederic Dale, *Islamic Society on the South Asian Frontier: The Mappilas of Malabar 1498–1922* (Oxford: Clarendon Press, 1980).

62 '*Demi-official*—to the General Officer Commanding dated the 11th August 1921, No. 258 S. Malabar Affairs,' in Tottenham, *Mapilla Rebellion*, 24.

63 Tottenham, *Mapilla Rebellion*, 20–21.

64 Tottenham, *Mapilla Rebellion*, 19–21.

65 Tottenham, *Mapilla Rebellion*, 27–29.

66 Tottenham, *Mapilla Rebellion*, 31.

67 'E.F. Thomas, Collector of Malabar, dated the 18th August 1921, No. 286-8, in Tottenham, *Mapilla Rebellion*, 31.

68 Knapp's 'Note on Malabar Affairs,' in Tottenham, *Mapilla Rebellion*, 32–34.

69 After his Malabar visit, Knapp prepared a note on Malabar affairs, which he submitted to the Chief Secretary on 18 August 1921. This note was later reproduced by Tottenham. See Tottenham, *Mapilla Rebellion*, 32–34.

70 Tottenham, *Mapilla Rebellion*, 32.

71 Tottenham, *Mapilla Rebellion*, 18.

72 Tottenham, *Mapilla Rebellion*, 23.

73 Knapp specified that Hitchcock's letter should be returned to Thomas and Thomas's draft order should be examined in detail. Tottenham, *Mapilla Rebellion*, 32.

74 Knapp's 'Note on Malabar Affairs,' in Tottenham, *Mapilla Rebellion*, 33.
75 Tottenham, *Mapilla Rebellion*, 33.
76 Temple swords were primarily used for ceremonial purposes during temple festivals. These swords were often large, but they were not designed for combat or intended to be as harmful as war knives or swords.
77 Tottenham, *Mapilla Rebellion*, 33.
78 Tottenham, *Mapilla Rebellion*, 34.
79 Hitchcock, *History*, 33; Tottenham, *Mapilla Rebellion*, 32–34.
80 Tottenham, *Mapilla Rebellion*, 33.
81 This list will be discussed in the next chapter in detail.
82 'Note On the Rebellion by Mr. F. B. Evans,' in Tottenham, *Mapilla Rebellion*, 44.
83 Hitchcock, *History*, 35–36.
84 K.K. Muhammed Abdul Kareem, *Ali Musaliar, K.M. Maulaviyude Khilafath Smaranakal* [K.M. Maulavi's Khilafat Reminiscences] (Tirurangadi: CH Muhammed and Sons, 2021), 70.
85 Muhammed Ali Musaliar personally showed me his private collections, which included the old books belonging to Ali Musaliar, bearing the grimy scars left by British soldiers' boots.
86 This transgression stands in direct violation of the clause stipulated in the approval for the raid in Tirurangadi. Furthermore, the collector and the police defied the explicit directive not to conduct searches within the confines of the mosque. Despite their actions, no knives were discovered within these premises.
87 Kareem, *Ali Musaliar, K.M. Moulaviyude Khilafath Smaranakal*, 72.
88 Field study.
89 'Letter—from the General Officer Commanding, No. S/250/72-G, dated the 25th August 1921,' in Tottenham, *Mapilla Rebellion*, 66–67; '*Letter*—from E. F. Thomas, District Magistrate, Malabar, No. 92/21, dated the 25th August 1921,' in Tottenham, *Mapilla Rebellion*, 68–71.
90 Interview with Muhammed Ali Musaliar.
91 Hitchcock, *History,* 35–40.
92 'Disturbances in Malabar—Letter from the General Officer Commanding, No. S/250/72-G, dated the 25th August 1921,' in Tottenham, *Mapilla Rebellion*, 66–70.
93 This excerpt is from the vernacular account collected during the field study.
94 Hitchcock, *History,* 195–196. The documentation provided by K.M. Moulavi, previously known as Thayyil Mohammed Kutty Musaliar, in 1921 offers insight into the events in Tirurangadi. The use of the term 'Ali Moulwiyar Thangal' in this context is significant, potentially indicating a British aversion towards individuals holding the title 'Musaliar'. K.M. Moulavi's account also highlights his admiration for Chalilakath Ibrahim Kutty, who was involved in printing pamphlets commissioned by British authorities. However, this affiliation with the colonial administration sparked a backlash among the populace, leading to the burning of the printing press. Interestingly, the biography of Thayyil Mohammed Kutty Musaliar (K.M. Moulavi) was published by Chalilakath Ibrahim Kutty's CH Press.

95 'Letter—from E.F. Thomas, I.C.S., District Magistrate, Malabar, No. 92/21, dated Calicut, the 25th August 1921,' in Tottenham, *Mapilla Rebellion*, 68–72.

96 'Letter—from N.E.Q. Mainwaring, Esq., Deputy Inspector-General of Police, Western Range, to the Inspector-General of Police, Madras, dated Camp, Calicut, August 23rd, 1921,' in Tottenham, *Mapilla Rebellion*, 72–73.

97 'From the District Magistrate, Malabar, dated the 21st August 1921. Despatched at 10-55 hours; received here at 11-7 hours. (Presumably sent in by hand on 20th August for despatch from Calicut),' in Tottenham, *Mapilla Rebellion*, 54.

98 'From the District Magistrate, Malabar, dated the 23rd August 1921,' in Tottenham, *Mapilla Rebellion*, 57.

99 Tottenham, *Mapilla Rebellion*, 54–55. The departure of troops from Tirurangadi on 21 August was accompanied by a few refugees and loyal Mappilas, whose safety, according to the British, was at risk in the area. Notably, among these loyal Mapillas were Kazhungunthottathil Moosa Kutti, the *adhikari*, Chalilakath Ibrayan Kutti (the owner of the Arabic press who had printed leaflets against the Khilafat Movement; Hitchcock mentioned that his house was completely looted and destroyed on 20 August) and his son Ahmed, Vettilakkaran Ahmed and Marakkarathodi Markkar Kutti of Tirkulam. See Hitchcock, *History*, 59. This illustrates how Muslims were also associated with the British, making them targets for resistance groups. To safeguard their lives, they sought refuge with the military team following the events of 20 August in Tirurangadi.

100 The tomb of Rowley and Johnstone stands in front of Tirurangadi Kacheri, commemorating their demise during the colonial action in Tirurangadi. Both names are inscribed on a single tomb, with one name on each side. 'We buried Rowley and Johnstone in the court house compound, where they rest as they fell, side by side'. See Hitchcock, *History*, 202.

101 Tottenham *Mapilla Rebellion*, 47–48; Hitchcock, *History*, 43.

102 Menon, *Kazhinja Kaalam*, 96–101.

103 Tottenham, *Mapilla Rebellion*, 38–40. Hitchcock noted in his book that martial law had been proclaimed on 26 August with effect from 19 August 1921. See Hitchcock, *History*, 60. This declaration was advantageous for the magistrate and police superintendent, granting them the leverage to cover up their brutal activities and massacres on 20 August in Tirurangadi under the umbrella of martial law.

104 'Letter from F. Thomas, District Magistrate, Malabar, No. 92/21, dated Calicut, the 25th August 1921,' in Tottenham, *Mapilla Rebellion*, 68–72.

105 'Letter from F. Thomas, District Magistrate, Malabar, No. 92/21, dated Calicut, the 25th August 1921. Tottenham, *Mapilla Rebellion*, 68–72.

106 Variations in the spelling of the name have been noted, with 'Johnstone' being the prevailing form in official communication. While alternative renditions such as 'Jonson' also exist, 'Johnstone' is the established orthography predominantly recognized within official contexts. On the tombstone, the official names were inscribed on both respective sides, as

they were buried side by side. This was due to the lack of time to dig two separate burial chambers, given the tense situation in the region. However, Hitchcock claimed they were buried as they were found dead. Hitchcock, *History*, 202.

107 'Letter from F. Thomas, District Magistrate, Malabar, No. 92/21, dated Calicut, the 25th August 1921,' in Tottenham, *Mapilla Rebellion*, 68–72.

108 'Letter from N.E.Q. Mainwaring, Deputy Inspector-General of Police, Western Range, to the Inspector-General of Police, Madras, dated Camp, Calicut, August 23rd, 1921,' in Tottenham, *Mapilla Rebellion*, 72–74.

109 The term *jutka* refers to bullock cart, and the person who drives it is called a *jutkawallah*. Bullock carts were popular vehicles in Malabar during that period, serving as essential modes of transportation for both goods and people.

110 Tottenham, *Mapilla Rebellion*, 69.

111 'From the Officer Commanding, Malabar, No. M.O. 106, dated Tirurangadi, the 1st September 1921,' in Tottenham, *Mapilla Rebellion*, 78; 'Reports from F.B. Evans, Special Civil Officer, Note on operations from 26th August 1921 to 6th September 1921,' in Tottenham, *Mapilla Rebellion*, 233–234.

112 'Judgment from the court of special tribune, Malabar, Calicut, 2nd November 1921,' in Hitchcock, *History*, 244–255.

113 Hitchcock, *History*, 249.

114 Hitchcock, *History*, 244–255.

115 Hitchcock, *History*, 244.

116 Hitchcock, *History*, 252.

117 Hitchcock, *History*, 253.

118 Captain Harry, 'Comment Fut Perimee La Revolt des Moplahs,' *Sciences et Voyages*, 10 August 1922, 5–9. This will be discussed in detail when we analyze the picture of Variamkunnath Kunhamed Haji in Chapter 3.

119 Henry Miers Elliot, *The History of India, as Told by Its Own Historians* (London: Trübner and Co, 1867); Mir Hussain Ali Khan Kirmani, *History of Tipu Sultan: Being a Continuation of the Neshani Hyduri. A Continuation of The Neshan-I-Hyduri*, translated from Persian by Col. Miles (London: Oriental Translation Fund, 1864).

120 Captain Harry, 'Comment Fut Perimee La Revolt des Moplahs,' *Sciences et Voyages*, 10 August 1922.

121 'Khilafat Rajah Installed in Mosque,' *Englishman's Overland Mail*, 13 October 1921, 3.

122 'Troops Restoring Order, Moplahs Flee to Jungle,' *Argus* (Melbourne, Vic.: 1848–1957), 5 September 1921. Most reports published in Australian newspapers were datelined from Allahabad or Simla (Shimla, the summer capital of British India). These reports were attributed to the Australian Press Association, with additional insights from Indian experts and perspectives from London being incorporated to underscore their gravity. Examples of such publications include: 'Many Moplas Yield,' *West Australian* (Perth, WA: 1879–1954), 9 December 1921, 7; 'The Malabar Revolt,' *Mercury* (Hobart, Tas.: 1860–1954), 30 August 1921, 5; 'Indian

Revolt,' *Maryborough Chronicle, Wide Bay and Burnett Advertiser* (Qld.: 1860–1947), 19 November 1921, 9; 'Malabar Revolt Troops in Action With Rebels A Five Hours' Fight Four Hundred Moplahs Killed Situation Still Serious,' *Mercury* (Hobart, Tas.: 1860–1954), 31 August 1921, 5.

123 'British Ultimatum to Moplahs,' *Nottingham Morning Post*, 5 September 1921. The *Guardian* also reported that the Ali Musaliar and forty other people, along with Hindus, were found looting at Cherpalacherry. See *Guardian*, 5 September 1921, 8.

124 'Ultimatum to Indian Rebels: Surrender Within 48 Hours,' *North Star*, 5 September 1921.

125 'Moplha Roundup: British Cavalry Capture Rebel Leader,' *Daily Mail*, 6 September 1921, 6; 'Indian Unrest,' *Lincolnshire Echo*, 6 September 1921, 2.

126 C.A. Innes, *Madras District Gazetteer—Malabar* (Madras: Government Press, 1951), 185–186; William Logan, *Malabar Manual* (Madras: Government press, 1887), 191.

127 Kathleen Gough, 'Mappilas in North Kerala,' in *Matrilineal Kinship*, edited by David M. Schneider and Kathleen Gough (Berkeley and Los Angeles: University of California, 1961), 442.

128 The tariqa refers to the spiritual path of individual Sufis (mystics) seeking direct knowledge (*ma'rifah*) of God or reality (*ḥaqq*).

Chapter 2: 'Moplah Amazons'

1 In the war memorial, a figure representing an Aboriginal Australian is the first carved face among the other indigenous animal faces and figures. Situated in Canberra, the Australian War Memorial is housed within a dedicated building, which hosts the majority of its galleries and commemorative spaces. See Australian War Memorial, accessed 20 May 2024, https://www.awm.gov.au/about.

2 'Moplah Amazons,' *Englishman*, 3 November 1921, 6.

3 'Bellary Alarmed Fears Moplah Prisoners May Escape,' *Englishman*, 3 November 1921, 6; 'Desecration of Temples,' *Englishman*, 3 November 1921, 6.

4 R.H. Hitchcock, *A History of the Malabar Rebellion, 1921* (Madras: Government Press, 1925), 84.

5 In some cases, the name of the reporter or author was not disclosed. However, the French magazine provided the name of the author as Captain Harry. Captain Harry, 'Comment Fut Perimee La Revolt des Moplahs,' *Sciences et Voyages*, 10 August 1922. This will be discussed in detail next chapter.

6 Hitchcock, *History*, 84.

7 Collected during my field study in Melmuri-Adhikarithodi, the protected group burial place, where the bodies of the family were buried.

8 Hitchcock, *History*, 84.

9 Hitchcock, *History*, 91.

10 Hitchcock, *History*, 115.

11 G.R.F. Tottenham, *Mapilla Rebellion, 1921-22* (Madras: Government Press, 1922), 27.

12 'Summary of the Important Events of the Rebellion by Under Secretary', in Tottenham, *Mapilla Rebellion,* 37–38.
13 'Judgment of Special Tribunal, Malabar, Calicut, 2 November 1921', in Hitchcock, *History*, 245.
14 This was quoted in the report from the Tiruvazhamkunnu *adhikari's* statement. See 'Note On the Rebellion by Mr. F.B. Evans,' in Tottenham, *Mapilla Rebellion*, 37–45.
15 List of persons to be treated under Sections 121 and 121-A and 122, Indian Penal Code, for whose prosecution sanction is required under Section 196, in Tottenham, *Mapilla Rebellion,* 316–317.
16 Tottenham, *Mapilla Rebellion*, 336.
17 'G.O. No. 867, Judicial, dated 15th November 1921,' in Tottenham, *Mapilla Rebellion*, 336.
18 'Note On the Rebellion by Mr. F.B. Evans,' in Tottenham, *Mapilla Rebellion*, 45.
19 K. Koyatti Moulavi, *1921-le Malabar Lahala* [Malabar Mutiny of 1921] (Kozhikode: IPB Books, 2020), 36.
20 Moulavi, *1921-le Malabar Lahala,* 37.
21 Case 4/21, Special Tribunal. See Hitchcock, *History,* 244–255.
22 Tottenham, *Mapilla Rebellion*, 336.
23 'The Malabar Revolt: Operations Of The Military, Dislocation Of Traffic,' *Mercury* (Hobart, Tas.: 1860–1954), 30 August 1921, 5.
24 'Malabar Revolt:Troops In Action With Rebels A Five Hours' Fight Four Hundred Moplahs Killed Situation Still Serious,' *Mercury* (Hobart, Tas.: 1860–1954), 31 August 1921, 5.
25 'The Moplahs of Malabar,' *Belfast Telegraph*, 30 August 1921.
26 Charles Alexander Innes, *Madras District Gazetteers* (Madras: Government Press, 1908), 198.
27 Hitchcock, *History*, 36.
28 'Moplahs Well Armed: Ferocious And Eager For Death,' *Western Daily Press,* 31 August 1921.
29 'Moplahs in Khaki: Preparations for Trench Warfare,' *Daily Herald*, 2 September 1921.
30 'Serious Rioting is reported in Ponani, Grave Situation Exists in India; Several Murders Reported; Military Aid is Summoned,' *New Britain Herald* (New Britain, Conn. 1890–1976), 24 August 1921.
31 '1000 are Killed by Natives in Indian Revolt,' *Washington Times* (Washington [D.C.], 1902–1939), 25 August 1921.
32 'Serious Rioting is Reported in Ponani, Grave Situation Exists in India; Several Murders Reported; Military Aid is Summoned,' *New Britain Herald*, 24 August 1921; '1000 are Killed by Natives in Indian Revolt,' *Washington Times*, 25 August 1921.
33 'Unrest in India, The Malabar Revolt,' *Warwick Daily News* (Qld: 1919–1954), 16 September 1921, 2.
34 'Unrest in India, The Malabar Revolt,' *Warwick Daily News* (Qld.: 1919–1954), 16 September 1921.
35 'Malabar Revolt,' *Observer* (Adelaide, SA: 1905–1931), 10 September 1921.

36 'Malabar Revolt,' *Register* (Adelaide, SA: 1901–1929), 3 September 1921.

37 'Moplahs Surrender to Gurkhas,' *Argus* (Melbourne, Vic.: 1848–1957), 12 December 1921.

38 Areekode is located along the Chaliyar River in the Areekode Grama Panchayat in Malappuram District, India. It was formerly a constituent of the Malabar District during the British colonial era.

39 'An Important Surrender,' *Observer* (Adelaide, SA: 1905–1931), 10 September 1921; 'Malabar Revolt,' *Register* (Adelaide, SA: 1901–1929), 3 September 1921; 'Malabar Revolt. Moplahs Surrender to Gurkhas,' *Argus* (Melbourne, Vic.: 1848–1957), 12 December 1921.

40 'Moplah Revolt Unbroken: Transport Troubles Delay British Troops,' *Herald,* (Melbourne, Vic.: 1861–1954), 20 September 1921.

41 'Malabar Revolt: Many Moplas Yield,' *West Australian* (Perth, WA: 1879–1954), 9 December 1921.

42 'The Malabar Revolt: Operations of the Military, Dislocation of Traffic,' *Mercury* (Hobart, Tas.: 1860–1954), 30 August 1921.

43 'Unrest in India: Malabar Rebellion Grave Development,' Australian Press Association, *Kalgoorlie Miner* (WA: 1895–1954), 31 August 1921.

44 'The Indian Revolt: Rounding Up Rebels in Malabar,' *Maryborough Chronicle, Wide Bay and Burnett Advertiser* (Qld.: 1860–1947), 23 November 1921, 5. The paper was known as the *Maryborough Chronicle, Wide Bay and Burnett Advertiser* until 1947. Afterward, it became the *Maryborough Chronicle* from 1947 to 1954.

45 Salem, located in present-day Tamil Nadu, is as a district that was established on 4 April 1792, encompassing the areas that currently constitute Namakkal, Dharmapuri and Krishnagiri. Alexander Reed served as its collector from 1792 to 1799.

46 Abbas Panakkal, 'Iruttu Muriyil Ninnu Choramanamulla Kathu' [A blood-scented letter from the dark room], *Varadhya Madhyamam*, 10 October 2010. The letter was found in the library of Edathola Bhavanam during the local history research in Vengara.

47 'Khilafat King Sentenced to Death at Calicut with Twelve Others,' *Englishman's Overland Mail*, 10 November 1921.

48 'More atrocities by the Rebels, Conflict with Military,' *Englishman's Overland Mail*, 10 November 1921.

49 'Moplah Trail: Case against Secretary of Khilafat Committee,' *Englishman's Overland Mail*, 13 October 1921.

50 Special Tribunal at Calicut, Evidence of Moplah Conspiracy,' *Englishman's Overland Mail*, 13 October 1921.

51 'Special Tribunal at Calicut: Evidence of Moplah Conspiracy,' *Englishman's Overland Mail*, 13 October 1921.

52 'Rebels Kill Villagers,' *Englishman's Overland Mail*, 8 October 1921.

53 Tottenham, *Mapilla Rebellion*, 247.

54 'Movement of Troops,' *Englishman's Overland Mail*, 13 October 1921.

55 'Movement of Troops,' *Englishman's Overland Mail*, 13 October 1921.

56 'Ultimatum to Rebels. Trouble Still Brewing in India,' *Courier*, 5 September 1921.

57 'Trouble Still Brewing in India,' *Dundee Courier*, 5 September 1921.
58 'Casualities in Wednesday's Fighting,' *Englishman*, 8 September 1921; 'How Moplah Leader Surrendered,' *Englishman*, 8 September 1921.
59 'Quiet Prevails in Military area, Looting Continues Elsewhere,' *Englishman*, 8 September 1921; 'Calicut Extremely Quiet: Railway Services Resumed,' *Englishman*, 8 September 1921; 'Quiet in North Malabar: Khilafat Activities Dying out, Hindus Migrating from Riot Area,' *Englishman*, 8 September 1921; 'Rioters Sentenced,' *Englishman*, 8 September 1921.
60 Field study.
61 'Trial of Arrested Rebels,' *Dundee Courier*, 5 September 1921.
62 'Quiet Prevails in Military Area, Looting Continues Elsewhere,' *Northern Whig and Belfast Post*, 14 October 1921.
63 'Calicut Extremely Quiet: Railway Services Resumed,' *Englishman*, 8 September 1921.
64 'Calicut Extremely Quiet: Railway Services Resumed,' *Englishman*, 8 September 1921.
65 'A Serious Affair,' [From A Special Correspondent], *Northern Whig and Belfast Post*, 14 October 1921.
66 'Three Days' Siege of Mosque. Moplahs' Scorn of Death,' *Dundee Courier*, 6 September 1921. The *Western Mail* also reported the same story of the surrender of Ali Musaliar with a similarly derogatory narrative: 'A good many of those killed received a number of rifle shots before they fell, their scorn of death being truly remarkable.' This uncivilized reporting reflects the British mindset at the time. See *Western Mail*, 6 September 1921, 5.
67 Judgment of Special Tribunal at Calicut on the 2 November 1921, the case Code no. 7 of 1921, in Hitchcock, *History*, 244–254.
68 Hitchcock, *History*, 244–245.
69 This is from an interview with Muhammed Ali Musaliar, who had a different perception of Ali Musaliar's final moments, although he agreed on the date. According to him, his grandfather died after his early morning prayer, and the British then tried to hang him to execute the judgment of the colonial court. K. Madhavan Nair, in *Malabar Kalapam*, mentioned the date of Ali Musaliar's execution as 17 February. See K. Madhavan Nair, *Malabar Kalapam* [Malabar Riots] (Calicut: Mathrubhumi, 1987), 193. Tottenham mentions another date: 'He was subsequently sentenced to death for waging war and after appealing for mercy to the Viceroy and after a great delay with the Government of India in passing orders, he was finally hanged at the end of January 1922.' See Tottenham, *Mapilla Rebellion*, 38.
70 Variamkunnath Kunhamed Haji, *Hindu*, 7 October 1921.
71 Variamkunnath Kunhamed Haji, *Hindu*, 7 October 1921.
72 Variamkunnath Kunhamed Haji, *Hindu*, 7 October 1921.
73 'Denies the Murder of Hindus—A Statement of Moplah says Report is British Propaganda,' *Baltimore Sun*, 7 December 1921, 6
74 'Denies Moplahs Forced Converts,' *Detroit Free Press*, 7 December 1921, 10.
75 'Denies Moplahs Forced Converts,' *Detroit Free Press*, 7 December 1921, 10.
76 Hitchcock, *History*, 78.

77 Hitchcock, *History*, 39, 65.
78 'Moplah Rising: Refugees Done to Death,' *Englishman*, 17 November 1921.
79 *Sphere*, 15 October 1921.
80 *Graphic*, 3 September 1921.
81 William Logan, *Malabar Manual* (Madras: Government press, 1887), 561–562.
82 Vincent Jos Ryder, *Two Years in Malabar* (Calcutta: Thacker and Spink Co., 1907), Introduction.
83 Ryder, *Two Years in Malabar*, 5.
84 Ryder, *Two Years in Malabar*, 12.
85 Field study. Also see Hitchcock, *History*, 55.

Chapter 3: Unveiling the Identities

1 The name of Variamkunnath Kunhamed Haji is transliterated in multiple forms in Roman script documents. 'Variyankunnath Kunjahammad Haji', 'Varian Kunnan' and 'Variyamkunnan' are popular.
2 Ramees Muhammed, *Sulthan Variyamkunnan* (Calicut: Twohorn Creation, 2021).
3 Abbas Panakkal, 'The Unknown Photo, and British Construction of History: Revisiting Captain Harry's Article,' *True Copy Think*, 18 November 2021.
4 Panakkal, 'The Unknown Photo'.
5 Text references to the article are from Captain Harry, 'Comment Fut Perimee La Revolt Des Moplahs,' *Sciences et Voyages*, 10 August 1922, 5–9.
6 It was mentioned in the last chapter how the term *Amazon* was used to denote the Malabar region, which was a polyglot centre of international trade for centuries before the British invasion.
7 The reader should bear in mind that this text strives neither to condemn nor to valorize Christianity, Islam or Hinduism at any level or individual Christians, Muslims or Hindus. Exercising both the objectivity and empathy incumbent on all serious historians, it aims to allow the sources to speak for themselves and capture the reader's interest, regardless of whether the reader is unconcerned or well-disposed to the doctrines of these faiths.
8 Pedro or Pero da Covilhã (1460–1526), hailing from Covilhã in Beira, received, in 1487, a notable document—a 'letter of credence for all the countries of the world'—accompanied by a navigational map delineating the contours of the Middle East and the expanse of the Indian Ocean. Embarking on a trading dhow, da Covilhã traversed the Indian Ocean and eventually reached the bustling emporium of Calicut, paramount hub of the flourishing spice trade. See 'Pero da Covilha,' Brittanica, accessed 15 May 2024, https://www.britannica.com/biography/Pero-da-Covilha-.
9 It is an effort to infer nefarious and malignant overseas influences on local events.
10 Field study in Vengara and Tirurangadi.
11 Reading initially underestimated the seriousness of the rebellion. He then tried to negotiate, but there were claims of a 'holy war' being declared by

the people of Malabar. This shows how complex the conflict was and how different parties responded.

12 This can be easily understood from Variamkunnath Kunhamed Haji's letter in which he states that the government was forcibly taking all Hindus out of villages. It was to make the ethnic cleansing easy in the region they identified as Amazon. *Hindu*, 7 October 1921.

13 The Sepoy Rebellion refers to the significant uprising among Indian soldiers, termed sepoys, within the British East India Company's army in 1857. This historical event, alternatively known as the Indian Mutiny or the First War of Independence, represents a pivotal chapter in India's fight for independence. It stands as a testament to the multifaceted resistance against British colonial rule, embodying various political, social and economic grievances. The term *Sepoy Rebellion* is often used interchangeably with other designations such as the 'Indian Rebellion of 1857' or the 'Great Rebellion' in recognition of its role in the struggle for India's freedom.

14 G.R.F. Tottenham, *The Mapilla Rebellion, 1921-22* (Madras: Government Press, 1922), 148–149.

15 Nilgiris, one of the districts in Tamil Nadu, is the name given to a range of mountains spread across the borders among the states of Tamil Nadu, Karnataka and Kerala.

16 'Moplah Train Tragedy,' *Pall Mall Gazette*, 31 August 1922.

17 The treatment of people by colonial officers in Malabar was inhumane and led to one of the most horrific episodes known as the Wagon Massacre, commonly narrated in colonial history as the 'Wagon Tragedy'. Regrettably, it was depicted merely as an unfortunate event without acknowledging the forceful actions of the colonial officers and their administration. See Tottenham, *Mapilla Rebellion*, 266. This incident reflects the overall attitude of the colonial authorities toward the inhabitants of the land. On 19 November 1921, 100 individuals were crammed into a closed goods wagon No. 1711 and transported from Tirur to Coimbatore. This wasn't just a tragedy; it was the British officers' inhuman treatment toward the people of Malabar that culminated in the massacre of numerous individuals.

18 Muhammed, *Sulthan Variyamkunnan*.

19 The advertisement featuring the film was published in *Kinematograph Weekly* on 5 January 1922, providing all these details.

20 'The Malabar Moplah Rebellion', official record film, directed by Major Robinson of 75th Carnatic Infantry, specially produced for the Government of India by A.W. Smith & Co, Imperial Theatre Bangalore, South India.

21 'Official Record film on Malabar Moplah Rebellion,' *Daily Herald*, 10 January 1922, 7.

22 *Motion Picture News*, January–February 1922.

23 Muhammed, *Sulthan Variyamkunnan*, 359–360.

24 *Kinematograph Weekly*, 5 January 1922.

25 Tottenham, *Mapilla Rebellion*, 28–29; R.H. Hitchcock, *A History of the Malabar Rebellion, 1921* (Madras: Government Press, 1925), 31–32.

26 The use of 'F' instead of 'J' in 'Fakeri' is a spelling error. Tottenham used 'Fakeri', but in a later publication, Hitchcock corrected it to 'Jakeri'.

It should be corrected to 'Jakeri' to align with Hitchcock's book. See Tottenham, *Mapilla Rebellion*, 28.

27 The event that Hitchcock refers to, where they agreed to suppress the movement, was the meeting at Jakeri Ahmed (Chakeri) house, which was also attended by Ali Musaliar. See Hitchcock, *History*, 45.

28 Kondanjanparambil was used in first report and then it was changed to Kondachamparambil. See Hitchcock, *History*, 31–32; Tottenham, *Mapilla Rebellion*, 28–29.

29 There is a discrepancy in the spelling of the name 'Lava Kutti' as documented by Hitchcock in the book in comparison to the version mentioned in the initial list quoted by Tottenham, which read as 'Chanimatel Lavar Kutti'. See Hitchcock, *History*, 31–32; Tottenham, *Mapilla Rebellion*, 28–29.

30 In the Hitchcock book, this name was recorded as Chittambara Kunhalan. See Hitchcock, *History*, 31.

31 In the first report, it was written as Asan Mammath, then it changed Ossan Mammad in Hitchcock's book. Hitchcock, *History*, 31–32; Tottenham, *Mapilla Rebellion*, 28–29.

32 Initially, this name was documented as 'Assan Moideen Kutii' and was later modified to 'Ossan Moideen Kutty'. Hitchcock, *History*, 31–32; Tottenham, *Mapilla Rebellion*, 28–29.

33 Tottenham spelled it incorrectly as 'Elamulasseri'. See Tottenham, *Mapilla Rebellion*, 29. Hitchcock corrected it to 'Elambulasseri'. Numbers five (5), six (6), seven (7) and eight (8) were portrayed as regular workers, but they were introduced as the linchpins of the movement and emerged as its most prominent figures. See Hitchcock, *History*, 31.

34 Tottenham, *Mapilla Rebellion*, 29; Hitchcock, *History*, 31.

35 His name was written in the first report as Meethal Panduth Narayana Menon. Tottenham, *Mapilla Rebellion*, 29.

36 Hitchcock, *History*, 32; Tottenham, *Mapilla Rebellion*, 29.

37 Hitchcock, *History*, 32; Tottenham, *Mapilla Rebellion*, 29.

38 Thayil Mammad Kuty Musaliar later adopted the name K.M. Moulavi. The usage of the term *Musaliar* presented considerable challenges, prompting him to abbreviate his pen name, Kathib Mammad, as 'K.M.,' while altering 'Musaliar' to 'Moulavi'. These narratives were gathered from the field study in Tirurangadi.

39 Hitchcock, *History*, 32; Tottenham, *Mapilla Rebellion*, 29.

40 Tottenham's book presented the name as Madambat Avaram Kutti Mussaliar, where the surname was spelled correctly, but the first name had an incorrect 'm'. In contrast, Hitchcock misspelled the surname as Marambat but corrected the first name to Avaran. Hitchcock, *History*, 32; Tottenham, *Mapilla Rebellion*, 29.

41 Hitchcock, *History*, 32; Tottenham, *Mapilla Rebellion*, 29. In the initial report quoted by Tottenham, the name was spelled as Munnayandakath Kunhi Khadir of Tanur. In the context of British officers, the phrase 'fanatical spirit' denoted behavior that ran counter to the directives of the colonial administration or actions that incited individuals to resist the injustices imposed by colonial rule.

42 Initially documented as 'Otakath Kunhi Koya Thangal' from Chembrasseri, it was later modified to 'Ottagath'. Hitchcock, *History*, 31–32; Tottenham, *Mapilla Rebellion*, 28–29.

43 The names in Hitchcock's list, as attached by Collector Thomas, were included without any alterations.

44 In the Tottenham report, the names were indeed documented as 'Theyil Assankoya Mulla of Calicut', 'Mulekandi Moidu of Calicut' and 'Unnayandakath Kunhi Khadir of Tanur'. Subsequently, these entries underwent modifications in later documentation. Hitchcock, *History*, 31–32; Tottenham, *Mapilla Rebellion*, 28–29.

45 Hitchcock, *History*, 32.

46 Tottenham, *Mapilla Rebellion*, 29–30; Hitchcock, *History*, 31–32.

47 In Tottenham's version, this name was spelled as Karath Moidin Kutti Haji of Pukkottur. Tottenham, *Mapilla Rebellion*, 29.

48 Those names were slightly different in Tottenham's book like Karath Moidin Kutti Haji of Pukkottur, Kaladi Isuf of Podiyat, Manethodi Kunhalan of Valluvambram, Kollaramban Abdu Haji Narukara, Parancheri Kunhiramutti of Pukkottur and Mozhikal Kunhamath Haji of Pukkottur, and it was modified in Hitchcock's book later. Hitchcock, *History*, 31–32; Tottenham, *Mapilla Rebellion*, 28–29.

49 Tottenham, *Mapilla Rebellion*, 29–30; Hitchcock, *History*, 31–32.

50 '*Demi-official*—from E.F. Thomas, Esq., I.C.S., Collector of Malabar, dated Calicut, the 16th of August 1921,' in Tottenham, *Mapilla Rebellion*, 29; see also Hitchcock, *History*, 51–52.

51 Their motivation appears to be to protect their employment and careers.

52 Judgment of the court of special tribunal Malabar, Calicut on 2nd November 1921, in Hitchcock, *History*, 244.

53 Tottenham, *Mapilla Rebellion*, 316–317.

54 '*Letter*—from E.F. Thomas, District Magistrate Malabar district to the Chief Secretary to Government of Madras, dated Calicut, Magistrate, the 19th September 1921, No. the 410,' in Tottenham, *Mapilla Rebellion*, 316–317.

55 Tottenham, *Mapilla Rebellion*, 316–317.

56 Tribunal report in Tottenham, *Mapilla Rebellion*, 44.

57 '*Letter*—from E.F. Thomas, District Magistrate Malabar district to the Chief Secretary to Government of Madras, dated Calicut, Magistrate, the 19th September 1921, No. the 410,' in Tottenham, *Mapilla Rebellion*, 316–317.

58 'Judgment of the Special Tribunal Malabar, Calicut., 18 October 1921,' in Hitchcock, *History*, 206–210.

59 Field study.

60 Mozhikunnath Namoodiripad, *Khilafath Smaranakal* [Reminiscences of Khilafat] (Calicut: Mathrubhumi Books, 2015), 12.

61 Hitchcock, *History*, 206–210.

62 There is a typo in the judgment against Kunhi Kadir, as the year of the Malabar War Knife Act is incorrectly written as 1845 instead of 1854.

63 J.W. Hugues, Judgment of Case Number 4 of 1921, Tuesday, 18 October 1921 in the court of special tribunal Malabar-Calicut, in Hitchcock, *History*, 206–210.

64 J.W. Hugues, Judgment of Case Number 4 of 1921, Tuesday, 18 October 1921 in the court of special tribunal Malabar-Calicut, in Hitchcock, *History*, 206–210.
65 J.W. Hughes, Judgment of case number 7, the court of the special tribunal Malabar, Calicut, 2 November 1921, in Hitchcock, *History*, 244–255.
66 'Moplah Trails,' *Englishman*, 13 October 1921.
67 'Moplah Trails,' *Englishman*, 13 October 1921.
68 Hitchcock, *History*, 38.
69 Field study.
70 Hitchcock, *History*, 38.
71 Tottenham, *Mapilla Rebellion*, 239.
72 Tottenham, *Mapilla Rebellion*, 242.
73 Tottenham, *Mapilla Rebellion*, 41.
74 '*Letter*—from E.F. Thomas, District Magistrate, Malabar, No. 92/21, dated Calicut, the 25th of August 1921,' in Tottenham, *Mapilla Rebellion*, 68–71.

Chapter 4: Enduring Legacy

1 Abbas Panakkal, *Islam In Malabar: A Sociocultural Study* (Kuala Lumpur: International Islamic University Malaysia, 2016); Sebastian R. Prange, *Monsoon Islam: Trade and Faith on the Medieval Malabar Coast* (Cambridge: Cambridge University Press, 2018); Wilson Chacko Jacob, *For God or Empire, Sayyid Fadl and the Indian Ocean World* (California: Stanford University Press, 2019); Abbas Panakkal and K.M. Baharul Islam, 'Cultural Integration in Muslim Communities,' in *South Asian Islam*, edited by Nasr M. Arif and Abbas Panakkal (London: Routledge, 2023).
2 Henry Miers Elliot, *The History of India, as Told by Its Own Historians* (London: Trubner and Co, 1869), v.
3 Romila Thapar, *Somanatha: The Many Voices of a History* (New Delhi: Penguin Books India, 2008,) 14–15.
4 M.K. Dhavlikar and G. Possehi, *The Pre-Harappan Period at Prabhas Pattan and the Pre-Harappan Phase in Gujarat* (Man and Environment, 1992), 17 (1), 71–78.
5 Pushpa Prasad, *Sanskrit Inscriptions of Delhi Sultanate: 1191-1526* (New Delhi: Oxford University Press, 1990), 12–13; Brajadulal Chattopadhyaya, *Representing the Other? Sanskrit Sources and the Muslims (Eighth to Fourteenth Century)* (New Delhi: Manohar, 1998), 28–43, 79–91, 92–97.
6 Nikki R. Keddie, *An Islamic Response to Imperialism: Political and Religious Writings of Sayyid Jamāl ad-Dīn "al-Afghānī"* (California: University of California Press, 1983), 5; Nikki R. Keddie and Ibrahim Kalin, 'Afghānī, Jamāl al-Dīn,' in *The Oxford Encyclopedia of Philosophy, Science, and Technology in Islam*, edited by Ibrahim Kalin (Oxford: Oxford University Press, 2014).
7 Keddie, *An Islamic Response*.
8 A.C. Niemeijer, *The Khilafat Movement in India 1919-1924* (Leiden: Brill, 1972); Gail Minault, *The Khilafat Movement: Religious Symbolism and Political Mobilization in India* (Columbia: Columbia University Press,

1982); M. Naeem Qureshi, *Pan-Islam in British Indian Politics: A Study of the Khilafat Movement, 1918-1924* (Leiden: Brill, 1999).

9 Home Department (Political) (A) Proceedings June 1919, No. 362-76, F.No. 16/192, National Archives of India (NAI), New Delhi.

10 Mushirul Hasan, *Nationalism and Communal Politics in India, 1885-1930* (New Delhi: Manohar Publications, 1991); Minault, *Khilafat Movement*; Andrew Tait Jarboe, 'War Losses (India),' in *International Encyclopedia of the First World War*, edited by Ute Daniel, Peter Gatrell, Oliver Janz, Heather Jones, Jennifer Keene, Alan Kramer and Bill Nasson, issued by Freie Universität Berlin, Berlin, 1914–1918; online, 19 October 2022.

11 I.H. Qureshi, *Ulema in Politics* (Delhi: Renaissance Publishing House, 1974), 261.

12 B. Pattabhi Sitaramayya, *History of the Indian National Congress (1885-1935)*, vol. I (Bombay: Padma Publications, 1946), 189–205.

13 M. Gangadhara Menon, *Malabar Rebellion (1921-22)* (Allahabad: Vohra Publishers & Distributors, 1989), 72.

14 Confidential Report on the Non-Cooperation and Khilafat Movement in India by Deputy Director, Central Intelligence Bureau, Home Department, Government of India, 240–242, National Archives of India (NAI), New Delhi.

15 P.N. Chopra, ed., *The Role of Indian Muslims in the Struggle for Freedom* (Delhi: Light & Life Publishers, 1979), xxv (Introduction).

16 Ram Gopal, *Indian Muslims: A Political History (1858-1947)* (Bombay: Asia Publishing House, 1964), 136–146.

17 Letter from F.C. Brown to the Chief-Secretary to the Government of Madras, January 1864, MJP. F. No. 980, 4 July 1864, Tamil Nadu State Archives, Chennai.

18 C.A. Innes and F.B. Ivans, ed., *Madras District Gazetteers* (Malabar [Madras]: Government Press, 1951), 4.

19 K.P. Keshava Menon, *Kazhinja Kalam* (Calicut: Mathrubhumi Books, 2024), 70.

20 R.H. Hitchcock, *A History of the Malabar Rebellion, 1921* (Madras: Government Press, 1925), 19.

21 Hitchcock, *History*, 19; Menon, *Kazhinja Kalam*, 69–71; C. Gopalan Nair, *The Moplah Rebellion 1921* (Calicut: The Norman Printing Bureau, 1923), 8–10.

22 G.R.F. Tottenham, *The Mapilla Rebellion, 1921-22* (Madras: Government Press, 1922), 2–3; C. Gopalan Nair, *The Moplah Rebellion* (Calicut: Norman Printing Bureau, 1923), 8–9.

23 K. Madhavan Nair, *Malabar Kalapam* (Kozhikode: Mathrubhumi Books, 2023), 64–68; M.P.S. Menon, *Malabar Samaram: M.P. Narayana Menonum Sahapravarthkarum* [Malabar Movement: M.P. Narayana Menon and His Companions] (Kozhikode: IPH, 2005), 60–61.

24 Hitchcock, *History*, 19; Menon, *Kazhinja Kalam*, 69–71; Nair, *Moplah Rebellion*, 8–10.

25 Menon, *Malabar Rebellion*, 77.

26 Menon, *Malabar Samaram*, 60–61.

27 R.C. Majumdar, *Struggle for Freedom* (Bombay: Bharatiya Vidya Bhavan, 1969), 316.

28 K.N. Panikkar, *Against Lord and State: Religion and Peasant Uprisings in Malabar, 1836-1921* (Delhi: Oxford University Press, 1989), 124.

29 Menon, *Malabar Samaram,* 62.

30 The discrepancy between the occurrence of an event in late April and its documentation in British newspapers, often presenting the information several days or even a week after the incident, led to the assignment of the date May 1920 instead of April 1920. This delay in reporting was a factor in chronologically situating the event within the context of historical records.

31 'A Serious Affair (From Special Correspondent),' *Northern Whig–Belfast Post*, 14 October 1921.

32 Graham Letter to Hannyngton, DO. No. 200-5, Dated 12 August 1920 in USSF. No. 307 Dated 01.10.1920, Tamil Nadu Archives, Chennai.

33 Hitchcock, *History,* 19.

34 Tottenham, *Mapilla Rebellion*, 1.

35 Bipin Chandra, *India's Struggle for Independence 1857-1947* (Delhi: Penguin, 2017).

36 Hitchcock, *History*, 21.

37 Report on the Administration of the Madras Presidency 1920-21, Tamil Nadu State Archives, Chennai; S.K. Pottekkat, P.P. Ummer Koya, N.P. Mohamed and K.A. Kodungallore, *Muhammed Abdurahiman: A Political Biography* (Calicut: Muhammed Abdurahiman Sahib Memorial Committee, 1978), 34, 36.

38 Menon, *Malabar Samaram*, 43–58; Pottekkat, Koya, Mohamed and Kodungallore, *Muhammed Abdurahiman*, 37, 43.

39 Nair, *Moplah Rebellion*, 23–24.

40 Tottenham, *Mapilla Rebellion*, 180; Hitchcock, *History*, 20.

41 Menon, *Kazhinja Kalam*, 76; Moyarth Sankaran, *Ente Jeevita Katha* [The story of my life] (Calicut: P.K. Brothers, 1965), 62.

42 A.R. Knapp, 'Notes on Malabar Affairs,' in Tottenham, *Mapilla Rebellion*, 32.

43 Letter from District Magistrate to the Chief Secretary, Dated 17 February 1921, F. No. 103-415, Tamil Nadu State Archives, Chennai.

44 Robert L. Hardgrave, Jr., 'The Mappilla Rebellion 1921: Peasant Revolt in Malabar,' *Modern Asian Studies* 11, no. 1 (1977): 57–99.

45 Hitchcock, *History*, 20.

46 S.F. Dale, *Islamic Society on the South Asian Frontier: The Mappilas of Malabar 1498–1922* (Oxford: Clarendon Press 1980), 188.

47 Hitchcock, *History*, 21.

48 Menon, *Malabar Samaram,* 72–73.

49 Fortnightly Report of the District Magistrate to Madras, March 1921, in Tottenham, *Mapilla Rebellion*, 4–5.

50 Menon, *Kazhinja Kalam*, 82.

51 Pottekkat, Koya, Mohamed and Kodungallore, *Muhammed Abdurahiman*, 38–40; Menon, *Kazhinja Kalam*, 68–84.

52 Ottapalam Conference and Police Atrocities (Pamphlet in Malayalam) 1921, Government of Madras, GO. No. 491, August 1921, Tamil Nadu Archives, Madras.

53 Menon, *Kazhinja Kalam*, 68–84; Tottenham, *Mapilla Rebellion*, 5.

54 'A Serious Affair [From Special Correspondent],' *Northern Whig-Belfast Post*, 14 October 1921.

55 P.K.K. Menon, *The History of Freedom Movement in Kerala*, Vol. II, 1885-1938 (Trivandrum: The Regional Records Survey Committee, 1972), 88–89; 'Street Brawl,' *Madras Mail*, 26 April 1921. See also Panikkar, *Against Lord and State*, 133.

56 Menon, *History of Freedom Movement*, 87–90.

57 Pub. Dept., G.O. No. 491, 3 July 1921, in Panikkar, *Against Lord and State*, 132.

58 Sitaramayya, *History of the Indian National Congress*, 209; Menon, *History of Freedom Movement*, 88.

59 K. Koyatti Moulavi, *1921-le Malabar Lahala* [Malabar Mutiny of 1921] (Kozhikode: IPB Books, 2020), 21–24.

60 Variyamkunnath Kunhamed Haji, *Hindu*, 7 October 1921.

61 Hitchcock, *History*, 21.

62 BEO 4175-313088, Başbakanlık Osmanlı Arşivi (The Ottoman Archives of the Prime Minister's Office), Turkey, hereafter referred to as 'Ottoman Archives'.

63 The First Balkan War (October 1912–May 1913) stands as a pivotal conflict where the Balkan League, consisting of Bulgaria, Serbia, Greece and Montenegro, confronted the Ottoman Empire. The outcome proved catastrophic for the Ottomans, who lost 83 per cent of their European territories and 69 per cent of their European population. During this period, Britain did not oppose the Ottomans, and there were no religiously motivated obstacles hindering aid efforts directed towards Turkey. Additionally, fanaticism did not impede the issuance of official checks from the British banking system in pounds, See Ottoman Archives.

64 The term *Mahratta* refers to the Maratha, and the war mentioned is the Third Anglo-Maratha War (1817–1819), a decisive encounter between colonial forces and the Maratha Empire.

65 'The Disbandment of The 77th Moplah Rifles Yielding up the Colours to the Bishop of Madras,' *Sphere*, 31 August 1907.

66 'The Disbandment of The 77th Moplah Rifles Yielding up the Colours to the Bishop of Madras,' *Sphere*, 31 August 1907.

67 Nair, *Moplah Rebellion*, 77.

68 Variyamkunnath Kunhamed Haji, *Hindu*, 7 October 1921.

69 Thomas Patrick Hughes, *A Dictionary of Islam; Being a Cyclopaedia of the Doctrines, Rites, Ceremonies, and Customs, together with the Technical and Theological Terms, of the Muhammadan Religion* (London: W.H. Allen & Co, 1885), 263.

70 Syed Mahmood, *The Khilafat and England* (Patna: Sidaqat Ashram, 1922).

71 T.W. Arnold, *The Caliphate* (Oxford: The Clarendon Press, 1924), 19–41.

72 Arnold, *Caliphate*, 163–184.

Chapter 5: Pathways of Freedom

1 Ibn Battuta, *The Travels of Ibn Battuta*, translated by Hamilton A.R. Gibb (Delhi: Goodword Books, 2000), 44.
2 G.F. Hourani, *Arab Seafaring in the Indian Ocean in Ancient and Early Medieval Times* (Princeton: Princeton University Press, 1995), 25.
3 Hourani, *Arab Seafaring*, 25.
4 G.R. Tibbetts, ed. and trans., *Arab Navigation in the Indian Ocean before the Coming of the Portuguese: Being a Translation of Kitāb al- Fawā'id fī uṣl al-baḥr wa'l-qawā'id of Aḥmad b. Mājid al-Najdī* (London: Royal Asiatic Society, 1971), 366–367.
5 Tibbetts, *Arab*, 366–367.
6 Sebastian R. Prange, *Monsoon Islam: Trade and Faith on the Medieval Malabar Coast* (Cambridge: Cambridge University Press, 2018), 30.
7 Battuta, *Travels of Ibn Battuta*.
8 Shaykh Zayn al-Din II, *Tuhfat al Mujahidin*, translated and edited by M.H. Hussayn Nainar (Madras: Madras University, 1942). The Zamorin dynasty remained a significant symbol of native power for Muslims throughout this era, even if the reality of the international European empires had diminished the potency of this symbol somewhat.
9 Qadi Muhammed ibn Abdul Aziz, *Fat'hul Mubin*,British Library MS, IO, Islamic 2807f, lines 401–403, British Library, London. Another copy of this manuscript was found in the personal manuscript collection of Sheikh Ahmed Koya Shaliyathi.
10 The contemporary manipulation and misinterpretation of the term *jihad* have resulted in a loss of its historical accuracy and coherence. Presently, this explosive concept, now laden with emotional connotations for both Muslims and non-Muslims, remains under discussion. However, it is crucial to acknowledge, without delving extensively into grammar, technical vocabulary or theological hermeneutics, the precise historical significance of this noun and how it shaped past societies.
11 Abbas Panakkal, *Islam in Malabar (1460-1600): A Socio-cultural Study* (Kuala Lumpur: International Islamic University Malaysia, 2016).
12 Shaykh Zayn al-Din I, *Tuḥriḍ Ahlul Iman*, Manuscript, Madin Academy Library, Malappuram.
13 Zayn al-Din II, *Tuhfat al-Mujāhidin*,.
14 Panakkal, *Islam in Malabar*.
15 Zayn al-Din, *Tuhfat*; Shaykh Zayn al-Din, *Tuhfat-al Mujahidin*, translated by M.J. Rowlandson (London: Printed for the Oriental Translation Fund, sold by J. Murray, 1883). Nainar's preface, however, reveals a notable error regarding Shaykh Zayn al-Din II's father's name, illustrating the complexities involved in historical documentation and translation.
16 K.M. Panikkar, *Asia and Western Dominance A Survey of Vasco da Gama Epoch in Asian History, 1498-1947* (London: G. Allen & Unwin 1959).
17 Ashin Das Gupta, *Merchants of Maritime India, 1500-1800* (Hampshire: Aldershot, 1994), 93.

18 Zayn al-Din, *Tuhfat-al-Mujahidin*, translated by S. Muhammad Husayn Nainar, 65.

19 William Logan, *Collection of Treaties, Engagements and Other Papers of Importance Relating to British Affairs in Malabar* (Calicut: Minerva press, 1879), 67.

20 Tellicherry' is the anglicized version of the vernacular name of the port town 'Thalasseri', which is situated in the Kannur District of the state of Kerala in South India.

21 K.K.N. Kurup, *History of the Tellicherry Factory, 1683-1794* (Calicut University: Sandhya Publications, 1985).

22 Irfan Habib, ed., *Confronting Colonialism: Resistance and Modernization under Haidar Ali and Tipu Sultan* (New Delhi: Tulika, 1999).

23 William Logan, *Malabar Manual* (New Delhi: Asian Educational Services, 2010), 469.

24 Logan, *Malabar Manual*, 476.

25 Logan, *Malabar Manual*, 469.

26 Logan, *Malabar Manual*, 469.

27 Logan, *Malabar Manual*, 468–470. William Medows (1738–1813) was a British Army officer who commenced his military career in 1756, engaging in military campaigns in North America, the Cape and India. He became the governor of Bombay in 1788 and later transferred to serve as governor of Madras in 1790. Notably, he was involved in leading attacks against Tipu Sultan of Mysore. See Alastair W. Massie, 'Sir William Medows (1738–1813),' Oxford Dictionary of National Biography, online version, accessed 15 May 2024.

28 The Arakkal kingdom was a Muslim realm situated in the Kannur District of South India. The ruler, known as Ali Raja, and the reigning queen, titled Arakkal Bibi, governed this kingdom. Their domain encompassed primarily the Cannanore town along with the southern Laccadive (Lakshadweep) Islands, namely Agatti, Kavaratti, Androth, Kalpeni and Minicoy. See Logan, *Malabar Manual*, 467.

29 Logan, *Malabar Manual*, 472.

30 Logan, *Malabar Manual*, 472–474.

31 Logan, *Malabar Manual*, 474.

32 This report took eight days (Monday, 28 May 1792) to get printed in the newspaper.

33 'From Tipoo Sultan,' *Sherborne Mercury*, 28 May 1792.

34 K.N. Panikkar, *Against Lord and State, Peasant Uprisings in Malabar, 1836-1921* (Delhi: Oxford University Press, 1989).

35 Roland E. Miller, *Mappila Muslims of Kerala: A Study in Islamic Trends* (Bombay: Orient Longman, 1976), 97.

36 *Reports of a Joint Commission from Bengal and Bombay, Appointed to Inspect into the State and Condition of the Province of Malabar in the years 1792 and 1793* (Madras: H. Smith at the Fort St. George Gazette Press, 1862).

37 These stories are abundant in the oral history of Malabar and are even visible in colonial records. For instance, when Mammad insisted on

getting money from his landlord, three Muslims of the locality, who were loyal tenants of the palace, stood surety for the amount and gave a jewel to Mammad with a promise to redeem it the next day. This is narrated in the first chapter in G.R.F. Tottenham, *The Mapilla Rebellion, 1921-22* (Madras: Government Press, 1922), 13. During my field study, I encountered many similar narratives, with people still speaking about their friendships and family bonds.

38 C.A. Innes, *Madras District gazetteers, Malabar* (Madras: Government Press,1908), 478. Innes and Logan used the spelling 'Haidros Kutti'. See Logan, *Malabar Manual*, 667.

39 See S.F. Dale, *Islamic Society on the South Asian Frontier: The Mappilas of Malabar 1498–1922* (Oxford: Clarendon Press 1980), 87–88.

40 Logan, *Malabar Manual*, 426–440.

41 Innes, *Madras District Gazetteers*, 440.

42 Logan, *Malabar Manual*, 472.

43 Logan, *Malabar Manual*, 534.

44 K.P. Padmanabha Menon, *History of Kerala* (New Delhi: Asian Educational Services, 1959), 26.

45 'Victory over Mysore,' *Courier Friday*, 31 January 1794.

46 'Victory over Mysore,' *Courier Friday*, 31 January 1794.

47 Nicole M. Hartwell, 'Framing Colonial War Loot: The "Captured" Spolia Opima of Kunwar Singh,' *Journal of the History of Collection* 34, no. 2 (2022): 287–302.

48 A Kanamdar held *Kanam* land tenure in erstwhile Malabar and was considered the highest tenant. Over time, kanamdars gained superior rights compared to the *jenmi* (landlord), who could only claim the land itself. Kanamdars had full rights over trees, structures, and buildings on the land. While it was easy to buy the *jenmi*'s land rights, purchasing the Kanamdar's improvements was often unaffordable. Innes, *Madras District Gazetteers*, 320–321.

49 Logan, *Malabar Manual*, 489–530.

50 Translation of Ola (leaf writing) from Unnimutha to Mr. Melling Chapwood, 9 April 1798, in Conrad Wood, *Moplah Rebellion and Its Genesis* (Delhi: People's Publishing House, 1987), 10.

51 Translation of Ola (leaf writing) from Unnimutha to Mr. Melling Chapwood, 9 April 1798, in Wood, *Moplah Rebellion and Its Genesis*, 10.

52 Logan, *Malabar Manual*, Vol. I, 485.

53 Wood, *Moplah Rebellion*, 105; Dale, *Islamic Society*, 136.

54 *Reports of a Joint Commission from Bengal and Bombay*, 1: 260–261.

55 Logan, *Malabar Manual*, 489, 504, 525; *Reports of a Joint Commission from Bengal and Bombay*, 1: 260–261; Wood, *Moplah Rebellion*, 105.

56 *Reports of a Joint Commission from Bengal and* Bombay, Diary IV 1243.

57 Logan, *Malabar Manual*, 485.

58 Logan, *Malabar Manual*, 489, 504, 525.

59 Logan, *Malabar Manual*, 492.

60 Logan, *Malabar Manual*, 504.

61 Logan, *Malabar Manual*, 504–505.

Chapter 6: The Legacy of Mamburam

1 Sayyid ‘Alawi Mawla al-Dawilah al-Ḥusayni Thangal (1752–1845) was a Hadrami scholar who settled in Mamburam, South India. To differentiate him from his son, Sayyid Fazal, who was also known as Fazal Pookoya Thangal and a renowned leader who fought against the British colonial powers, Sayyid ‘Alawi Mawla al-Dawilah al-Ḥusayni Thangal was respectfully referred to as Valiya Thangal, which translates to ‘Big Sayyid’.

2 In the local dialect, she was referred to as ‘Che’rekki’, and I noticed that people, except her children and close relatives, called her ‘Chere’kkei’, despite her advanced age. This could reflect the caste-oriented society, where individuals from lower castes face discrimination and are denied consideration or respect by others. The use of different names for individuals based on their caste or social status highlights the prevailing inequalities and biases within the society. It is a reminder of the challenges faced by marginalized communities in attaining equal treatment and recognition.

3 Mudal is a ritualistic tradition that involves purchasing special linen to auspiciously cover the tombs of saintly personalities. This is typically done at the shrine of Sayyid Alawi Thangal Mamburam.

4 Edavappathi refers to the latter half of the Malayalam month *Edavam*. It is when the rain arrives in Kerala, marking the onset of the southwest monsoon.

5 The traditional family tree of the Jifri family is preserved in the Jifri house in Calicut. I closely examined their family tree, which branches out to Sheikh Jifri from Prophet Muhammed.

6 This is located on the western side of Jumath Palli in Kuttichira, which also boasts centuries-old traditions. It served as the headquarters of Muslim judges in the region. Nearest to this mosque, the tomb of Qazi Muhamed is identified.

7 Wilson Chacko Jacob, *For God Or Empire: Sayyid Fadl and the Indian Ocean World* (Stanford: Stanford University Press, 2019). The Ba’ ‘Alawi i Tariqa represents a distinguished Sufi order, with its historical roots firmly anchored in Hadhramaut, Yemen. Its influence extends significantly throughout the Indian Ocean rim, primarily because of the Hadhrami diaspora. Of note is the close association of this Sufi order with the Baʿ Alawi Sayyid families. The chain of *ijazah* (a spiritual authorization for Sufi transmission) that emanates from al-Faqih Muqaddam Sayyid Muhammad traces its origins back to the Islamic prophet Muhammad himself, progressing through the lineage of his cousin Ali and, subsequently, his son Husain.

8 Vaughan to Secretary to Government, Judicial Department Madras, 10 April 1817, BL India Office Records/P/323/33, British Library, London.

9 A Sufi Sayyid is a descendant of the Prophet Muhammad’s family who follows the mystical dimension of Islam.

10 Thangal wielded substantial influence in the region, assuming a leadership role encompassing all communities. Regardless of their religious or caste

affiliations, individuals sought his counsel and mediation to address their personal and communal concerns. His stature transcended religious and social boundaries, positioning him as a revered figure entrusted with the resolution of various societal issues.

11 Vaughan to Secretary to Government, 10 April 1817, India Office Records/p/323/33, British Library, London.

12 Vaughan to Secretary to Government, 10 April 1817, India Office Records/p/323/33, British Library, London.

13 Vaughan to Madras, 29 April 1817, India Office Records/323/33, British Library, London.

14 *Mamburam Mala, Maulid Kitab—Volume of Maulid and Malas* (Tirurangadi: Amirul Islam Press, 1995), 573–583. This volume also includes Mamburam Maulid, reflecting narratives about the Sayyids of Mamburam. See *Mamburam Mala,* 335–345.

> A common religious observance is the celebration of what is called a maulad or muulad. A maulad is a tract or short treatiso in Arabic celebrating the birth, life, works and sayings of the prophet, or some saint such as Shade Mohiuddin, eleventh descendant of the prophet, expounder of the Koran, and worker of miracles, or the Mambram Tangal, father of Sayid Fasl.

See C.A. Innes, *Madras District Gazetteers, Malabar* (Madras: Government Press, 1933), 190.

15 K.N. Panikkar, *Against Lord and State: Religion and Peasant Uprising in Malabar, 1836-1921* (Delhi: Oxford University Press, 1989), 61.

16 S.F. Dale, *Islamic Society on the South Asian Frontier: The Mappilas of Malabar 1498–1922* (Oxford: Clarendon Press 1980), 116.

17 Richard M. Eaton, *Indo-Muslim Traditions, 1200-1750: Towards a Frame Works of Study,* Volume 22, Issue 1 (New Delhi: South Asia Research, 2002), 2.

18 Richard M. Eaton, *India in the Persianate Age 1000–1765* (London: Allen Lane, 2019), 3.

19 Malabar Dist. records, Police 1817, 435–436, TNA, Chennai.

20 Vaughan to Madras, 10 April 1817, BL IOR/P/323/33, British Library, London.

21 Vaughan called Mamburam Thangal 'Taramalle Coya Tangal', which is the vernacular colloquial version of 'the sayyid from Tarim', referring to Sayyid Alawi. See Vaughan to Secretary to Government, 10 April 1817, IOR/p/323/33, British Library, London.

22 Conrad Wood, *Early Mappila Rebellion 1800-1802* (Delhi: People's Publishing House, 1987), 45.

23 Innes, *Madras District Gazetteers*, 445; Wood, *Early Mappila Rebellion*, 48.

24 Innes, *Madras District Gazetteers*, 445.

25 Dale, *Islamic Society,* 117–118.

26 Logan, *Malabar Manual* (New Delhi: Asian Educational Services, 2010), 558–562; Innes, *Madras District Gazetteers*, 444–445.

27 Panikkar, *Against Lord and State*, 60–62.
28 Benedict Anderson, *Imagined Communities: Reflections on the Origin and Spread of Nationalism* (New York: Verso, 1991).
29 Panikkar, *Against Lord and State*, 61.
30 Wood, *Early Mappila Rebellion*, 114.
31 Logan, *Malabar Manual*, 557–558.
32 Logan, *Malabar Manual*, 559–560.
33 MJP. 21 December 1841, No. 5, India Office Records, British Library, London.
34 Elder brother
35 MJP. 21 December 1841, No. 5, India Office Records, British Library, London.
36 See also Panikkar, *Against Lord and State*, 69–70.
37 Local vernacular accounts from Cherur during the field study.
38 Logan, *Malabar Manual*, 102–103.
39 Logan, *Malabar Manual*, 558–562.
40 Logan, *Malabar Manual*, 560–570.
41 Field study.
42 Logan, *Malabar Manual*, 560.
43 Field study.
44 Nijeesh Narayanan, 'For Over 100 Years, a Temple and a Masjid in Kerala Have Stood by Each Other,' *News Minutes*, 23 December 2020, accessed 15 May 2024, https://www.thenewsminute.com/kerala/over-100-years-temple-and-masjid-kerala-have-stood-each-other-140154.
45 Jihad-al-nafz is a personal struggle to lead a more upright, pious life and to resist forbidden temptations.
46 Malabar Deputy Collector C. Kanaran provided these reports to W. Logan. See *Malabar Special Commission 1880-82: Malabar Land Tenures.* Vol. 2 (Madrass: Government press, 1882), 48.
47 *Correspondence on Moplah Outrages in Malabar for the Years 1853–59* [*CMO*] (Madras: United Scottish Press, 1863), 1: 273–277.
48 T. Clarke, Magistrate of Malabar, wrote to T. Pycroft, Chief Secretary to Government, in *CMO*, 1: 279–288.
49 *CMO*, 1: 276.
50 Panikkar, *Against Lord and State*, 61–62.
51 'An Indian Tribe,' *Morning Advertiser*, 14 August 1851.
52 'An Indian Tribe,' *Morning Advertiser*, 14 August 1851.
53 The friendship between Mamburam Thangal and the Hindu community is well known, and his friendship with Konthu Nair is particularly celebrated. Another testament to this bond is the numerous Hindu pilgrims who visit Thangal's shrine. This is a common sight in Mamburam. During the annual *nercha* celebrations, members of the Hindu community actively participate in the week-long program. See 'At Mumbaram Interfaith Friendship Blooms,' *Times of India*, 7 October 2016, accessed 20 May 2024, https://timesofindia.indiatimes.com/city/kochi/at-mambaram-interfaith-friendship-blooms/articleshow/54727413.cms.
54 'An Indian Tribe,' *Morning Advertiser*, 14 August 1851.

55 J.F. Thomas, Minutes, 18 Oct. 1851 in *CMO*, 205.

56 'Indian and China-Another Outbreak,' *Newcastle Guardian and Tyne Mercury*, 25 October 1851.

57 Indian and China-Another Outbreak,' *Newcastle Guardian and Tyne Mercury*, 25 October 1851.

58 'Indian and China-Another Outbreak,' *Newcastle Guardian and Tyne Mercury*, 25 October 1851.

59 'Indian and China-Another Outbreak,' *Newcastle Guardian and Tyne Mercury*, 25 October 1851.

60 'Another Outbreak,' *Tyrone Constitution*, 24 October 1851.

61 *Morning Post*, 18 October 1851.

62 'A Correspondent Down the Coast Writes Us,' *Bombay Gazette*, 14 February 1852.

63 Panikkar, *Against Lord and State*, 97; Robert Hardgrave, Jr., *The Mappila Rebellion, 1921: Peasant Revolt in Malabar* (Cambridge: Cambridge University Press, 1977).

64 Logan, *Malabar Manual*, I: 566–567.

65 Panikkar, *Against Lord and State*, 99–100.

66 'C.J.D. Cole Vice Council and East India company agent in Jeddah to Pycroft Secretary to the Government Fort Saint George. 29 July 1853,' in *CMO* 2:12; I_DH_01295_3_102066_001_001, The Ottoman Archives.

67 'Charles J.D. Cole, addressed to T. Pycroft, dated 29 June 1853,' in *CMO* 2: 7.

68 Conducting an interview with the descendants of Sayyid Fazal in the region was a pivotal step in elucidating the nuanced dimensions of his legacy. Notably, the presence of Sayyid Fazal's portrait in their residence serves as a tangible artifact, attesting to the enduring impact and reverence attributed to him within his family. This visual representation not only offers a poignant insight into the personal and familial facets of his influence but also underscores the intergenerational transmission of historical and cultural significance, thereby contributing to the broader academic discourse on the sociocultural dynamics of religious transitions and familial legacies.

69 Robinson to Pycroft, 18 November 1856, in *CMO*, 2: 388; Edmonstone to Pycroft, 5 December 1856, in *CMO*, 2: 389. Janet Ewald and William G. Clarence Smith, 'The Economic Role of the Hadhrami Diaspora in the Red Sea and Gulf of Aden, 1820s to 1930s,' in *Hadhrami Traders, Scholars and Statesmen in the Indian Ocean*, edited by Ulrike Freitag and William Clarence-Smith (Boston: Brill, 1997), 280–296.

70 In Ottoman records, the name 'Sayyid Fazal' is transcribed as 'Seyyid Fazıl Pasha'. This transcription reflects the Ottoman Turkish rendering of the name, highlighting the formal title 'Pasha' denoting a high-ranking governmental or military position.

71 MBI-00071_00177_001_001, Ottoman Archives.

72 DH-SFR-00127_00174_001_001, Ottoman Archives.

73 MF-MKT-00095_00099_001_002, Ottoman Archives.

74 I-HUS-00098_00085_001_001, Ottoman Archives.

75 Y-A-HUS-00325_00104_001_001, Ottoman Archives.
76 IML-00035_00043_001_001, Ottoman Archives.
77 IML-00029_00069_001_001, Ottoman Archives.
78 IML-00027_00024_001_001, Ottoman Archives.
79 IML-00015_00041_001_001, Ottoman Archives.
80 ASBU History Talks: Dr. Abbas Panakkal 'Sayyid Fazal Pasha: Bridging Continents with Harmony and Anti-Colonial Values from India to Ottoman Empire,' https://www.asbu.edu.tr/en/node/2684.
81 MV-00122-00037-001-002; I-DH-01200-093905-001-001, Ottoman Archives
82 A-MKT-MHM-00148_00034_001_001, Ottoman Archives.
83 BEO 3450-258677, Ottoman Archives.
84 Y-EE-KP-00038_03782_002_001, Ottoman Archives.
85 I-DH-01295_3_102066_002_001, Ottoman Archives.
86 *CMO*, 2: 387.
87 BEO 4714-353515, Ottoman Archives.
88 I-DH-00883_070384_001_001, Ottoman Archives.
89 I-TAL-00183_00040_001_002, Ottoman Archives.
90 I-DH-00865_069187_001_001, Ottoman Archives.
91 I-DH-00811_065534_001_001, Ottoman Archives.
92 I-DH-01237_096875_005_002, Ottoman Archives.
93 Y-PRK-AZJ-00003_00105_002_001, Ottoman Archives.
94 *Tercüman-ı Hakikat*, 27–28 October 1900; *Iqdam*, 27–28 October 1900.

Chapter 7: Conolly's Death

1 Born in 1806, Conolly embarked upon his career trajectory as a writer in the civil service of the East India Company in 1824, culminating in his ascent to the distinguished position of principal collector in Bellary. His linguistic adeptness extended to Kannada translation, enhancing his multifaceted profile. Between 1842 and 1855, Conolly became the magistrate and collector of Malabar, a designation that would ultimately be marked by a poignant tragedy.
2 The Nilambur teak plantation and the extensive waterways connecting various regions were named by the colonial administration after him. These landmarks still bear his name today, serving as living examples of the colonial historical legacy. See William Logan, *Malabar Manual*, Vol. I, (Madras: Government Press, 1887), 13.
3 V. Aksan, 'Locating the Ottomans in Napoleon's World,' in *Napoleon's Empire: European Politics in Global Perspective*, edited by Ute Planert (New York: Palgrave Macmillan, 2016), 277–290; Talal Asad, *On Suicide Bombing* (New York: Columbia University Press, 2007), 92.
4 Henry Pottinger, 'Minute', 16 December, 1851, in response to 'Letter from the Magistrate of Malabar, No. 1,014,' 29 November 1851, located in Colonial Office Records, 1: 231, Tamil Nadu Archives (TNA), Chennai; Conolly to Sec., Judicial, 11 February 1852, Madras Judicial Proceedings (MJP), No. 125. 20 February 1852, 696, Tamil Nadu Archives (TNA), Chennai.

5 Conolly to Montgomery, Secretary to Government, Judicial Department, 1849, in *Correspondence on Moplah Outrages in Malabar for the Years 1853–59* [*CMO*] (Madras: United Scottish Press, 1863), 1: 33–135.
6 Conolly, Correspondence to Montgomery, Secretary to Government, Judicial Department, 12 October 1849, in *CMO,* 1: 33.
7 Conolly, Correspondence to Pycroft, 29 January 1852 in *CMO,* 1: 241.
8 Conolly to Pycroft, January 29, 1852, in *CMO*, 1: 240–241.
9 Conolly to Strange, 10 September 1852, MJP No. 56, 27 January 1853, 399, TNA, Chennai.
10 J.F. Thomas, 3 November 1852, MJP No. 483, 23, TNA, Chennai.
11 Conolly to Sec., Judicial, 16 October 1851, MJP No. 720, 2 December 1851, TNA, Chennai.
12 H.V. Conolly, Malabar Magistrate to Sec., Judicial, 12 October 1849 P/527/22, MJP No. 794, 1 December 1849, 4729, TNA, Chennai.
13 Local history collected in field work.
14 Logan, *Malabar Manual*, 576.
15 The letter written by G.B. Tod, assistant collector, Malabar, to the chief secretary to government, dated 1 a.m., 12 September 1855, in *CMO*, 76–77.
16 On 13 March 1940, during a joint meeting of the East India Association and the Central Asian Society at Caxton Hall in Westminster, London, Michael O'Dwyer was shot by Indian revolutionary Udham Singh in retaliation for the Amritsar massacre. O'Dwyer succumbed to two gunshot wounds instantaneously. Lord Zetland, then secretary of state for India, presided over the meeting and sustained injuries. Following his recovery, Zetland chose early retirement from his position, and Leo Amery succeeded him as secretary of state for India. Udham Singh, making no effort to escape, was apprehended at the scene and was subsequently arrested. O'Dwyer was later laid to rest at Brookwood Cemetery near Woking. See Gordon Honeycombe, *The Murders of the Black Museum, 1870-1970* (London: Hutchinson, 1982); Louis E. Fenech, 'Contested Nationalisms; Negotiated Terrains: The Way Sikhs Remember Udham Singh "Shahid" (1899–1940),' *Modern Asian Studies* 36 (2002): 827–870.
17 'Murder of Mr. Conolly,' *Sheffield Daily Telegraph*, 5 November 1855.
18 'Murder of Mr. Conolly,' *Sheffield Daily Telegraph*, 5 November 1855.
19 'Murder of Mr. Conolly,' *Sheffield Daily Telegraph*, 5 November 1855.
20 'India and China,' *The Constitution*: or *Cork Advertiser*, 6 November 1855.
21 'India and China,' *The Kendal Mercury,* 10 November 1855.
22 'Murder of Mr. Conolly,' *Durham Chronicle*, 9 November 1855.
23 'Murder of a Government Official at Madras,' *Bolton Chronicle*, 10 November 1855.
24 'Murder of a Government Official at Madras,' *Bolton Chronicle*, 10 November 1855.
25 'Murder of a Government Official at Madras,' *Bolton Chronicle*, 10 November 1855.
26 'Murder in Madras,' *Bicester Herald*, 10 November 1855.
27 Field study.

28 The *Reading Mercury*, the *Oxford Gazette*, the *Newbury Herald*, and the *Berks Country Paper* published a report on the same day: Saturday, 10 November 1855.
29 C.A. Innes, *Madras District Gazetteer—Malabar* (Madras: Government Press, 1951), 80.
30 From G.B. Tod, assistant Magistrate of Malabar to T. Pycroft, Chief Secretary to Government, on 14 September, in *CMO*, 79–82.
31 Logan, *Malabar Manual*, 575–580.
32 Mawlid originates from an Arabic term signifying 'birth' or 'birthday'. Specifically, 'Mawlid al-Nabi' denotes the 'birth of the Prophet'. In Malabar, Mawlid refers to the recitation of eulogies written to honor the Prophet, typically done during the birth month and on special occasions.
33 Logan, *Malabar Manual*, 565–580.
34 Logan, *Malabar Manual*, 576.
35 W. Logan attributes personal grudge of the assailants and probably a revenge on deportation of Sayyid Fazal. See Logan, *Malabar Manual,* 579.
36 Report of T.L. Strange, Special Commissioner, Malabar, 25 September 1852, MJP No. 483, 23 August 1853; 4618–4619, TNA, Chennai.
37 H.M. Winterbotham, Acting Malabar Magistrate to Chief Sec., 10 July 1886, MJP No. 2236, 23 August 1886, 72, in Logan, *Malabar Manual,* 582–585.
38 Conolly to Secretary, Judicial, on 16 October 1851, MJP No. 720, dated 2 December 1851, 340–341, mentions that 'Shernad' or 'Chernad' was a taluk located in the south-western region of Malabar until it was merged with Ernad in 1860. This merger resulted in the creation of a new taluk, which retained the name Ernad.
39 Logan, *Malabar Manual*, 595.
40 W. Logan, Malabar magistrate, wrote to the chief secretary on two occasions: written on 30 June 1835 (MJP No. 1830), the letter was received on 13 July 1886 and can be found on page 35; written on 1 May 1835 (MJP No. 1337), the letter was received on 21 May 1885 and can be found on page 98. Madras Judicial Proceedings, TNA, Chennai.

Conclusion

1 Field study in Vengara.
2 The yearly celebration at Vengara Temple is a vibrant event, attracting both devotees and the general public from distant places. The festivities encompass various dimensions, incorporating rich rituals, cultural performances and a grand communal procession. Throughout this celebration, the temple effigies of bulls are adorned with vivid colors, accompanied by resonating music and the fragrances (traditionally perfumed with various flowers), creating a truly captivating atmosphere.
3 R.H. Hitchcock, *A History of the Malabar Rebellion, 1921* (Madras: Government Press, 1925), 31–32.
4 Hitchcock, *History*, 21.

5 Proceeding of the court of the special Judge, Calicut, Malabar, No. SJE-128, 25 September 1922, in Hitchcock, *History*, 217–243.

6 B.H. Baden-Powell, *Land Systems of British India*, Vol. III (Oxford: Clarendon Press, 1892), 159–60; William Logan, *Malabar Special Commission 1881-82, Malabar Land Tenures Report*, Vol. 1 (Madras: Government Press, 1882), 32; William Thackeray, *Report on Revenue Affairs Malabar, Canara and Ceded Districts*, 1807 (Calicut, 1911), 15.

7 G.R.F. Tottenham, *The Mapilla Rebellion, 1921-22* (Madras: Government Press, 1922), 15.

8 Tottenham, *Mapilla Rebellion*, 15, 275, 281.

9 'Women Get the Vote,' UK Parliament, accessed 15 May 2024, https://www.parliament.uk/about/living-heritage/transformingsociety/electionsvoting/womenvote/overview/thevote.

10 'Viceroy Addressed the Council of State,' *Liverpool Daily Post*, 6 September 1921, 5.

11 In the adjudication pronounced on Monday, 9 October 2023, by Judge Daniel Thulare at the re-examined inquest held at the Western Cape High Court, the preceding findings of the initial inquiry were set aside. Judge Thulare conclusively determined that Imam Haron met a tragic demise due to grievous acts of torture perpetrated by members affiliated with the Security Branch of the South African Police. My direct communication with Muhammed Haron, the progeny of Imam Haron, revealed the family's contentment and sense of fulfilment regarding the court's decision—a culmination of prolonged anticipation. This sentiment signifies the attainment of justice and closure after an extended period of waiting.

BIBLIOGRAPHY

Aksan, V. 'Locating the Ottomans in Napoleon's World.' In *Napoleon's Empire: European Politics in Global Perspective*, edited by Ute Planert, 277–290. New York: Palgrave Macmillan, 2016.

Anderson, Benedict. *Imagined Communities: Reflections on the Origin and Spread of Nationalism*. New York: Verso, 1991.

Arnold, T.W. *The Caliphate*. Oxford: The Clarendon Press, 1924.

Asad, Talal. *On Suicide Bombing*. New York: Columbia University Press, 2007.

Baden-Powell, B.H. *Land Systems of British India*. Vol. III. Oxford: Clarendon Press, 1892.

Başbakanlık Osmanlı Arşivi (The Ottoman Archives of the Prime Minister's Office), Turkey.

Battuta, Ibn. *The Travels of Ibn Battuta*. Translated by Hamilton A.R. Gibb. Delhi: Good Word Books, 2000.

Buchanan, Francis. *A Journey from Madras through the Countries of Mysore, Canara and Malabar from London*. London: Cadell and Davies, 1807.

Captain Harry. 'Comment Fut Perimee La Revolt Des Moplahs.' *Sciences et Voyages* 3, no. 154 (10 August 1922).

Chandra, Bipin. *India's Struggle for Independence 1857-1947*. Delhi: Penguin, 2017.

Chattopadhyaya, Brajadulal. *Representing the Other? Sanskrit Sources and the Muslims (Eighth to Fourteenth Century)*. New Delhi: Manohar, 1998.

Chopra, P.N., ed. *The Role of Indian Muslims in the Struggle for Freedom*. Delhi: Light & Life Publishers, 1979.

Colonial Office Records. Tamil Nadu Archives, Chennai.

Confidential Report on the Non-Cooperation and Khilafat Movement in India by Deputy Director, Central Intelligence Bureau, Home Department, Government of India, 240–242. National Archives of India (NAI), New Delhi.

Correspondence on Moplah Outrages in Malabar for the Years 1853-59. Madras: Graves and Cookson, 1863.

Dale, Stephen Frederic. *Islamic Society on the South Asian Frontier: The Mappilas of Malabar 1498–1922*. Oxford: Clarendon Press, 1980.

Das Gupta, Ashin. *Merchants of Maritime India, 1500-1800*. Hampshire: Aldershot, 1994.

Dhanagere, D.N. 'Agrarian Conflict, Religion and Politics: The Moplah Rebellion in the Nineteenth and Early Twentieth Centuries.' *Past and Present* 74, no. 1 (1977): 112–141.

Dhavlikar, M.K., and G. Possehi. *The Pre-Harappan Period at Prabhas Pattan*. Man and Environment, 1992.

Eaton, Richard M. *India in the Persianate Age 1000–1765.* London: Allen Lane, 2019.

———. 'Indo-Muslim Traditions, 1200-1750: Towards a Frame Works of Study.' *South Asia Research* 22, no. 1 (2002): 1–19. https://doi.org/10.1177/026272800202200101.

Elliot, Henry Miers. *The History of India, as Told by Its Own Historians.* London: Trübner & Co, 1867.

Ewald, Janet and William G. Clarence Smith. 'The Economic Role of the Hadhrami Diaspora in the Red Sea and Gulf of Aden, 1820s to 1930s.' In *Hadhrami Traders, Scholars and Statesmen in the Indian Ocean*, edited by Ulrike Freitag and William Clarence-Smith. Boston: Brill, 1997.

Fenech, Louis E. 'Contested Nationalisms; Negotiated Terrains: The Way Sikhs Remember Udham Singh "Shahid" (1899–1940).' *Modern Asian Studies* 36 (2002): 827–870.

Gopal, Ram. *Indian Muslims: A Political History (1858-1947).* Bombay: Asia Publishing House, 1964.

Gough, Kathleen. 'Mappilas in North Kerala.' In *Matrilineal Kinship*, edited by David M. Schneider and Kathleen Gough. University of California, 1961.

———. 'Peasant Resistance and Revolt in South India.' *Pacific Affairs* 41, no. 4 (1968): 526–544.

Graham Letter to Hannyngton, DO. No. 200-5, Dated 12 August 1920 in USSF. No. 307, Dated 01.10.1920. Tamil Nadu Archives, Chennai.

Habib, Irfan, ed. *Confronting Colonialism: Resistance and Modernization under Haidar Ali and Tipu Sultan.* New Delhi: Tulika, 1999.

Hardgrave, Robert L., Jr. 'The Mappila Rebellion, 1921: Peasant Revolt in Malabar.' *Modern Asian Studies* 2, no. 1 (1977): 57–99.

———. *The Mappila Rebellion, 1921: Peasant Revolt in Malabar.* Cambridge: Cambridge University Press, 1977.

Hitchcock, R.H. *A History of the Malabar Rebellion, 1921.* Madras: Government Press, 1925.

Home Department (Political) (A) Proceedings. National Archives of India (NAI), New Delhi.

Honeycombe, Gordon. *The Murders of the Black Museum, 1870-1970.* London: Hutchinson, 1982.

Hourani, G.F. *Arab Seafaring in the Indian Ocean in Ancient and Early Medieval Times.* Princeton: Princeton University Press, 1995.

Hughes, Thomas Patrick. *A Dictionary of Islam; Being a Cyclopaedia of the Doctrines, Rites, Ceremonies, and Customs, together with the Technical and Theological Terms, of the Muhammadan Religion.* London: W.H. Allen & co, 1885

India Office Records. British Library, London.

Innes, C.A. and F.B. Evans, eds, *Madras District Gazetteers.* Malabar (Madras): Government Press, 1908.

Jacob, Wilson Chacko. *For God or Empire: Sayyid Fadl and the Indian Ocean World.* California: Stanford University Press, 2019.

Kareem, C.K. *Kerala Muslim Charitram.* Edappally: Charithram Publications, 1991.

Kareem, K.K. Muhammed Abdul. *Ali Musaliar, KM Moulaviyude Khilafath Samranakal.* Tirurangadi: CH Muhammed and Sons, 2021.

Keddie, Nikki R. *An Islamic Response to Imperialism: Political and Religious Writings of Sayyid Jamāl ad-Dīn "al-Afghānī".* California: University of California Press, 1983.

Keddie, Nikki R. and Ibrahim Kalin. 'Afghānī, Jamāl al-Dīn.' In *The Oxford Encyclopedia of Philosophy, Science, and Technology in Islam*, edited by Ibrahim Kalin. Oxford: Oxford University Press, 2014.

Kirmani, Mir Hussain Ali Khan. *History of Tipu Sultan: Being a Continuation of the Neshani Hyduri. A Continuation of the Neshan-I-Hyduri.* Translated from Persian by Col. Miles. London: Oriental Translation Fund, 1864.

Kurup, K.K.N. *History of the Tellicherry Factory, 1683-1794.* Calicut University: Sandhya Publications, 1985.

Letter from District Magistrate to the Chief Secretary, Dated 17 February 1921, F. No. 103-415. Tamil Nadu State Archives, Chennai.

Logan, William. *Collection of Treaties, Engagements and Other Papers of Importance Relating to British Affairs in Malabar.* Calicut: Minerva press, 1879.

———. *Malabar Special Commission 1881-82, Malabar Land Tenures Report.* Vol 1. Madras: Government Press, 1882.

———. *Malabar Manual.* Madras: Government Press, 1887.

———. *Malabar Manual.* New Delhi: Asian Educational Services, 2010.

Madras Judicial Proceedings. Tamil Nadu Archives, Chennai.

Mahmood, Syed. *The Khilafat and England.* Patna: Mohemed Imtyaz, Sidaqat Ashram, 1922.

Majumdar, R.C. *Struggle for Freedom.* Bombay: Bharatiya Vidya Bhavan, 1969.

Malabar Dist. Records, Police 1817, 435–436. Tamil Nadu Archives, Chennai.

The Malabar Moplah Rebellion. Official record film, directed by Major Robinson of 75th Carnatic Infantry. Specially produced for the Government of India by A.W. Smith & Co, Imperial Theatre Bangalore, South India.

Mamburam Mala, Maulid Kitab—Volume of Maulid and Malas. Tirurangadi: Amirul Islam Press, 1995.

Menon, K.P. Keshava. *Kazhinja Kalam.* Calicut: Mathrubhumi Books, 1969, New Edition 2024.

Menon, K.P. Padmanabha. *History of Kerala.* New Delhi : Asian Educational Services, 1959.

Menon, M. Gangadhara. *Malabar Rebellion (1921-22).* Allahabad: Vohra Publishers & Distributors, 1989.

Menon, M.P. Narayana. *Malabar Samaram M.P. Narayanamenonum Sahapravarthakarum* [Malabar Movement: M.P. Narayana Menon and His Companions]. Calicut: IPH, 1994.

Menon, M.P.S. *Malabar Samaram: M.P. Narayana Menonum Sahapravarthkarum.* Kozhikode: IPH, 2005.

Menon, P.K. Keshava. *History of Freedom Movement in Kerala*, Vol. II. Trivandrum: Kerala Regional Records Survey Committee, Government Press, 1972.

Miller, Roland E. *Mappila Muslims of Kerala: A Study in Islamic Trends.* Bombay: Orient Longman, 1976.

Minault, Gail. *The Khilafat Movement: Religious Symbolism and Political Mobilization in India*. Columbia: Columbia University Press, 1982.

Moulavi, K. Koyatti. *1921-le Malabar Lahala.* Kozhikode: IPB Books, 2020.

Muhammed, Ramees. *Sultan Variyam Kunnan.* Calicut: Twohorn Creation, 2021.

Nair, Gopalan. *The Moplah Rebellion 1921.* Calicut: Printed at the Norman Printing Bureau, 1923.

Nair, K. Madhavan. *Malabar Kalapam.* Calicut: Mathrubhumi Books, 2022.

Namboodiripad, E.M.S. *A Short History of the Peasant Movement in Keralam.* Calcutta: National Book Agency, 1985.

———. *Keralam Malayalikalude Mathrubhumi.* Thiruvananthapuram: Chintha Publishers, 2009.

Namboodiripad, Mozhikunnathu. *Khilafath Smaranakal.* Calicut: Mathrubhumi Books, 2015.

Niemeijer, A.C. *The Khilafat Movement in India 1919-1924.* Leiden: Brill, 1972.

Ottapalam Conference and Police Atrocities (Pamphlet in Malayalam) 1921, Government of Madras, GO. No. 491, August 1921. Tamil Nadu Archives, Madras.

Panakkal, Abbas. 'Iruttu Muriyil Ninnu Choramanamulla Kathu' [A blood-scented letter from the dark room]. *Varadhya Madhyamam*, 10 October 2010.

———. *Islam in Malabar (1460-1600): A Socio-cultural Study.* Kuala Lumpur: IIU Malaysia, 2016.

———. 'Transformation of Admiral to the Sainthood and Sacred Stories of Chinese Sanctum Sanctorum from Malabar Coast.' In *Sacred Sites and Sacred Stories Across Cultures*, edited by D.W. Kim. New York: Palgrave Macmillan, 2021.

———. 'The Unknown Photo, and British Construction of History: Revisiting Captain Harry's Article.' *True Copy Think*, 18 November 2021.

———. 'Sayyid Fazal Pasha: Bridging Continents with Harmony and Anti-Colonial Values from India to Ottoman Empire.' ASBU History Talks, 2023. https://www.asbu.edu.tr/en/node/2684.

Panakkal, Abbas and K.M. Baharul Islam. 'Cultural Integration in Muslim Communities.' In *South Asian Islam*, edited by Nasr M. Arif and Abbas Panakkal. London: Routledge, 2023.

Panikkar, K.M. *Asia and Western Dominance: A Survey of Vasco da Gama Epoch in Asian History, 1498-1947.* London: G. Allen & Unwin,1959.

Panikkar, K.N. 'Peasant Revolt in Malabar in Nineteenth and Twentieth Centuries.' In *Peasant Struggles in India*, edited by A.R. Desai. New Delhi: Oxford University Press, 1979.

———. *Against Lord and State: Religion and Peasant Uprisings in Malabar, 1836-1921.* Delhi: Oxford University Press, 1989.

Pottekkat, S.K., P.P. Ummer Koya, N.P. Mohamed and K.A. Kodungallore. *Muhammed Abdurahiman: A Political Biography*. Calicut: Muhammed Abdurahiman Sahib Memorial Committee, 1978.

Prange, Sebastian R. *Monsoon Islam: Trade and Faith on the Medieval Malabar Coast.* Cambridge: Cambridge University Press, 2018.

Prasad, Pushpa. *Sanskrit Inscriptions of Delhi Sultanate: 1191-1526.* New Delhi: Oxford University Press, 1990.

Qadi Muhammed ibn Abdul Aziz. *Fat'hul Mubin.* British Library MS, IO, Islamic 2807f. British Library, London.

Qisssat Shakruti Farmad. MS. IO Islamic 2807d. British Library, London.

Qureshi, I.H. *Ulema in Politics.* Delhi: Renaissance Publishing House, 1974.

Qureshi, M. Naeem. *Pan-Islam in British Indian Politics: A Study of the Khilafat Movement, 1918-1924.* Leiden: Brill, 1999.

Report on the Administration of the Madras Presidency 1920-21. Tamil Nadu State Archives, Chennai.

Roy, M.N. *India in Transition.* Bombay: Nachiketa Publications, 1971.

Ryder, Vincent Jos. *Two Years in Malabar.* Calcutta: Thacker and Spink Co., 1907.

Sankaran, Moyarth. *Ente Jeevita Katha* [The story of my life]. Calicut: P.K. Brothers, 1965.

Sitaramayya, Pattabhi. *History of the Indian National Congress (1885-1935)*, vol. I. Bombay: Padma Publications, 1946.

Tagore, Soumyendranath. *Peasant Revolt in Malabar.* Bombay: People's Publication, 1937.

Thapar, Romila. *Somanatha: The Many Voices of a History.* New Delhi: Penguin Books India, 2008.

Tibbetts, G.R., ed. and trans. *Arab Navigation in the Indian Ocean Before the Coming of the Portuguese: Being a Translation of Kitāb al- Fawā'id fī uṣl al-baḥr wa'l-qawā'id of Aḥmad b. Mājid al-Najdī.* London: Royal Asiatic Society, 1971.

Tottenham, G.R.F. *The Mappila Rebellion, 1921-22.* Madras: Government Press, 1922.

Wood, Conrad. 'The Moplah Rebellion of 1921-22 and Its Genesis.' PhD thesis submitted at School of Oriental and African Studies, University of London, 1975.

———. *Early Mappila Rebellion 1800-1802.* Delhi: People's Publishing House, 1987.

———. *Moplah Rebellion and its Genesis.* Delhi: People's Publishing House, 1987.

Zayn al-Din, Shaykh, I. *Tahrid Ahlul Iman.* Manuscript, Madin Academy Library, Malappuram.

Zayn al-Din, Shaykh, II. *Tuhfat al Mujahidin.* Translated and edited by M.H. Hussayn Nainar. Madras: Madras University, 1942.

INDEX